ALSO BY CONNIE BRUCK

Master of the Game

The Predators' Ball

WHEN HOLLYWOOD
HAD A KING

WHEN HOLLYWOOD HAD A

KING

The Reign of Lew Wasserman,
Who Leveraged Talent into Power and Influence

CONNIE BRUCK

RANDOM HOUSE / NEW YORK

RANDOM HOUSE and colophon are registered trademarks of Random House, Inc.

LIBRARY OF CONGRESS CATALOGING-IN-PUBLICATION DATA
Bruck, Connie.
When Hollywood had a king : the reign of Lew Wasserman, who leveraged talent into
power and influence / Connie Bruck.
p. cm.
Includes index.
ISBN 0-375-50168-1
1. Wasserman, Lew. 2. Chief executive officers—United States—Biography. 3. Music
Corporation of America—History. I. Title.
PN2287.W4525B73 2003
338.7'617914'092—dc21
[B]   2003041418

Random House website address: www.atrandom.com

Printed in the United States of America on acid-free paper

24689753

First Edition

Book design by Casey Hampton

To Ari Schlossberg

and

Mel Levine

Contents

Introduction

For the better part of the last fifty years, aspirants to great power in Hollywood imagined themselves in the chair of one man. It was not just that Lew Wasserman ran MCA—"the largest talent agency the world has ever known," as its founder, Jules Stein, liked to say—and the biggest television production company. Or, later, that Wasserman headed one of the first diversified entertainment companies, which included the world's largest motion picture studio, Universal, and the country's leading supplier of television programs. These were only the facts on his résumé, and they did not begin to convey the scope of Wasserman's power. Like other pioneering businessmen with an appetite for dominion, Wasserman shaped his world, ruled it with a free hand, and tried to control whatever forces impinged upon it.

From the start, he prized disciplined troops, and he succeeded in creating legions of followers within his enterprise who were willing to live by his dictates, generally regarding him with both fear and awe. As an agent, he engineered changes within the industry that contributed to the fall of the studio system, a demise from which he benefited—and later, when he found himself on the studio side, he sought to re-create his own version of that system. Labor struggles had ravaged Hollywood in the thirties and forties, and studio heads such as Jack Warner and Louis B. Mayer regarded the unions as their bitter enemies. Wasserman, however, established strong relationships with labor leaders, from Jimmy Hoffa on down, and with the underworld that controlled some of them; Sidney Korshak, the Chicago mob's representative in Hollywood, was probably Wasserman's closest friend.

Wasserman also developed a healthy respect for the government's power to intrude on his domain. He had watched as the major studios were forced to sell their cinema chains under the so-called Paramount Decree, a Supreme Court decision issued in May 1948. And he experienced the impact of antitrust enforcement firsthand in 1962, when the Justice Department sued MCA. He decided, therefore, to make Hollywood a political force far more potent than it had ever been, so that it could help thwart governmental attacks and bring about regulatory help and legislation that could mean billions of dollars to the entertainment industry. Wasserman built a machine for political contributions, conscripted Hollywood stars to appear at fund-raisers, and became an indefatigable presence on Capitol Hill. He took pride in his closeness to presidents, from Lyndon Baines Johnson to Ronald Reagan to Bill Clinton; Wasserman didn't care for Richard Nixon, but he gave the assignment of courting Nixon to another MCA executive, and Nixon probably did more for the industry than any other president, with the possible exception of Reagan. In Hollywood it was widely known that Wasserman's reach extended from the White House to the underworld, which added to his aura of invincibility.

For decades, Wasserman did more to affect the course of the entertainment industry than any other individual. It was a historically fractious community; moguls such as Warner and Mayer had ruled their fiefdoms and treasured their prerogatives, refusing to yield to one another, and there had been no recognized industry leader. But that was what Wasserman became, through his deft maneuvering. He maintained that position for so long that by the time he surrendered it, the role he had created for himself was an anachronism. By the mid-nineties, a trend that had begun with the creation of diversified enter-

tainment companies such as MCA had led to media entertainment be-
hemoths far larger and more all-encompassing than even Wasserman
might have predicted. The Hollywood studios, subsidiaries of these
giant conglomerates with varying agendas, had to defer to their respective parent companies—not to someone from their own ranks. For
years, people in Hollywood had wondered who "the next Lew Wasserman" would be. The answer, now, was no one.

Despite his extraordinary ambit, Wasserman managed over the
years to maintain a surprisingly low profile outside his Hollywood and
Washington circles, his name barely recognized by the general public.
He had been schooled by Jules Stein, who believed that talent agents
should cultivate visibility for their clients and anonymity for themselves. It was a business principle, and also a deep personal proclivity;
both Stein and Wasserman were congenitally secretive men. However,
Wasserman eventually bent the rule somewhat. He realized that public
relations, like political clout, would be another weapon in his arma-
ment; although he spoke to the press infrequently, he did talk to select
reporters when it served his purposes. The consummate Hollywood
agent, Wasserman was well aware, too, that his elusiveness—a rare
commodity in the hot center of the celebrity culture—strengthened his
mystique.

Because Wasserman had been able to operate so commandingly for
so long, while revealing so little of either his modus operandi or him-
self, I found him an alluring subject. Moreover, he was absolutely singular: if there was any person through whom the larger story of
Hollywood in the past five decades could be told, it was Wasserman. I
met him only at the end of his remarkable run, in early 1991, when
MCA had just been sold to the Japanese consumer-electronics giant
Matsushita, and I was interviewing him for a piece I was writing for
The New Yorker about that transaction. About seven years later, when
I called to tell Wasserman that I was writing this book about MCA, he
agreed to see me, and over the course of the next four and a half years
I had a series of interviews with him. He was plainly ambivalent about
the process. He had always sworn, very publicly, that he would never

write a book, nor would he cooperate with one. But there we were. In the beginning he said he would talk to me only about Jules Stein, not himself. Then he said he would talk to me about the company, not himself. Inevitably, though, he did talk about himself, and though much of what he said had a distinctly prerecorded quality, stories told and retold, there were surprisingly spontaneous, candid moments. Once, when I had seen him a number of times and called to set up another appointment, he declined; he said he had realized he was "cooperating sideways"—and that was something he didn't want to do. But after several months I called again, his secretary made the appointment, and when I arrived at his office he greeted me warmly as usual, and never referred to his earlier refusal. I assumed he had decided that he wanted his story told (though probably only parts of it), and that he would take his chances. He was extremely frail—but I succumbed to the popular illusion that Lew Wasserman was bound to endure indefinitely. So I was caught painfully off guard when he suffered a stroke in May 2002 and died a few weeks later. I was left with the regret that I had not seen him more often—and that he would never read the book that I believe he would have felt, on balance, gave him his due.

I did not have the opportunity to meet Jules Stein, who died in 1981. But I was fortunate to have access to hundreds of pages of a rough draft of a Stein memoir, written by former *New York Times* reporter Murray Schumach, and drawn from many hours of interviews with Stein near the end of his life (he would not have contemplated such a thing earlier). So Stein's idiosyncratic voice can be heard, along with Wasserman's, in the pages of this book. Stein said he realized early on that Wasserman was a "pupil who was surpassing his teacher." His statement was accurate; Stein did not mince words, or flatter. But it was Stein who had imprinted the Music Corporation of America, the band-booking agency he founded in Chicago in 1924, with the characteristics that powered its remarkable trajectory—and who provided Wasserman the platform from which to launch his own.

WHEN HOLLYWOOD
HAD A KING

Jules Caesar Stein seated at his desk in the office of the Music Corporation of America—just opened for business, in 1924. *Courtesy of Jean Stein*

Chapter 1

THE TWO CAESARS

On a spring day in Chicago in 1922, two young men stood deep in conversation on the sidewalk outside the headquarters of Local 10, a branch of the American Federation of Musicians union. They might have conferred inside the building instead—one of them, James Caesar Petrillo, was the local's vice president—but he thought the walls had ears, and the message he wanted to deliver was confidential. He had sent word to his companion, Jules Caesar Stein, that he wanted to see him. Stein was a recent medical school graduate who booked bands on the side, and, in his relatively short career, he had already run afoul of the musicians union, and gotten caught in the crossfire of Chicago's ongoing, internecine labor wars. It seemed, moreover, to be Petrillo's fire that had caught Stein; the bombs that had recently exploded at several Chinese restaurants where Stein was booking bands were Petrillo's handiwork, Stein was convinced. At one of them, the Canton Tea Garden on Wabash, the damage had been especially severe. But the nature of the band-booking business—and more, of the city itself—was such that Stein had little recourse. If he wanted to continue in this business, he had to make his peace with this, the dominant musicians union. So he was eager to hear what Petrillo had to say.

Stein had entered this business at a young age—he was only seventeen when he began assembling and booking bands as a means of putting himself through school—but he had grasped the power of the union from the start. In the first few years, he had booked bands mainly in summer resort areas, always employing members of the Federation (AFM). But one summer, unable to fill an orchestra for a resort engagement at Lake Okoboji in Iowa, he had engaged a nonunion musician, hoping his transgression would remain secret. The information, predictably, leaked out; he was brought before the board of Local 10, then headed by its president, Joseph Winkler, fined $1,500 (a sum he could not hope to pay), and expelled from the union. So Stein had joined a rival union, an independent group called the American Musicians Union (AMU), which was far less powerful than the AFM. And he began to book Chinese restaurants with AMU musicians. To Petrillo, this was tantamount to a declaration of war; he considered the Chinese restaurants his personal fiefdom. When he had joined Local 10 in 1919, he had been assigned the task of organizing the musicians in these restaurants. Other union members had been trying to do this, off and on, for nearly two decades; Petrillo had it wrapped up in about one month. According to one story, perhaps apocryphal, Petrillo had walked into one of these restaurants, placed a time bomb on the table, and demanded that the owner sign a contract before the device exploded.

Now, the very capable Petrillo was offering Stein a truce. He said he would cancel Stein's expulsion and allow him to pay a reduced fine, $500, over a period of months, to rejoin the AFM. If Stein felt any anger at Petrillo for his violent acts, he was too pragmatic to let it show. He promptly agreed to Petrillo's proposition, and thanked him. How Petrillo had the authority to lift Stein's punishment—inasmuch as Winkler, who had levied it, was still the president—is not clear. But not long after this exchange, a series of dramatic events took place at Local 10. Winkler, while presiding over a board meeting, was attacked by the union's business agent, who hit him over the head repeatedly, apparently with metal knuckles, fracturing his skull, while all the assembled directors watched; and about six weeks later, as Winkler was slowly recovering, a bomb exploded in Local 10's offices. Shortly after the bombing, a union member wrote a letter to the editor of the *International Musician*, in which he declared that the violence was due to a faction within the union opposed to Winkler, which "seemingly had but one desire, namely, to advance their own selfish individual interests"—and he implied that this faction included Petrillo. Stein, moreover, would recall years later that, after he and Petrillo had had their rapprochement, Petrillo "ousted" Winkler. In December 1922, Petrillo was duly elected president of the local.

The alliance that had been forged between Stein and Petrillo on the sidewalk that day would last the rest of their lives. To a casual observer, they were the strangest of consorts. Stein, who was very conscious of his professional status, cultivated a rather formal, even courtly mien, and a gentleman's image—dressing in dark, double-breasted suits, parting his hair in the middle, sporting a pince-nez; and he was singularly self-contained, betraying little emotion, choosing his words as warily as though he had to pay for them. Petrillo, on the other hand, a rough type who looked very much the saloon-keeper he'd been until he decided to make his way in what he called "the union business," had devoted nine years to school but never could get beyond the fourth grade—something suggested in his signature, which always remained an exemplar of beginning penmanship, and, most noticeably, in his speech. He was a stubby volcano of a man, erupting at the slightest provocation in streams of tortured syntax peppered with profanity, and delivered, raspingly, out of the corner of his mouth. But the two men did share other characteristics, less immediately evident: shrewdness in their judgments about people, organizational skills, and (as suggested by their middle names) a taste for empire building. Though they were both instinctively suspicious, distrusting virtually everyone, they knew at least some of each other's secrets. And, in these critical, early years, each would do more to pave the way for the other's steep ascent than any other individual. Much later, when Stein was a world-famous businessman and philanthropist, he would attempt to distance himself from some of his early Chicago connections, and he would substantially revise that history. But he would never turn his back on Petrillo.

Petrillo was given the name Caesar at birth, but Stein took it for himself when he was a teenager. Later, he would regret this adolescent gesture as too flamboyant and, worse, revealing. But at the time, it was his declaration that he was impatient to put the torpor of life in South Bend, Indiana, behind him, and to conquer the world. He was born on April 26, 1896, to Rosa and Louis Stein. Louis (whose family name was changed from Seimenski) had emigrated from Lithuania; initially he made his way as a peddler, carrying a heavy pack of goods on his back, and ultimately he opened a dry goods store in South Bend; and Jules's mother, Rosa Cohen, also from Lithuania, was sent here by her parents to be Louis's bride. Orthodox Jews, Rosa and Louis had five children; Jules was the second son. The family lived in a run-down neighborhood with vestiges of past elegance; their two-story house adjoined Louis's general store, where all the children worked. The value of money was inculcated in them early. Stein would learn much later that one of his grandfathers had been a rabbi, and a great-grandfather a scholar of some renown (and so devout that when he was told, during a Sabbath service, that his daughter had just died, he displayed no emotion and simply continued with his prayers); but this came as a surprise to Jules, who had believed that he was the first of his family to be well educated. In his parents' household, it was not scholarship but business acumen that was prized; Jews from Lithuania, who were called Litvaks, were known for their financial prowess. As Shalom Aleichem, whose sayings reflected the sentiments of many Middle European Jews, wrote: "If you have money, you are not only clever, but handsome too, and can sing like a nightingale."

The store where Jules spent much of his childhood was a narrow, cluttered space—twenty-five by one hundred feet—overflowing with merchandise. In the long showcases, and on the shelves that lined the walls from the floor to the ceiling (a ladder on wheels ran on a railing along the shelves, so even the children could reach the high items) were piles of men's and women's clothing, shoes, dress patterns, cloth, balls of wool. In a cage in the center stood the cash register. The customers were workers and farmers; barter was common, negotiation constant. Always vigilant for theft, the family developed secret codes in order to communicate. Spotting a possible shoplifter, one family member would call out the name of another, closest to the suspect, and shout, "21!" They also devised what they called the GOLDBERKS code, in which G stood for 1, O for 2, and so forth; P or X stood for 0. (Many years later, when Jules would make his younger sister, Ruth, his financial assistant—the only person he trusted in this capacity—he would use this code to send her messages from abroad.) They used the code to mark merchandise so that, when the inevitable negotiations ensued, they would know what they had paid for it but the customers would not. It was almost scriptural that one must never be taken advantage of, but, rather, must get the better end of the deal. And it followed, too, that money so hard-earned was to be spent frugally; thus, since the bus to school cost a nickel, Jules and his siblings often chose to walk rather than spend the five cents.

It was not lost upon Jules that, hardworking as his father was, the family remained poor; if business acumen was the measure of a man, his father fell short. Perhaps Louis Stein knew his son viewed him critically. Louis was adept with his hands, and had wrought an iron fence that stood in front of their house; he liked to make constructions out of pipes, which Rosa viewed as a vulgar hobby. Jules, who also enjoyed crafts and gadgetry, sent away for a kit for making an English antique-style desk; when he brought it home from carpentry class, his father ridiculed it, declaring it should be thrown out, but his mother placed it in the center of the living room, where it remained for many years. Jules, in any event, felt an affinity for his mother—a warm, open-faced woman with a clear gaze—but not his father. He was a child who never seemed childlike; he never learned to swim because his mother warned him the water was dangerous, he trudged to school in the company of his thoughts, alone, and from an early age he seemed to feel responsible for his siblings. "Jules was like a father," his sister Ruth said, recalling how her older brother would reward her with money for excellent report cards. He was intent on making money; when he was about eleven, he began playing the violin, and within a couple years he had found a way to make that pastime pay. He formed an orchestra with four or five other youngsters, and they performed for small parties—their favorite number was "Alexander's Ragtime Band." Jules also accompanied a pianist in a nickelodeon movie theater, for which he received seven passes per week. Soon, he added the saxophone to his repertoire to increase his marketability.

Because Jules was in a great hurry to escape the confines of South Bend, he enrolled in summer school at Winona Lake Academy to accelerate his high school schedule. It was his first time away from home, and he was so homesick he almost quit; but then he decided to promote Saturday night dances for the students of his school and also the University of Indiana summer school, and he became so engrossed in this activity he forgot his homesickness. He found a dance hall in Warsaw, a few miles away; arranged for a streetcar line to run a special car from Warsaw back to Winona at midnight; printed postcards announcing these dances and sent them to all the students. "This was my first dance promotion," he recalled in a series of interviews conducted by former *New York Times* reporter Murray Schumach in the 1970s. Upon graduating from high school at sixteen, Stein commenced what he later referred to as "negotiations" with colleges—proposing that he would play in the school band in exchange for free tuition. The best offer came from the University of West Virginia—not only free tuition and books but a job playing in the local Swisher Theatre two nights a week, for about $5 a night. During the two years he spent there, Stein came up with another business venture; realizing that students had trouble locating one another, he solicited ads from merchants and put out a student guide—in which his name appeared in letters larger than all the rest. ("That was a mistake," he said later. "I never did anything like that again." Stein seemed to consider it vulgar. Indeed, cultivating personal anonymity would become one of the hallmarks of his business life.) The following summer, he formed his own band and played in hotels; he also gave dance lessons in the fox-trot, two-step, and waltz. After graduating at eighteen from the University of West Virginia, Stein attended the University of Chicago for a year of postgraduate study; he continued to receive tuition free in exchange for playing in the band, and he found Chicago a far more lucrative market for booking other band dates. Soon, Stein realized he could make more money booking bands than playing in them; and, when he booked them for a summer stint at a resort, he found other opportunities as well. At Charlevoix, Michigan, in the summer of 1919, he not only provided musicians for the season but also paid to lease the hotel beauty parlor and barbershop and haberdashery, which he then ran—an instinct for dominating numerous venues that would become more pronounced over time.

Thanks to his band booking, Stein was able to put himself through medical school in Chicago (it was said that during his internship at Cook County Hospital he set the record for the greatest number of tonsillectomies performed in one day), and was even able to spend a year in eye research at the University of Vienna. Traveling through Germany during a period of extreme inflation, he kept a detailed diary of his expenditures, which were minimized by the relative strength of the dollar (for example, he spent 65 cents for an overnight train from Leipzig to Berlin). While Stein took great satisfaction in recording his economies, he also developed a lasting fear that inflation might someday wipe out all his savings. By 1924, he had completed his studies, and he was working for well-regarded Chicago ophthalmologist Dr. Harry Gredel. But medicine was not what compelled him; money was. So that year, with $3,000 in capital, Stein started a band-booking agency he called the Music Corporation of America. And if it had a familiar ring—like, say, the Radio Corporation of America—that is just what Stein intended. The Radio Corporation of America was the consortium of five huge corporations—United Fruit, General Electric, Westinghouse, AT&T, and Marconi—that had decided to join together in 1919 in order to divide the nascent radio business among themselves. It was a preposterous analogy—the implicit suggestion that this company, which had opened for business in a tiny, two-room office in Chicago's old Capitol Building, might become to the band-booking business what these corporate giants were to the radio business—but Stein's expectations had always been vaulting. When he was still in college, he had vowed that one day he would drive a Rolls-Royce and own a seat on the New York Stock Exchange. Now, the letterhead for this fledgling booking agency featured a sketch of the globe, with a short musical phrase (about three measures of "My Country 'Tis of Thee") stretching across the equator.

It did not appear to be a particularly propitious moment to go into the band-booking business. Prohibition had closed many cabarets and beer gardens, putting thousands of musicians out of work, and radio was widely perceived as a medium that would displace musicians even more. America's first commercial radio station had opened in 1920, and by the start of 1922 more than five hundred of them were broadcasting; the explosion of radio, said Herbert Hoover, then secretary of commerce, was "one of the most astonishing things that have ever come under my observation of American life." In fact, radio would become a boon to musicians generally, and to the fledgling Music Corporation in particular; but this was not yet apparent. Petrillo was outraged by the fact that musicians were not paid for their performances—something that would be detrimental to Stein as well. In early 1924, the rough-spoken Petrillo released a statement to the press that was plainly ghostwritten: "With the exception of brewers and distillers, no class of men have felt the blow of Prohibition more keenly than the musicians. . . . If no check is made, it is only a matter of time until music as a profession is relegated to history. Parties, banquets, and social functions now use the radio for music. . . . Free advertising of orchestras given by broadcast stations doesn't feed the large majority of musicians affected." Following Petrillo's declaration, a vote of the membership of Local 10 prohibited union musicians from playing on the radio for free in the Chicago jurisdiction. The broadcasters attempted to fight, but not for long. A triumphant Petrillo recalled later: "They told me to see their lawyer. The lawyer was usually an ex-Judge So-and-So. He had a lot of books on the table to prove the Government owned the air. I said, 'I know the Government owns the air. What I want to find out is who pays the musicians!' " Petrillo bargained hard for radio musicians' pay and union jurisdiction, and eventually radio musicians would be brought to the top scale of the music industry—something that probably stimulated the growth of big bands (and worked to Stein's advantage).

In hard times, in any event, the astute discern opportunity; that was a Stein-like maxim, one that he would put into effect again and again in his life, as an entrepreneur and an investor. And the opportunity he spied at this moment was the one-night dance band tour. It was terribly simple. If a band or orchestra were to be booked at a café or hotel for a long engagement, as most were, then they did not necessarily need an agent. But if they were to travel from one-night stand to one-night stand, an agent was a virtual necessity. And if these bands became successful and numerous enough, then the bigger, famous bands would come under the sway of Music Corporation as well. The demand for these traveling bands, moreover, was there, for dancing had become the biggest single factor in the entertainment business; there were hundreds of new halls, pavilions, and ballrooms going up in communities across the country. The potential existed to draw as many as five thousand dancers to a single affair, grossing as much as $10,000 a night. Over the next couple of years, thousands of new orchestras would come into being, and radio would make many of them nationally famous. There had been some one-night tours before Stein started Music Corporation—he had booked a couple himself—but they were poorly organized, haphazard affairs. Stein saw he could make it into a business.

Here, as in other critical situations over the years, he would need the support of the musicians union—particularly Petrillo, and also the national president of the AFM, Joseph Weber. For the locals had, Stein already knew, a "hatred . . . for the imposition of traveling dance bands." He needed Petrillo to waive his injunction against traveling bands coming into Chicago, and he needed Weber to persuade locals across the country to relent. Stein felt it was imperative for him to be a delegate to the AFM national convention, and in order to increase his chances of becoming one, he joined five different locals, including Chicago's Number 10. For ten years, he was a delegate to these conventions, and he introduced a number of resolutions favoring or protecting the traveling dance bands. All lost. Some of the other delegates' proposed resolutions would have put him out of business if they were passed. But Stein cultivated his relationship with Weber, and they became good friends, though they did not enjoy the same bond he had with Petrillo. And, as Stein commented, "Weber was able to convince the delegates of the folly of their thinking."

Meanwhile, Stein was building the business from scratch. The earliest clients were, unsurprisingly, the hardest to sign. One night at the Lincoln Tavern, a busy roadhouse on Chicago's North Side, Stein was captivated by the Coon-Sanders Nighthawks, a band headed by Joe Sanders at the piano and Carleton Coon on the drums. The two were noted for their singing, especially their duets; they had already made some Victor records and had become popular, especially through nightly radio broadcasts from the Muehlebach, a hotel that was the premier dance spot in Kansas City. Stein eagerly fastened on them, but they tried to shake him off. They'd done well enough on their own, and were already signed at the Congress Hotel in Chicago for the next season. Stein, however, told them he had a different idea. Since radio had already built them an audience in the Midwest, he would send them on a one-night tour of small towns, and with clever booking and good advertising, the box office receipts should far exceed what they could make in a fixed locale. Still disinclined, Sanders asked for an advance of $10,000, to be deposited before they left Chicago. To his amazement, Stein agreed. He didn't have the money, but he decided he would demand a 50 percent advance from each of the promoters. The tour was such a hit that Stein netted about $10,000 after his costs.

The first associate Stein hired was William Goodheart, a part-time musician whom Stein had first met when he was still in school, and he had booked the band in which Goodheart, a student himself, was the piano player. Goodheart was a humpbacked gnome of a man who devoted himself to his tasks with a kind of infernal energy, and so terrorized his associates that orchestra leaders' wives were said to hush their youngsters by warning them that not the devil but Goodheart would get them. His mission for Music Corporation was to comb the territory and compile information on every possible locale, no matter how remote, for a traveling dance band; and, at the same time, to try to win bookings in major hotels. One of Goodheart's stops was the Muehlebach Hotel. As he later described to Karl Kramer, a Music Corporation employee who wrote a memoir about these early days, "I stopped off there intending to sell Ted Weems, which was one of the few top orchestras we handled. I spent three days getting the run-around from the front offices until somebody tipped me off that I was talking to the wrong parties and that all the Muehlebach bands were booked out of the men's washroom. It sounded like a joke until I sounded out the chief attendant in that august department. It cost me a good part of my meager travel funds to find that the hotel management, before making any decisions on booking or changing bands, always had the washroom boy conduct a sort of Gallup poll among his customers. He queried each visitor about his particular likes and dislikes in dance orchestras, and these plus all the overheard comments and conversations, he passed on upstairs. Such opinions were considered as unbiased and factual and probably were an exact measure of customer opinion. So I spent a lot of time and some money in this department extolling the merits of Ted Weems's wonderful orchestra, and, at the same time subtly conveyed that the financial welfare of the washroom staff would be assured when linked to the booking of MCA bands in the Muehlebach." The Weems booking was made, and the Muehlebach became one of MCA's most important customers for many years.

Over the next couple of years, Goodheart and a small cadre of additional Music Corporation employees compiled the mailing list of buyers that became the engine of their one-night business. At first, it dealt only with the Midwestern states, but eventually it covered the country. California, for MCA, was especially unknown territory, until one clever young employee, Taft Schreiber, came up with the idea of persuading Western Union executives to sponsor a plan to have each branch manager send a list of all the dance jobs in his town. He argued that it would build wire business for the company, since so much of MCA business was conducted by telephone and telegraph—and what would have taken years to amass by sending MCA salesmen as scouts was done in short order. Each name on this list was stamped on an Addressograph plate, tabbed with individualized notations as to the customer's idiosyncrasies, and these were kept in locked cabinets. It was a top secret but storied property. (Once, a competitor approached the MCA employee in charge of these plates and offered him $500 for a duplicate roll; it was decided that a new list should be made from the morgue of obsolete and discarded plates in MCA's back room, and proffered in place of the real thing. The $500 was credited to "miscellaneous one-night bookings.") With the mailing list in hand, the process became quite methodical. A decision was made about what territory would be best for a given band; then, sample packages of advertising were sent to promoters. Stein and his team prided themselves on their marketing materials, which were, indeed, innovative in this area; each booker was provided flyers, window cards, circulars, news stories, and original posters, done by a team of poster artists employed by MCA.

The one-night business was lucrative, but it needed to be complemented by bookings at nightclubs and, especially, deluxe hotels—these provided prestige and, also, the radio time that enabled bands to become famous more quickly. And when Stein founded Music Corporation, the biggest booking agency in the Midwest, and the one that booked nearly all Chicago's hotels and cafés, was the Edgar A. Benson Company. Stein spotted vulnerability in the Benson operation, however. For no matter how well known were the bands Benson was representing, he insisted that each one be billed primarily as a "Benson Orchestra." Even on some phonograph recordings, that was how they were named. In Stein's view, it seemed like a foolish egoism; Benson failed to realize that a dance orchestra could attain the same fame as a movie star, and that fame, in turn, would only increase box office earnings. Soon, Stein started winning some Benson clients away, promising them that not Music Corporation but *they* would be the stars, under his direction. It was a principle he would continue to apply over the years. And there was no obstacle to his winning these clients away because Benson had no contracts with them, only casual mutual agreements. Not so, Stein. The Stein contract was "a thing of beauty," wrote Karl Kramer. It was not only exclusive but, in most cases, lifelong. For it contained a paragraph that said the contract was in effect until the band leader had grossed $1 million. ("A lot of leaders took this to mean that they were guaranteed a million, which in those days was a lot of money," Kramer added.) Stein may have had other gambits, too, like the Muehlebach sweetener, for capturing Benson's clients, for soon most of them had joined the MCA fold; the big jobs, therefore, became MCA's as well; and within several years, the Benson agency disintegrated. Years later, Benson, sick and destitute, would write Stein a letter, asking for financial help.

Now that Stein had acquired much of the hotel- and nightclub-booking business, his goal was to obtain "exclusives" from these buyers. If they agreed to buy all their talent from him, he would of course have far more bookings available, and his competition would effectively be shut out. Why these buyers should agree was a harder proposition. He started by promising them a steady flow of performers who were right for them, at the right prices; and he assured them that they would get first call in their area on his top talent. If the logic of this arrangement was not compelling enough, there were other benefits available, as Goodheart had suggested in recounting his dealings at the Muehlebach; there were, for example, Christmas presents for those who hired talent, large sums of cash given with no quid pro quo, in the spirit of the season. The more exclusives Stein was able to obtain, the more important clients flocked to him; the more important clients were his, the more he obtained exclusives. It did not happen overnight, but it was a machine that would keep feeding itself, growing larger and larger, and with it came a great deal of leverage. This was the dawn of "tie-ins," a practice that later would become almost synonymous with MCA. Harry Sosnik, who signed with MCA in the late twenties and eventually became a well-known composer-conductor, recalled in an oral history that MCA initiated this system in this early period. It operated on the principle, Sosnik said, that if you wanted Guy Lombardo—which *everyone* did—you had to take some unknown orchestra for a couple weeks. "The big names were the ones that opened the door for MCA's lesser-known orchestras, which created a very big MCA."

A highly profitable extension of exclusives and tie-ins was called "packaging." Stein would ask an exclusive buyer for a lump sum for all the season's entertainment; then Stein would pay the bands himself out of these monies. And if he were able to juggle effectively—mixing expensive bands with less-expensive, and maybe putting a high-cost band in for less money because he couldn't find them any other bookings (or so he told his musician clients)—then what he pocketed at the end was much more than the usual agent's commission of 10 percent. It was a natural evolution; first Stein, as a youth, realized he could make more money booking bands than playing in them; and then he realized that, in many instances, he could make more money employing them than booking them.

Through Music Corporation, Stein was able to fulfill his early sense of responsibility for his siblings; ultimately, he would employ all of them (directly, or indirectly through a spouse). He hired his sister Adelaide's husband, Charles Miller, in the first couple of years, and, not long after, his brother Bill. Though Bill was older, it was Jules who had always been the provider; when Bill had wanted to start a dress business, Stein—then still in his late teens—had given him money he'd saved; the business failed. And when Jules was seventeen, he had obtained a summer job for Bill, playing with Jules's band, in its engagement at the Hotel Ottawa, in Ottawa Beach, Michigan. "Since Bill could not play any instrument, I rented a string bass and rubbed soap on the bow so there was no sound," Jules recalled. "Bill was a good singer, so he got by for a while by energetically sawing away on his silent bow until one night the hotel people got suspicious of so much activity resulting in so little music. That was the end of Bill's first and only employment as a musician. . . . But really he was born to be an agent and after he joined us in 1925 he became our number one talent scout, probably bringing into the MCA fold more big attractions than any other single individual." Bill, who had no direct duties or responsibilities, and kept no regular hours, spent his nights making the rounds of the dance spots. Karl Kramer later wrote that Bill Stein "knew everybody and talked to everybody: head waiters, song pluggers, secretaries to hotel managers, phonograph record bosses and trade journal reporters." His extreme sociability, so different from his brother Jules's reticence, paid off; among those he was responsible for signing were Guy Lombardo and the Royal Canadians (he discovered them in Cleveland when they were little known) and Kay Kyser, who would later become famous as the quizmaster in the *Kollege of Musical Knowledge* radio show.

By May 1926, Stein and his troops had moved to new quarters in the Oriental Theater building, part of the Balaban & Katz chain, which owned large, rococo-style movie houses throughout Chicago. Barney Balaban and Stein were good friends, and they did business together as well; for motion picture theaters had become major bookers of orchestras, which played during intermission, and Stein booked Balaban's theaters. This Music Corporation office displayed, for the first time, what would be a signal penchant of Stein's—creating an office that made a statement, and one distinctly at odds with the tawdry, flesh-peddling image of an agent. The mundane wooden desks and stiff chairs from the two-room Capitol office had been banished. Instead, Stein had an ornate, Spanish-style desk and comfortable chairs in his office, and on his walls there were none of the usual amusement business photos but, rather, Viennese etchings he had acquired during his medical study abroad. Karl Kramer stressed that the appearance of the office—opulent and glamorous for that time, and one that created a general impression that the young company was intensely prosperous—didn't quite match reality. Music Corporation's profits in 1926 were $12,000. Its half-dozen employees all lived in modest rented apartments, and not one owned a car. When Stein bought his first car, it was indeed a Rolls-Royce, as he had vowed it would be; but it was secondhand, owned by one of the band leaders, Zez Comfrey, and all Stein's men had to go for a ride and put their approval on the deal before Stein paid the $1,800. "There were many times that our bank account was strained to the last buck, and on some occasions we even had to wait months to cash our bonus checks, small as they were, because there were not sufficient funds available," Kramer wrote. "But you never would have known it from the front office."

Stein's apparent prosperity made it inevitable that he would attract the attention of Chicago's ruling class, the gangsters who controlled the city in the twenties—and who were, in addition, his customers, at many of the nightclubs he was booking. Stein would later claim that it was in 1928 that they began demanding payoffs and a piece of Music Corporation. The only surprise is that it took that long.

There were rival gangs, led by men like Bugs Moran, Dion O'Bannion, and Roger Touhy, and they certainly had their territories and perquisites, but by the late twenties Al Capone was supreme. And if Capone or those operating on his behalf made a demand of a businessman or labor union official, there was no meaningful authority to appeal to, so thoroughly had Capone subsumed the majority of the police and the politicians. The price of resistance, of course, was well known. Someone who had the opportunity to observe Capone close up during this period was a member of his entourage—filled in the main with triggermen like Machine Gun Jack McGurn—who was rather out of place: a young piano player and law student (he was at the time clerking for a federal district court judge) named Luis Kutner. Kutner had gone to Lane Tech High School in the heart of the Black Hand, or Mafia, district; status there came from being accepted at the Buffalo Ice Cream Parlor, where the gangsters recruited. Although Kutner was a slight, blond kid who played in the school orchestra and led literary discussions, he also became a good fighter and cultivated the right friends; so he eventually made it into the ice cream parlor and, from there, to Colosimo's, the famous eating and cabaret spot at Wabash and 22nd Streets, which had been run by Big Jim Colosimo, the Chicago overlord of crime, until he was killed there in 1920. Johnny Torrio had taken Colosimo's place in the crime hierarchy, as well as the café, and he hired young Kutner to play piano there a couple nights a week. As Kutner tells it, a lowly foot soldier named Al Capone, moody and withdrawn, sitting by himself in a corner, asked Kutner if he could play "Roses of Picardy," which, as it turned out, was Capone's favorite song. Kutner did—for the first of many hundreds of times. "Piano was my open sesame," Kutner said in a series of taped interviews conducted with him in the seventies.

Kutner learned from Capone that he had quit school after the fourth grade and started out as a shoeshine boy in Brooklyn, then graduated to looting trucks and warehouses on the wharves, then to hijacking and murder. Torrio, who had been one of the original heads of the Five Points gang in Manhattan, wrote to Capone to come to Chicago, and soon Capone was able to invite other members of his family to move there and work for Torrio, too. "It seemed to be a good town to hustle in, because the police and politicians were so thoroughly owned by the gangs that every imaginable manner of larceny, skullduggery, and illegitimate enterprise could flourish in Chicago in relative safety," Kutner said. "Only chicken stealers and common bandits went to jail. The gangs bought their freedom at so much a head." In Kutner's view, it was Torrio who had the acumen to spot the business potential in Prohibition, and who created the structure of the crime empire that Capone simply inherited. After Torrio was shotgunned and nearly killed, he decided to retire, and left for Italy. "Al had never dreamed at any time that he would suddenly be the one to be head of the gang. He had not displayed particular talents, or leadership, or anything else of that sort except muscle . . . he didn't have a head for business . . . he squandered millions out of everything that came in and eventually died penniless, supported by the Outfit." But, with Torrio suddenly gone, "nobody was around to give orders. They began to ask Al for answers to their questions. Where was the booze for 41st Street? What garage was repairing Tortorelli's truck? Was the precinct sergeant supposed to get a hundred or a thousand? A million little facts that Al had at his fingertips because he had been Torrio's aide-de-camp. It was as if the secretary to the president of IBM had suddenly become the chief officer.

"Even then I had the mind of a lawyer," Kutner added, "and I told Al very strictly, 'Don't pass out information freely, make them struggle for it. Hold in everything that you can.' And he did this. He wasn't sure that I knew what I was doing, because I was just a punk. But fellows in the rackets have a tremendous respect for anybody with an education. So he listened to me."

Kutner said he became a fixture in Capone's headquarters, on the fourth floor of the Metropole Hotel. There, Capone—always very particular about the chair in which he sat—presided in an elaborate high-backed throne (lion heads with open, menacing mouths protruded from its arms), which had been taken from a Balaban & Katz theater. Often, after midnight, Kutner would bring kosher corned beef to the Metropole, make Capone a sandwich, and play the piano softly, while Capone talked a little, or just stared out the window. Capone, who spoke with a thick Brooklyn accent, wanted to improve his diction; Kutner advised him to do this by reading aloud whenever he was in the john; he says that Capone followed his instructions (to the amusement of his listening henchmen), and became well spoken, with a good vocabulary. Kutner told him how to dress—persuading him to give up white socks, and to buy a velvet-collared coat at Marshall Field's. ("All the salesmen gulped when he pulled out this tremendous wad, because he had about a hundred $100 bills and about fifty $1,000 bills, all held together by a little rubber band.") No matter how gentlemanly the rest of his attire, Capone sported a diamond ring that was like a search-light—a symbol of power that would continue to be worn by Chicago businessmen and politicians for many years.

Capone discovered that he loved the limelight, and he cultivated the press. "He threw press conferences like confetti," Kutner said. "He was the original gangster-showman. Can you imagine Sam "Mooney" Giancana making these statements to the press the way Al did? . . . Nobody showed such disregard for the traditional rule of silence. He operated with complete disdain and utter braggadocio." And, Kutner continued, "Once the publicity machine got going, a lot of guys wanted to work for Al for the glory. You were a Capone man; that was important. Better than being a movie star, in Chicago of those days."

Colonel Robert McCormick, who was the owner of the *Chicago Tribune,* seemed to agree. In 1928, when a strike of the *Tribune*'s chauffeurs and drivers union was threatened, Max Annenberg, the *Tribune*'s director of circulation, called Capone, who attended a meeting with Annenberg and Daniel Serritella, a city official who was a Capone protégé (and, also, a good friend of Petrillo's for many years). According to a signed statement by Serritella, Capone agreed to use his influence to stop the strike, and Annenberg then brought in McCormick, who thanked Capone and said, "You know, you are famous like Babe Ruth. We can't help printing things about you, but I will see that the *Tribune* gives you a fair deal."

At that time, Capone appeared invincible. The strength of the system over which he presided was that it was based on mutuality, a perfect mesh of interlocking needs: the gangs' operations provided the aldermen and committeemen with thousands of patronage jobs, as well as the gunmen to supervise the polls on election day; and the aldermen and committeemen chose the police captains in their districts. So the politicians and the gangsters and the police were all bound to one another. "By 1928, Al's police payroll was topping $30 million," Kutner said. "Mayor [William 'Big Bill'] Thompson alone got a million a year. On [Capone's] payroll were over half the police force, and the remaining half would have liked to be. . . . Money was delivered in O'Connor and Goldberg shoe boxes in bills of one thousand denominations. The weekly lineup of police at various warehouses was common knowledge, but no one cared. . . . The bribery was really complete, always in-

cluding the chief of police, detectives, state senators and state representatives, and right into the governor's office, where pardons awaited
Capone's friends on the first day of their arrival at Joliet penitentiary.
This was Governor Len Small, of whom it was said that he belonged in
jail more than the gangsters he pardoned. . . . Al made and broke
politicians at will, and many of their mouthpieces were in due course
elevated to the bench, state and federal. Jury fixing became an art, usually with the rolled-up money stuffed into a cigarette which was
handed to a juror in the men's room by a cooperative judge's bailiff."
It was an expensive system to operate, but the money was pouring in
from Capone's interests in booze, vice, gambling, and labor racketeering; Kutner claims that at one point Capone had a gross income of as
much as $10 million a week.

Nightclubs were the center of Capone's business and, also, his
source of relaxation. Kutner recalled that he went along with Capone
time after time to hear Isham Jones at the College Inn, "a big hangout
for the boys." And he remembered when Bing Crosby, then an unknown from Spokane, Washington, was in town with Paul Whiteman's
Rhythm Boys, and showed up at the Three Deuces (a Capone cabaret).
"He came into the Three Deuces with Bix Beiderbecke, who said that
some dude had invited them to play in Cicero. They had been told they
would be picked up at the Deuces. . . . Crosby sat there biting his nails
and drinking Coke. Chicago made him nervous, he said. . . . Finally
one of Al's limousines called for them. I went out with them and introduced myself to the driver: 'You know me, I play piano for Mr. Brown
[Capone's pseudonym].' Capone had set up the Greyhound Club for
them to play in, with his boys patrolling the streets armed to the teeth
like a small army. Bing stepped out of the door of the limousine, looked
around at all the mugs toting submachine guns in the open, and asked
me, 'Is this a jazz joint or World War II?' He had never before seen men
carrying arms like this in the heart of an American city." Capone
would hand out cash freely to the bands—often a thousand to a band
leader, and at least a hundred to each musician. And he was a great fan
of some entertainers, like George Jessel (Capone grabbed him and

kissed him on both cheeks after he saw him in *The Jazz Singer*) and Joe E. Lewis, who was a kind of forerunner of Lenny Bruce.

Still, business was business. Lewis was working for Capone at a nightspot, Green Mill Gardens, and had promised Capone that he would work for him at the Vanity Café as well. The Vanity Café was run for Capone by a man named Mike Fritzel, who had arrived in Chicago on a cattle train in 1898, gotten a job as a bartender, and, eventually, operated a string of cafés. "Now, if someone couldn't do a job for Al, you were supposed to tell him in advance," Kutner said. "Because once a promise had been made, Al expected one to keep it, very definitely. When Joe E. Lewis reported that he had been offered a better job and wouldn't be available for the Vanity Café, Al was furious. . . . He told Jack McGurn, 'Take care of it.' That was all the instruction Jack ever needed. . . . So Lewis was cut up, and his tongue was hanging out of his open jaw. . . . Actually it was not intended to kill Joe, but just to let him know that next time he was to keep his word. Do you suppose that if Jack McGurn had wanted to kill someone he wouldn't have known how? But this was just a warning. The scar on Lewis's face was a big Z, like Zorro's, a slash from the eye down to the mouth and coming across the jaw." Lewis never identified his assailant—and continued to be employed by Capone and his successors for the rest of his life.

When Stein many years later would reminisce about this period, he repeatedly asserted that he "had the guts of a fool"—because he had rebuffed the gangsters when they had wanted a piece of his company; and when, in the early thirties, he was informed he was a kidnapping target of theirs, he had not tried to appease them or even deigned to hire bodyguards, but had merely taken out a life insurance policy and gone about his business. His compatriot Petrillo, too, would make it a point to boast of his stubborn independence back in those fearsome days. "About 1924 or '25, a guy comes to see me . . . says he's a cousin of Al's and I should get him a job," Petrillo recounted when he was interviewed by Murray Schumach. "I listened to him play and he wasn't so bad, and I thought there was no use getting into a fight with the Capone gang so I got him a job. Pretty soon another guy turns up, then another. . . . I got to thinking that this Capone is going to have ten thousand cousins and my men need those jobs. They would take over . . . so I had to throw them out . . . to protect the union."

The story of that era, however—and of the parts that Petrillo and Stein played vis-à-vis the gangsters—appears more complicated. A close friend of Petrillo's for nearly fifty years who delivered the eulogy at his funeral, U.S. District Court Judge Abraham Lincoln Marovitz first met Petrillo in the late twenties, when Marovitz was a young lawyer in the state attorney's office in Chicago. "Petrillo was a tough guy, but I was lucky—he took a liking to me," Judge Marovitz said. "He made me an honorary member of his union." They discovered that they had grown up in the same neighborhood, a West Side ghetto ward that had gone from Irish to Jewish to Italian, and was so riddled with gang violence that it was known as the Bloody Twentieth. They were the children of immigrants; Petrillo's father was a sewer digger, Marovitz's a tailor, and his mother ran a small candy store on Maxwell Street; both families had barely subsisted. Petrillo had played the trumpet in a band, sold newspapers, operated elevators, and helped run a saloon before spotting opportunity in the unions when he was twenty-two. Marovitz's world was limited, too, but he was a bright, ambitious youth, and he caught the eye of well-placed people. A speech he gave at a boys club led to an $8-a-week job in the law library at Mayer, Meyer, Austrian & Platt; senior partner Al Austrian then offered to pay his tuition at night law school (the only prerequisite at that time was a high school diploma), and, upon his graduation, got him a job in the state attorney's office; and Jacob Arvey—an alderman during the Capone era who was a protégé of ex-convict and political boss Moe Rosenberg, and who would in turn become the boss of Chicago, and then the entire state—tapped Marovitz for his ward organization and, over the years, would support him for all his posts: state senator, superior court judge, and, ultimately, federal district court judge.

Judge Marovitz was a local personage in Chicago, someone whose nearly century-long history was intertwined with that of the city, and of the politicians and businessmen and gangsters who controlled it for so long. He was on good terms with most of them. More, he was supported by them, or he would not have been able to rise politically as he did. Arvey, whom Judge Marovitz called his "godfather," had among his closest associates men who were connected to the Syndicate, or Outfit, as it was long known in Chicago. One long-standing member of that organization, a contemporary of Judge Marovitz's who would not allow his name to be used, said that Marovitz was "a great person"— and while he would not answer questions himself for fear of being labeled a "stool pigeon," he insisted that Marovitz "knows everything." Another longtime associate of former Mafia head Sam Giancana declared that Marovitz was more powerful than the Outfit because he had legitimacy, and could serve as a bridge between his world and theirs. Using an expression that refers to the Hanukkah candle with which one lights all the others, this person said, "Marovitz was the shamas."

Over the course of several interviews in the office he occupied as a senior-status judge in the federal district court building—an office whose walls were lined with the likenesses of Abraham Lincoln that he had collected over the years, and also with photographs of his famous friends, including many show business people, like Frank Sinatra, Joe E. Lewis, Bob Hope, Tony Bennett, Jimmy Durante—Judge Marovitz talked about the past. After he left the state attorney's office in 1932, he went into private practice. "I made more money in the first few months of that practice than I expected to make in my lifetime. But it was very, very tough in those days. I represented all sides—mobsters, unions, management. I represented Petrillo for years. Petrillo was with the Outfit—but when Capone left [he was convicted of tax evasion and went to prison in late 1931], Petrillo was able to get out a little. They were trying to dominate him too much. And he got his own tough guys, former mob guys, around him." Under Capone, Judge Marovitz added, there was mainly one group to deal with, which made it easy in a way; but once he was gone, there were many different factions, all trying to move in.

This state of gang anarchy was what led to Petrillo's kidnapping in mid-1933, Marovitz continued—an event that was much rumored, but that Petrillo denied had occurred. It was a particularly tumultuous time. With Prohibition just ended, the mob was intent on finding new sources of revenue; labor racketeering was intensifying, and kidnapping became a popular form of extortion. "There *was* a plot [to kidnap him]," Judge Marovitz said. "It's hard to talk about it. I was involved in resolving it."

How so?

"I would talk to the mob. Some I had helped. If I had to ask them for something, they would listen."

Several months later, the kidnapping provided ammunition for a challenge to Petrillo's union presidency. In December 1933, just days before an election at Local 10, a suit was filed by two union members charging that Petrillo and his officers had abused their authority in numerous ways—essentially, misappropriating union funds for their own use and aggrandizement, and then refusing to allow members to see the union's books. Questions were raised about the rumored kidnapping. The plaintiffs alleged that about six months before it was said to have taken place, Petrillo had declared at a union meeting that he believed he was in danger of being kidnapped, that it was likely a ransom demand of $50,000 would be made—"and you boys would in all probability pay for my release, and if there are no objections to that, we will consider that the opinion of the membership." In the event, $100,000 was supposedly paid for his release. The plaintiffs wanted to know: had there been a kidnapping, or had this been a ruse to obtain $100,000 of union funds? And if the kidnapping had indeed occurred, was this a legitimate use of the money? After its rumored occurrence, the complaint continued, Petrillo had hired five bodyguards, placing them on the union payroll; four were his relatives. They also alleged that Petrillo was buying votes in the coming election, using money from a $40,000 relief fund. Petrillo immediately hired an auditor, obtained a clean report, and took out a full-page ad in the newspaper to publish those findings. He won reelection overwhelmingly, and his challenger, a musician, was unable to find work in Chicago for several years and finally left the city. After the election, the plaintiffs did not pursue the case, and it was dismissed. According to Marovitz, the lawsuit was a bid for power by another gang faction, which wanted to replace Petrillo with their man. The attorney for the plaintiffs in this case was a young man named Sidney Korshak.

"Sidney and I were rivals in the thirties," Judge Marovitz said. "I represented the unions, and the muscle guys. So did he. He had silent partners in his law firm—he was with the hoodlums. The mob tried to move in on everybody. They tried to move in on me. I carried a pistol." Marovitz paused, and leaned down to open his bottom desk drawer. He took out a black pistol—small enough to fit in a woman's evening bag—and aimed it playfully at his visitor. "You'd be *amazed* to know the people they were able to reach. When I became chief justice of the criminal court, two lawyers came to see me, and they said, 'We'll make you a rich man.' I said, 'I *am* a rich man. I came in with my self-respect, I'm leaving with it.' After that, they sought a change of venue every time they came before me. Korshak came before me sometimes, but he almost never took a case to trial—he was always making deals.

"I was approached so many times," Judge Marovitz continued. "I got a lot of verbal abuse—'Who do you think you are?' Well, money was never my god."

Petrillo had been well acquainted with violence for many years before his kidnapping. In 1924, his front porch had been bombed (a front-porch bombing was a favored expression of mob interest, usually after their initial advances had been rebuffed; it made a strong impression, and generally did not kill the person they were attempting to enlist). He had moreover not been above using violent means himself—in the Chinese restaurants, for example. And after he was president of the local, he apparently continued to find it a useful tool. In 1929, Maurice Wells, owner of the Adams Theater, was quoted in the *Chicago Herald and Examiner,* saying, "This is a racket. My company

Stein's cohort James Caesar Petrillo in 1928—when he was president of the Chicago local of the American Federation of Musicians. *Corbis-Bettmann*

bought this theater about five years ago. The previous owners had once employed an organist but had discontinued music. Some time ago, I installed an automatic organ. Six weeks ago, Petrillo visited me in company with two other men. He said, 'Shut off that organ and don't start it again.' I kept it silent for four days and then I started it again. Then the stench bomb business started. A friend of mine went to see Petrillo. He came back with the word, 'They mean business. They say that they have just started.' "

But it was only after the kidnapping that Petrillo behaved like someone who was at odds with the mob and thus feared for his life—which squares with Marovitz's statement that it was then that Petrillo was trying to "get out a little" from the Outfit. Not only did Petrillo hire bodyguards at that time, but he began riding in a limousine that had bulletproof glass. The storm windows at his office were made bulletproof, too. And in order to reach his office, located on the third floor of the musicians union building, one had to walk past the bodyguards' station on the second-floor landing, and then—if one were not expected—search for his office door, which was hidden, and opened only from the inside. In this period, too, Petrillo installed a machine gun in the building's auditorium.

In September 1933, about three months after Petrillo's kidnapping, Petrillo learned that Stein was targeted for kidnapping as well. Petrillo's informant was George Browne, an official of the stagehands union who had been a friend and business ally of Petrillo's for years—and who, in partnership with Willie Bioff, would shortly be carrying out a huge extortion plot on behalf of the Outfit, targeting the Hollywood movie studios. Petrillo would only divulge that his informant had been Browne many years after both Browne and Bioff were dead. Recalling his conversation with Browne, Petrillo began, "He says to me, 'What do you know about this guy Jules Stein?'

"I tell him, 'He's a good guy.'

"Then George gives me the word. He says the snatch will be for $50,000. So I call Jules and tell him to come to my office. That is natural. It's not something you discuss on the phone. Jules asks me how I know. I wasn't going to tell Jules. How can I? What happens to George if that gets known? He gets killed. I was in the middle. I had to protect both of them. I never knew for sure which mob it was. People always like to say it was Capone. Why say Capone? No one knows. It could be O'Bannion. It could be Touhy.

"Well, I give the news to Jules. He is cool. That's Jules. He just sits and bites his fingernails, the way he does when he's excited.

"What people don't realize is what it was like in those days," Petrillo added. "It's almost impossible for an outsider to realize that in those days if a guy sneezed everybody went for his gun. It was a son of a bitch. Guys would come to you to buy tickets and say, 'Al sent me.' Or, 'Touhy sent me.' Then they would send someone around a few days later and he'd tell you, 'Everybody's paying. So you pay, too.' There was lots of that. Nobody was bluffing in those days. If a guy said he would shoot you, you could bet on it. You would be shot."

The day after receiving Petrillo's warning, Stein went to see his insurance broker. Stein had never heard of a kidnap insurance policy before, but he thought it seemed only logical. He told his broker he wanted a $75,000 policy, $25,000 more than the ransom demand was supposed to be; that way, if he *were* kidnapped, it would only cost him the $650 premium. It was an idiosyncratic approach to the situation, and one that was utterly characteristic of Stein. He tended to view almost everything through a financial prism, always trying to protect his downside, ceaselessly computing his gain or loss; it was the position in life, once removed, with everything reduced to what was quantifiable, where he felt most comfortable. The policy, dated September 29, 1933, stipulated that nothing would be paid if Stein were killed; Stein would later have it framed, displaying it to visitors as evidence of his temerity. "I'd always known that Lloyd's gives insurance on chancy things—like the weather," Stein said later. "So I decided they would do this. I didn't know who else to go to. I was pretty sure the Touhy gang was behind it. And the big gangsters in Chicago in those days had deals with the politicians and the police and the judges. I figured there was no sense going to the cops."

It is interesting that Stein was convinced his would-be kidnappers (who never did materialize) were the Touhy gang; in all likelihood, the reason that he did not suspect the Capone gang is that they were his partners. For while it is not clear whether Stein gave them a piece of the Music Corporation when they first demanded it, by the early thirties he did appear to have interests in properties they controlled. The most famous of these was the Chez Paree, which opened its doors in November 1932, when the Depression had barely begun to lift, to the sounds of Ben Pollack's orchestra playing "Happy Days Are Here Again." Featuring showgirls known as the Chez Paree Adorables, and such performers as Joe E. Lewis and Sophie Tucker, the Chez Paree fast became the hottest nightspot in Chicago—a mecca for Chicago's trinity of businessmen, politicians, and the mob. "The Chez Paree was the meeting place for the Outfit," said Irving Kupcinet, a columnist for the *Chicago Tribune* who was friendly with its members, and who was himself a regular at the Chez Paree, as was his close friend Sidney Korshak; Marovitz, too, rarely missed a Saturday night there. Unprepossessing from the outside, the Chez Paree was on the top floor of a three-story building; the first and second floors were a warehouse, and a liquor store and butcher shop were in the basement. It was a large space, big enough to seat about 650 people, with a bandstand on the east side of the room; there was also a gambling room in the back—ignored by the police and politicians for nearly twenty years—that some gambling connoisseurs rated the best in the country. Singer Tony Martin, who began his entertainment career playing the saxophone in the Tom Gerun orchestra, recalled that they were booked by MCA at the Chez Paree in the mid-thirties. During his stint there, Martin became a friend of Korshak's, who he knew was a lawyer for the Outfit, and they would remain close for the rest of their lives. "Of course the boys owned the nightclubs, the saloons, the hotels—they owned everything!" Martin said. "They were very nice with me. I was a performer, I wasn't a competitor, I just contributed to their fun. I worked for them in Chicago, in New Orleans. I knew never to ask questions."

The nightclub's major owners were the Fischetti family, Capone's cousins, who continued to be powerful members of the Capone gang long after Al had left Chicago for the penitentiary. But, as was always the case, the major owners' names did not appear on any publicly available documents; their front men were Mike Fritzel—who had run other Capone clubs, including the Vanity Café where Lewis had been performing at the time of his assault—and Joey Jacobson, a Capone underling. And Marovitz said that Stein had an interest in the Chez Paree as well. "I know Jules had an interest, because I represented Mike Fritzel," Judge Marovitz said. "Jules made deals with Fritzel and Jacobson to provide the entertainment, and then he demanded a piece. Jules was very powerful." And it was his accommodation with Capone and his successors that allowed Stein that power. "Jules had to be with Capone," Judge Marovitz commented, "or be shot in the head."

Asked about the ownership of the Chez Paree, Kupcinet said, "It was owned by Fritzel and Jacobson, and the mob had a piece. Fritzel and Jacobson were businessmen, but with a taint—because they were partners with the Outfit. In nightclubs in those days, they had to buy their liquor from one place, their meat from one place—the Outfit dictated all aspects of it."

Was he aware that Stein had a piece of it, too? "Yes, Jules may well have," he replied. After a pause, he added, "Jules had private investors in Music Corporation in the early days." He said he did not recall their names.

According to Marovitz, Stein had acquired interests in several other nightclubs as well in this period—among them, the French Casino and the College Inn. "He had a piece of the clubs and the mob had a piece," Judge Marovitz said. The only nightclub that Stein ever was publicly identified as having an interest in, however, was the French Casino. In what was his first step into the personal appearance and act business, Stein had brought the Folies Bergère to the Pabst Blue Ribbon Casino at the 1933 World's Fair in Chicago, and after that he opened the French Casino and moved the show there. Karl Kramer claimed in his memoir that the French Casino thus became this country's original theater-restaurant—a place with food, dancing, and a big, lavish theatrical spectacle (in this case, replete with an almost-all-nude chorus line). "The impact upon the café business was instantaneous and shattering," Kramer wrote. "From the opening number to the final chorus, the Folies Bergère was an unqualified smash hit."

Perhaps it was *too* successful not to draw unwelcome attention. In the midst of a performance on a summer night in 1934, when there were about two thousand people in the nightclub, several unions' representatives appeared and ordered all the employees out on strike. As Kramer tells it, Stein was told by the representative of the waiters union that for $10,000 under the table they would call off the strike. Stein refused. Visits to the state attorney's office and the police offered no help for a quick resolution; but then Kramer was told by a lawyer who "represented rather the seamier side of the amusement business" to go to the Chicago World's Fair the next night, and have dinner at the Italian Village. There, Kramer and his wife enjoyed dinner, along with a bottle of Asti Spumante wine, sent to their table, and then their host appeared. The apparent proprietor of the restaurant was Alex Louis Greenberg, whom Kramer later determined was the treasurer of the Capone syndicate, and "the financial brains behind the entire Capone operation." (He would be murdered in a gangland killing in 1955.) Kramer told Greenberg the whole story, including the fact that the unions had made no prior demand and had called the strike in the middle of the performance, thereby preventing the collecting of receipts from that night's attendance—several thousand dollars that would have been helpful in reaching a richer deal with the unions. "Now this money was gone forever," Kramer, a notorious penny-pincher, recounted his having lamented to Greenberg, who "knocked his knuckles on his head and said, 'No brains, no brains.' This Mr. Greenberg had a very unusual personality," Kramer continued. "He had coal black hair, and very piercing green eyes. It was apparent that he was a personality of great force and vitality, and the type of man you wouldn't care to tangle with."

At Greenberg's suggestion, Kramer met with him the next day, at the offices of the waiters union—a forbidding place, behind a heavy locked door with a little grilled iron window, through which strangers were interrogated. Kramer found all the unions' representatives seated around a long table, with Greenberg presiding; and after some desultory conversation, Greenberg asked Kramer whether MCA would pay the workers a small token raise, about $5 per week, per man. Of course they would, Kramer responded. After a private consultation with the various union representatives, Greenberg said the French Casino could reopen the following day. Kramer was amazed—could it be true? Didn't they need some letter or legal agreement? "He looked at me with those piercing green eyes and said, 'Will you take my word for it that it is okay to open?' I looked back at him, and I had only one answer to make—yes, I would take his word. He said, 'Then open.' "

They did, and they had no further problems. Kramer was mystified as to why Greenberg would have chosen to help them as he did. And he never speculated, at least in his memoir, about whether Greenberg might have intervened because of the Outfit's connections to Stein—or, also, whether Stein might have quietly turned over some interest in the French Casino that he had previously withheld.

Within just a few years, in the depths of the Depression, Stein had metamorphosed from the owner of a promising but often cash-poor young company to a powerful player in the entertainment world who was flush with cash. Instead of buying a secondhand Rolls, he traveled to England to buy one new and, in order to obtain a dealer's discount, he bought several and shipped them back to this country to resell. He had lost about $10,000 in the stock market crash in 1929 and, looking for a more scientific approach to buying stocks, he had begun keeping charts on past market trends and the behavior of stocks; he then met an investor, Bob Rhea, who taught him his method for interpreting the market, using a modified Dow theory. In early July 1932, following Rhea's method, Stein—betting that the Depression bear market had reached its nadir—invested about $100,000. At about that time, too, he bought an estate, styled as a French château, on a bluff overlooking

Lake Michigan in Deere Park, just north of Chicago—reported in the newspaper as one of the largest residential sales to have taken place in recent months. From there, he would often commute by speedboat to MCA's elegant new offices on Michigan Avenue, adjacent to the Wrigley Building. (Stein said he became "addicted" to speedboats, buying increasingly faster ones, until in 1935 he had one built with airplane engines that could go over sixty-five miles per hour—at that time the fastest boat ever to travel Lake Michigan. After an accident, Stein—who couldn't swim, and had to be rescued from the water—sold his beloved boat to Guy Lombardo.) He began what would be his lifelong avocation, buying English antiques; Alastair Stair, an antiques dealer, recalled in an interview with Schumach that when they first met in Stair's London shop, "The Depression was on and he had cash. That made for some interesting transactions. He would offer you substantially less than you asked. You generally took it because he had cash." Stein traveled through England in a convertible Rolls-Royce, buying antiques and piling them in the back of his car. "I was amazed at the number of pieces" Stein bought at that time, Stair added, estimating that he must have bought about "fifty or sixty pedestal desks alone." And in 1936, Stein bought a seat on the New York Stock Exchange—fulfilling his youthful ambition. "I thought it would bring me prestige," he remarked later. In the view of some of his associates, however, Stein had another motive as well: saving money on brokers' commissions. For even though he now lived in baronial style and possessed large amounts of expendable cash, he never spent it freely but, rather, seemed to weigh each penny. Indeed, Stein once reproached Stair, who had become his business partner, for mailing him two letters in one day—thus wasting one stamp.

The Depression had not hurt the entertainment business much, so the fact that Stein's band booking continued to prosper was not surprising. What was remarkable, however, was the expansiveness of Stein's activities. He had opened an MCA office in New York in 1927; that was followed by offices in Los Angeles, Dallas, and Cleveland. His dominance of the band-booking business he had started was almost complete; in 1934, Walter Davenport wrote in *Collier's* that Stein (whom he described as "a smallish, dapper man, with cold, direct eyes") "manages the affairs of more than ninety percent of the country's dance bands." Radio had been a great catalyst for this business, and also an opportunity in itself. By 1931, MCA booked dance orchestras for more than a dozen sponsored radio programs. But the greatest hit was the *Lucky Strike Magic Carpet* program, sponsored by the American Tobacco Company; it aired three nights a week, featuring bands in cities across the country. As Karl Kramer wrote, "Every band clamored to ride on the *Magic Carpet,* and many orchestras eagerly sought MCA management in the hope of getting on this radio program." Stein also sold bands to provide the music for variety or comedy programs; and, in a further extension of what he had already started doing with nightclubs and hotels, he offered radio advertisers a package deal, including not only bands but also comedy writers, singers, producers, guest stars. Thus, he became the employer, presenting the network with a show ready to go on the air—and pocketing the difference between what he charged the advertisers and his cost, often recouping three times what he would have made as a mere agent.

There seemed no end to Stein's interests. Just as he was an undisclosed partner in some of the nightclub venues where he booked his bands, so he was, too, in radio. According to Karl Kramer, the radio networks, NBC Red and Blue and CBS, began to encroach on MCA's territory in the early thirties. Bands by this time considered radio exposure a necessity, and the networks, which had the radio lines in the major hotels and cafés, also began booking dance bands, so they could promise the bands much desired exposure, and they could threaten the hotels that they would remove their radio lines if they didn't buy the network's bands. It was an MCA kind of two-step—but now, if Kramer is right, being carried out by a competitor with a big advantage. Whether defensively or not, this is what Stein did: he entered into what Kramer called "an informal agreement" with the powerful Chicago radio station WGN, a subsidiary of the Tribune Co., to install their

lines in every Chicago hotel or café that used MCA bands. Since WGN
offered excellent coverage—stronger in the Midwest than the networks'—some of those nightspots that had network lines switched to
WGN. Then, Stein focused on the West Coast. The fourth national network, the Mutual Broadcasting System, was formed in 1934, and was
controlled by the Tribune Co.—Stein's informal partner—and R. H.
Macy & Co. Plans quickly developed to expand Mutual to the West
Coast, and Stein decided he could use Mutual to establish a beachhead
for orchestra broadcasts there. So MCA made what Kramer called a
"nonreturnable loan" of $50,000 to Mutual to finance this develop-
ment. Up against an agent who, one way or another, controlled more
than 90 percent of the country's dance bands *and* the radio stations
that aired many of them *and* had exclusives at the hotels that booked
them, NBC soon capitulated and gave up the band-booking business;
CBS stayed at it longer, but ceased to pose a real threat.

With the Folies Bergère, Stein had begun to move into the floor
show business as well; this was timely since Repeal led to the prolifer-
ation of new nightclubs across the country, all hungry for entertainment. Stein started supplying clubs with liquor, too—something that,
were he not partners with the Outfit in some of these clubs, would have
been almost unimaginable, considering the mob's control of the liquor
business. He also created a company that sold novelties; soon, his customers at the clubs and dance halls could obtain everything they
needed from MCA—party hats, ashtrays, confetti, highball stirrers,
admission tickets. And this one-stop shopping was not simply a matter
of convenience. Harry Sosnik, the composer-conductor who signed on
with MCA in the late twenties, recalled that it was a kind of block-
booking sideline; MCA would say, "You want Guy Lombardo? You've
got to buy your liquor from us, you've got to buy your novelties from
us . . ." Stein's commercial opportunism extended to his employees and
clients as well. They could buy insurance from an insurance company
in which he had an interest; cars from one of his automobile dealer-
ships; and homes through a real estate firm of his. He owned music-

publishing companies, too—sheet music was a big business—and he had a ready market in his clients' music. Stein believed in leaving virtually no need unexploited.

And he was always alert to meeting a new one as it emerged. In 1935, a successor program to the *Magic Carpet,* called the *Lucky Strike Hit Parade,* began. Twenty winning musical pieces were played on each program, and, according to the sponsor, American Tobacco, 75 percent had been selected by the public. "*None* of the numbers was selected by the public," recalled Sosnik, who was a conductor on the *Hit Parade.* "There was quite a racket going on at that time. The MCA controlled . . . all the commercial conductors in New York on radio. They also controlled this hit parade. They booked all the orchestra leaders and the orchestra, and they had a contract with which they collected a certain amount of money, I heard it was $1,000 a week, from American Tobacco, for taking care of the selection of those numbers for the public. Now, their sales pitch to the client was that they had so many orchestras all over the country that they would have the orchestra leaders ask the dancers what their favorite songs were, and then fill out the forms and send them in to New York, and that was supposed to be a legitimate and fair way of doing this. Well, it was anything but fair, because the orchestra leaders put in whatever they felt they wanted to put on the list to send. Not only that, most of them, if not all of them, were paid off by the music publishers. . . . It meant a lot to them, you know. A performance on the *Hit Parade* made a song a hit, because everybody tuned in . . . to try to find out what was number one. You see, then each week the selections moved up, and number one would be a big seller in the stores." MCA's control and profit potential in this situation was even greater than Sosnik realized, however—because of Stein's interest in music publishing through his phalanx of privately owned companies not publicly associated with MCA.

Sosnik knew MCA was powerful, but it was not until he ran afoul of the agency that he understood just how powerful it was. He had been a docile client. He had paid commissions to MCA even when he had gotten conducting jobs on his own. And when he had worked at the Edge-

water Beach Hotel in Chicago, where the manager refused to deal with
MCA and where Sosnik had been given the responsibility for engaging
orchestras for private parties, he had quietly turned that business over to
MCA, and asked nothing for it. Now, in 1935, he was working on the
Hit Parade—another job he had gotten without MCA's help—and he received a call from an agent in MCA's New York office, Harold Hackett,
asking him to come over. When he arrived, he found another MCA client
there, Carl Hoff, who was very close to Hackett. "Harold excused himself, and then Carl said, 'Harry, you know, we all pay Harold.' I said,
'What do you mean?' . . . He said, 'Well, every orchestra leader who
works out of the MCA here pays him $100 cash under the table every
week.' I said, 'You mean to say that after my paying commission on two
programs, which they had nothing to do with, I'm supposed to pay
Hackett $100 a week?' Now, $100 was a lot of money then. This is
1935. . . . So I hit the ceiling. I said, 'I've never heard of anything like
this. I pay all the legitimate commissions. I just don't understand it, and
I refuse.' I got up and walked out." Suddenly, Sosnik found that he was
out of work. He had a contract with the *Hit Parade,* but it was canceled.
He called George Washington Hill, Sr., the head of American Tobacco,
with whom he had a good relationship—and found he couldn't get
through. When he met advertising people on the street whom he knew
quite well, they were cool. He had no idea what was happening. Then
Hackett called him and said he had a job for him in California—Sosnik
was so desperate that he went to Los Angeles, only to find that there was
no job. Eventually, he found work. And about two years later, his wife
took a trip back to New York and went to "21," the restaurant popular
with the show business crowd. There she saw Hackett, who told her,
"You know, if it's the last thing I do, I'm going to see that Harry never
works again in radio. I got him off the *Hit Parade*. I took him to California. I didn't want him to get anything out there."

    "Then I started talking to people," Sosnik continued, "and I found
out the story, which they had refused to tell me. Everybody had been
warned not to touch me." He had had no inkling of his blacklisting. He
had been out of work for nearly two years.

Sosnik wanted to return to New York—but he didn't want the MCA contract hanging over his head. He had signed it as a young man, without understanding it. "It went on page after page. If I had read it, I wouldn't have been able to understand it. . . . It was a contract which committed me to permanently pay a commission on everything I did until they reached $1 million in commissions. . . . That would be a couple of lifetimes." His lawyer told him it was not binding, because it did not contain a time-period clause. Sosnik went with his lawyer to see Jules Stein, and asked to cancel the contract. Stein refused. "He said, 'We've got a contract. Business isn't done that way.' " Sosnik pointed out that he had always paid his commissions, and even sent business to MCA from the Edgewater Beach Hotel, behind the manager's back. "I said, 'I can't go back with that crook you've got in New York, Harold Hackett, after what he did to me.'

"He said, 'I don't know anything about that.' He refused to release me." Sosnik went to see Joseph Weber, the president of the American Federation of Musicians union, who happened to be in Los Angeles at the time. "He read the contract, and he said to me, 'Harry, this contract isn't worth the paper it's written on, but if you try to break it in a court of law without going through the union board of directors, I'll kick you out of the union.' " Like Petrillo, Weber was extremely close to Stein. Sosnik's lawyer urged him to sue Stein, but Sosnik said he couldn't afford it, and Stein was too powerful. (Several years later, the union would outlaw this type of contract.) Sosnik returned to Stein's office. "I said to Jules, 'I just have to get out of this contract. I'm not saying that I won't do business with you in New York, but I want to be able to make up my own mind.' So it wound up where I bought my contract. He named a figure, I wrote out a check. It was all the money I had at the time. And I walked out a free man."

Even as his business expanded, the principles Stein had utilized from the start continued to apply. Thus, what gave Music Corporation its singular power was Stein's cultivation of that sublime circle, in which exclusive bookings led to more top clients which led to more exclusive bookings—which, over time, led to almost no meaningful competition. Martin Baum, who began his career as an agent in New York in the forties—not working for MCA—recalled the system as he knew it. "MCA got exclusives with many of these clubs, first in Chicago and then in every big city in the country. I mean, other agents could place people here and there—but *nothing* like MCA." The system was built on the commonality of interests between the owners of the clubs (mainly, the Syndicate), Stein, and Petrillo, Baum continued. The Syndicate wanted to be protected from escalating musicians' salaries, and the threat of strikes; these were things Petrillo could deliver. Stein wanted the booking business; this, the Syndicate could deliver, and to someone who was, in at least some enterprises (if not Music Corporation itself), a partner. And Petrillo wanted ever more power as a union leader, and perhaps—something always speculated, even asserted in government documents, but never proven—money. "What do you *think* Jules gave Petrillo," Baum asked rhetorically. "I'll tell you a story. In 1943, I was working as an office boy for Blaine Thompson, which did all the advertising for theaters. And every Friday afternoon I was given envelopes full of cash to bring to [the offices of] Warner and Shubert. It was kickbacks for the advertising—all cash."

Certainly Petrillo by the mid-thirties was living in a style not commensurate with his salary of $26,000 a year. He took his wife to Europe, stayed at the Waldorf-Astoria hotel when he was in New York, wore expensive silk shirts, and—in the sovereign style of Capone—sported a two-and-a-half-carat blue-white diamond on the index finger of his left hand. He also had a country home. As Petrillo told the story, he had wanted a place in the country and his "boys" had learned of his desire; so they bought him the old Edward G. Uihlein estate at Fontana on Lake Geneva, Wisconsin. In 1937 alone, according to Local 10's books, these expenditures were made on behalf of Petrillo: $25,000 for the country house, $12,000 to furnish it, $1,700 to take care of its evergreen grove, $16,000 to pay income taxes, $25,000 for a bulletproof car and bodyguards, and $5,000 for incidental expenses. (The bulletproof car and bodyguards were not without reason; in 1936, an assassination attempt was apparently made on Petrillo—bullets chipped but did not pierce his windshield.) Over the years, there was continued speculation that at least some of the funds that supported Petrillo so lavishly came from Stein. It was also rumored that Stein had helped raise the $100,000 to ransom Petrillo when he was kidnapped. In an interview in a *Collier's* article in 1947, Petrillo (who by this time had succeeded Joseph Weber as international president of the AFM) responded to a question about Stein's financial favors this way: "They said the same thing about my predecessor [Weber], that he was a stockholder in MCA. It ain't true. Would I lie to ya?" But Herbert Rosenthal, a longtime MCA executive who had joined the agency in 1940, said, "Petrillo retired and never had to work again, because of MCA stock."

The relationship between Stein and Petrillo continued to flourish for decades in a kind of happy symbiosis, though its benefit to Stein was more visible. Petrillo was fiercely protective of his turf—or, as he would have put it, his boys' welfare; and although his audacity would reach new heights with his ascension to international president (he would put a stop to all recording activity in the U.S. for over a year, until the record companies finally caved in to his demands), he had already been nicknamed "the Mussolini of Music" when his sole dominion was Local 10. In 1931, for example, Chicago's new mayor, Anton Cermak, decided he wanted a high school band to play for his inauguration. Petrillo was outraged. He protested to Cermak, but got nowhere. When he learned that Cermak was to deliver his speech over the National Broadcasting Company, however, he sprang into action. He gave the local radio station an ultimatum: either Cermak hired a union band, or he could not broadcast. When the network officials objected, Petrillo said, "Ya hafta deal wit' me 365 days in the year and with Cermak on Sunday. What'll it be?" As usual, Petrillo got his way. But when it came to Jules Stein, Petrillo was the soul of flexibility. If someone other than Stein had a piece of a nightclub and also booked musicians there, Petrillo would almost certainly have deemed that a conflict of interest. But for Stein, there was no problem. AFM bylaws did prohibit a booking agency from also functioning as a production company—as in the case of Stein and his radio shows—but Stein was able to perform this dual role because Petrillo had helped him to obtain an exclusive waiver. And while there were also severe restrictions on traveling bands appearing in Petrillo's jurisdiction, these, too, became negotiable for Stein. Stein's ability to hold sway over Petrillo was a well-known feature of the local landscape. And it apparently was a factor in the strike at the French Casino that Kramer described, though he did not mention it. For in July 1934, several unions went on strike at the popular Edgewater Beach Hotel, but the musicians continued to perform; the Edgewater's striking unions then called the strike at Stein's French Casino—and, according to a bill of particulars later filed by the government, their business agents told Stein that they would call off the French Casino strike on the condition that he induce Petrillo to call a musicians strike at the Edgewater.

Whatever else Stein may have provided Petrillo, he clearly made him the beneficiary of his political instincts and clout—strategizing to keep Petrillo in power, seeing to it that he was elevated when the time came. Stein did this quietly, however, moving almost imperceptibly behind the scenes. He had watched as a conflict began to fester between Petrillo and the aging Weber, who had held the position of international president for nearly two decades. It was plain to Stein that Petrillo would eventually challenge Weber for the presidency; in the resultant turmoil, Stein worried, other candidates would inevitably emerge and one of them might beat Petrillo. What Stein wanted was a smooth, controlled succession. In 1938, the conflict burst noisily into the open. Weber, who had grown tired of hearing Petrillo refer to himself as "the tail that wags the dog," wrote a front-page editorial in the union newspaper charging that Petrillo was not "the big cheese" in the union and that all the benefits he claimed he had won for the musicians were "pure bunk." Stein stepped in. He knew that Weber was dependent on the income from his job to survive, and also that the AFM had no pension plan. He approached Weber and asked him whether—if

Petrillo would support a resolution of compensation to Weber and his wife for the rest of their lives—Weber, in turn, would not run for re-election and would designate Petrillo his preferred successor. Weber agreed. Next, Stein went to Petrillo, who quickly saw the wisdom of avoiding an open conflict on the floor of the convention (and, proba-bly, of passing a resolution that would one day benefit him in his re-tirement as well). At the AFM convention in Asbury Park, New Jersey, in 1940, therefore, Stein watched as Weber stepped down and his anointed successor, Petrillo, was elected by a resounding majority.

"Everything was carried out as planned," Stein declared.

Stein had gravitated to the entertainment business from the time he was a boy, but there was nothing wide-eyed about this fascination; he ap-proached entertainment in the same clinical, dispassionate way he did investing—studiously analyzing the past and present in an attempt to identify those patterns that would enable him to exploit the future. And by the early thirties, he had concluded that it was time to diversify from the traveling band business. For while its rate of increase had been tremendous through the twenties, and had even persisted after the onset of the Depression, by 1931 the road business had changed. Only famous orchestras could draw large crowds, and less important groups were harder and harder to book; if promoters couldn't have a top or-chestra, they tended to use local bands instead. Many of the smaller traveling bands were going out of business. The dollar volume of book-ings for MCA was nevertheless high, due to the success of the top or-chestras, strongly amplified by radio; and that volume would even reach a new peak when the swing era began in 1935, and bands like the Dorseys, Benny Goodman, Glenn Miller, Harry James, and Casa Loma became great hits on the road. But Stein knew that—however res-olutely upward its dollar trajectory—the one-night business he had es-sentially invented would eventually be obsolete.

He had expanded to booking floor shows—and even providing liquor, and quietly owning an interest in nightclubs; but these were mere sidelines (rather déclassé for something as grandly named as the Music Corporation of America) and dangerous besides. In the aftermath of Capone's reign there was so much gang factionalism that it was harder to chart a safe course. Stein had, after all, been threatened with kidnapping. His friend Petrillo had been kidnapped, and several years later had narrowly escaped assassination. When the business agents had muscled Stein at the French Casino, apparently in an attempt to reach Petrillo, there were several different gangs trying to move in on Petrillo, according to Marovitz. Perhaps they were trying to move in on Stein as well. And it could not have pleased Stein, who so coveted prestige, that he was identified in the press in 1935 as an owner of the French Casino. Stein was intensely secretive about his business dealings—whether it was the mailing list of MCA customers or his interest in the Chez Paree—but Chicago (where he was known as "Julie" Stein) was in many ways like a small town, in which within a certain milieu everyone knew everyone else, and their business, too. Secrets were hard to keep.

In 1936, Stein decided to shift the major focus of his talent agency to the movie industry. If there was a past he wanted in some measure to leave behind, Hollywood was the place for that. It was a movie colony, a still embryonic, highly fluid society, where even the most prominent—Eastern European moguls and movie stars from Dubuque —tended to shed old skins. And it fairly radiated opportunity. The movie industry was young (talkies had come in just a few years earlier), but it was already the nation's eleventh-largest, producing about four hundred new movies a year. The studios had weathered a downturn during the Depression but were recovering nicely; much of their strength derived from the fact that they were run as a cartel, controlling not only production and distribution but also exhibition, through their own movie theater chains—and their power over independent theaters as well. (Stein, with his promotion of exclusives and packaging, could appreciate the virtue of being able to control the buyers of one's entertainment.) And money flowed freely in Hollywood—most freely to the studio executives (Louis B. Mayer, the president of Metro-

Goldwyn-Mayer, would be the highest-paid in the country in 1937, with a salary of $1.3 million), but also to the stars, on whose sizable salaries Stein would be taking commissions. There was a major national talent agency rooted in Hollywood—the William Morris Agency, headed by Abe Lastfogel—which had started in vaudeville, and now had several hundred actors on its roster; but Stein had already proven that he could defeat his competition. The largest studio was Warner Bros.; the richest and most powerful, Metro-Goldwyn-Mayer; but the most complex and far-flung of the eight major studios, and the one Stein knew best, was Paramount Pictures. Stein's good friend, Barney Balaban, had sold two thirds of the Balaban & Katz theater chain to Paramount in 1926, since then becoming one of Paramount's largest stockholders. The company had gone through a six-year epic of mismanagement and a wasting bankruptcy. During that process, Stein had become a major shareholder, acquiring a great deal of stock at a very cheap price. In July 1935, Paramount had emerged with a new corporate structure; one of the powers behind that restructuring was another good friend of Stein's, a lawyer from Chicago named Edwin Weisl, Sr. When the dust had cleared, Weisl was head of Paramount's executive committee; he brought in Balaban to be Paramount's president in 1936, but in the coming decades no major decision would be made at Paramount without Weisl's approval. Stein concluded the timing was right for him, too, to move to the new frontier of show business; his plan was to begin representing the talent in movies, and—as he had done with musicians and radio programs—eventually to move into production as well.

Primitive though it was, Hollywood already had the patent on glamour in this country. This was an added bonus. For while Stein was not enthralled by glamour, his wife certainly was. In 1928, Stein had married Doris Jones Oppenheimer, a divorced mother of two from Kansas City. That description, however, evokes far too matronly an image of Doris—a strikingly beautiful brunette, with a heart-shaped face and coquettish look, who no doubt felt as stymied by the confines of Kansas City as Jules had by South Bend. They had first met when she

Doris and Jules in 1928, shortly before they were married. *Courtesy of Jean Stein*

was not quite fifteen and the twenty-year-old Stein was playing with his orchestra at the Muehlebach Hotel. At the time, however, Stein was seriously involved with another Kansas City girl—he was said to have intended to marry her—but she died a short time later. When Doris and Jules met again, it was in 1927, at a dance in Kansas City during the Christmas holidays; by this time, Doris, twenty-six, had been married and divorced. A tightly controlled man who instinctively kept his emotions at bay, Stein was a thoroughgoing romantic when it came to Doris. Seeing her at this dance, he later recalled, "I realized how attractive and beautiful she was. She was dressed in a tight long dress with a black velvet bodice covered with orchids, beautifully groomed and most appealing. We danced together several times and much to my surprise she told me she was going to New York early the next month for a few weeks or longer." Stein was spending most of his time there, too, since he had just opened MCA's office in New York, on the top two floors of the new Paramount skyscraper at Times Square. He was there to meet her train at the New York Central station, and Doris never went back to life in Kansas City. She remained in New York, taking a job in the handbag department at Bergdorf Goodman, and introduced the sober Jules to delectable new pleasures (including shellfish, forbidden in his parents' kosher household). Doris was Jewish, too— her father's name was Jonus before it was changed to Jones—but it was not something she generally acknowledged. Jules was mesmerized by what he saw as her exoticism and joie de vivre (deriving, he told himself, from her French and Portuguese ancestry)—"I was the introvert, she, the extrovert," he commented—and in November of that year they were married. On their wedding night, they sailed on the Île de France for a month-long honeymoon in Europe.

Upon their return, they lived in Chicago and also New York. Their daughter Jean was born in 1933, and Susan two years later. ("I wanted girls," Jules said, "since I was concerned that no boy would have lived up to my expectations.") Doris was very eager to mingle in New York society, but found it unreceptive. Hollywood, however, was far more open. There was really no significant social establishment there, and at the moguls' mansions—where many guests made an art of pretending to be what they were not—Doris and Jules were eminently acceptable. "Here in Hollywood," Jules declared, "is where Doris came into herself." Richard Gully, a well-born Englishman who arrived in Hollywood at about the same time as the Steins, recalled meeting them at a party at Mary Pickford's estate. Pickford, who had been the nation's biggest box office draw for many years, had married Douglas Fairbanks in 1920; the marriage was seen as a union of Hollywood royalty, and their estate, Pickfair, was legendary. When the Steins arrived in 1936, Pickford had just divorced Fairbanks, but the aura of Pickfair had not dissipated. "It was like being invited to the White House," said Gully. "Everyone else there knew each other, there were all these great stars—and Doris and Jules and I were the three unknown people, huddled in a corner."

Gully, who became Jack Warner's assistant (and a lifelong confidant of Doris's), continued, "Doris made up her mind in the very beginning that she had to be in the social swim. The three most famous hostesses at that time were Mary Pickford, Mrs. Jack Warner, and Mrs. Sam Goldwyn. Most of the great movie people at that time had a court jester—at Pickfair, the jester was Sonny Chalif. So Jules Stein employed him as an agent at MCA—and from then on, the Steins were always included at Pickfair." Jules, who had been a good dancer since his years as a young orchestra player, especially loved to dance with Pickford, and they became lasting friends (he eventually arranged for their plots at Forest Lawn cemetery to be adjacent, saying that he imagined himself dancing with her there on moonlit nights). And, over the next ten years or so, Doris so excelled as a hostess that she ultimately surpassed her role models. "People think being a hostess is having money and giving a party," sniffed Gully, who missed the glamour of Hollywood in its golden age. "But it's much more than that. Doris had an instinct for who had social prestige, who had glamour, who had flair. Doris," he added, "had flair from the word go." Even before she had the wherewithal, she had an eye for style (that was, in part, what Jules had noticed); and now its presentation—in Jules's offices, in their homes, in herself—became her specialty. A fashion columnist, describing Doris on a visit to her hometown of Kansas City, wrote, "And speaking of rubies and diamonds—did you see the bracelet worn by Mrs. Jules Stein of Hollywood. . . . Necklace, earrings and rings repeated the diamond and pink ruby theme. Her platform-soled sandals were of pink ruby satin, silver bound. The glittering tunic gown of lame alternated pink ruby and true blue stripes, and was run through with soft pink ruby bands at neckline and waist. . . . Her satin bag matched her slippers; even the orchids pinned to it were of just the right shade."

MCA had opened an office in downtown Los Angeles in 1930, but now Stein decided to build a headquarters worthy of his ambitions— and not on Sunset Strip, where most agents' offices were, but in Beverly Hills. He had believed from the start that a well-appointed office was key; it presented one's face to the world. And it reflected, too, his determination to professionalize this most denigrated occupation—there were notable exceptions, but talent agents in Hollywood generally occupied the lowest rung on the social ladder, perceived as poorly educated, vulgar, obsequious, venal. Stein's agents broke the mold; like him, they had to dress conservatively, in dark suits; as a rule they were college-educated; and they were not to wear their venality on their sleeve. To Stein and his men, the Randolph Street office had seemed the height of tastefulness; but Doris—who came on the scene after the office had been decorated—disapproved, deciding that Stein's heavy, dark Flemish and Spanish furniture should be replaced. She had gone to New York (to the store that would become Stair and Company, their eventual partner) and found an eighteenth-century English Chippendale desk. It cost $900. (This was in the midst of the Depression; it had sold for $2,900 several years earlier.) Jules had been pleased with this desk (and, no doubt, the bargain), so Doris had returned to New York and bought an eighteenth-century English breakfront for $1,800, which also was shipped to the Randolph Street office.

"I kept looking at the desk and breakfront in my Chicago office," Stein said many years later, "and I realized how much more beautiful they were than what I used to have. I became infatuated with English

antique furniture. I found it was not only beautiful, but also comfortable and utilitarian. I have come to love these pieces so much that I
have a terrible time disposing of them. I like to buy them, but I hate to
sell them. It's the way some people feel about disposing of beautiful
paintings. We are known to have one of the largest collections of English eighteenth-century furniture in the world." From the start, too,
Stein had been struck not only by the antiques' beauty and utility, but
also their tax benefit. Always searching for an edge, Stein scoured
books on finance, reports on tax legislation; this was his idea of reading for pleasure. And he concluded that antiques had a singular advantage: one could buy them for one's offices, depreciate them at a rate of
10 percent a year for ten years—thus, the government paid about half
their cost—and they would go up in value all the while! As if that were
not enough, he leased the furniture—which, eventually, would fill all
MCA offices—to the company.

Doris and Jules decided to create this office together, supervising the
design, construction, and decor from the ground up. The result was
quite remarkable. Situated on a large piece of property in the center of
Beverly Hills and designed by architect Paul Williams (whose neo-
Colonial mansions were becoming a distinctive town feature), the
MCA building was a white, columned mansion with black-shuttered
windows and a bell tower. Seeing it for the first time, one might have
taken it for a small museum, or perhaps a diplomatic consulate—never,
a talent agency. As Stein said, "It was the only time in history that a
building that looks like a Colonial mansion was constructed to be an
office building." A huge Irish Waterford crystal chandelier hung above
a sweeping double circular staircase in the entry hall (a competitor later
recalled how cowed he felt when he drove by the MCA building at
night and saw that blazing chandelier through the windows). Jules's office was an eighteenth-century pine-paneled room from London that
had then been used as a background for selling antiques in Wanamaker's in New York; when Wanamaker's went out of the antiques
business, Jules bought the room. And on a shelf behind his desk was
something he would keep there always, which must have reminded him

of his youth and, perhaps, his ancestry: a Middle European music box in which violinists and other instrumentalists played, and dancers (one wearing a powdered wig) turned slowly to the music.

The furnishings throughout the building were, of course, English antiques—dark-paneled offices were filled with partner's desks, breakfronts, bookcases, leather club chairs, hunting prints—and Doris selected everything, from upholstery to picture frames. One problem with the abundance of breakfronts and bookcases in the MCA offices was that they demanded books. Leather-bound books. Initially, Stein bought a few thousand books in England—"furniture books," they were called—for about a dollar apiece. But then, having exhausted his source, he advertised for such books in the British newspapers, and soon he was inundated with them. He filled every breakfront and bookcase and still had an overflow of about forty thousand books, which he stored in the basement of a building he owned in Manhattan. (After a visit to his MCA agent, Tennessee Williams is said to have told friends, "When you go to MCA, take a book. They'll never miss it.") Stein had of course wanted to gentrify the image of an agent, but this building was so grandiose (and so at odds with the reality of the business it housed) that it had all the integrity and verisimilitude of a Hollywood stage set. The only clue to what went on inside was the MCA symbol over the front door—a globe with music running around the world (better designed but conceptually unchanged from that first letterhead). At the opening of the building, Jerome Kern approached the entrance and, looking at the MCA insignia, remarked, "There is a sour note in 'Home Sweet *Home*.' " Stein, however, seemed impervious to any detractors; he took such evident pleasure in his showplace that the producer David O. Selznick dubbed him, sardonically, "The Curator of the White House."

With his inveterate formality, passion for English antiques, and medical training, Stein was a rarity in the talent business—but instead of trying to adapt to his environment, he underscored whatever set him apart. And he was convinced, oddly enough, that his medical training was a particular asset when he got to Hollywood where, he said, he

Jules Stein (rear, second from right) with Bette Davis (right), the first big Hollywood star to sign with MCA. *Gene Lester Collection/Screen Actors Guild*

viewed his artists as a doctor does his patients. "A doctor's attitude is one of understanding the patient," Stein said. "He must be able to analyze their reactions, make suggestions and recommendations; mollify them when they have tantrums. He must never show emotion.

"I was always cool," Stein added. "This attitude, in which I was trained . . . gave me an advantage over my competitors. And I instilled the same attitude in my associates."

Stein pointed to his dealings with Bette Davis as a case in point. His signing of Davis in June 1939 was the most momentous event that had occurred since he had opened the Beverly Hills office; it rang through the industry like the starting bell of a world-title fight. Until then, MCA had not been able to sign a single major star; after that, others began to follow Davis's lead. There was much speculation, at the time and long afterward, about how Stein achieved it. The most prevalent story was that Davis had succumbed to Stein's entreaties after MCA had put Davis's husband's best friend, who was out of work, on the company payroll. Another was that Stein had offered to invest Davis's money and promised her a great return. (He had been investing other clients' money for a number of years; he is said to have invested part of Guy Lombardo's paycheck, without his knowing, and turned over the profits to him when they amounted to $1 million.) Yet another—which had considerable currency even within Stein's family many years later—was that Stein and Davis had an affair. However her MCA representation had come about, its chances of being long-lasting were slim; Davis was notorious for her temper, and the Hollywood landscape was littered with agents she had discarded. Of Davis, Stein said, "She can fly into a rage at the drop of a hat. She would fight over her properties with her producers (particularly Warner Bros., where she was mostly under contract), her directors, her cameramen, and her agent, which in this instance meant me. I had the benefit of understanding her tantrums particularly because of my medical background, which included psychology and psychiatry. She would often send for me to come to her house immediately to discuss some serious picture problem. I always did, and usually agreed with everything, only to return within a few days when her reaction was more normal and solve the issues. . . . Many people would think she was a manic-depressive, and while the reactions are often similar, Bette was simply a highly emotional, sensitive individual whom I considered more as a patient than an artist on those difficult days. It never occurred to me that she not only admired me, but might also be falling in love with me, even though I never gave her any encouragement.

"On one occasion when I was asked to come to her home immediately, she was sitting in her bed clothed in magnificent white lingerie. She complained about some insignificant studio problem, while the balance of the time it was chitchat. She was too much of a lady to invite me into bed with her but it was obvious she expected me to do so. The next half hour or so was very uncomfortable," Stein concluded, "but I finally left like I came in."

The interlude did no irreparable damage to their relationship. Stein continued to represent Davis for many years. The two of them were also the prime movers behind the Hollywood Canteen, the wartime club on Cahuenga Boulevard where soldiers on leave could go for free entertainment and a chance to dance with movie stars. Not long after Stein joined the Canteen's board, filled with leaders of the Hollywood community, the club's financial director was relieved of her responsibilities and Stein took over that role. Regarding it more as a business than a charity, he quickly saw the opportunity to make money for the Canteen by appealing to the general patriotic fervor—convincing radio chains to pay for the right to broadcast Canteen shows commercial-free, for example, and persuading Warner Bros. to agree to make a movie, *Hollywood Canteen,* in a profit-sharing deal (from which the Canteen made $750,000). By the time the war ended in 1946, the Hollywood Canteen had a $500,000 surplus—used to start a foundation for wounded soldiers' rehabilitation.

Even before Stein relocated to Beverly Hills, his sometime partners in the nightclub business in Chicago had recognized Hollywood's potential. The studios were, in a way, a natural next step from the nightclubs for the mob. "The mob infiltrated the studios," said Shelly Schultz, who started his career as an agent at MCA in Chicago, and whose uncle had worked at Colosimo's. "They selected that industry. It was a new business, with so much money to be made, and it was glamorous (don't forget the gangsters were celebrities themselves, they were in the columns). You could control it from the bottom up, through the unions—with the ability to make it function or stop functioning. And also from the top down. The guys who started these studios, like Jack Warner and Harry Cohn, were rough, uncouth—the boys could sit with them. They understood each other. It was all about relationships. If the boys said we don't like this guy, cancel his contract—they would!" And, perhaps most important, the studios always needed money, and the mob was looking for legitimate investments in which their cash could be laundered. Indeed, when Harry Cohn—struggling with his brother, Jack, for control of Columbia Pictures in 1932—needed $500,000, he turned to his friend and gambling partner, Johnny Roselli. Roselli, a henchman for Johnny Torrio who had become close to Capone and others in his organization, had arrived in Los Angeles in the twenties, establishing himself in its criminal underworld and eventually in Hollywood, through his relationship with Cohn, Joseph Schenck, who founded Twentieth Century Studios, and many others as well. Roselli relayed Cohn's request to New Jersey rackets boss Abner "Longy" Zwillman, who forwarded the $500,000 in cash.

Over the years, it would be handy for Cohn, having the mob as his backer. Gangster Mickey Cohen, who achieved some celebrity in Los Angeles, wrote an autobiography late in his life, in which he recalled Frank Costello's telling him to call Harry Cohn, and "go along with him in every way ya can." Going along with Cohn, in this instance, meant killing Sammy Davis, because he was romantically involved with Kim Novak, and Cohn said he was "worried that her image doesn't get ruined in the country." Mickey Cohen said he refused, because he liked Sammy Davis—and he threatened that if anything happened to Davis, he would inform on Cohn.

In 1934, Johnny Roselli visited Chicago to propose a plan for the Outfit's obtaining a cut from the Hollywood studios. The plan was not novel, except in its scope. Once the end of Prohibition stanched an almost limitless flow of cash, the Outfit had focused more intensively than before on labor unions, which often had large reserves of loosely controlled cash; and, during the thirties, the organization would intimidate or take outright control of numerous local and international unions (siphoning off membership dues, putting relatives on payrolls, extorting money from company managements). In 1934, the Outfit placed its own man, George Browne, in the presidency of the stagehands and projectionists union, known as the International Alliance of Theatrical Stage Employees (IATSE). Browne, of course, had informed his friend Petrillo of Stein's planned kidnapping; he and Petrillo had worked hand in hand, since Browne had been head of the stagehands local, and they often dealt with theaters together. Browne quickly installed Willie Bioff—an erstwhile pimp who took his orders from the mob—as his assistant. Before they were thus elevated, Browne and Bioff had been freelancing on their own. Representing the stagehands, they had threatened Barney Balaban with a strike in his theaters, and he had responded by giving them a cash payoff in exchange for peace. It had become almost routine; Balaban had been initiated into this way of doing business earlier, having made a similar deal with the head of the projectionists union—something for which he was investigated by a grand jury, though charges were not brought.

The latest idea was to carry out the Bioff-Balaban scheme but on a much bigger scale. Since most of the studios owned chains of theaters, they were vulnerable to strikes not only on the movie lot, where production could be halted and a perishable product lost, but also at theaters, from which they needed box office receipts to fund production. Moreover, their relations with labor were abysmal. They had just experienced a very violent strike in 1933; Roselli had commandeered his thugs to help break it, and from then on was employed by the studios' labor liaison on a confidential basis. Conservative businessmen who detested the union leaders on principle and also feared their power, the studio owners had never tried to establish the kind of rapport Stein had with Petrillo. (Actually, Stein was just as politically conservative as they, but when it came to his business interests he was a pragmatist.) So it was entirely plausible that these men would make the same calculation Balaban had made earlier; payoffs to union officials were the cost of doing business—and far cheaper than meeting real demands on wages, or taking a strike. (Interestingly enough, Balaban would become the head of Paramount in 1936, and Leo Spitz, his Chicago lawyer who had arranged for those earlier payments to be made to Bioff, would head RKO; so these were men who knew from personal experience how the game was played.) What the studio heads had no way of knowing, however, was the Outfit's audacious long-term plan: 20 percent of studio profits within five years, and, ultimately, a 50 percent interest in the studios themselves.

Nearly ten years later, in 1943, seven high-ranking members of the Chicago organization would be indicted on federal charges of extortion—Roselli, Frank Nitti (who committed suicide when the indictment came down), Paul Ricca, Louis Campagna, Charlie Gioe, Phil D'Andrea, Ralph Pierce, and Frank Diamond. During the trial, the studio heads, testifying for the prosecution, claimed that they had made payoffs to Bioff out of fear for their lives. That seemed unlikely; each major studio had been paying out $50,000 a year through the mid-thirties, and not one had ever complained to law enforcement. Harry Cohn, moreover, admitted his closeness to Roselli on the witness stand—testifying that they used to go to the Santa Anita racetrack together, that Roselli had found him an apartment and for several years they had lived in the same building, and that they had exchanged valuable gifts (Cohn was wearing a ruby ring Roselli had given him). Moreover, on one occasion, when the union had struck the Columbia lot (Bioff had ordered the strike in a fit of anger, because Cohn had not made his payment), Cohn had immediately called Roselli, who ordered Bioff to call off the strike, which he did. The mob's lawyers argued that what had occurred here was not extortion by their clients, as charged, but bribery by the producers, who wanted to buy labor peace at a bargain; but the truth probably lay somewhere in the gray region between the two.

Bioff, in any event, was such an excellent, expansive witness that he evidently dispelled any gray from the jurors' minds. He and Browne had been tried and convicted of tax evasion and racketeering in 1941, and now he testified about how he had been coached in concocting his story for that earlier trial by the lawyer for the Outfit, Sidney Korshak. A couple of years earlier, with his legal troubles escalating, Bioff had had a series of conferences with members of the Outfit, including Frank Nitti, Charles Gioe, and others at the Bismarck Hotel in Chicago; and at one of these meetings, Bioff testified, Gioe had introduced him to Korshak, saying, "Willie, meet Sidney Korshak; he is our man. . . . I want you to pay attention to Sidney when he tells you something, that he knows what he is talking about. Any message he might deliver to you is a message from us." After that, Bioff and Korshak met frequently ("I had lunch with him and went to cafes with him I would say a dozen times," Bioff testified). Bioff was indicted on May 23, 1941, and a day or so later, Korshak called, wanting to see him. By this time, federal investigators had found evidence of a $100,000 payment that Joe Schenck, of Twentieth Century, had made to Bioff; Schenck, who claimed it was a loan, had been convicted of tax evasion and sentenced to three years in prison. When he and Korshak met, Bioff testified, Korshak asked him if he had prepared a defense; when Bioff responded that he had not, Korshak told him that he had studied the transcript of Schenck's trial and it had shown many transactions Schenck could not explain. Therefore, Korshak had continued, Bioff's alibi should be that he had collected the money from the producers to give to Schenck, to be used as a legislative slush fund for the industry "so Joe Schenck could fix things in Washington." Korshak also said that "Joe would be a good victim, for he is known as the playboy of the industry, and the politician of the industry; to dump it into his lap, and think in that direction, and collect everything I can that would point in the direction that Joe Schenck would be the man I gave the money to," Bioff testified.

Before Bioff went to trial, he began to have second thoughts, and he told Charlie Gioe that he might resign from the IA, as the IATSE was known—which amounted, in effect, to a statement that he wanted to go his own way. Shortly, he received another visit from Gioe, this time accompanied by Louis Campagna. "Campagna said, 'I understand from Charlie that you told him you were going to resign; is that right?' " Bioff testified.

"I said, 'Yes, sir.'

"He says, 'Well, anybody resigns, resigns feet first . . . you understand what that means.'

"I says, 'I do.'

"He says, 'Now go ahead,' and that was the end of it, and I didn't resign."

At his trial, Bioff presented the fiction about having collected the money for a slush fund. He and Browne were both convicted. Korshak—who, according to Bioff, had brought him $15,000 from Gioe to be used to pay his defense lawyers—continued to make himself useful. He represented Browne for a time after he was convicted, and brought messages to him from members of the Outfit. The critical question was whether Bioff and Browne, facing ten- and eight-year prison terms, respectively, would cooperate with the government and expose their bosses. The same question pertained to a confederate of theirs, Nick Dean, an Outfit member who had been placed in the IA and was indicted at the same time as Bioff and Browne. He had gone underground; been arrested after they had been tried; pled guilty; and was sentenced to eight years in jail. Assistant U.S. Attorney Boris Kostelanetz, who had tried the case against Bioff and Browne, was trying to prod the three to cooperate; Dean, wavering, began to talk a little; and the fact that he was doing so leaked out. The response in Chicago was swift. The body of Dean's mistress, Estelle Carey, was found in her apartment; she had been beaten, slashed, ice-picked, and then set afire. Dean's cooperation ended. But Bioff, rather surprisingly, reacted differently. "We sit around in jail for those bastards and they go around killing our families," he told Kostelanetz. "To hell with them. Whataya want to know, Boris?"

Three weeks later, the indictments were handed down. At trial, one of the defense lawyers, trying to undermine Bioff's credibility, confronted him with his perjury about his transactions with Schenck at his earlier trial. Bioff responded with an unvarnished self-appraisal. "I am just a low uncouth person. I'm a low type sort of man. People of my caliber don't do nice things." But when pressed about having lied, he emphasized, again and again, that he had done so "on advice of a member of your profession. . . . I had no choice much. They were my orders." He also admitted that he had lied to the lawyers who had represented him during that trial. But he said he had never lied to Korshak. "He was in my confidence, sir. . . . I was ordered to discuss the truth and facts with him."

It was one thing to be a lawyer who represented members of the

Outfit, another to be someone who spoke as though they and he were one, conveying messages and orders from them—and suborning perjury on their behalf. Korshak could have been prosecuted, Kostelanetz acknowledged years later, but all he had was Bioff's word, and he had other targets that, at the time, were bigger. All the gangsters but Pierce were convicted and given ten-year terms. These were cut to a third, at least in part through the efforts of Korshak, who obtained a letter recommending their parole from the Illinois state superintendent of crime prevention, Harry Ash, who happened to have been Korshak's former law partner. Their release in 1947 was sufficiently shocking that it triggered a congressional investigation—and elevated Korshak's standing within the organization.

This kind of status carried a price. Another lawyer in Chicago, Harry Busch, recalled that he had known Korshak since the thirties, and used to see him frequently in those early years. "We had our law offices in the same building as Sidney's, and it had an opening into the Bismarck Hotel. On Fridays they had a filet of sole lunch that was so good, you used to see *everyone* there. I liked Sidney as a person. Whom he advised, what he did—that was different." Over the years, Korshak would tell some friends that he had gotten his start with the Outfit by advising Capone when he was still in law school. Now, Busch commented, "However Sidney got his start, I think it was inadvertent. Something that was just too tempting, and then he couldn't get out. I remember once I was walking down the street—this was probably in the forties—and he said, 'Wait, I'll walk with you, where are you headed?'

"I said, 'It's a court recess—I'm going to pick up my car.'

"And he said, 'How I envy you!'

"I said, 'Why? I know you're making far, far more money than I am—'

"He said, 'I'd rather make less money, and be out of this.' Well, I didn't ask what 'this' was—I mean, I knew, but I didn't want to know any more. The thing was, by then, he *couldn't* get out."

And, thanks to Bioff, Korshak had become a known quantity, his relationship to the mob no longer just a part of Chicago lore. The trial received heavy coverage in newspapers across the country; and in some papers, like the *Herald-American*, it was headline news ("Bioff Names Sid Korshak as Mob Aide"). In 1943, Korshak married an ice skater and dancer, Bernice Stewart, and the couple lived in Chicago; but by the mid-forties, Korshak was coming to Hollywood quite regularly. "Already the word was that he was a spokesman for the underworld," Richard Gully recalled. "So people were leery, though fascinated. Mervyn LeRoy [the director who, among other things, had started the Warner Bros. cycle of gangster movies in the thirties, and who was working with Stein on the Hollywood Canteen] launched Korshak. Mervyn's wife, Kitty, was from Chicago, and she talked Mervyn into giving a party for Korshak. Now Jules was very close to Mervyn—but he said, 'As fond as I am of you, Mervyn, I will not come to your party.' And he stuck to that always. Jules barred Korshak socially." Indeed, many years later, when Korshak's annual Christmas party had become the ultimate event of the season in Hollywood—the one where everyone who was anyone wanted to be—Stein's daughter Jean decided to go. Stein was furious at her, and told her that he would never think of setting foot in Korshak's home.

It was an odd fastidiousness, considering Stein's own relationships in Chicago. When Judge Marovitz was told of Stein's outspoken avoidance of Korshak, he said he did not find it difficult to understand. "Jules had to do certain things, to not be harmed, to be able to do business," he said. "But some of these guys want to brag that somebody's their friend—and Jules wouldn't want someone like Korshak bragging that Jules is his friend. So Jules kept him distant."

Such scruples were uncommon in Hollywood. Even Johnny Roselli had been accepted to a degree; and while he had remade himself (he dressed in an understated way, avoided using profanity, and cultivated an appreciation for fine wines), one could still see, beneath the veneer, the thug he was. At one time he even held the job of associate producer, despite the fact that he was illiterate. (Arturo Pettorino, a maître d' for the Outfit at many of the clubs and restaurants they controlled, recalled

Roselli one night summoning him into the men's room, where he showed Pettorino a note a woman had just written him, and demanded to know what it said.) And Ben "Bugsy" Siegel—so nicknamed because as a youth, in league with Meyer Lansky in New York's Lower East Side, he had killed with such ferocity that even his cohorts questioned his sanity—had arrived in Los Angeles in 1937, and he, too, had found a measure of social acceptance. He was handsome, meticulously groomed, and favored cashmere suits. Hillcrest Country Club, where the Jewish moguls belonged, was their elegant, nicely understated answer to the posh clubs that barred them, and it mirrored those clubs in reverse: only Jews were eligible, and they had to be sponsored by existing members and approved by a committee. Siegel was duly nominated, and he passed the test. (According to club legend, however, the members had not realized who he was, and when they did, he was asked to resign—by someone chosen for the task because of his advanced age and infirmity.) In the late thirties, Richard Gully began seeing Siegel socially because Siegel was having an affair with Gully's friend, Countess Dorothy del Frasso, an American heiress who had married an Italian nobleman. Gully mentioned to Siegel that he needed a job. "He said, 'You'll have a job tomorrow,' " Gully recalled. "He called Mark Hellinger, a producer who did gangster pictures for Warner Bros., and said, 'Put Gully on the payroll.' I had nothing to do, I used to wander around the sets. The power of the underworld!"

In the early forties, Siegel was having an affair with another woman, Virginia Hill, notorious for her liaisons with a number of mobsters; and her brother had an apartment at Hollywood's Chateau Marmont (then home to many writers, including Dorothy Parker and Robert Benchley), where Siegel and Hill often stayed. Screenwriter Edward Anhalt lived there at that time as well; a New Yorker, he had known Frank Costello and Charles "Lucky" Luciano fairly well, and he and Siegel became good friends. "Ben Siegel was fearless," Anhalt said. "He drove around in this convertible woodie, the only one I ever saw. For a guy who shouldn't have been so visible, it was crazy. I said that to him, but he said, 'Nobody's gonna bother me.' " They would go to Rothschild's barbershop together ("It was above a clothing store," Anhalt recalled, "but you wouldn't have known it was there—the wiseguys all went there, and the owner didn't want anyone there he didn't know") and to dinner at Dave's Blue Room. They talked a lot about Anhalt's writing a script about Siegel. Siegel was keen on the idea—he had theatrical ambitions, and was taking voice lessons, in an effort to overcome his Brooklyn accent. "Ben introduced me to Sidney Korshak, who he said was his consigliere," Anhalt said. "He said Korshak would help on the movie." These plans, however, were cut short on June 20, 1947, when Siegel was killed by several shotgun blasts as he sat in the living room of a Spanish-style mansion Virginia Hill had rented in Beverly Hills. Over the years, Anhalt continued, he came to know Korshak fairly well. "People *were* afraid of him, of course, but he was meticulously polite, unlike many of his contemporaries," Anhalt commented, smiling. "And I thought he was fascinated with crime, and with show business."

Well integrated in the Hollywood social scene as the mob's emissaries had been before, Korshak would achieve a level of recognition and respect that was different not only in degree but in kind from his predecessors'. The fact that he was a lawyer gave him a patina of legitimacy, particularly for those who wanted to rationalize their association with him. But legitimacy really was not the coin of the realm. Korshak had *presence* ("When he entered, it shook up the room," recalled Pettorino); and in this community, that counted for nearly everything. His physical attributes were passable—he was tall, with regular enough, if rather fleshy features, in an undistinguished countenance—but this one barely noticed. For Korshak had perfected the intimation of power (and dark power, at that), subtly conveyed. He exhibited none of the clichéd attributes of his compatriots, in their white ties on white shirts, with their icy eyes, bejeweled, meaty hands, and hair-trigger tempers. Korshak, one felt, wouldn't deign to raise his voice; his kind of threat was, "I wouldn't do that if I were you," uttered ever so quietly; he was debonair, beautifully dressed in hand-tailored suits, and so smooth that the boys in Chicago called him "Mr. Silk Stockings."

Lew Wasserman, an MCA agent who arrived in Los Angeles in 1939, recalled that he, Korshak, and a young actor named Ronald Reagan, who was one of MCA's handful of movie clients at the time, used to socialize together. "In those days, money was not something people talked about. It didn't matter that Reagan was making $200 a week, I was making about $300, and Sidney, much more." Wasserman paused, seeming to consider. "We didn't know just what Sidney was making, or what he was doing. He was a lawyer, very accepted in the community. And he was a good friend of mine for fifty years."

When Wasserman, a candidate for MCA's publicity department, had appeared in the doorway of Stein's Chicago office in 1936, Stein made a quick appraisal. A tall, spindly twenty-three-year-old in a suit Stein considered tasteless, Wasserman had not gone to college; hiring him, therefore, would mean an exception to the rule. But Stein's brother Bill was keen on Wasserman. So before Wasserman even stepped into his office, Stein agreed to give him a chance, but warned him that the position might be only temporary, and he should "arrange his personal affairs accordingly." Wasserman did not have much to arrange. He was doing advertising for the Mayfair Casino in Cleveland, making $100 a week, and living with his wife's parents. He'd already worked at several Cleveland theaters, including the Palace and the Hippodrome (where he did a publicity stunt using hearses and caskets for a *Dracula* show); and he had been booking MCA bands for several years. It had become standard practice: MCA would send Wasserman its advertising materials, a source of considerable pride at the company—and he would redo them. "Finally, Bill Stein came down to see me and asked why I was doing that. And I said, 'Because I don't like it, I think it's old-fashioned.' You know," Wasserman added, "when you're twenty, you know everything."

His taking the MCA job meant a move to Chicago and a pay cut (Stein would pay him only $60 a week)—but Wasserman was well aware that MCA was a national powerhouse in the band-booking business, and that Stein had just decided to break into the movie business as well. He was very impressed by Stein. "He was a new breed of agent. He was a doctor, he wore a pince-nez, he dressed like a doctor—not like those guys in plaid jackets hanging around the Brill Building in New York," Wasserman remarked. In addition, Wasserman's prospects at the Mayfair Casino were bleak, despite its having opened with great fanfare just the year before. "They spent eight to ten million building the Mayfair," Wasserman said. "It was modeled on the Chez Paree. It was really beautiful, with a dramatic entryway, a long narrow lobby, a big oblong-shaped bar. There was to be gambling—but then a new mayor was elected, and he said, no gambling!" The Mayfair was limping along at the time Stein interviewed Wasserman, but by the following year it went bankrupt. As at the Chez Paree, there were front men and then the real owners. Herman Pirchner, who sold his interest in the Mayfair Café, a family restaurant, to the new owners, was quoted in *The Last Mogul* by Dennis McDougal as saying that those with the biggest stake were four members of the Syndicate: Moe Dalitz, Sam "Sambo" Tucker, Lou Rothkopf, and Morris Kleinman, all members of the Mayfield Road Gang, who had controlled much of Cleveland's gambling, bootlegging, and prostitution during Prohibition. Since Wasserman had married Edie Beckerman the previous summer, he had family ties to Dalitz, too. Edie's father, Henry Beckerman, was a lawyer and power broker in Republican political circles in Cleveland, often referred to as one of the "powers behind the throne" of GOP county boss Maurice Maschke. Beckerman and Maschke were close friends as well as political allies, and Maurice Maschke, Jr., was in business with Dalitz. Beckerman had made a small fortune in the stock market and the real estate market as a shrewd speculator. Before the crash of 1929, he was a millionaire, he later testified. But he had been hit hard by the crash—and since then he had been indicted for attempted arson and embezzlement. He was acquitted in a trial on the embezzlement charges, but a mistrial was declared in the arson case because of efforts at jury tampering. Beckerman was indicted on the arson charges again. At that time, an editorial in the Cleveland *Plain Dealer* commended the prosecutor for his perseverance. "For years Beckerman's name has been dodging in and out of the local picture," the editorial said. "His Beckley Realty Co. has more than once figured in improvement projects in which the city was interested. Mystery has clouded the public understanding of some of his operations. . . . It has never appeared that the whole story of the arson case has been told." Ultimately, Beckerman was acquitted—but the cost of his defense in these cases had further depleted his funds. Unlike her older siblings, Edie had not been able to afford to go to college. When she met Wasserman, she was working at the May Company for $18 a week.

Wasserman may have felt some pressure to succeed from a new wife who remembered what it was to be wealthy and wanted to be again— but the real drive plainly came from within. His background was somewhat similar to Stein's, though even more destitute and restrictive, in that he had to work to help support his family from an early age and was unable to obtain a scholarship to go to college. His ambition, thwarted, had been to become a lawyer; and no amount of success would ever erase a lingering self-consciousness about his lack of education. His parents, Isaac and Minnie Weiserman, were Yiddish-speaking Orthodox Jews who had emigrated from Russia, arriving in this country in 1907; a few years later, they changed the family name to Wasserman. Along with approximately 35,000 other Russian Jews arriving between 1905 and 1912, they settled in the bleak, overcrowded Woodland Avenue area of Cleveland. William Zorach, who grew up in this neighborhood in the early 1900s, wrote in his autobiography, *Art Is My Life,* that "Woodland Avenue, once a beautiful, wide, tree-lined street with handsome houses," had by this time become "a dilapidated slum, a market street where farmers lined their produce up along the sidewalks and cried their wares. Across the street, houses seemed a long way off, set in back of dried up lawns. . . . A small boy seldom walked across the street." Wasserman had two older brothers, Max— who was born in Russia in 1906, and who died of epilepsy at sixteen— and William, born here in 1908. Louis Wasserman was born on March 22, 1913—though he later would use March 15 as his date of birth instead. His father worked as a paper cutter, a book binder, a box maker; he tried opening small restaurants but they failed. By the time he was twelve, Louis was selling candy in a theater, and at fifteen he had a regular job, working as an usher in the Palace movie theater from 3:00 P.M. to midnight, seven days a week. "I wanted to get out of things like gym, so I could work that schedule. I went to my principal, and I said, 'If I can raise money for school athletic uniforms, will you let me out?' Yes. So I brought movies to the school, and charged each kid 3 cents to go. Eight thousand kids times 3 cents! I knew they'd go. Because what the principal didn't realize and I did was this: to show movies, it has to be dark. And don't you think kids would pay 3 cents to sit in the dark?" Wasserman demanded, deadpan. "Then I went to my chemistry professor—I've always been pretty good in math," he added, with wry understatement, "and I said, I'll make you a deal. Will you allow me to miss class, as long as I pass every test? So, for two years, the only times I went to chemistry class were to take a test." In his family Louis became the acknowledged star. Lou Ratener was a longtime close friend of Bill Wasserman's; regarding the two brothers, Louis and Bill, he said, "They were two different personalities. Bill was a nice young man, but not charismatic like his brother, Lou. They were not close. And their parents were very ordinary people. Isaac, their father, was a very pious Jew, went to shul, the mother kept a kosher home. Isaac's only pleasure was Cleveland baseball—he listened to the Cleveland Indians games, day and night—and his son Lou. Lou was *god* to his parents."

Soon after Wasserman joined MCA (he had changed his name by this time from Louis to Lew), Stein began to notice his energy and resourcefulness. Wasserman went to Detroit and came back with a signed contract for a show at the Michigan State Fair, subject to Stein's approval; Wasserman had opened up a new area of business for MCA, and he wasn't even an agent. "Can you believe in those days you could put a DC-3 on a fairground, and people would come to see it?" Wasserman marveled. "They would, because they'd never seen a plane—the only people who did were those who traveled!" What he liked to call his claim to fame came about with Kay Kyser. Kyser and his orchestra had been performing at the Blackhawk restaurant in Chicago; he was very popular, but his fame was strictly Midwestern, because the radio broadcasts from the Blackhawk were not on a network. Chicago's WGN was a powerful station, but it was the networks that spanned the country. And by the late thirties, one needed a rich sponsor to get on a network. Kyser, therefore, had to distinguish himself in some way—and the way he could occurred to Wasserman one night as he was driving back from the Edgewater Beach Hotel, on the shores of Lake Michigan, with several executives. They were all listening to the radio. "There was a quiz show on the air. People in the car would act like they knew the answers but they wouldn't say anything— they were afraid of being wrong. Then, when they heard the answer, they would say they'd known it. You know," Wasserman paused, looking at his visitor, "you've been in groups like that. So I thought, let's do something where they *know* the answer. Because music is something that a lot of people know a lot about." It was an intuition that may have sprung from his own insecurity listening to that quiz show; but it was, in any event, a very clever idea. Wasserman took an audience participation routine of Kyser's, added musical quiz elements to it, and named the program *Kay Kyser and His Kollege of Musical Knowledge.* Soon, he and Stein had persuaded the American Tobacco Company to sponsor this show on Mutual Broadcasting, the smallest of the national networks (and with which Stein had some affiliation). Within a few months, it became such a hit that it moved to NBC, where it would remain on Wednesday nights for years, with over 20 million listeners a week.

Relieved of his publicity position, Wasserman became an MCA agent. He began working closely with Bill Stein, selling shows in Detroit, Kansas City, and Fort Worth. In 1938, Stein sent him to New York, to work under Billy Goodheart. MCA's success had not mellowed Goodheart; if anything, he was more tyrannical than he'd been in the pioneering days in Chicago. Irving "Swifty" Lazar, who had begun working as an agent in MCA's New York office in 1936, later described Goodheart, his boss, as someone "who had an ice tong for a tongue and reverence for no one." He was famous for abusing his subordinates. David "Sonny" Werblin would eventually become one of MCA's most powerful executives and, later, the owner of the New York Jets football team, but he had started out as one of Goodheart's lackeys, whose responsibilities included keeping Goodheart's pencils freshly sharpened. On occasion, Goodheart would start his day by breaking all the pencils and scattering them about his office; as soon as Werblin appeared for work, he would scream at him for being so derelict. Others tolerated Goodheart (he was, in fact, a remarkable agent), but Wasserman would not—the job, important as it was to him, was not worth being treated that way. He developed a strong dislike for Goodheart and, after working for him for a few months, called Stein and said he wanted to be transferred, or he would quit. Stein told him to join him in Los Angeles.

When Wasserman arrived in 1939, MCA's Hollywood business was still nascent. "We had about seven agents in the picture department," Wasserman said. "Our biggest clients then were Ronnie Reagan, Richard Dix (whose career was almost ending), and Hattie McDaniel (she had just been in *Gone With the Wind*). The total income of the theatrical department was less than one day's income for the band department." Wasserman found this anything but dispiriting; to him, it meant a clean canvas. Director George Sidney recalled the first time he saw the tireless young agent. "I was staging a big affair at the Coliseum, and I had eighteen or twenty of the top people in the industry at a planning session. I was saying, 'I want a marching band here.' This guy at the end of the table said, 'I'll take care of that.' 'I want planes to fly over March Field.' 'I'll handle that.' 'I want pink lemonade.' 'I'll handle that.'

"So I said to my assistant, 'Who *is* that tall, skinny guy?'

" 'It's Lew Wasserman. He's a PR guy for Kay Kyser.'

"There were a lot of fellows ahead of him," Sidney concluded, "but he was just faster and sharper."

Stories about just how fast and sharp Wasserman was began to make the rounds of the tight Hollywood circles. He was not only so fast with numbers that, as one associate said, "he was a walking computer before there were computers," but he was creative; he could invent deals that did something for everyone. He began to study tax law, and eventually came up with suggestions about deferred compensation and structuring of transactions that neither Stein nor the company's lawyers had thought of. He was not a loquacious person, certainly not given to small talk—and yet, when the need arose to win over an actor or a radio sponsor, he could exhibit great charm. He seemed never to tire; the more he worked, the more energized he became. And though he was a young, untried newcomer in this fabled industry, he was not afraid to go his own way. Wasserman recalled that not long after he arrived, N. Joseph Ross, who was Stein's lawyer, took him to lunch at Hillcrest. "He said, 'To be successful here, you have to join.' (It cost $3,500 to join, and $250 a month.) Jack Warner and Harry Cohn belonged." Wasserman said he took some materials home, read them, and—realizing that one had to be a Jew to join—told Ross, " 'I'm not joining. It's restricted.' And Joe Ross said, 'No, it's not. It's for Jews.' " According to Wasserman, he declined because he disagreed with the policy.

The enterprising young agent even came to the attention of L. B. Mayer, the head of MGM, who—with the legendary Irving Thalberg, as supervisor of production—had made MGM into Hollywood's most prestigious and glamorous studio in the thirties. "I looked up tremendously to L. B. Mayer, because I watched his operation," Wasserman told director Steven Spielberg in the course of an oral history interview. "Mayer's theory was very simple . . . he bought the best. If he thought you were talented, he bought you." Wasserman recalled his first meeting with Mayer. Wasserman had become fast friends with Eddie Mannix, a former bouncer who was general manager of MGM. After they had lunch one day, Mannix told Wasserman to come with him, and they walked down a corridor at MGM and entered an office. "We were in L.B.'s office—a fairly large office," Wasserman recounted. "He sat on a platform behind the desk so he could look down at you. He was a short man. Mannix said, 'This is the young man I've been telling you about.' " Mayer told Wasserman to sit down, and handed him a yellow pad. "He said, 'Write this down.' I took out my pen. I turned around, and Mannix was gone. I'm all alone! *L. B. Mayer,* I'd never met him.

"And he said, 'A firm seven-year contract.' I was thinking, Jesus, are they going to do a sequel to *Gone With the Wind* for Hattie? We don't have anybody that's worth a seven-year contract.

" 'Five thousand dollars a week.' Now I know it's got to be Hattie.

" 'Vice president in charge of marketing.' That was the third thing. And he stopped. He said, 'Well?'

"I said, 'Well, what, Mr. Mayer?'

" 'That's what I'm offering you to come to work here next Monday.'

"I said, 'Why would you do that? I only get $350 a week at MCA.' I told him the absolute truth.

"He said, 'I don't care what you get. That's a firm offer to start Monday.'

"I said, 'Thank you, I'm not interested.' He didn't talk to me for two years. But then we became very friendly."

Wasserman turned down Mayer, he said, because "I liked what I was doing. They let me alone at MCA, let me do what I wanted." And the kind of freedom Wasserman was describing at MCA—which would become far greater before long—was not something he would have found at a studio. At MCA, Wasserman really had only to answer to Stein. But the autonomy that the most powerful studio heads, including Mayer, seemed to have in Hollywood was illusory. They had bosses in their corporations' New York headquarters (for Mayer, it was Nicholas Schenck); and ultimately it was those executives, and the banks and other entities that financed the film corporations, that controlled their destinies. Wasserman also said, "I never cared about the money—I know it sounds like I'm saying it because it's the thing to say, but it's true. Mayer couldn't believe I didn't have a contract at MCA—but I didn't! I never had a contract, from 1936 to 1976. I had a strange relationship with Jules, one that's hard to explain."

It was a relationship that would remain largely opaque to others, and perhaps even to the two men themselves. What was already plain, however, was their extreme compatibility—not in the customary sense of enjoying each other's company, for neither of them had much of an instinct for that generally—but in the ability each had to further the other's goals: a virtual paradigm of utilitarianism. Stein offered Wasserman a vehicle for the full exercise of his talents; and Wasserman, Stein had begun to believe, offered him the chance to expand his empire. Neither, moreover, would really conflict with the other; for Stein, while he was highly secretive and distrustful of nearly everyone, did not need to exercise hands-on control over every aspect of his business. Indeed—inasmuch as it would involve establishing the kinds of relationships with union representatives that he earlier had with Petrillo—he did not want to. Within a year of Wasserman's arriving in Hollywood, therefore, Stein gave him essentially free rein.

Wasserman did not believe in trying to build their movie talent business from scratch. MCA was cash-rich. And if they had to buy stars in order to sell them, they would; they were merchants, after all. "The Selznicks [pioneering agents] wouldn't buy contracts. They felt they didn't need to, they were king," Wasserman said. "William Morris wouldn't either. They felt it was beneath them." Wasserman had no such compunction. If he had his way, MCA would become the agency analogue to MGM, with most of Hollywood's top talent under its control. Shortly after Stein persuaded Bette Davis to sign on, Wasserman bought up a slew of contracts, bringing in Errol Flynn, Joan Crawford, Basil Rathbone, and Paulette Goddard. But Wasserman also told Stein he believed it made even more sense to buy existing agencies, and the bigger the better. "I was more acquisition-minded than Jules, but he let me. I acquired a lot of agencies, here and around the world." In the early forties, they merged a number of agencies into MCA, including Alan Miller; Casting Consultants; Liebling-Wood; Alexander and Silman; Martonplay; Myron Selznick, Ltd.; William Meiklejohn; and Linnit & Dunfee, Ltd. It was surprising, in a way, that there were so many willing sellers; some may have felt it was an offer they couldn't refuse. For as Martin Baum commented, recalling this period, "MCA was saying, 'Take this money, come with us, you'll be part of the biggest agency—and if you don't, we'll take away your clients. You'll have nothing!' " MCA, everyone knew, was the juggernaut. In 1943, when Leland Hayward, one of the very small group of elite Hollywood agents, was recuperating in the hospital, he received a note from another member of that fraternity, Charles Feldman, which read: "Relax—don't give business a single thought, for in a few months Jules Stein will have all your clients, anyway."

Leland Hayward was even more antithetical to the stereotype of an agent than Jules Stein. Hayward, who came from an aristocratic New York family and had been educated at Eastern private schools and, for a year, at Princeton, was one of those rare people who seemed to carry out everything, in business and in life, with a kind of effortless grace. He was partial to white flannels and yachting sneakers. As his daughter Brooke Hayward later wrote in *Haywire*, he had what Stein described as "that radiant effervescent smile—rarely ever saw him when his face wasn't shining—ready to tell you something or sell you something." Both he and his partner, Nat Deverich, had started out at the Myron Selznick agency and then had gone off on their own. Hayward-Deverich's client list was appropriately sterling. It held three hundred established performers—including Greta Garbo, Myrna Loy, Ginger Rogers, Margaret Sullavan (Hayward's wife), Fred Astaire, Joseph Cotten, Henry Fonda, Oscar Levant, and Fredric March; producers and directors such as Billy Wilder and Joshua Logan; and writers including Dorothy Parker, Ben Hecht, Dashiell Hammett, Walter de la Mare, and Arthur Koestler. Billy Wilder, also in *Haywire*, said of Hayward, "In my opinion, his enormous success in this town, beyond his being very bright and knowing it inside out, was due to the fact that the wives of the moguls were crazy about him. I do not mean to imply that he had an affair with Mrs. Goldwyn, but Mrs. Goldwyn was just crazy about him. So was Mrs. Warner. *All* the wives were crazy about him and kept talking about him, because he was a very attractive, handsome, dashing man. He should have been a captain in the Austro-Hungarian army—something like that. He was certainly miscast as an agent. If I were to make a picture about an agent, a very successful agent, and my casting director brought in Leland Hayward, I would say, 'You're out of your mind! This is not the way an agent looks!' That was part of his success. Just charmed the birds off the trees, the money out of the coffers, and ladies into their beds."

Even Hayward, however, must have felt the hot breath of MCA's—especially Wasserman's—competition. Thus, one day in the early spring of 1945, Deverich told Wasserman that he should make an appointment with Hayward. "I went over to see Hayward," Wasserman began, seeming still to relish a story he had told associates countless times. "He had an office four times the size of mine today. He was lying on a couch without a tie and with no shoes on. He said, 'Hi. I haven't got a lot of time. My partner thinks you're a genius. Why don't you join us? We'll give you one third of the business.' I asked why, and he said he was not happy in the business and wanted to do less of it. I said, I'll buy your company. He wanted to know if I had the authority—I was pretty young. It was a very large business. It was done in an hour." The basic terms of the agreement were that Hayward and Deverich would each have ten-year contracts at MCA at roughly $100,000 a year, and they would also receive 50 percent of the commissions on the clients they brought with them, as well as sharing in MCA's bonus system on future business. With a single stroke, MCA had become not only the most important and largest agency in the world, but also the most powerful organization in the motion picture business.

The transfer of Hayward-Deverich's superb talent was not done painlessly, according to Larry White, who was Hayward's young assistant. "Getting some of the artists to go there was hell—Leland said, send them flowers, candy, do whatever you have to do," White recalled. "Generally speaking, you had an agent like Leland, he took 10 percent. But with MCA, you didn't know *what* they would take. And the artists were afraid of them. They let you know they could destroy your career." However, White continued, "I would say that many of the artists did better with Lew than they'd done with Leland."

Once the merger was completed, Hayward moved into the MCA

Jules Stein (center), shown with (left to right) Leland Hayward, Lew Wasserman, Nat Deverich, and Taft Schreiber, after the merger with Hayward-Deverich made MCA the largest and most powerful talent agency in the world. *Gene Lester Collection/Screen Actors Guild*

building. Wasserman, who was too practical to care much about the conventional signs of station, said, "I told Hayward he could have any office at MCA he wanted, including mine—just not Jules's or Taft Schreiber's [Schreiber was very senior to Wasserman, and close to Stein]." Hayward, however, did not take Wasserman's. "He picked out an office with French wallpaper—*real* wallpaper—but he didn't want it. So I had it torn off. He wanted it to be maroon (he had very modern furniture). Jules was angry—*maroon?* Then, Jules told me, 'I've worked it all out with Leland. I'm going to panel his whole office.' "

Stein gave Wasserman all the credit for having achieved this remarkable deal, and he felt it confirmed his judgment about Wasserman's talents. It was at this point, Stein later said, that he realized he had a "pupil who was surpassing his teacher." Stein was not alone in this assessment. Within the organization of MCA, Stein had already begun to recede somewhat; it was Wasserman, after all, who pulled off the master deal that catapulted them to preeminence, and Stein who was distressed about Hayward's maroon walls. Stein had begun to focus more of his attention on investing, applying the tenets of the Dow theory not only to his portfolio but to operating MCA; when he saw signs of an impending bear market, for example, he would exhort his executives to firm up their commitments. Stein's work was still his life—he would comment once that "Saturdays and Sundays were always my worst days"—but the force that was driving MCA, certainly in Hollywood, was Wasserman.

All the heat emanated from Wasserman's office; so, too, did the dictates about how life within the company was to be lived. It was a very tightly controlled environment. The dress code had become rigid: dark suits, white shirts, dark blue or gray ties. Wasserman had needed instruction in dress when he had first come to MCA, but he was a fast learner. Now MCA agents, in their dark uniforms, were commonly referred to as the "MCA Mafia." Desks were to be left clear at night; if Wasserman and Stein, patrolling, found papers on them, they would sweep them into the wastebasket. "Messy desk, messy mind," was the credo. There were strict rules for the agents' secretaries. They went up the back stairs, while the agents ascended the winding staircases in the front of the building. And there was a prohibition on fraternization. Helen Gurley (Brown) went to work at MCA as a secretary in 1942. She recalled how frustrated she and her colleagues were at not being able to date the agents. "I remember for Valentine's Day, we decided to wear pink and red—we were a *flower house* of color in the secretarial pool. Still, we couldn't attract any attention. The agents were all business." Wasserman provided an example for his troops. "Lew was very attractive, and he could have had anyone," Gurley said, "but that didn't seem to interest him." Lew's wife, Edie, had given birth to their only child, a daughter, Lynne, in 1940; but he seemed almost as uninterested in home life as he did in office dalliances. Gurley added, too, that the temper that would become notorious was already in evidence; the screams coming from his office could be heard down the hall. Eventually, Gurley did manage to attract some attention, and she began having a clandestine affair with Herman Citron, whose clients included Frank Sinatra, Dean Martin, and Jerry Lewis; when her relationship with Citron was discovered, she was fired.

It was Edie Wasserman who had spotted Dean Martin and Jerry Lewis, according to longtime MCA executive Herbert Steinberg. But it would appear, from Steinberg's account, that Edie was stepping outside her prescribed role and realized it was best to approach her husband obliquely with regard to her talent scouting.

"Dean Martin and Jerry Lewis were being handled by Abby Greshler, and they were booked into the Copacabana," Steinberg said. "Edie went to their opening night. She realized this was a great talent team. She started to bring people in every night. Then, Lew came to New York. 'Where do you want to go tonight?' She'd been there every night for two weeks—but she was careful in the way she suggested things to Lew. So she said, 'I hear there's a good act at the Copacabana.' Jack Entratter, who was later co-owner and general manager of the Sands, was managing the Copacabana. When Edie and Lew came in, he said, 'Oh, hi, Mrs. Wasserman. You're here *again!*' Lew bought out their contract with Greshler," Steinberg concluded.

In these days, the term "corporate culture" had not yet become part of the lexicon, but MCA's was, unmistakably, survival of the fittest. And this was true company-wide. Shelly Schultz recalled his indoctrination in MCA's Chicago office. "There were two guys in adjacent offices. They were both selling to nightclubs, and were given the same territory. And you'd hear one of them, on the phone, talking to a customer and saying, about the guy in the next office, 'Don't buy from him! I can give them to you $200 cheaper!' " It was a brutal arrangement, but it successfully weeded out those who were hampered by personal ethics, or friendship with their colleagues, or the lack of a killer instinct. Thus, MCA agents, by and large, were trained to be as ruthless with one another as they were with outside competitors. They would display their mettle in gladiatorial combat—shouting and going for each other's throats at company meetings, while Stein, presiding, listened quietly, and in the end ruled up or down. The premium placed on aggressiveness—and, of course, productivity—was institutionalized through the compensation system. Sliding scale bonuses were calculated according to a formula that included the amount of business brought in by the agent, the gross done by each department and each branch office, and some other esoteric factor employed by Stein. In many cases, these bonuses constituted the lion's share of an agent's income. In 1943, for example, Sonny Werblin, kingpin of the New York office and its highest-paid member, received a salary of $5,200 and a bonus of $49,300. Second to Werblin was Harold Hackett, vice president in charge of radio, who received a salary of $5,200 and a bonus of $37,300. According to Harry Sosnik, of course, Hackett had considerable under-the-table income as well. Sosnik's informing Stein of Hackett's conduct had obviously not hurt his career at MCA; indeed, Hackett had prospered dramatically since that time.

Irving "Swifty" Lazar, who had worked in MCA's New York office in the thirties under Goodheart, left the agency but decided he would like to return in 1945. Stein had a general rule that no one who left could be rehired, but he thought so highly of Lazar's talents (he had been given his nickname by Humphrey Bogart, after he made three deals for Bogart in an afternoon) that Stein gave him special dispensation. As Lazar described in his autobiography, *Swifty*, he asked Wasserman, who headed the Hollywood office, if he could work there, and Wasserman agreed. Lazar quickly learned how MCA had changed under Wasserman's aegis. Since Wasserman "was answerable only to Jules Stein, he could run the agency pretty much any way he pleased. The way that pleased Lew was very different than anything ever seen in Hollywood. MCA was more like the Central Intelligence Agency than a talent business." First, there was the uniform. Second, there was the code of secrecy; MCA agents were instructed to be strictly close-mouthed, on the grounds that whatever information they had related to their clients' business.

Wasserman had also instituted a system, unique to MCA, in which agents covered not only their clients but a particular studio; so there would be, for example, an MCA agent who covered Warner Bros., and was responsible for everything that happened there that affected an MCA client. Lazar, who was friendly with Darryl Zanuck, the head of Twentieth Century-Fox, was assigned to Fox.

"My first day on the lot, an actor hailed me. 'Are you the new MCA guy?' he asked.

" 'Yes.'

" 'My name's Bob Sterling. I don't like the color of my dressing room. It's green. I want yellow.'

" 'I don't handle dressing room colors,' I replied.

" 'But you're my agent.'

" 'I handle contract matters, or any disputes you might have with the director or your co-stars,' I told him, 'but I don't handle paint.' "

Wasserman reprimanded him, but, as Lazar said, "I wasn't accustomed to the lengths to which an agent was obliged to go to help his client." It was, however, Wasserman's insistence on regimentation and his hunger for information that Lazar found most invasive. "Lew wanted to know everything his agents did, so he required us to write a daily report on all our clients and activities. These reports were distributed to MCA executives at the end of the day. At a weekly meeting, Lew would choose highlights from these memos for discussion.

" 'What were you talking to Norman Krasna about?' he asked me one day.

"I thought for a moment, and then, just to be ornery, I said, 'I didn't tell him to go to the Morris office, I know that.'

" 'The Morris office? Why would he go to the Morris office?'

" 'I don't think he will. I told him not to.'

"Lew failed to see the humor. 'I wish you would remember your conversations,' he said. 'The way I run this office, I need all the information.'

"... When the meeting was over, I explained to Lew that I couldn't possibly do it his way. 'You have a Mafia-type routine here with all these guys reporting to you,' I told him. 'I'm no robot. I do my own thing.' "

That, of course, was the ultimate heresy. Wasserman wanted him out; and before long—with a noncompete contract whose terms were rich, because Lazar was already an agent of considerable standing—he left MCA for the second, and last, time. Life inside MCA under Wasserman may have had more and more of the oppressiveness of a totalitarian regime; but it was halcyon compared to life outside as a competitor. Sam Jaffe, who wanted to emulate Leland Hayward, had opened his own agency in the mid-thirties. William Morris at that time was the largest agency, but Jaffe did not feel threatened by them. They did not raid other agencies for clients, for example. "The raiding was done by MCA," Jaffe said in an oral history. "They were new, so they had to get a stronghold and they were very successful. . . . They offered everything to a client in those days. An automobile, a painting, insurance. They had no hesitancy about taking your clients away. . . . I remember driving by MCA at night, I'd see the lights on in the MCA building, and I'd say, I'm sure somebody up there is trying to figure out how to entice my clients. In the days that MCA came in, I think every client I had was contacted almost daily, trying to entice them. They had a mass talent. They had many people working, and they were eager beavers. You know, eager beavers scurrying on the ground, trying to take . . ." Jaffe broke off. "I hated that part. I did it, but it was different. It was competition, it was different. When MCA came in the business, they became a real force. I'm not condemning them, that's what they wanted to do, and what they started out to do, they did. But they were merciless, they were cruel.

"Some people create, and will do anything to destroy you," Jaffe continued. "I often told Wasserman and Stein, 'You can put me out of business. You're very strong. I can't compete with you in that way.' I mean, they could take one of my people and offer all kinds of advantages [long contracts, bonuses, insurance] that we couldn't as a young company. We had to depend on a personal relationship or effect. That was our only hope."

The subject of competition was a sensitive one at MCA. Exclusives, for example—whereby an amusement operator agreed to get all his entertainment attractions through MCA and, in return, got first option on the most desirable talent in his area—had been a cardinal building block of the business. These arrangements were not committed to paper, but they were common knowledge in the industry. One amusement operator, Larry Finley, had finally raised the issue in a court case, which was tried in federal court in Los Angeles in February 1946. Finley charged that MCA refused to offer him talent because it had an exclusive with a rival operator—and that even when he offered to pay more for certain attractions, MCA would book them with his competitor instead. His amusement park and ballroom lost money, he alleged, because he had been denied access to MCA clients—which included a majority of the best talent on the West Coast. The jury had found in his favor and awarded him substantial damages; the judge cut out the damages, agreeing with the contention of MCA lawyers that it was impossible to calculate Finley's loss; but he also ruled that there was "ample and substantial evidence to support and sustain the implied findings of the jury to the defendants having conspired to . . . monopolize interstate commerce." Indeed, he likened MCA to an "Octopus," its "tentacles reaching out . . . and grasping everything in show business." (Apt as the image was, it was not original; it had been used to describe Music Corporation by a lawyer in a Chicago trial back in 1935.)

The *Finley* judge did not know the half of it. Starting in the early thirties, Stein had started accumulating so much Paramount stock that he had become its major shareholder, second only to his friend Balaban in his holdings. While Stein's owning both a talent agency and such a substantial share of a studio to which he sold talent was not illegal, it could be compellingly presented as part of a larger, anti-competitive picture. That picture could also include his relationships with his purported competitors—relationships that Stein, concerned about his vulnerability to antitrust enforcement, had gone to some lengths to disguise. By the mid-forties, MCA, William Morris, Associated Booking Company, and General Artists Corporation (GAC) were among the biggest agencies in the country. Of the four, only William Morris was truly unaffiliated.

Associated Booking was headed by Joe Glaser. A rough character who kept his considerable wealth in a safe-deposit box, Glaser had grown up in a bordello in Chicago, promoted fights for the Capone mob, and managed a nightclub, the Sunset Café. He hardly projected the desired image of an MCA agent. But in the early thirties he had, oddly enough, been employed by MCA; and, even more, when he started Associated in 1940 he had done so with a loan from Stein, who thus acquired an interest in the company (this was subsequently noted in the trade press). Personal style aside, it was perfectly complementary. Talent agencies at this time tended to book either black or white clients, not both; MCA's clients were white, while Glaser specialized in booking black jazz musicians, including Duke Ellington and Louis Armstrong. "Joe Glaser was very powerful," recalled Bob Carruthers, who worked for Petrillo for a number of years. Petrillo and Glaser were good friends, he said. "He tried to buy his way in everywhere. I remember once he came to me—there was some problem with one of his clients and the union. He said, 'How much would it take to fix this? One thousand? Twenty-five hundred?' I said, 'Forget it, Joe—and vamoose outa here!' " What made the Stein-Associated connection ironic was the identity of another person with an interest (probably the controlling interest) in Associated: Sidney Korshak. Korshak was close to Glaser personally, and—since even after he moved from Chicago to Los Angeles he never opened a law office there—he often worked out of the Associated office in Beverly Hills. So while Stein loudly refused to attend the same party as Korshak, he nonetheless was his secret partner.

GAC was also rumored to be linked to Stein; he was said to have bailed out GAC when it was on the verge of going out of business in the early forties. Stein denied the persistent rumor. But, in *Swifty,* Lazar wrote about that period, "I heard an amazing rumor that turned out to be true: Jules Stein was secretly keeping his rival afloat with MCA money, in order to create the appearance of competition and not bring the government down on MCA for being monopolistic. Long after the dust had settled, I asked Stein about it. A bit sheepishly, he admitted it had been true." In his memoir, Karl Kramer confirmed Lazar's assertion, saying that while the "tie-up" of the two companies was never made public, Stein had taken Petrillo into his confidence. "The role Jules Stein played was so powerful, behind-the-scenes—he *was* funding his competitors," said Herbert Siegel, who would acquire GAC in 1960. "He loaned GAC the money, the controlling stock was placed in a vault." And, Siegel continued, a senior MCA agent "would get all the information on GAC's clients and numbers every week. He did the same thing with Joe Glaser," Siegel added, noting that he had gotten to know Glaser and examined his books because he had at one point considered buying Glaser's company. "I don't think it was legal—but Jules knew he had better be sure to have some competitors around, to be able to point to."

In 1944, Frank Sinatra—who had recently emerged as one of the country's hottest performers—moved his agency representation from GAC to MCA. His switch sparked quite a flurry in the trade press, where it was portrayed as an example of client theft by MCA. Considering MCA's general pattern, it was a fair enough extrapolation—but, apparently, mistaken. The story began with the contract Sinatra had signed with band leader Tommy Dorsey in the late thirties—a contract that gave Dorsey an exorbitant share of Sinatra's earnings. In 1942, Sinatra succeeded in terminating the contract. "Sinatra went to the mob, and the mob got him out of the Dorsey contract," said agent Martin Baum, "and he retained his relationship with the mob for the rest of his life." According to an unpublished biography of Manie Sacks, a onetime MCA agent and a close friend of Sinatra's, Sinatra extricated himself from that contract by paying $60,000—much of which Jules Stein provided. Then—in a move that would seem almost inexplicable but for the story's subtext—Sinatra went not to his benefactor MCA, but to GAC. It was about two years later that he made his much reported move from GAC to MCA; most likely, because Sinatra had become such a star by that time, Stein preferred to have him under MCA's own roof, not that of its covertly controlled subsidiary. "That whole story about how MCA 'stole' Frank Sinatra from GAC—I thought Jules must have had a good laugh. It was all part of the deal!" Siegel said.

Orchestrating from the wings was nothing new for Stein, but by the forties his stage had grown much larger. His instinct for secrecy, too, had grown apace. MCA's corporate structure was positively byzantine, with interlocking companies incorporated in many different states; in addition, there were Stein's myriad companies, also far-flung; and it was almost certain that no one but Stein and an accountant in New York named Harry Berman, who had started working for Stein in 1930, were familiar with all of it. None of the standard business references, such as Moody's or Poor's, offered any information on MCA. Dun & Bradstreet could not glean enough to compile a credit rating on the company. Stein, unlike most of his peers in show business, shunned publicity (by 1946, he was not listed in *Who's Who,* or even *Who's Who in the Motion Picture Industry*), and he demanded that his employees at MCA cultivate anonymity as well. Complete client lists were guarded as though they were state secrets.

There were of course plenty of secrets to protect, including Stein's interest in the Chez Paree and other Chicago nightclubs. Frank Sinatra was lambasted in the press when, in January 1947, he went to Havana in the company of Joey Fischetti to perform at the Hotel Nacionál (there was also a rumor that the small valise Sinatra was carrying when he and Fischetti got off the plane held $2 million in cash, which Sinatra was delivering to the mob). Sinatra would be forced to try to explain this trip and his association with Fischetti for years afterward. And while Sinatra was a star, he was just an entertainer after all; for

Jules Stein, one of America's most successful businessmen, to be exposed as a partner of the Fischettis would have caused a furor.

Nor did Stein's partnerships with the mob end with the nightclubs. In the forties, Stein held in a trust account shares of various private companies he controlled—and one that he didn't. That one, a private company named Kirkeby Hotels, Inc., was controlled by Meyer Lansky. Its nominal head was A. S. Kirkeby, who in the mid-thirties had been a used car dealer and then, within a few years, was transfigured into the president of a hotel chain that included the Blackstone and Drake hotels in Chicago; the Gotham in New York; the Beverly Wilshire in Beverly Hills, and the Hotel Nacionál in Cuba. (Stein would often bemoan how he had missed a chance to buy the Beverly Hills Hotel—but he would never mention that he owned, through Kirkeby, a piece of the Beverly Wilshire.) Kirkeby had lived in Chicago in the late thirties; then he moved to Beverly Hills where he built an estate in the style of Versailles, and amassed a fabulous collection of Impressionist art. Stein, too, had constructed an elaborate facade by this time, and the extent of the artifice made his secrets all the more perilous. Stein, after all, was not Harry Cohn, going to the racetracks with Johnny Roselli, or even Lew Wasserman, social chum of Korshak's. Stein and his family lived at the top of a high canyon in Beverly Hills, behind blue iron gates and a long drive lined with cypresses, in a Spanish-style, semicircular villa, Misty Mountain, which had been designed by Wallace Neff, a California architect with a select clientele that included Mary Pickford, Darryl Zanuck, Cary Grant, and Barbara Hutton. Doris—who was named one of America's Ten Best-Dressed Women in 1946—had achieved her aim of becoming the town's preeminent hostess. In their home, filled with exquisite seventeenth- and eighteenth-century English furniture, Doris and Jules gave parties that were famous—seated dinners of fifty to a hundred, where the guests were an eclectic mix, including Mary Lasker, Jack Benny, Sam Goldwyn, Howard Hughes, Jimmy Stewart, the Duke and Duchess of Bedford, Artur Rubinstein, Diana Vreeland, the Reagans, Mae West,

Maurice Chevalier, Armand Hammer, Lady Fairfax. Only the cream of Hollywood society was invited, and that did not, as a rule, include MCA employees.

Secrecy, of course, is double-edged; if one cultivates it too assiduously, one attracts the very attention one is seeking to avoid. And that is what was happening to Stein. He was becoming famous for his secretiveness. In the spring of 1946, David Wittels, a writer for the *Saturday Evening Post,* set out to shine some light on the shadowy businessman. Stein, as usual, refused to grant any interviews. But then, according to Wasserman, Stein became concerned about the scope of the article, and reports coming back to him about questions Wittels was asking. It was, moreover, to be an in-depth, four-part series. And Stein was also well aware that the Antitrust Division of the U.S. Justice Department was conducting an investigation of MCA, and anything damning that was published would lend heat to that investigation; indeed, an internal Justice Department memorandum noted that the article was soon to appear, and that it should be significant because the reporter, Wittels, had interviewed over one hundred people. So a few days before the first piece was to appear, Stein flew to Philadelphia to meet with Wittels, to whom he spoke on the condition that he not be quoted. From Stein's perspective, the results could not have been better. Regarding Sinatra's move from GAC to MCA, Wittels wrote, "There is a legend on Broadway—which always believes there's a hidden ball somewhere—that MCA secretly owns half of General Amusement, ostensibly its bitter rival, and that at the proper moment MCA merely took over what it already half owned [Sinatra]. The legend has no foundation in fact." Wittels mentioned Stein's standing up to the mob in Chicago, and his taking out an insurance policy in the face of the kidnapping threat. He mentioned an interest through corporate setups in hotels and other real estate, but divulged no names. And, in a section with a subhead entitled, "The Secretive but Stainless Mr. Stein," Wittels wrote, "The natural result of this studied secrecy has been a hair-raising motley of rumors and conjectures, some of them downright libelous, as to Stein's origin and early career. No obvious reason for such secrecy reveals itself, however, when his history is laboriously dug out and pieced together."

This piece functioned as something of an amulet with which to ward off suspicion; more than fifty years later, Wasserman was still pointing to it as the best extensive piece ever written on MCA (though he cautioned that the numbers were not right, implying that they were low). Certainly, it was salt in the wounds of its rivals. It estimated MCA's annual profit, before taxes, at $4 million a year, and declared Stein one of the richest men in America. It *did* mention that competitors referred to MCA as the Octopus—but it softened that appellation by suggesting that, given the glamour of its talent list, MCA should be seen, instead, as "a star-spangled octopus" (the title of the series). "No movie company, no producer, no radio chain, no other agency, no impresario of any sort has such a galaxy of stars." After acquiring Hayward-Deverich, with its three hundred established stars, MCA had a movie list with nearly seven hundred on it—including, in addition to those mentioned earlier on the Hayward-Deverich roster, Betty Grable, Gregory Peck, Jimmy Stewart, Jane Wyman, Boris Karloff, Clark Gable, Shirley Temple, Maureen O'Hara, Dick Powell, Frank Sinatra, Joan Fontaine, John Garfield, Abbott and Costello, Eddie Cantor, and Marlene Dietrich. MCA was a force in theater, too. Fredric March starred in *A Bell for Adano,* Carol Bruce and Buddy Ebsen in *Show Boat,* Ethel Merman in *Annie Get Your Gun,* Maurice Evans in *Hamlet.* There were hundreds of MCA clients working on Broadway and in road shows, as performers and also directors, playwrights, scene designers. MCA also backed plays, and Leland Hayward, now producing plays, functioned both as agent and employer. And MCA was still dominant in radio, and in bands. Conveying a sense of just how ubiquitous MCA had become in the entertainment world, Wittels wrote that "the odds are rather good that any time you go to the movies or theater, tune in a major radio program, visit a night club or cocktail lounge, listen to a famous dance-band or attend a large-scale lodge benefit, MCA either put the show together or had a hand in it somehow." No matter how vast the enterprise, however, it was Hollywood that was now "the mainspring of MCA activities." There, Wittels pointed out, MCA controlled more than one third of the important stars—"far more than any of the highly publicized producers such as Darryl Zanuck, David O. Selznick or Samuel Goldwyn, and perhaps more than the three of them together."

And Hollywood *was* Wasserman. There were other contenders to become head of MCA, all older and more senior in the company than he. Sonny Werblin, in the New York office, expected that he might become president; and Taft Schreiber, who had started out with Stein in Chicago, and was close to him personally, believed he surely would be president. But Schreiber had opened the L.A. office in 1930 and it had remained a backwater for eight years; Wasserman had arrived and within a year was laying siege to every agency in town. And it was not just that he managed to swallow so many, by dint of muscle and money. He was, as Leland Hayward put it, "the best agent I ever saw."

So in early December 1946, Wasserman and Schreiber traveled by train to Chicago. It was ten years, almost to the day, since Stein had hired Wasserman, with his warning it might not last. Now, the thirty-three-year-old was to be named president. But it was, not surprisingly, a secret. Stein wanted to announce it in Chicago, in the offices of the First National Bank, where a Jewish banker, Walter Heymann, had backed Stein early, and where important company meetings would continue to be held for decades. Schreiber and Wasserman had an uneasy relationship; Wasserman was careful to be deferential to him (he had, after all, offered Hayward any office but Stein's and Schreiber's) but he knew that Schreiber did not like him, and would like him far less once he learned that Wasserman was to supersede him and become president. So, during the long trip, Wasserman said nothing about it. Walking down the street in Chicago, the two men ran into Petrillo. "Jimmy said, 'Lew, what the hell are you doing here?' " Wasserman recalled. "And then he said, 'Oh, I remember, you're going to be named president!' "

MCA president Lew Wasserman in 1958. *Corbis-Bettmann*

Chapter 2

MONOPOLY POWER

When Wasserman took the helm of MCA, Hollywood was engulfed in one of the most bitter, violent battles in its long-running labor war. Labor in the band business had been powerful, but that power had come to rest in the hands of one man—and a man with whom, as Stein had found, he could do business. Labor in the movie business was far more complicated; in fact, it was more complicated than anything in the labor world. There were no fewer than forty-three crafts and talent unions—which meant there was endless fodder for jurisdictional disputes. On the crafts side, the IATSE (recently the fiefdom of Bioff and Browne) was the behemoth—a fifty-three-year-old union with sixty thousand U.S. members, ten thousand of them in Hollywood, ranging from photographers to florists to camera crane operators to makeup artists; opposite the IATSE, in the current struggle, was the Conference of Studio Unions (CSU), a five-year-old group of twelve unions, with close to ten thousand members, primarily carpenters and painters. On the talent side, there were the actors, writers, directors, and musicians; they were weighing in from the sidelines on the IATSE-CSU battle.

Perhaps one reason the management-labor struggles in Hollywood were historically so fierce was that labor essentially held the key to the viability of the business; not only could a strike in the midst of a production cause it to be aborted, with all the millions spent to that moment lost, but labor costs were generally between 70 and 80 percent of the overall cost of a movie. Studio bosses like Jack Warner and Louis B. Mayer viewed labor as a force to be vanquished, and their approach was to fight bitterly over every penny they gave in negotiations. They were much hated in turn by many of the workers. (Jack Warner's daughter, Barbara Warner Howard, would recall that during the forties strikes, "a note was sent to my family threatening to scatter our bones all over our golf course; a map was enclosed to show where the different pieces would be buried.") Wasserman was a relative newcomer to this violently antagonistic scene, and he, like Stein, viewed it differently than the patriarchs of the business did. Labor wars hurt both sides; in times of peace, everyone made money. And one way to achieve peace was to establish relationships with those labor leaders who were strong enough—and complaisant enough—to deliver it. Petrillo had done this for Stein, and (thanks to Stein's machinations in ensuring he would not be ousted in his fight with Weber) continued to. Bioff and Browne had done this for the studios in a far cruder, less effective way, which had ended badly, with a black eye for Hollywood. But with the right kinds of leaders, who had at least a semblance of legitimacy but could be properly cultivated, a new era of labor relations in Hollywood might be ushered in.

Herbert Sorrell, chief of the CSU, was unquestionably the wrong man for the part. A brawny onetime fighter, rough-looking, with a bashed-in nose and a general readiness for both verbal and physical confrontation, Sorrell had started working in a factory at the age of twelve and, after holding a string of jobs, became a painter at Universal Studios in 1923. Two years later, the painters in the studios were organized; Sorrell, whose father had been a diehard union man, quickly joined the union, only to be fired when he was asked by his boss if he held a union card, and he responded that he did. He began to recruit union members, and was fired from jobs at other studios as well. But when an agreement was reached in late 1926 that the studios would no longer discriminate against union men, Sorrell returned to work there. He eventually became a union leader. However, unlike many of his more autocratic counterparts, particularly at the IATSE, who had little use for the will of the rank and file, he was a passionate believer in trade union democracy. He often referred to himself as a "dumb painter," apparently self-conscious about his lack of formal education; but he was, in fact, very keen, and capable of a raw eloquence. He had denounced Bioff and Browne early on (according to Sorrell, Bioff tried to appease him by offering him $56,000), and fought to oust them for years; they, in turn, had called him a Communist. Even after Bioff and Browne were incarcerated, Sorrell continued to speak his mind in ways that won him no friends among the studio bosses. He charged that they had been Bioff's and Browne's collaborators, not their victims, and that the IATSE leadership was still corrupt, since virtually all its top hierarchy had served with Bioff and Browne. And in July 1946, in the flush of victory after leading a two-day CSU strike that won every wage and hour demand, including a 25 percent increase in base pay, from the studios, Sorrell had struck a decidedly noncomplaisant note. "From now on," he had declared, "we dictate."

It may have been at that heady moment that Sorrell's fate was irrevocably sealed. It had long been evident to the producers that it would be far easier to deal with one group of unions, not two, on the crafts side—and, certainly, with the IATSE, not the CSU. During the last couple of years, the studios had maneuvered to weaken the CSU by helping to promote jurisdictional confrontations between the CSU and IATSE; indeed, the CSU had been provoked into a strike in 1945—one that had depleted its treasury and caused its workers to go without paychecks for nine months. But the union had endured, and Sorrell had just emerged from these most recent negotiations stronger, and perhaps even more intemperate, than before. If he and his union were to be eliminated for good from this unmanageable triangle, what was required was not a desultory fueling of jurisdictional disputes, but a fully concerted, covert plan of attack, two (the studios and the IA) massed against one.

It would be a tricky and unlawful business—management conspiring with one union to destroy another. But Roy Brewer, the head of IATSE in Hollywood, seemed peculiarly suited to the task. After Bioff and Browne had been deposed, the new president of IATSE, Richard Walsh—who had been a vice president and member of the executive board during the Bioff-Browne regime, and who had publicly defended both men and castigated their critics—sent Brewer from his union post in Nebraska to present a fresh face in Hollywood. Upon his arrival there in 1945, Brewer sought out the opinions of some of his colleagues, and he quickly became convinced that the most insidious influence in Hollywood was not the mob's, but, rather, the Communists'; and he decided that Sorrell (just as Bioff had charged) was indeed a Communist, and his CSU a Communist hotbed. His view was unequivocal, and sweeping. As he would subsequently testify at congressional hearings, "We have a very sincere and positive conviction that a substantial portion of the trouble that has existed in Hollywood during the past ten years arises out of the efforts and the activities of those persons who are Communists, Communist-dominated, or influenced by Communists." Whether his conviction derived from genuine belief or ambition or, more likely, some mix of the two, it certainly enabled him to present his desire to destroy the CSU as principled rather than craven. He was the studios' perfect proxy.

Opportunity quickly presented itself. In the aftermath of the 1945 CSU strike, the American Federation of Labor (AFL) executive council had appointed a three-man committee to define jurisdictional lines in Hollywood in an effort to eliminate this perpetual source of conflict among the myriad craft unions; and the three men (from postal worker, barber, and trainmen unions, respectively) were given thirty days to master the arcana of labor in Hollywood that tended to confound those who had been immersed in it for decades. When they produced their directive, it was, unsurprisingly, ambiguous. One section in particular—which addressed the issue of construction work on sets—provided an opening for the IA. Despite the fact that this work had historically been done by the CSU carpenters, the IA's Walsh interpreted the opaque language of the directive to mean that these jobs had now been given to his union. The CSU carpenters protested, and in August 1946, the committee issued a clarification—making it clear that they intended the construction to continue to be done by the carpenters, as it had been in the past. The IA and the producers, however, ignored the clarification; the producers continued to assign construction work to the IA.

One day in late September, the producers put a match to the smoldering conflict. CSU workers were taken off their customary jobs and ordered to work on the hot sets where IA men were performing the contested work (sets from which the CSU had resigned in protest). The CSU men refused. Picket lines went up, and other CSU workers refused to cross them. Technically, it was a lockout, not a strike—but the effect was the same: nearly ten thousand people out of work. Production, however, continued virtually uninterrupted; the IA moved in to cover all the CSU jobs, and strikebreakers were transported through the picket lines in buses driven by the Teamsters, whose muscle in such situations was indispensable.

The strike dragged on for months. Picket lines were forcibly broken; hundreds of the strikers were arrested, jailed, and tried in mass trials. Repeated proposals for arbitration met a uniform response: Sorrell and the CSU would accept the suggestion and agree to abide by an arbitrator's decision; the IA would ignore it; and the producers would express their regret at being unable to interfere in a dispute that was, they said, between unions. In early 1947, Father George Dunne, a Jesuit professor of political science at Loyola University in Los Angeles, began trying to find a resolution to the conflict. Dunne had been requested months before to write an article about Hollywood's labor troubles for *The Commonweal,* a publication of the Catholic Church. Thus, in August, shortly before the lockout occurred, he had interviewed both Sorrell and Brewer. As Dunne would later testify in congressional hearings, Sorrell had been quite sanguine at that time. He had told Dunne that in light of the just-issued clarification by the AFL committee, he thought the last major problem had been cleared up; the carpenters would be restored to the jobs they had been performing before. He also said that he thought the CSU and the IA could coexist peacefully in Hollywood. Brewer, however, fervently disagreed, Dunne would recall. Brewer had expounded at length on the allegedly Communist origins of the CSU, and "made it clear that the IATSE was engaged in a war, and he said a war to the finish, with the Conference of Studio Unions. . . . He said, 'The Conference of Studio Unions was born in destruction and it will die in destruction.' "

Dunne followed the gripping events that unfolded that fall, as Brewer's war-mongering words became prophecy; and in January 1947, when Dunne was invited to address a meeting of CSU members, in their fifth month out of work, he told them that he believed theirs was a fight for justice. He expressed the same view in a radio interview a few days later. He said, moreover, that he believed the Screen Actors Guild (SAG) held the key to the conflict's resolution—because the IA could fill in for the CSU jobs, but no one could replace the actors and actresses. If *they* refused to cross the picket lines, the strike would be settled in twenty-four hours. Dunne added, too, that he considered such action the performers' "moral obligation," inasmuch as "their careers, highly successful careers, and financially remunerative careers, would not have been possible without . . . these people [striking workers], and if these people had justice on their side they [SAG] ought to refuse to cross the picket line." Dunne's remarks had considerable impact. He was told by the manager of the radio program that the producers and the IATSE had reacted with "bitter anger," and had brought such pressure to bear on the owner of the radio station that this program was canceled for the time being. As for the Screen Actors Guild, it was an executive vice president, Ronald Reagan, who rose to Dunne's challenge.

Reagan had been one of Wasserman's first clients, and Wasserman continued to play an important role in Reagan's life. In 1941, Wasserman had sought to extend Reagan's deferment from active military duty by writing a letter for Jack Warner to sign. Shortly before Reagan was drafted, Wasserman had obtained a new seven-year contract for him with Warner Bros.—one that tripled the salary Reagan had been earning under his original contract. Just after Wasserman had concluded this deal, the movie *Kings Row* (in which Reagan uttered his famous line, "Where's the rest of me?") opened. Reagan received such praise for his performance that Wasserman succeeded in renegotiating Reagan's just-signed contract with Jack Warner. This time, it had one peculiarity; it covered forty-three weeks, not the standard forty. As Reagan later told the story, "When all the commas were in place, J.L. [Warner] said to Lew, 'Now will you tell me why I've given him the only forty-three-week deal in the whole industry?'

"Lew grinned like a kid with a hand in the cookie jar. . . . 'I've never written a $1 million deal before—so three extra weeks for seven years makes this my first $1 million sale.'"

Their relationship, however, went beyond the usual symbiosis of agent and client. From the time Wasserman had arrived in Los Angeles in 1939, Reagan and he had socialized together, often joined by Sidney Korshak. And Wasserman had also guided Reagan through the political thickets of Hollywood. Upon his return from military service in late 1945, Reagan—along with Helen Gahagan Douglas, who would be a Democratic senatorial candidate in 1950 and who was the wife of actor Melvyn Douglas—had agreed to appear at one of Hollywood's first anti-nuclear rallies. Jack Warner, whose politics were hard right, sent a telegram objecting to Reagan's participation. Wasserman quickly took command; he told Reagan not to go to the rally, and he assured Warner that Reagan would not attend. Reagan, no doubt mindful of his career, followed Wasserman's instructions. And now, some months later, in this strike situation—volatile, high-stakes, with Hollywood's spotlight fixed upon it—Reagan no doubt received Wasserman's blessing before taking center stage.

The night after Dunne's radio interview, Reagan arrived at Loyola to see him, Dunne would recall many years later. Reagan was accompanied by his wife, actress Jane Wyman (also a Wasserman client), the actor George Murphy, and Jack Dales, executive director of SAG; but it was Reagan who was the spokesman. The group sat and talked in the parlor of the Loyola residence until the early hours of the morning. Reagan's message was twofold. First, he told Dunne he had recently traveled to Indianapolis to meet with the AFL committee that had issued the directive, and he insisted that the committeemen had told him that it "was definitely their intention that this work should go to the IATSE union." (That statement, Dunne added, would be directly contradicted by those three committeemen in the subsequent congressional hearings.) Second, he sought to persuade Dunne "that Herb Sorrell and the CSU and all these people were Communists, and this was a Communist-led and -inspired strike, and that I was simply being a dupe for the Communists.

"He was very aggressive, of course . . . and very articulate," Dunne continued. "I remember very distinctly that when it wound up I had the very definite impression, this is a dangerous man. . . . Murphy was totally harmless . . . but Reagan, I had a definite view, this is a dangerous man, because he is so articulate, and he's sharp. But he can also be very ignorant, as he clearly was, in my judgment, interpreting everything in terms of the Communist threat." (Several years after his meeting with Reagan, Dunne would write a lengthy article about the strike in which he said that Reagan's "Rover Boy activities helped mightily to confuse the issues." What he meant, Dunne later explained, was Reagan's "running back to Indianapolis to see [the committeemen] and then coming back and saying that he had the answer to all the questions in the strike. . . . I think I called it 'Rover Boy' because it seemed to me . . . the night I met with him here, that he didn't know what he was talking about. He had his facts all wrong both as to the alleged Communism of Herb Sorrell and the CSU union and as to the rectitude of the jurisdictional issue. He was all wrong.")

On March 9, 1947, Dunne addressed a union meeting at the Olympic Auditorium. Sorrell had been kidnapped several days before—stopped by men dressed as policemen, handcuffed, put in a car where he was badly beaten, and then left in the desert. (His kidnappers were never apprehended.) Sorrell had just been released from the hospital, and this gathering was a kind of welcome home. Dunne told the assembled crowd about his meeting with Reagan and the others from SAG, and he made concrete proposals to settle the strike—calling not only for an agreement by both sides to abide by the decision of an arbitrator, but for major concessions, in advance, from the CSU. A day or so later, the CSU accepted the proposals; the IATSE and the producers never responded to Dunne's telegrams. The Screen Writers Guild took out a full-page newspaper ad, stating that "Father Dunne's proposals and their acceptance by the CSU mean that the current dispute, which is daily disgracing our industry and bringing misery to thousands of rank and file workers, could be settled by negotiations begun here and now. . . . The producers' silence indicates to us that they are unwilling to make an honest try for labor peace in Hollywood. We are forced to this conclusion: A lock-out exists in our industry." Nearly two weeks after Dunne had appeared at the Olympic Auditorium, *The Tidings* (an organ of the archdiocese) published a report that had been prepared for Archbishop John Cantwell by two men, his film industry representative and a professor of labor relations. They concluded that the strike could be settled if all parties were determined to do so, but that the producers "have taken a most negative attitude by doing little to settle the dispute"; and they said, further, "the strike issues cannot be beclouded with cries of Communism and radicalism if a settlement is to be accomplished."

Five months later, in mid-August 1947, with the strike nearly a year old, hearings were conducted in Los Angeles by a subcommittee of the House Committee on Education and Labor, chaired by Representative Carroll Kearns. The greatest revelations came only near the close of this set of hearings, in the beginning of September, when Kearns learned of the existence of notes of meetings held between the producers, their agents, and Roy Brewer in the days leading up to the September 1946 lockout of CSU. How Kearns learned of these notes was a mystery at the time; but, in any event, he ordered them produced. As Dunne would later write, the production of these notes threw "a bombshell into the smug ranks of the producers and their battery of

lawyers. Those who were present the day [the] minutes were introduced will not have forgotten the signs of consternation and the flurry
of activity . . . [or] the squirming of Roy Brewer when recalled to the
stand and confronted with the record of the part he had played in for-
mulating producer strategy, a record which flatly contradicted his previous testimony." The minutes certainly seemed to bear out what both
Dunne and Sorrell had long believed, but been unable to prove: that the
CSU's ongoing troubles were rooted not in a bona fide jurisdictional
dispute but in a conspiracy between the producers and the IATSE to destroy the CSU. According to the notes, Brewer assured the producers
that he would supply IA men to take the jobs of CSU workers; that if
his men hesitated to cross the picket lines he would "use the full power
of the IATSE to force them to"; and that, in order to spark the crisis,
they should "put IA men on sets so carpenters and painters will quit."

Damning as the minutes seemed, they were only an incomplete
paper record. Confronted with them, Brewer said he didn't recall having made the statements, or that they meant something different from
what they seemed to mean, or that he didn't recall having been at a
meeting at all; and other participants in these meetings were similarly
aphasic. The hearings, therefore, continued their somewhat desultory
course, reconvening in February 1948. At that time, they offered another glimpse of the backdrop of this struggle, when the role of Joseph
Tuohy was examined. Until recently, Tuohy had been the head of
Teamsters Local 399, the powerful studio transportation drivers union;
he was from Chicago, where he was said to be well connected to the
Outfit, and he had been a longtime friend of Bioff's. Tuohy and Sorrell
had been at loggerheads for years. In 1940, when California Governor
Culbert Olson was presented with extradition papers to send Bioff
back to Chicago to face charges there, Tuohy had spent a week in
Sacramento, pleading on Bioff's behalf; Sorrell had also gone to see the
governor, arguing that he sign the papers; and Bioff had been sent.

Here in the strike, Tuohy's efforts to aid the producers and the
IA—and to subvert Sorrell's CSU—had been far more successful than
his attempt to aid Bioff. The Teamsters' transporting busloads of

Herbert K. Sorrell, head of the Conference of Studio Unions. *Screen Actors Guild Archives*

strikebreakers through the picket lines had been absolutely vital to the studios' ability to continue to run smoothly. It now emerged, however, that the members of Local 399 had voted overwhelmingly to observe the picket lines—but had nonetheless been ordered by Tuohy, backed by his superiors, including Teamsters head Dave Beck, to cross them. It was, really, not so surprising that the Teamsters officials would have done this, considering the coziness of their relationship with the producers and with the IA. But the producers, in any event, had not depended merely on goodwill. For in March 1946, months before the strike began, Joe Schenck of Twentieth Century-Fox (who had served time in prison for his role in the Bioff scheme) had offered Tuohy a job at the studio—one that, however, would not begin until the following January, after the strike was well underway. Tuohy, who had been making a salary of $175 a week in his Teamsters job, would make between $400 and $500 a week over the course of his seven-year contract with Twentieth Century. It was, of course, just another version of the kind of payoff presumably made to Petrillo, certainly to Bioff and Browne— and routinely being made to business agents of many unions across the country by the mid-forties. Even many who did not themselves take the payoffs—for example, the continuing board members of the IA who had presided along with Bioff and Browne but probably did not share in their profits—learned to avert their eyes so as not to make trouble.

Herb Sorrell, however, specialized in making trouble. He was almost religious in his trade unionism, and its corruption enraged him. (During the hearings, he told one congressman who was cross-examining him, "I think you should pass legislation that labor leaders who accept bribes or gratuities from the employer should be shot.") Since those whom he attacked (starting with Bioff, continuing with Walsh and Brewer) had long sought to discredit him by calling him a Communist, that issue became a leitmotif of these hearings—and, also, a small companion piece to what was about to transpire before the House Un-American Activities Committee (HUAC), which would have such a terrible effect in Hollywood in the coming years.

Dunne, predictably, was Sorrell's defender. As he testified, "I have come to know Mr. Sorrell quite intimately. I am completely convinced in my mind Mr. Sorrell is not a Communist. . . . I know there are Communists, undoubtedly, in the CSU, as there are in the IATSE and almost every other group in the country. It is not a Communist group and not Communist led." When he completed his direct testimony, Dunne was asked numerous questions prepared by IA attorney Michael Luddy. Luddy had been a lawyer for IATSE throughout the Bioff-Browne regime; he had represented Bioff at trial and would, in all likelihood, have consulted with Korshak, Bioff's other counsel, during that period. And in the last few months, he had phoned Loyola to complain about Dunne's statements, and most recently had attempted to exert pressure to prevent Dunne's testifying at these hearings. Now, a number of Luddy's questions were designed to expose what listeners might construe as Dunne's Communist leanings. For example, the priest was asked about having spoken to a meeting of the strikers from the same platform as Vicente Toledano, the allegedly Communist leader of Mexican trade unions. Dunne said, "I learned Mr. Toledano was to speak at the meeting, so the question arose in my mind, 'Should I appear at the meeting or should I stay away simply because he was there?' I saw no reason then and I see no reason now for staying away. As a matter of principle, I am not afraid of Communists. I am not a Communist. I am not a Communist fellow-traveler. I sympathize with them . . . I sympathize with anybody that is intellectually confused. I subscribe to the doctrine that we cannot hate anybody . . . I maintain personal relations of the friendliest kind with Communists, or anybody else. That is part of my philosophy." Another question from Luddy was whether Dunne had received money other than expenses for the trips he made in an effort to settle the strike. "I have received not a red penny from anyone," Dunne responded, with some heat. "I should say this has cost me considerable, not in terms of money, but in terms of peace of mind and sleepless nights, and my reputation being seriously damaged in a smear campaign. I have gotten nothing out of it except the satisfaction of a clear conscience and awareness I was trying to do something for people that were deprived of their jobs for months."

Pat Casey, who had only recently retired from his long-held post as the chairman of the labor committee of the Motion Picture Producers Association, a trade association made up of the major Hollywood studios, and who had employed Johnny Roselli for a time during the Bioff regime, was a less likely defender of Sorrell. But he, too, testified that he did not believe Sorrell to be a Communist. He had dealt with Sorrell for many years, he continued, and "I have considered him honest in the first place, which covers a multitude of sins. In the second place, I will take his word for anything he says in a deal. He has never broken it with me." When Casey was asked, at another point, whether he believed there was anything in this jurisdictional dispute that had been Communist-inspired, he responded, "I don't think so. My God, I have heard Communist, Communist, Communist. It gets down to where if you do not agree with somebody, you are a Communist."

On the subject of his putative Communism, however, Sorrell was probably his own best witness. He plainly saw this occasion as his opportunity to right the record, and his words came in a torrent, filling hundreds of pages of transcripts. As he said, "My name has been dragged in mud throughout these United States as a Communist, as a subversive element, and people who have known me all my life think that something is wrong and they do not understand it. People who have fought me have had access to the press. . . . They have a large staff of publicists. They get their word out much better than I do." The self-portrait he now drew, however, was warts and all. He testified about arrests for participating in strikes, or fights, that the committee would probably not otherwise have known about. He described how in his early days working in the studios he had been prejudiced against foreigners who could not speak the language well, and against Jews, but then he had gotten to know these people and visited their homes and he realized that they were no different than he was, working hard to own a home and be able to put children through college, and he vowed he would do anything he could to benefit them. He even confessed that when he was really young he had attended a Ku Klux Klan meeting, where he had found the drills and regimentation impressive, and he had considered joining; but when he returned with a Catholic friend and learned Catholics were ineligible, he had rejected the idea. "I explain these things to you," Sorrell declared, "because I want you to know that I am not holding back anything. If I joined the Communist Party, I could just as well tell you . . . [but] I tell you now, so that you will not be in any suspense, that I am not now nor ever have been a member of the Communist Party. I say that under oath." Sorrell traced the history of the allegations that he was a Communist, beginning with Bioff and his supporters. "The minute Bioff stepped in, the cry of Communism came in. It has been that way, and continues to be." In the present regime, he continued, "Exactly the same line is followed by Walsh and Brewer. They come in with the charge of Communism to protect themselves."

Anti-Communist as he declared himself to be, however, he was opposed to the growing move to deprive Communists of their rights. "I have no use for them . . . but I think they are a minority group, and if we allow ourselves to become so embittered against our enemies, who are minorities, pretty soon it moves from one thing to another. . . . It follows just like night follows the day, that when you eliminate any small minority it soon becomes a larger minority, and you and I know that right today when the move is on to eliminate Communists, the move is on to eliminate Jews. . . . The next thing is to eliminate labor unions. The next thing is to eliminate Catholics. . . . Look, that's Hitler's plan. You know what he did. And it always follows that way."

In the end, the congressional investigation produced three volumes of testimony but did nothing to alter the ineluctable tide of events. The CSU was crushed, Sorrell faded into obscurity, and many of the roughly ten thousand workers he had represented did not recover from the financial losses they sustained. In an interview for an oral history in 1981, Dunne spoke at length about this epoch, and also divulged something that he had kept secret until then. During the hearings, Pat Casey had asked to meet with him privately. When they met at the Wilshire

Country Club, Dunne recalled, Casey had led him to the veranda and chosen the table farthest away from the others. After eliciting Dunne's promise that he would not reveal what he was about to hear, Casey told Dunne that what the minutes had seemed to substantiate was indeed true: "that the strike had been deliberately promoted, manipulated, by the producers, together with the IATSE leadership, in order to force the CSU out, and then keep them out, of the studios. He said this was a definite conspiracy on the part of the producers and the IATSE union, and he gave me facts in support of that, their secret meetings, and so on." In the lengthy piece on the labor wars that Dunne had written in 1950, he had not divulged what Casey had told him; but now that Casey had been dead for decades, Dunne said he felt he could reveal it. He also said he was certain that it was Casey who had made Kearns aware of the existence of the incriminating minutes. Casey's breaking rank, though, was all covert; on the witness stand, he had given no hint that he had any knowledge of conspiracy. Dunne speculated that Casey had been unwilling to testify truthfully about what he knew because he might have been afraid of jeopardizing his pension—or even his life, inasmuch as "this was a violent [situation]—when dealing with the Hollywood strike, you were dealing with Chicago gangsters." It was their hired gunmen, Dunne asserted, who had kidnapped Sorrell.

Not long after Dunne had testified at the hearings, he was transferred out of the Los Angeles diocese, and sent to Phoenix, Arizona. He was certain at the time that his expulsion was "the result of direct intervention by the Hollywood producers and their friends in the archbishop's office." The church, he said, likes to have good relations with those in the community who are wealthy and powerful. ("After all, when Archbishop Cantwell died, not long after I was expelled from the diocese, one of the honorary pallbearers at his funeral was Louis B. Mayer.") And about two years after his expulsion, he was playing golf with another Jesuit in Phoenix, when he spotted Clark Gable with Eddie Mannix—Wasserman's close cohort from MGM—who had been in the thick of the labor war. Mannix asked Dunne what he was doing in Phoenix, and Dunne replied, "I'm here thanks to you." Dunne recalled that Mannix laughed, saying, "Well, you were getting under our feet over there in Hollywood, we had to do something to get you out of there."

The key players on the other side went on to enjoy close relationships with Hollywood's powerful, and to prosper—Reagan, most of all. Although much attention would be paid by Reagan chroniclers to his appearance as a friendly witness before the House Un-American Activities Committee in the fall of 1947, it was this strike that was really his political debut. It gave him the chance to insert himself aggressively into the center of the action. It marked his rightward shift (a threat from a striker to throw acid in his face was a defining moment in his political change, Reagan has said). And it presented him with the opportunity to address a crowd of several thousand, at a Screen Actors Guild mass meeting in October 1946 in Hollywood Legion Stadium—a performance that probably laid the groundwork for his election as president of SAG the following year. It was not an altogether *popular* speech—Reagan argued that SAG had never involved itself in craft union disputes before, and should not now—and there was so much hissing and yelling that Reagan seemed glad a bunch of Teamsters were there at the end to get him to his car. But SAG members voted (many by mail because of fear of physical reprisal) overwhelmingly in favor of continued neutrality. And it established Reagan as a strong persona, with a talent for presentation.

And that talent was one he would be able to display with some frequency as SAG's president. Robert Gilbert, a labor lawyer who began practicing in Los Angeles in the late forties, recalled an experience he had had with Reagan during the 1949 consultations between SAG and AFTRA (the American Federation of Television and Radio Artists) regarding who would represent performers in the new medium of television. Reagan, as head of the SAG delegation, had come to New York for a critical meeting, and Gilbert phoned him to schedule a briefing. "Brief me in the cab," Reagan said. Gilbert protested that the cab ride would not allow nearly enough time and they should meet before that;

but Reagan was adamant. "He said, 'I've got to meet this lady and her daughter to give her my autograph.'

"I said, 'This is a very important meeting!'

"He said, 'Gilbert, you're not an actor. When they stop asking for your autograph, that's when you're in trouble.'

"So I briefed him in the cab," Gilbert continued. "He made a two-hour speech based on a fifteen-minute briefing—and it was fabulous. This guy could absorb what he was told and regurgitate it. He was *very* glib and articulate—even if he didn't understand it."

Over the course of the years, as Reagan made his remarkable climb, Dunne had ample opportunity to observe him in new roles; but his view of Reagan remained unchanged. "I have never had much use for him ever since my dealings with him in the Hollywood strike," Dunne commented, "because he played a key role in cooperation with what, in my judgment, were the thoroughly immoral Hollywood producers in league with the thoroughly immoral Chicago gangster Outfit. . . . At least," he amended slightly, "the union had been controlled by those gangsters and, in my judgment, it was still. And it was operating in conspiratorial cooperation with the Hollywood producers to destroy what was the only honest and democratic trade union movement in Hollywood. Reagan played a key role in that destruction.

"It's been difficult for me to believe that he wasn't aware of what he was doing and with whom he was cooperating," Dunne went on. "And I also have been convinced that he was rewarded for it. I don't pretend to charge that he had a prior arrangement with the producers, that the producers agreed, 'We will do this for you if you do this for us.' No, I don't charge that . . . [but] he was at the end or near the end of his acting career, such as it was, and it's from this period on, after having done this very effective job in the interests of the producers, that his whole success stems. . . . The producers don't forget their friends, any more than the crime syndicate people forget their enemies." Dunne alluded to the example of Willie Bioff, who—after having testified for the government in the Hollywood racketeering trial—lived in Phoenix under an assumed name for years, until the morning of November 4, 1955, when he turned on the ignition of his pickup truck and it exploded. "They didn't forget Willie Bioff," Dunne concluded, "and the producers didn't forget Ronald Reagan."

The IA's Roy Brewer and Richard Walsh, and the Teamsters' Joe Tuohy and Ralph Clare thrived, too. They all sang from the same hymnbook—in the tradition established by Willie Bioff in his heyday—blaming the Communists when any criticism was leveled at them or their allies. Tuohy was no longer even nominally a union man, having been employed by the producers; his place at the head of Teamsters Local 399 had been taken by his assistant, Ralph Clare, who had accompanied him to the secret meetings with the producers in the days just before the lockout. Clare had served on the board of the Hollywood Canteen with Jules Stein, and was a good friend of Wasserman's. In 1947, Clare became the chairman of an ultraconservative group called the Motion Picture Alliance for the Preservation of American Ideals (Roy Brewer and Joe Tuohy were members of its executive board). The alliance had been created, according to its statement of purpose, because, "in our special field of motion pictures, we resent the growing impression that this industry is made up of, and dominated by, communists, radicals, and crackpots." Clare's affiliation with the organization allowed him, a Teamster, to wear two hats. For example, he wrote a letter to *The Tidings,* which was published, objecting to the March 1947 report to the archbishop that had blamed the producers for the strike's continuing. Clare argued that the authors of the report had reached erroneous conclusions because they had not gathered sufficient evidence from all sides. "There are many unions which have close contact with the motion picture studios, although they are not primarily engaged in motion picture work, and whose leaders have intimate knowledge of the personalities involved, of their political adherence, and of the issues. Such a union is the Teamsters," Clare wrote, unabashedly. "Yet, this informed and unaffected source of information has not been tapped for your report." He signed his letter, "Ralph Clare, Chairman of the Motion Picture Alliance for the Preservation of American Ideals."

Victorious allies in the struggle against the CSU—Roy Brewer (left), Ronald Reagan, and Richard Walsh (right)—with Kenneth Thomson, co-founder of the Screen Actors Guild (to Reagan's right), at the Truman White House in 1949. *Screen Actors Guild Archives*

Clare was a good soldier, but Brewer evidently saw himself as a general. And he *was* one during the dark years of blacklisting that now began to unfold in Hollywood—when MCA, like other agencies, did nothing to fight the blacklist. Robert Gilbert, the labor lawyer, knew Brewer well. "The IA needed somebody squeaky-clean to come out to the Hollywood office, because the CSU was attacking the IA as corrupt—so they brought out Roy Brewer, who had never been in Hollywood in his life," Gilbert recalled. "They threw him into this very complicated strike situation—which some said was a dress rehearsal for revolution. That led to a close friendship between Brewer and Clare, Brewer and Reagan. When Reagan got that acid threat, he turned to Brewer for protection and support. Reagan thought Brewer was the be-all and know-all in labor. (Indeed, Brewer later claimed credit for Reagan's moving right, declaring, "I was the man who persuaded Reagan he was on the wrong side.")

"Brewer was the keeper of the blacklist," Gilbert added. "Here's this little guy from Nebraska. Studio heads would call him up and say, 'I want to hire this guy—is he okay?'

"He was *powerful!*" Gilbert declared. "Truth is stranger than fiction."

And on the labor front, harmony ruled. An article in *Fortune* in November 1949 stated that "relations between Hollywood labor and major producers are bathed now in a calm so colossal that the eventful signing in August of a five-year basic agreement between the major film producers and the unions that control most of the technical labor in film production created only a slight ripple of new interest." For decades to come, neither the IA nor the Teamsters (which would negotiate together, essentially as a unit, with the producers) would call a major strike against the studios. The Screen Actors Guild would, but rarely. And the men who had been shoulder to shoulder in the IA-CSU war—Reagan, Brewer, Clare, Walsh—would eventually find in representing their unions that there was one man among the producers so dominant that he could speak for all the rest; and, powerful as he was, he made them feel that he was not their adversary but their friend. As Brewer said, "Lew was always ready to meet with me, and listen. He worked with me. And he understood me better than most people."

———

It was at this moment, with Hollywood's labor situation pacified, that Wasserman was preparing to steer MCA into its next great business. Once again—just as when Stein had started the Music Corporation of America—it was a dispirited time in entertainment. Although the labor peace was certainly a boon to the studio bosses, they had been badly shaken by what was known as the Paramount Decree: in May 1948, the U.S. Supreme Court had ruled that the major studios had to sell their cinema chains, because they had conspired to fix admission prices and had used block booking to force small exhibitors, especially, to take their bad movies along with the good. The roots of this decision extended back to a case brought in 1938 by Thurman Arnold, head of the Justice Department's antitrust division. Arnold, whom Franklin Delano Roosevelt had chosen to launch his attack against the cartels, had sought to dismantle the vertical integration of production, distribution, and exhibition that had enabled the studios to wield power over the international movie industry since the early twenties. The studio bosses had fought this case, and its successor, for the better part of the decade; but in the end, most of what Arnold had envisioned was done (though the studios were, importantly, allowed to keep control over distribution), and the structure was broken apart. It was a radical break. As David Puttnam pointed out in *Movies and Money,* in 1948 investment in cinemas accounted for 93 percent of all investment in the American movie industry, and production only 5 percent; therefore, "the studios were more akin to real estate companies than to creators of entertainment; and the cinemas served as collateral, which underwrote their activities in production and distribution." Now, with the forced sale of their cinemas, the studio system gradually began to come apart; studios could no longer afford the vast payrolls required to maintain their long-established stables of talent employed in multiyear contracts, and many of the stars and directors—with the encouragement of MCA—left the studios to form independent production companies. For men like Louis B. Mayer and Adolph Zukor and Jack Warner, their long-accustomed hegemony was fading into memory.

The Paramount Decree had another effect, too, on the beleaguered studios. In the mid-forties, when television was still embryonic, Warner Bros., Twentieth Century-Fox, and Paramount had each attempted to start building TV networks of their own; but the Federal Communications Commission had blocked their efforts, awaiting the outcome of the antitrust action. Now, with that decree, the studios' desire to create networks of their own—a version of cinemas, through which they could control the exhibition of this new medium—was stymied. They could have made filmed product for TV, but that was considered heresy; if they could not control it, then TV was the enemy—and why feed your enemy? Movie attendance fell off dramatically (in 1951, movie admissions were as low as twenty years earlier) and TV was commonly viewed as the culprit. Because the studio bosses were already weakened, reeling from the Paramount Decree and the unraveling of their empires, they may have ascribed to television an even greater destructive force than it actually possessed. But whatever the cause, the industry was filled with doomsayers. David O. Selznick, the producer of *Gone With the Wind,* made a pronouncement many thought oracular at the time: "Hollywood's like Egypt, full of crumbling pyramids. It'll never come back. It'll just keep on crumbling until finally the wind blows the last studio prop across the sands."

Wasserman did not share this view. Indeed, what was anathema to the moguls was enthralling to him. He would later say he had believed in television's potential from the start; he liked to mention that he had owned a set in 1940, when he believed there was only one other in all of California. It was an unprepossessing contraption—a big set with a tiny screen that was a mirror when the lid of the machine was raised, and it had images like sticks. "I would take people up to my office to see this box, and all that was on it was a cartoon, *Aesop's Fables.* I'd say, don't you understand it's going to be in your home? And they'd say, let's go to the projection room." While that may have been the reaction of the entertainment cognoscenti, the public's response was different; in the early forties, Wasserman observed crowds of people standing in front of store windows to watch the TV cartoons, and seeing them so mesmerized, he became even more convinced that TV, like radio before it, was the future.

It was really not surprising that Wasserman would respond so differently to this new medium than Jack Warner and his compatriots. They were the old guard, defending their fortress, and it was Wasserman, more than any other individual, who had begun to scale the walls. It was he who had advised Olivia de Havilland, repeatedly suspended by Warners for refusing roles, that the Hollywood custom of adding suspension time to stars' contracts was probably illegal; de Havilland had sued to get out of her contract, and she'd won in a

1944 California Supreme Court decision that undercut the power of
the studio system. And it was Wasserman who dealt the studio system
an even more decisive blow when he constructed a revolutionary deal
for his client Jimmy Stewart in 1950. Wasserman recalled that he
made a two-picture deal for Stewart to star in *Harvey* and *Winchester 73*; Universal was either to pay Stewart a salary of $200,000 per
movie, or half of the movies' profits. ("Universal didn't *have* the
$400,000, that's why they paid the percentage," Wasserman said.) At
a time when the postwar tax rates were as high as 90 percent, the deal
was especially advantageous to Stewart, because his income would
be spread over the life of the films. Wasserman said that *Harvey* saw no
profits for many years, but *Winchester 73* brought him about $800,000
to $900,000. It was a bonanza for Stewart, making him Hollywood's
best-compensated star. By this time, Wasserman had driven stars' salaries
so high that, little by little, studios began to grudgingly accept this new
sliding scale. Thus, for the first time, the fact that stars were largely responsible for the success of a movie was reflected in the bottom line. As
more and more stars demanded such treatment, their power grew, and
the studios' diminished. And the agent who had shaped this new system
(and controlled so much of it through the talent) was, of course, the most
powerful of all.

This altered reality must have been difficult for the autocratic
Warner to assimilate—sometimes he seemed to react reflexively, as
though he still ruled. In April 1950, he barred Wasserman and all his
MCA agents—whom he referred to, contemptuously, as "the MCA
blackbirds" for their sartorial style—from the Warner lot. According
to Wasserman, the trouble had started when Warner had been slow to
respond to a deal Wasserman had proposed for Charlton Heston—and
Wasserman made the deal with producer Hal Wallis instead. *That*
added insult to injury. (The history between Warner and his former employee, Wallis, was acrimonious; the two had worked together on
Casablanca, and "at the Academy Awards, they both started down the
aisle but Wallis picked up the award! So Warner fired him," Wasserman recalled.) The day after Warner barred MCA, Wasserman

arranged a lunch across the street from the studio lot, with about thirty MCA clients who were working there that day. "Bette Davis showed up, and she said, 'F— Jack Warner! Let's have a drink!' No one left until four that afternoon. And when I got back to the office," concluded Wasserman, "there was a call from Warner . . . he was so upset I couldn't tell what he said, I had to call his secretary back and ask her." The ban was lifted. "It was an emotional thing," Wasserman continued. "I think he got worried, I might have luncheons once a week— and what would happen to his shooting schedule?" He paused, and added, "Studio heads were funny in those days—so isolated and eccentric."

Years later, this would be one of the stories Wasserman would tell and retell with discernible relish. However, while it did serve to demonstrate the power he had been able to lord over Warner, it was not as unprecedented as it might have sounded. In an oral history given to Columbia University by Dore Schary, the producer, screenwriter, and director, Schary recounted a strikingly similar confrontation that had occurred in the thirties between the famous agent Myron Selznick and L. B. Mayer. "Mayer felt that he didn't have to bother with agents— and he wouldn't allow Myron Selznick on the lot to talk to some of his stars. Myron had Jean Harlow, and William Powell, and Wallace Beery, and a whole big rack of them. Selznick said that he was now barring MGM. . . . His stars would go off the lot for lunches, and when they were asked where they were going, they'd say, 'I have to go see my agent. He won't come on the lot. You don't want him on and he won't come on the lot.' Finally, Mayer had to make an appeal to Myron Selznick. Selznick finally agreed that he would no longer bar MGM."

Schary, a Wasserman client, had been a writer at MGM in the thirties and early forties and returned as chief of production from 1948 to 1956. It was a very difficult time; MGM, for so long the richest studio, was suffering badly from the dramatic drop in movie attendance—and the studio system on which it had prospered was in extremis, its troubles exacerbated by Wasserman's efforts. Regarding the issue of stars' participation, Schary commented, "This was a trend MGM was very loath to accept. . . . There had always been a feeling that Metro was above and beyond what appeared to be casual trends, that they could keep the company going by stars under contract, and that they did not have to submit to this. . . . It became very apparent that we were beginning to lose people and that we could no longer attract certain people to the studio because we would not give them participation." While the producers were stubbornly resisting this change, the agents embraced it. "If the producers had been wise enough—and I think in their younger days they would have been wise enough—they would have taken the initiative. You must remember, when all these things happened, L. B. Mayer, the Warner brothers, Harry Cohn, the Paramount group, were all older men. . . . They wanted to be left alone, 'leave things as they are.' Twenty years before, those same men would have been sharp enough to anticipate all this, and to move quickly. They would have made arrangements with stars, given them a piece of the picture, done this and that, and prevented the agents from taking over the entire operation. . . . So you had Lew Wasserman, who is . . . the smartest individual man I have ever met in pictures. He's sharp, he's wise, he has great imagination, and he exudes confidence and enthusiasm. Mr. Schenck once said to me that he would never see Lew Wasserman after 12:00 noon, because he said after 12:00 he could no longer cope with his very bright mind."

Warner, too, evidently admired Wasserman, even if he infuriated him. And an exchange of telegrams in April 1951, a year after Warner attempted to bar Wasserman from the lot, shows Warner still trying to exert the kind of control over stars that he had been accustomed to—as well as, half seriously, offering to hire Wasserman.

"Dear Lew: Didn't know that Jules was back in business again. You told me he was retired. Why all of a sudden is he in charge of Russell Nype. We have a script he wants to do and we want to make a deal that is satisfactory to all concerned. Needless to contact Jules in Nassau or Palm Beach because we can't do business in these two ports. We are extremely interested in an exclusive long term motion picture contract with Nype. Would permit him to do state shows and personal appearances at stipulated periods. Television and radio subject our consent. Let me hear from you by return wire how soon we can make this deal and when are you returning. Warm personal regards. Jack Warner."

In his return telegram, Wasserman was his succinct self. First, he said, Jules was not in Nassau or West Palm Beach, but Cuba. Second, Jules handled Russell Nype himself. Third, he would be returning from Cuba on Saturday, at which time he, Wasserman, would immediately raise this issue with him. And fourth, if Jules were to fire Wasserman after reading Warner's telegram—because he so objected to the suggestion that he was even partly retired—"I will look to you for a job."

"Dear Lew: Thanks for your wire. Will certainly appreciate your getting into the Nype situation with Jules as soon as he returns. If the fourth condition of your wire ever happens you can certainly hook up with us. Expect to hear from you on your return. Best Wishes. Jack."

Five days later, Jules—still very much the boss—weighed in, also by telegram, and dashed Warner's hopes for control.

"Dear Jack. Have been discussing Nype matter. Lew and I meeting with Nype tomorrow. However to avoid any misunderstanding and to make certain you have all the facts months ago both Fox and Metro offered Nype exclusive motion picture contracts with radio theatre freedom. Nype refused these offers and has repeatedly stated he will not make motion picture agreement for more than one picture per year with complete radio theatre and television freedom. Will phone you tomorrow after meeting with Nype. Kindest personal regards—Jules."

Gratifying as it was to Wasserman that he had so shifted the balance of power from the producer to the agent, it was only a preliminary goal. He wanted to *be* the producer *as well as* the agent—and that was consistent with what Stein had done before him, when he went from booking bands to producing shows for radio. Stein had kept his eye on movie production since arriving in Hollywood, and in the early forties had even tried to talk Balaban into an MCA-Paramount merger. But it wasn't movie production that Wasserman wanted to enter, at least not yet—it was television. The talent business had already been well established in Hollywood by the time Wasserman had arrived; he'd had to buy up a lot of it, and, eventually, he was able to shape it to his liking. But the television industry was so new that he could almost create it from whole cloth.

Even territory claimed during its infancy now was tantalizingly available. For in the late forties, programming was controlled not by the TV networks but by the advertisers; it was they who produced the programs they wanted (mainly quiz shows, audience participation shows, and talent shows) and put them on the air in the time slots they wanted. But in 1950, the head of NBC's new television operation, Sylvester "Pat" Weaver, desperate to improve the quality of programming, decided that the network would have to control it; advertisers would no longer be allowed to buy an entire program, but only short segments of time for their commercials. Ad agency executives were apoplectic, but before long Weaver's ruling at NBC became the norm for the other networks as well. This development left a vacuum in the TV production business—and an ever-growing one. In 1946, there were only 11,100 TV sets in the U.S., but by 1952 there were 14 million. "The appetite of television is like the great maw of the sperm whale," wrote Milton MacKaye in the *Saturday Evening Post* in January 1952. "Thousands of hours of entertainment must be available to the television public, and any guess as to where it will come from is . . . as good as another."

It would come largely from MCA, if Wasserman had his way. But first he had to win an internal struggle. Stein had made him president just a few years before, but since Stein controlled all the company's stock, he was still the de facto ruler. And some of Wasserman's colleagues, bitter about this junior executive's elevation, were hoping to persuade Stein that his young president's obsession would be the company's undoing. The contest became defined as East versus West. It was not yet clear whether TV programming was going to be predominantly live or filmed—that is, produced mainly in New York or in Hollywood. In the early fifties, the majority of TV shows were live, and agents in MCA's New York office, led by Sonny Werblin, argued that live programming would prevail, and the center of TV production would remain in New York. Stein agreed with them. Wasserman, however, was adamant that filmed TV would prevail; it was more expensive, but it also offered a more consistent product—*and* it could be reshown. Its home would be Hollywood, he swore, and its master should be MCA. "They were selling live TV in New York, and they said, we should confine ourselves to this, it's a bird-in-the-hand story—why should we risk what we have today?" Wasserman recalled. "I said, but this is *tomorrow.*" After a number of MCA's classically savage encounters—where the combatants tried to inflict mortal wounds on each other, while Stein, imperial, self-enclosed, surveyed the spectacle—Stein supported his president.

Only one major hurdle remained. Screen Actors Guild regulations had long prohibited talent agencies from producing motion pictures, because of the inherent conflict of interest in simultaneously being agent and employer. Television, however, was so new that SAG had not yet adopted comparable restrictions in TV production. Thus, MCA had started producing television shows in 1949, through its newly formed subsidiary, Revue Productions; but Revue's output was fledgling compared with what Wasserman now had in mind. He knew, too, that the Guild was shortly to adopt rules for TV production. Its existing regulations did contain a mechanism by which an agent could apply for a waiver to produce a movie on a case-by-case basis, and that, presumably, could be applied to television as well; but it would be far too restrictive for him. What Wasserman wanted was untrammeled freedom: a blanket waiver that would allow his talent agency to engage in television production for many years to come. It would in fact guarantee him, in this new field, the kind of edge that MCA had had in its old band-booking and radio days. His control of talent would give him an unbeatable advantage in TV production, and his TV production would only strengthen his hand with talent; these intertwining activities would create a system so powerful that someone not similarly situated could not compete in any meaningful way. As a business model, its only weakness lay in its transparency; it was impossible not to see how overreaching it was. Petrillo, of course, had given Stein a similar kind of waiver years before (and he would give an exemption to Stein now, too, allowing MCA to use not live musicians but recorded music for their TV productions, to help keep expenses down at the start). Petrillo, however, ruled by fiat. The president of the Screen Actors Guild could issue no such diktat. But the president of the Screen Actors Guild *was* Ronald Reagan.

During the next few months, in early 1952, Wasserman navigated this process in ways so characteristically deft and traceless that even FBI and grand jury investigations undertaken later would be unable to fully reconstruct it. No matter how many times they were questioned over the years, Wasserman, Reagan, and longtime SAG executives John "Jack" Dales and Chester "Chet" Migden would always insist that the waiver was granted solely on the merits of the argument Wasserman had made—namely, that if MCA were allowed to go into television production in an unlimited way, it would create badly needed jobs; and, on a more parochial note, the increase in those jobs in filmed television would mean that SAG would stop losing its members to a rival union, AFTRA, which had jurisdiction over live TV.

Wasserman no doubt made this argument. It was also true, however, that SAG was in the late spring of 1952 engaged in negotiations with the Association of Television Producers over the issue of "reuse payments"—to be paid to performers when TV programs in which they had appeared were reshown. The idea was blasphemy to the producers—but not to Wasserman. According to Billy Hunt, a lawyer who would work closely with Wasserman on industry labor matters for many years, it was Wasserman who inaugurated the reuse payments, in an agreement that was secret at the time. The closely held arrangement was handled by Lawrence Beilenson—a lawyer who had been one of SAG's founding members and who, a couple of years before this transaction occurred, had left SAG and, after consultation with Jules Stein, started a law firm that would handle the bulk of MCA's legal work. Beilenson was also Reagan's personal lawyer. In 1954, Beilenson wrote a letter to Wasserman outlining the secret terms of the deal that had been struck two years earlier. The waiver, he wrote, "was executed under a specific set of circumstances where Revue [MCA's production arm] was willing to sign a contract giving the guild members reuse fees when no one else was willing to do so." (In 1962, Reagan—subpoenaed to appear before a federal grand jury investigating alleged antitrust violations by MCA—was questioned about the apparent quid pro quo. He testified that there was none. When Beilenson's letter was read to him, he said, ". . . It's quite conceivable then if he says it in this letter." Asked whether that refreshed his recollection, Reagan responded, "I don't recall it, no.")

It may well be that the sweetener made Reagan feel Wasserman's desired waiver was palatable; but the waiver still needed to be voted on by board members (who would be unaware of the backroom dealings). And Reagan could not afford to appear to be steamrolling his board. As lawyer Robert Gilbert commented about the process at hand, "SAG is not a rubber-stamp board. It's not like the IA. Reagan couldn't just make the deal one-on-one with Lew. They could have an understanding—but someone else would have to bring the board along."

That person, as it turned out, was actor and SAG vice president Walter Pidgeon—"whom everyone loved, he was the father image on that board," SAG's Chet Migden said. Pidgeon, an MCA client, had recently had his long-standing contract at MGM terminated, along with a host of other actors and actresses. What ensued at the fateful meeting in mid-July 1952 was a debate that raged for several hours, in which virtually all the actors were vehemently opposed to the idea of talent agents becoming involved in production. Migden continued, "Indeed, the waiver was going down, Reagan didn't say anything, he was in the chair, he was presiding over the debate that was going on. Until Walter . . . said, 'Look around, so they want to produce, what do we have to lose? Is anybody working?' He turned to the board members and said, 'Is anybody working? There's no work. Where is this town going to go? How are we going to survive? What am I supposed to do, pack

Ronald Reagan and Walter Pidgeon. *Gene Lester/Screen Actors Guild*

my bag and go to New York and work in live television for beans?' His impassioned speech turned the whole debate around, and suddenly everybody said, Somebody wants to create some work, what the hell is wrong with that?" And the board voted, unanimously, to grant the waiver.

The board's action that night would arguably influence the history of television—and it certainly changed the life of Ronald Reagan. Wasserman had been doing his best to find Reagan movie jobs, but Reagan's performances, unfortunately, spoke for themselves (in 1951, he was reduced to playing the chimpanzee-raising professor in *Bedtime for Bonzo*). Las Vegas was just becoming a new mecca for entertainers, and Wasserman tried Reagan there, too; but as MCA agent George Schlatter, who handled Reagan's engagement at the Frontier casino, said, "He was an omelet." Now that MCA was not only booking talent but also producing TV shows, however, it had far greater latitude in its search for a successful venue for Reagan; and, before long, it found one. Beginning in 1954, Reagan hosted and often starred in the *General Electric Theater* drama anthology programs, ultimately becoming a producer of the show as well. There was much talk around Hollywood about how Reagan had managed to land this fancy new job, which resurrected his career. The connection was hard to miss. Jack Dales, a longtime friend of Reagan's, whom Reagan in later years would appoint to state government positions after Dales retired from SAG, always tried to put the best face on it. In handling the waiver situation, Dales said, "I think Ronnie did more or less what he thought he should—and then he *was* rewarded for it, with the GE job."

Billy Hunt was less equivocal. "Lew always told me the waiver was Ronnie Reagan."

With the waiver won, Wasserman launched MCA into the TV production business. The television industry, still relatively nascent, was populated with many neophytes, but Wasserman was not one of them. He had a sophisticated understanding of the broadcasting business from his years of experience in radio. He and other MCA agents had well-established relationships with the major advertisers and their advertising agencies. And, most important, MCA by and large controlled the talent. Other agents had become producers (Leland Hayward, for one), but none had gone into production with the force of a talent agency behind them. It was a really remarkable coup. Now, in order to square the circle in signature MCA style, Wasserman needed only to achieve a liaison with one of the three major TV networks. Many years had passed since Stein had negotiated his exclusives, whereby a dance hall owner agreed to buy only from the Music Corporation of America and in return got first pick of the top bands in his area. This was a different era, to be sure, with different players, and a different business. But the basic tenets Wasserman was applying remained unchanged.

By the early fifties, CBS had established itself as the premier network—and it had done so with the help of MCA. William Paley had become fascinated with radio when he was buying advertising time for his father's cigar company in Philadelphia, and he had acquired the Columbia Phonograph Broadcasting System in 1928. During World War II, the most competitive arena for the networks was news, and CBS radio—with Edward R. Murrow, Eric Sevareid, William L. Shirer, and others—produced programs that drew the largest audiences in broadcasting. But CBS had been second to NBC in entertainment programming for roughly twenty years, and it was not until the so-called Paley Raids of 1948 and 1949 that CBS, overtaking NBC, was really launched. The blueprint for those raids was created in mid-1948, when Wasserman and Taft Schreiber suggested to Paley over lunch that he could have the *Amos 'n' Andy* show—one of NBC's most popular radio programs—if he were willing to pay for it in a tax-friendly structure they had dreamt up. MCA represented the creators of *Amos 'n' Andy*, Freeman Gosden and Charles Correll. Like so many of MCA's high-earning clients, they were affected by the staggering income tax rates—as high as 90 percent—introduced by the Revenue Act of 1941. But if they were to incorporate and sell their assets (their show's scripts and characters) to CBS for a given sum and a percentage of future profits, then their income from CBS would be taxed at a capital gains rate of only 25 percent. Paley jumped at the idea.

Immediately after the announcement of the *Amos 'n' Andy* deal, Wasserman returned to Paley and offered him Jack Benny—the linchpin of NBC's impregnable comedy schedule on Sunday night. The Benny deal, though, proved much more expensive and complicated. David Sarnoff, the longtime chairman of RCA, NBC's parent, had not fought the *Amos 'n' Andy* defection, but now he authorized a move to retain Benny by offering him nearly twice as much as CBS. Paley countered—and Sarnoff decided, ultimately, that the prize was simply not worth the cost. Hovering over the transaction was a legal question—*would* the Bureau of Internal Revenue consider the capital gains scheme an evasion?—which worried Sarnoff more than it did Paley. (Indeed, the bureau ruled against the transaction, but that ruling was subsequently overturned in the courts.) The more fundamental reason that Sarnoff did not fight harder to keep Benny, however, was his view of the business. NBC had been created primarily to help sell RCA radios and, later, television sets; and Sarnoff, a pioneer in communications technology, resisted the notion that a mere star could be the engine of his business. Wasserman was summoned to see Sarnoff (who, since his wartime service, chose to be referred to as "General") in his executive suite at the RCA Building in New York's Rockefeller Center. "He said, 'Nobody tunes in to Jack Benny—they tune in to NBC. We're not making this deal,' " Wasserman recalled.

But Paley, the inveterate showman, understood the importance of talent. And within months, in deals brokered mainly by Wasserman, most of NBC's top entertainers—Burns and Allen, Edgar Bergen, Red Skelton, and Groucho Marx—flocked to CBS. By the end of 1949, CBS Radio had twelve of the top fifteen radio programs, and for the first time CBS was number one in commercial broadcasting—a position it would hold long into the television era. It was by no means an unmitigated blessing. CBS had been home to many of the finest, if money-losing, programs in broadcasting, such as those created by Norman Corwin, the accomplished radio dramatist; but with these raids, Paley began to implement his decision to operate the network on more strictly commercial terms. If the game were only about profits and power, though, Paley emerged from this match the undisputed champion.

One might have expected the role Wasserman had played in Paley's triumph to forge a bond between them. Paley had been in the entertainment business nearly as long as Jules Stein, and he knew MCA well. Indeed, when the Justice Department in 1941 had brought pressure upon the radio networks to divest themselves of their talent management activities, arguing that they should not be both carriers and providers of talent, CBS had sold its Artists Bureau to MCA. If anything, Paley knew MCA too well. "Paley did not like the MCA guys," longtime CBS programming executive Michael Dann said. "He was as tough as Lew. He was a *killer,* as much as Lew. But he wore the gray suit with the perfect tie, and he had the home in Lyford Cay with the French chef, and he had married the most beautiful and elegant woman in the world, and he had his Matisses and Monets and Picassos, perfectly placed. It was quite a jump for a guy from Philadelphia, whose father was a cigar maker. And the MCA guys *embarrassed* him. They were too crude, too blatant."

"Paley had a great distrust for just about all agents and everything in Hollywood," said Frank Stanton—the man chosen by Paley in 1946 to be president of CBS, who then ran the network with Paley for more than a quarter century, earning a reputation for his acumen and integrity. Stanton added that he and Paley would on occasion have dinner with Stein and Wasserman, but "it was strictly for business reasons. There was no rapport." He recalled, though, that after one of these dinners, Paley had remarked to him how good Wasserman was at handling people—which was no small compliment from Paley, master of the art. "Lew could be very charming—that was part of his effectiveness," Stanton commented.

Beneath the charm, though, what Stanton perceived in Wasserman was mainly muscle. "Anything you wanted in the colony, he could get for you. He had all the connections, he knew where all the bodies were. And people had such fear of Lew. Because he played rough—blocking careers, pulling talent out of one picture into another. If a producer were reluctant about something, Lew would do something over here"—Stanton gestured, as though pulling at an invisible web strand—"to make the guy do what he wanted over there."

Hollywood might have come under Wasserman's dominion, but in many Easterners' eyes it was indeed a mere "colony," and a shady one at that. CBS, Paley's vaunted Tiffany network, would never allow Wasserman the kind of propinquity he had in mind. And NBC, in the early fifties, was scarcely more congenial. Its president was Pat Weaver—the most original, innovative executive in the broadcast business, and the one who had decided that networks had to wrest control of their programming from their advertisers. Weaver had been in broadcasting for roughly twenty years, in jobs ranging from radio scriptwriter, to advertising director for the American Tobacco Company, to a vice president at the Young & Rubicam advertising agency, where he produced numerous radio shows. He, too, knew MCA; he had done shows with many band leaders, including Isham Jones, and he had crossed paths with Wasserman early on—at the American Tobacco Company, he had worked on *Kay Kyser and His Kollege of Musical Knowledge*. And it was true that both men were ardent believers, early, in the new medium of television. But there the commonality ended.

Weaver had come up differently from Wasserman. His father was one of the founding members of the Jonathan Club, an elite social club in Los Angeles. A graduate of Dartmouth who majored in philosophy and made Phi Beta Kappa in his junior year, Weaver continued as president of NBC to have a lively curiosity about the arts, sciences, industry, the latest discoveries in astrophysics, the state of the Cold War, the cybernetics theories of Norbert Wiener, the technological forecasts of Arthur C. Clarke, the complete works of Albert Schweitzer—as well as the Nielsen ratings for a rival CBS program schedule. And Weaver was positively messianic about the potential of television for bettering mankind. "Television is a miracle," he wrote in an article in *Television*

Magazine. "The grand design of television . . . is to create an aristocracy of the people, the proletariat of privilege, the Athenian masses—to make the average man the uncommon man. . . . Television makes diversity the natural law, not conformity." In a profile in *The New Yorker* by Thomas Whiteside in 1954, Weaver referred to himself as a "communications optimist"; he routinely exhorted his employees that "NBC must do *good,*" and in one of the many hundreds of memos that he was continually firing off to staff, Weaver wrote, "Every writer, every director, every producer is having an influence upon upwards of ten million people when he goes on the air for NBC. It is therefore more than just his self-interest as a creative artist that is challenged in this day. It is his self-interest as a member of the human race. For he can do something personally that will increase . . . the individual's ability to meet and decide his own future."

One of the shows Weaver created—which he thought would "establish NBC as it ought to be"—was *Wide Wide World,* the first live attempt to capture the American experience on coast-to-coast television. As usual, Weaver wrote evangelical memos to his colleagues about this new concept, his ideas tumbling over each other, uncontainable; but they seemed to fall on fallow ground. The General had made his son, Robert Sarnoff, the executive vice president of NBC in 1953, at the same time he had made Weaver president; Weaver's forte was programming, Bobby Sarnoff's was thought to be business, and the two were meant to be a team. In a meeting at NBC described in the *New Yorker* profile, Weaver was listing the places to be visited on *Wide Wide World*—Dismal Swamp, the Sadler's Wells Ballet, Los Angeles's Greek Theatre for classical Greek drama.

"Suppose you went to the Greek Theatre in Los Angeles," Sarnoff interjected. "Would most people *want* to go to the Greek Theatre?"

"This show is not just about what the public wants to do but what you want them to do, Bobby," Weaver said. "You *take* the American people to see the Greek drama, you *take* them to see *King Lear* at Stratford, Ontario. It would be good for them to see Shakespeare, whether they liked it or not."

After a further exchange, Weaver said earnestly, "I think I know what I want but I'm not sure that you all do. I want a show that will give people a chance to go out of their homes to almost every part of our wide world that is America and participate in all of our activities—a show that people will say has enabled us to become more mature, more cultured, and more urbane, and that will be the conversation piece wherever people meet. . . . Nobody would watch *Wide Wide World* all the time unless he was paralyzed, but he would see it occasionally and it would do him good. Fellows, don't you see I'm trying to get something *civilized?*"

Weaver had lofty aspirations for television, but he also had the commercial track record to be taken seriously by those who viewed it from a strictly dollars-and-cents perspective. He fathered both the *Today* and *Tonight* shows, and *Matinee Theater,* as well as *Wide Wide World;* and probably his most publicized innovation was his ninety-minute "spectacular"—a cultural or entertainment special that pre-empted regular prime-time series shows, and was intended to keep television (and its viewers) in a state of creative flux. Even in NBC's mass appeal programs, Weaver insisted that some cultural ingredient be slipped in, so that the "average man" would, through his TV watching, become the "uncommon man."

In the aerie of corporate power, Weaver was an anomaly—cerebral, unorthodox, highly literate, obsessed with the desire to use these new technological tools for the public good. The press gravitated to him, and he became something of a star in his own right. That was to prove his downfall. For he was not meant to outshine Bobby Sarnoff, and he was certainly not meant to outshine the General. Weaver, moreover, had never been politic. He was notorious for having treated George Washington Hill, Sr., the irascible, hard-to-please head of American Tobacco, with a convivial directness that amazed his colleagues; Hill and he were bonded by mutual respect, however, and Weaver never suffered for his boldness. But with Bobby Sarnoff, it was different. Michael Dann, who was Weaver's assistant at NBC, recalled one meeting in which the junior Sarnoff—a man who was sensitive about having inherited his job—made some insubstantial remark. "And Weaver said, in a low stage voice, '*Down,* boy!' I could not believe it. So he rubbed the General the wrong way, because of the way he treated Bobby, among other things." The General chose not to fire Weaver outright, because he was self-conscious about NBC's history of executive turmoil. In 1955, he made Weaver chairman of NBC, and Bobby president—and, a year later, eased Weaver out.

That was the opening Wasserman needed. Leonard Goldenson, the chairman of ABC—which ranked a distant third among the three networks—had recently dismissed its president, Robert Kintner. Kintner, a former journalist, was a talented executive, well respected particularly for his leadership in broadcast news; but it was rumored in the industry that the reason for his firing was a drinking problem. He was one of those people whose awkward, even forbidding physiognomy—short, bulky, slightly hunched, his homely countenance partly obscured by big, thick-lensed glasses (he was sometimes called "Quasimodo" behind his back)—seemed to reflect some inner disproportion as well. It was, in any case, at this trying moment in Kintner's life that Sonny Werblin came to his rescue.

Werblin had lost out in his bid for the presidency of MCA, but in the New York office he was the leading man. He was a slightly picaresque character—a great raconteur, a devoted sportsman, a man's man in a time when that required no apology—and he held court at his table at the fabled "21," hosting the chairmen of Coca-Cola, American Tobacco, AT&T. Younger MCA agents were awed at his social versatility, and how it translated into business. ("We would get a call about a deal he had just struck with Charles Woodruff, the chairman of Coca-Cola, while he was sitting in Woodruff's box at the Kentucky Derby," his young associate Al Rush recalled.) The peripatetic Werblin was so close to the advertisers that often he would make a deal with them before going to a network. One network executive recalled, "Sonny would come to me and say, 'The Chesterfield people are very keen on this show, they *love* it!' MCA knew every advertiser better, they knew the talent better, than we did." Werblin had also cultivated a good relationship with General Sarnoff and, especially, Bobby. His old mentor, Billy Goodheart, had retired, but now Goodheart wanted to work again and Werblin got him installed as head of sales at NBC. More important, Werblin had helped to move Manie Sacks, the former MCA agent who had been at Columbia Records, to a dual post—head of RCA Records and vice president in charge of programming at NBC. And now—most important of all—he persuaded Bobby Sarnoff that Kintner would bring NBC the programming savvy that was needed; he could be brought in as a vice president, with the understanding that within the next year or so he would be named president. For Kintner, it meant that he had been thrown from ABC's top executive floor and, miraculously, landed on his feet. But for MCA, it meant even more. As Mike Dann summed up the situation, "The three most powerful people at NBC were Bobby [Sarnoff], Manie [Sacks], and Bob Kintner. Sonny was very close to all three, and he had a role in bringing two of the three to the company." He paused, and added, "As television grew, later you couldn't control it in that way."

Shortly after Kintner became president of NBC, Wasserman invited him to a party in Hollywood—a birthday party for him given by his wife, Edie, Wasserman told Kintner. When Kintner arrived, he found himself surrounded by a dazzling array of actors and actresses—an experience that had a very pleasing, tonic effect on Kintner, as he tended to be rather starstruck. And then Wasserman announced to his guests that this was in fact not his birthday party. "This happens to be a surprise party for my good and true friend, Robert Kintner, to celebrate his having taken over the throne at NBC."

The relationship between MCA and NBC—particularly, Werblin and Kintner—quickly became the subject of industry chatter. Most remarkable was its brazenness, which was epitomized in an NBC programming meeting called by Kintner and Bobby Sarnoff in the spring of 1957. After the programming executives were assembled, their projected season schedule on the magnetic board before them, Werblin strode into the room—which was in itself shocking, since a network's projected scheduling is considered highly proprietary. And then, instead of banishing him, Kintner declared, "Sonny, look at the schedule for next season; here are the empty slots; you fill them." Werblin proceeded to rearrange the magnetized show squares while the executives watched; when he was finished, he had placed in prime time fourteen series that were either produced or sold by MCA. And that became the season's schedule.

There was some question about the legality of what had occurred, inasmuch as networks were licensed by the Federal Communications Commission, and, as licensees, they were to exert full control over their programming, including its scheduling. But the real point was less technical. MCA was unmistakably in bed with NBC, occupying a position of such favor and dominance that no other seller of product could truly compete. In return, MCA generally treated NBC more favorably than other buyers. "Sonny brought Kintner all MCA's top stuff," MCA agent Al Rush said. As usual, the situation worked to MCA's advantage in multiple ways. It provided a major, dependable outlet for MCA's production. It gave MCA a ready buyer for its clients' shows as well. And it won MCA even more clients, since the common perception was that the way to get a show on NBC, or to get roles in Revue's constant flow of productions, was to be represented by MCA—much as the bands had flocked to Music Corporation in the thirties in order to get on the air in the *Magic Carpet* program. Once these clients signed on with MCA, moreover, they were tied to the agency, one way or another, for the long term. MCA had finally revised its early, unenforceable contract that stipulated it could not be terminated by clients until they had made $1 million; the new contracts were more sophisticated, but no less advantageous to MCA. Clients had to sign an "omnibus" contract, giving MCA the right to represent them in all facets of show business for many years.

The MCA-NBC relationship was unique; but by the late fifties, MCA could impose its will on other networks, too. Even, surprisingly, CBS. Unlike NBC, which produced very few of its own shows, CBS prided itself on its in-house production, and its executives routinely derided MCA, whose Revue staple was formulaic Westerns, as a "sausage factory." It was well known within CBS, moreover, that Paley had no interest in buying MCA-produced shows, and would never countenance the kind of surrender NBC had made. "We didn't want to deal with those guys, we wanted to control our own destiny," said Salvatore Ianucci, a lawyer in business affairs at CBS in the fifties and sixties. "Lew's method was intimidation. But we had the power, we didn't *need* their productions." What they did need, however, was MCA talent.

Not all radio stars had been able to make a successful transition to television, but Jack Benny certainly had—his was one of the highest-rated TV shows at CBS in the fifties. Wasserman, therefore, had enormous leverage when he went to CBS to renegotiate Benny's deals. And, according to both Dann and Ianucci, Wasserman not only demanded a specific time slot for the Benny show but, even more remarkably, *another* specific time slot, for another season-long show. "He'd say, 'Jack must have the next half hour'—it would be for some unnamed project!" Dann said. "And of course it wasn't Jack who had to have it, it was Lew. Power leads to power." Nor was Benny the only client for whom Wasserman could exact such a price. "It was no secret. We all knew who had the time commitment—Benny's commitment, [Red] Skelton's commitment. The president of the network would say, 'Go to MCA, they have the commitment for that time,' " Dann continued. But it was not something that either party would have acknowledged publicly then. "If you lose control of your scheduling, that is very questionable," Dann said. MCA's Al Rush, asked whether MCA demanded specific time slots for their clients and, also, additional slots for other season-long shows, responded without hesitation. "It was done all the time. But it had to be a handshake. It could never be in the contract."

In these TV deals, too, Wasserman adapted the concept of packaging that Stein had implemented in his band-booking days. In producing, or packaging, a show for radio, Stein would put together all the talent for a given sum, out of which he would then pay them—often pocketing three times as much as he would have had he charged a straight agent's commission of 10 percent. Wasserman now inaugurated his version of that, putting director, star, story, and supporting talent in a single deal, and demanding a 10 percent commission on the whole package. But eventually he carried this idea even further, and became, in a sense, a *virtual* packager. For MCA would demand its commission on the cost of the entire show—including all above-the-line (talent) costs, as well as all below-the-line (facilities, production) costs—even when the network was supplying much of the talent, and producing the show. They just demanded their 10 percent on the whole thing as if they were responsible for every element. As Rush said, grinning, "We took our commission on everything—above-the-line, below-the-line, and *sideways!* If the whole show cost $300,000, we got $30,000."

MCA could make up the rules because, as always, no one in the commercial world was strong enough to challenge them. By the 1959–60 season, MCA produced or co-produced more television series than any other company; and it got some cut from about 45 percent of all TV network evening shows. Among those it produced were *Wagon Train, General Electric Theater,* and *Bachelor Father.* It was the agent for many others made by independent producers, including *Alfred Hitchcock Presents, Tales of Wells Fargo,* and *Ford Startime.* The system Wasserman had devised produced a perpetual stream of money, flowing from multiple sources to MCA. MCA continued to be so secretive (its full client list had still never been seen by more than a few top MCA executives) that it would not say which television series it represented, or even how many series it handled. Indeed, in 1959, when the Federal Communications Commission began an inquiry into the reasons for the poor quality of American television programming and subpoenaed the lists of shows packaged by various producers, Taft Schreiber, called to testify, refused to turn over a full list of MCA's shows unless it was kept confidential—despite the fact that he was threatened with being held in contempt. MCA's competitors, including the William Morris Agency, turned over their lists.

In July 1960, *Fortune* magazine attempted to lift the veil—at least enough to offer a glimpse of MCA's TV economics. *Fortune* calculated that MCA was likely to earn $7 million from a thirty-nine-week, half-hour TV series that it produced at its Revue Studios. The early stages of this enterprise were straightforward enough. MCA would sell first-run rights in advance to a network for a fee of $40,000 a week. MCA TV would receive a commission of 10 percent, or $4,000. Revue would then take 20 percent of the remaining $36,000 ($7,200) as "over-head," and roughly $20,000 for other production costs such as studio rental and camera crew. The remaining $9,000 or so would be paid as salaries to performers. Therefore, MCA would get $31,000 out of the original $40,000; in a thirty-nine-week season, that would total approximately $1,200,000. Thus, the show would probably earn MCA before taxes (on an 18 percent return) roughly $220,000 the first year, although the series itself would merely make back its production costs (and the star, an MCA client, who owns half of the show, would make nothing but salary). But the key to profit was the show's longevity. If it were successful, it would likely run for three years. And then the true bonanza would come—one that Wasserman had imagined years before when he was fighting so hard, within MCA, for a stake in filmed TV. For in its reruns, the show would likely gross as much as it did in initial showings—and at almost no cost to the producers. Now the show would plainly be making a profit, and the star would begin to cash in. But before that happened, MCA would cut itself many more slices. MCA would take 40 percent off the top of any income from network reruns; 30 to 50 percent from other earnings in domestic syndication (non-network showings); 50 percent of any income from foreign syndication; and 50 percent of any income from merchandise tie-ins. Thus, MCA would take about 40 percent of the price per episode on reruns—leaving only the remaining 60 percent to be split with the star.

And for a successful hour show, *Fortune* estimated, MCA would earn much more. The first three years of *Wagon Train,* budgeted at $100,000 a week, would probably bring MCA about $17 million. It was easy to understand, then, why Wasserman had been so determined to enter this business. To earn $17 million as an agent, MCA would have to collect $170 million of client salaries—an astronomical sum, notwithstanding all Wasserman had done to drive up stars' earnings.

Even as MCA extended its reach across the TV industry, its relationship with NBC continued to be the keystone. And yet—vital as NBC was to MCA—there was no question about which was the dominant partner. This dynamic was nicely illustrated in the story of *Wagon Train*. Don Durgin, then an NBC executive, described the episode. Revue's *Wagon Train*, a one-hour Western, had become a great hit at NBC, garnering top ratings for four years. When its next contract was being negotiated, MCA wanted NBC to buy the new episodes as well as a package of the old as reruns. The network had a contractual right of first refusal (the right to bid on renewing the show before it could be sold elsewhere), and, according to Durgin, NBC fully intended to make the deal. And then, one day, Durgin and his colleagues heard that Wasserman had gone to Leonard Goldenson of ABC and sold him the whole package. "Wasserman just took it away!" Durgin said. "And when we screamed, he said, 'You didn't act.'

"We said, 'Wrong! Wrong!'

"So he said, 'Look, in our opinion, you didn't act. Anyway, it's gone. But now we're going to do a show, *The Virginian*, and it's going to be great, and you can have it.' "

Durgin, who would become president of NBC in the late sixties, had worked for Kintner at ABC and then had been recruited by him to NBC; Durgin would always defend his former boss when questions about NBC's relationship with MCA were raised. Now, he tried to explain how that relationship had developed. CBS was king of the half-hour comedies—a high-risk, high-reward business. These shows were hard to create, and there was little middle ground; they either became outright failures or hits. The failures were expensive, but the hits were gold mines. NBC had tried them repeatedly, without success. So NBC executives decided to concentrate on the long form, an hour or ninety-minute show, such as a Western or detective drama; these were more formulaic than the half-hour comedies, so far less risky. This was MCA's specialty. "MCA *was* derided as a sausage factory," Durgin said. "They were thought to be uncreative, boilerplate. But we couldn't get the great half-hour comedies, so we were dependent on the long form, and MCA was the biggest supplier of it. Then, because we were a big customer, they'd say, 'If you don't want that, we'll do this'—and they tended to lock us in an unholy embrace."

Dealing with Wasserman was unlike anything Durgin had experienced in his network career. "I had been used to dealing with honest guys. But Lew would misrepresent and let you draw a conclusion at your peril. Anything he had a legal duty to disclose, he'd disclose in full detail. That would make you feel he was honest, and maybe let your guard down. But then you'd discover later that the package had shifted—and if you complained, he'd say, 'Okay, forget it! We'll take it back!'" In retrospect, Durgin continued, it seemed that he and his colleagues were "little boys in kindergarten dealing with Darth Vader." Wasserman, he thought, was the smartest executive he had ever known. He had a way of negotiating that let you know he had assessed his advantage to the decimal point ("if he thought he had a 50.1 percent advantage he would be merciless, threatening, *nasty*—though not in a vulgar way"), and he was always willing to walk away. "He never had any briefcase, never any notes," Durgin recalled. "Dark suit, white shirt. A handkerchief in his breast pocket, another in his back pocket. He would pat his forehead occasionally, though he was never perspiring—it was just a habit. He was so *finished*. A very attractive man. I didn't like him because he was such a shark—but it was a shark you almost had to admire as he circled you."

Durgin was fascinated, too, by Billy Goodheart's reminiscences of the early days at Music Corporation of America. "He told me about how they made bookings for Coon-Sanders. They dressed up several guys as Coon and Sanders and sent them out across the country. They figured that, with the exception of some traveling salesman, who would be likely in those days to be in such distant places in such a short time? And Billy told me, also, about the time they were having big troubles with orchestras in theaters, some union dispute. Billy resolved it. In his next expense report, he wrote, $10,000 in cash to bribe some union official. The accountant said, Billy, *what is that?* What do you think you're doing, writing that down? Billy said, Okay, okay—he never wrote it again.

"Well, that was MCA," Durgin concluded. "It never changed."

Speculation about some lucre in the MCA-NBC relationship was endemic in the industry. "Let's be realistic," said Sal Ianucci of CBS. "Agents did whatever it took—girls, money. I know, because as an executive I was offered it." Alan Livingston joined NBC as vice president in charge of programming in 1955 and worked on the West Coast, where he was supposed to produce pilots in house. But, he said, "Kintner had no interest in my pilots. He would ask me to do them—it was my job—but he didn't want to buy them. It was all MCA." He continued, "There was a lot of speculation that Kintner got payoffs. But did they just flatter him? All I know is that they *controlled* NBC." Livingston added that executives at NBC in those days were not so highly paid; he estimated that Kintner might have been making $250,000 to $300,000. "There are different ways of paying off, too. A vacation? A car? A case of scotch every week?" Certainly, MCA was known for its extravagance in gift giving; it had come a long way since the days of paying off attendants in the washroom of the Muehlebach Hotel, or others with Christmas money. Harris Katleman, who was an MCA agent in the fifties working closely with Wasserman, said, "At Christmastime, so much money was spent, you could have run a small country. There were A, B, and C lists. The A list got cars, mainly Cadillacs."

However much comment it provoked, MCA's dispensing of favors was only a small part of the system Wasserman had engineered. "Lew was an entertainment mogul without peer," commented Mike Dann. "I don't think he was a great recognizer of talent, but he knew how to acquire it and implement it and negotiate for it. Part of the problem was that network executives (me included) were novices about dealing with talent. So it wasn't just that Lew was brilliant—but also that he was dealing with people who were not professional in the beginning. He came in with a blank canvas." Dann added, too, that the television industry was largely a white Anglo-Saxon Protestant preserve, populated by executives who had graduated from prep schools and Ivy League colleges—and they were no match for MCA. "The MCA guys did not play by the Marquis of Queensberry rules! They had started out in the nightclubs, and you know who owned them. The early days of MCA's existence left an imprint on the personality of the company—and it was very different from William Morris, for example. The MCA agents always wore the white shirts and the black suits, but underneath they were guys who were much too smart, too aggressive, too street-wise for most broadcasting executives.

"As a unit, they were the shrewdest people in the history of the entertainment world," Dann declared. "You wouldn't want to take a Greyhound bus trip with them, or model your children after them—but they could *deliver* for themselves."

If television represented the future for MCA, Las Vegas was the past, revivified—for MCA was at least as big a player in the booming entertainment scene of Las Vegas in the fifties as it had been in Chicago's in the thirties. It had been a natural progression, from booking performers in nightclubs and hotels to booking them in Las Vegas; the performers were, by and large, the same, and the owners of the entertainment spots were, in a generic way, too. Bugsy Siegel's Flamingo had opened in 1946; after that came Meyer Lansky's Thunderbird, and then, in 1950, Moe Dalitz's Desert Inn. Actually, the Desert Inn was *called* Wilbur Clark's Desert Inn; Clark had begun its construction, but when he ran out of money, Dalitz and his friends from the Cleveland syndicate came in. They were happy, though, to have Clark out front, since he had no police record. By the time it was finished, the Desert Inn cost $4.5 million—a Bermuda pink hotel with green trim and a circular drive leading to the entry, ringing a fountain that sprayed water sixty feet high. Wasserman had known Dalitz since he was a young man in Cleveland. For the Desert Inn's opening night on April 24, 1950, Wasserman booked the floor show—Edgar Bergen and Charlie McCarthy, supported by Vivian Blaine, Pat Patrick, and the Don Arden

Dancers. Dalitz had made sure that the crowd was full of high rollers; 150 "$10,000 men" had been invited—that is, men with credit lines of at least $10,000. Wasserman recalled that it was a tense moment for him; it was just hours before the opening that Jack Warner had announced he was barring MCA from the lot (in his temper over the Charlton Heston–Hal Wallis deal), and Wasserman felt he needed to stay in L.A. to handle that crisis. "I told my friends from Cleveland, 'I can't come, I have this problem,' " Wasserman said. "They said, 'Fine, you got a problem, you don't come, we don't put the show on.' They wanted me *there*. So I had to call Howard Hughes, and get a flight on his plane to get back that night."

Las Vegas in the fifties was paradise for the mob. Although most of the owners operated behind semilegitimate fronts who were the licensed "owners," that was about the only subterfuge required. (Even Meyer Lansky operated from the offices of the Thunderbird; agent Martin Baum, who worked exclusively for the Thunderbird for a time, recalled that "Lansky did not want to overpay. He checked every place an act I booked had been booked before. God forbid he found anyone had even once paid less!") The casinos were the economic lifeblood of the town, and in this insular world, mob members were accorded the respect they felt they deserved. Years later, a longtime Las Vegas resident would express a nostalgia for these days, saying, "It was a real Western town, where people took care of their own. Yes, there was skimming, and the government didn't get its full share. But if you worked in a casino and anyone in your family was sick, there was money to take care of that—it was all so personal, everyone knew everyone." And the skimming—the process by which cash is taken after it leaves the tables and slot machines and before it is officially counted—was carried on with ease, as couriers fanned out with suitcases of money to Chicago, Miami, New York, and Geneva. For performers, too, Las Vegas represented a kind of windfall; they could make more money there than anywhere else. And MCA, as usual, controlled most of the major bookings. No other talent agency even had an office in Las Vegas.

"MCA ruled Las Vegas. You couldn't take on MCA," a former MCA agent told me. "Yes, there was some competition, here and there—but MCA was *it*." He explained the facts of life in Las Vegas during this period. "There was all this cash. The way it worked was that performers would get salaries, and then they would get 'salad'— maybe they'd get $7,500 in salary, and $50,000 in salad. Now, the agents obviously had to make some arrangements, because they were aware of the salad and they of course got their commission off the salad as well as the salary. For the performers, what to do with the cash was a problem. You couldn't spend it on tangible assets, like a house or a Rolls-Royce—because then they'd say, you made $100,000 this year, how'd you buy that car? You had to spend it on jewelry, furs, or some- body's rent." If you spent it on jewelry, for example, and the IRS ques- tioned you, he continued, "you could say, 'I got a great deal, but I never knew how great it was. I paid one thousand for that ring, you're telling me it's worth fifty thousand? My God, I wish that guy was still in busi- ness!' "

Like any closed society, Las Vegas had its own system of reward and punishment. "This was a world in which favors were done all the time," this former agent continued. "And if you were working in this milieu, you were friendly with the guys. . . . I remember once I did a favor for some of the guys, and they said, 'What can we do for you?'

"I said, 'No, nothing, that's okay.'

" 'No, really, what can we do?'

" 'No, I'm telling you, I'm fine.'

" 'But we want to do something.'

" 'No, it's okay, glad to do it.'

" 'Well—is there anybody you really don't like?' "

When debts were owed to a casino, he continued, legal action was not generally contemplated; rather, each casino owner had his own ways of dealing with the delinquency. Beldon Katleman, the owner of the El Rancho—who had booked Reagan as an emcee in his casino in 1953—had a distinctive approach. (He was a longtime friend of Wasserman's and the uncle of Harris Katleman.) "Beldon Katleman was a tough, tough guy—nobody wanted to mess with him," this former MCA agent said. "He had this box he always kept with him, and there was supposed to be enough in there to put everybody away. When people owed the El Rancho money, first they'd get the bill. Then they'd get a bill, marked 'late.' Then they'd get another one, marked 'overdue.' Then they'd get another one, marked 'final bill.' Then they'd get a picture of their house. And then they'd pay."

One of the top MCA agents in Las Vegas was a man named Jim Murray, who did a good job for MCA but was decidedly not cast in the Jules Stein mold. "We were the personal appearance guys, we were not part of the 'snob berets,' as we used to call the guys in radio and TV," Murray said. He had started out in MCA's New York office as a fifteen-year-old office boy in 1943, and eventually graduated to become an agent. "I went from the New York office to Chicago to Miami [where he booked Havana, too] to Vegas. I knew how to talk to the crooked noses. I was a saloon-booker, and dealt with the boys." He arrived in Las Vegas in 1956. "They shielded who was who in Vegas by having an entertainment director—but I was so close to the guys I would go to them (the entertainment director was sometimes the third man down)." The symbiotic relationship between the mob and the stars, he explained, went beyond the hotels where they performed. "The boys ran the jukebox business. They could *make* a star, by putting nine of her records in their jukeboxes. Then the boys would say, 'If I do you this favor, you play my club.' " After the Desert Inn, many other hotel-casinos had opened—the Sands, the Tropicana, the Riviera, the Fremont, the Stardust—and they were all vying for top entertainment. Recalling how he had had to juggle the competing interests of Moe Dalitz, Jack Entratter [the Sands], Morris Lansburgh [the Flamingo], and others, he rolled his eyes, saying, "It wasn't easy."

Decades later, it was plain that he was still proud of his MCA affiliation—though he had had to pay a personal price for it. Reaching into his jacket pocket, Murray brought out a navy leather billfold, embossed with gold lettering, "MCA Profit-sharing Trust," and the name, "Murray Fusco." He said that after he had worked at MCA for a number of years, his department head had announced to him one day, "You're now Jim Murray." He had not wanted to change his name, and his father had not been able to accept it. "But there were *big* Fuscos," Murray explained—Joseph Fusco was indicted along with Capone in 1931 on five thousand Prohibition law violations. "And the name Fusco just wouldn't do."

From the time Stein made Wasserman president, he had stepped back from the day-to-day running of MCA. He still kept a sharp eye on what transpired, but he no longer had to engage in the rougher side of the business, and he was free to concentrate on what absorbed him most. That, as ever, was money—but now, money in its finer, post-acquisition phases. Its investment, and its securitization, and its retention, through one intricate tax-saving structure after another. Asked once how he spent his leisure time, Stein responded in his cut-and-dried manner, "I don't live on the golf course. I would rather deal with corporate tax problems and the intricacies of corporate structure. I relax that way."

Stein had of course invested clients' money since the early days, and while he personally did not come up with all MCA's tax schemes, he encouraged and rewarded others' ingenuity. MCA had become increasingly tax-savvy; its incredibly complicated structure, with ultimately more than two hundred subsidiaries incorporated in many different states as well as abroad, had been designed that way largely because of tax considerations. The English antiques that filled every MCA office were being depreciated as they gained in value. In the forties, when taxes were so high, MCA had focused on tax-saving measures for its clients; there was the capital gains idea that Wasserman and Taft Schreiber had taken to Paley, and there was also another, conceived by Wasserman, through which talent—if they remained outside the U.S. for eighteen months or longer—could receive all monies tax-free. And there were oil-drilling partnerships that sheltered income for Stein, his MCA executives, and other business friends.

The creation of MCA's profit-sharing trust in 1944 had given Stein the chance to indulge himself in the pleasures of corporate finance. Judging from his correspondence when he was negotiating the terms of this trust with the Treasury Department, it is clear one reason he was establishing it was that he was worried about losing his best people—Wasserman, above all. In the fall of 1944, Stein pointed out in a letter to his attorney that Metro-Goldwyn-Mayer had recently instituted a pension plan, one that was much talked about in Hollywood. (Louis B. Mayer, of course, had already tried to hire Wasserman several years earlier.) And Stein was disturbed about the government's suggestion of a ceiling on salary. "If you have to settle for a top of $100,000, it would be feasible, however anything less than $75,000 would be trouble. I am hopeful I will get approvals to pay a few of our men $75,000 this year otherwise I will really be sweating. . . . Wasserman is worth $150,000 a year to many companies here and Jack Warner asked me the other day if I could spare him."

As the trust was ultimately constructed, MCA's contributions (15 percent of the employees' annual compensation) and any profits earned by their investment were tax-exempt until they were distributed to the employees. Stein, therefore, had a very large pot of money to invest—by 1955, he was directing the trust's capital mainly into the stock market, and its assets were over $4 million—and one over which he enjoyed virtually complete control. (His fellow trustees were his brother-in-law, Charles Miller, and his close friend from Chicago Edwin Weisl.) This trust did benefit MCA employees; but it also worked as a restraining device. For if an employee were to leave MCA less than six years after arriving at the company, he would forfeit all his interest in the trust; after six years, he would receive a mere 20 percent; after seven years, 40 percent. Only if an employee were to leave after ten years at MCA would he be entitled to 100 percent of his interest in the trust. It was a considerable financial deterrent to jumping ship.

It seems to have been Stein's preoccupation with estate planning that eventually led him to think about taking the company public. The idea of MCA as a public company was almost an oxymoron; Stein had made secrecy the company credo, and Wasserman was, remarkably, even more secretive than Stein. (Stein, at least, would write letters; Wasserman made it his practice to commit almost nothing to paper personally—he would return correspondence with "O.K." or "No" scrawled in the margin.) Indeed, Wasserman was said to have opposed the idea of going public, for this very reason; but the prerogative was Stein's. It would establish a market for estate tax purposes—and it would also mean a further step toward legitimacy, and away from the shadowed past. As a prelude to this projected undertaking, Stein made the company's stock available to nine key executives in the spring of 1954, to be followed by distributions to others over the next few years. He may have felt some pressure to distribute the stock at long last— one former MCA agent, Herbert Rosenthal, who was one of the first nine executives to receive the stock, insisted that "Jules *had* to do it. He knew we would have left if there was no stock distribution." But it also suited his larger purpose.

Certainly the event Stein created for the distribution of the stock gave no hint of his having been pressured to do so; it seemed, more, al- most feudal, a ceremony for the lordly bestowal of patronage. Wasser- man was the only one whom Stein had taken into his confidence beforehand. It would become one of Wasserman's vintage anecdotes— how Stein had walked into Wasserman's office one day and said, "I'm going to distribute the stock. I'm keeping 40 percent, you take 20 per- cent, and you decide how to divide up the rest." Except that, according to Stein's account, Stein had kept control of not 40 but 53 percent, and he and Wasserman together had decided what percentages the other men should receive. Furthermore, the stock was nonvoting; only when MCA eventually went public would the executives, Wasserman in- cluded, receive voting stock. In later years, Wasserman would always insist, as a seeming point of pride, that from the time he became presi- dent Stein gave him a completely free hand, and never challenged his decisions. But that was, evidently, an idealized version of the relation- ship between the two men and the balance of power they struck. Look- ing back on this period, Stein commented in his blunt way, "I was not going to let anyone else run the company."

The day before the event, Stein had summoned each executive into his office and asked them to come to his home the following afternoon. No one but Wasserman had any idea why, and it was rare for these executives to go to Misty Mountain; Stein did not socialize with them. Upon driving through the blue iron gates, high on Angelo Drive, higher even than Rudolph Valentino's Falcon's Lair, they were led into the library by the Steins' longtime butler, Charles, who had worked at Hearst's San Simeon. The bookcases were lined with masses of Stein's leather-bound books, and some of the Queen Anne tables, opened, had vertical extensions—reminiscent, in a way, of the ladders that used to run on wheels along the shelves in the dry goods store in South Bend. Before him, Stein had a stack of ten thin books, which he distributed to each executive. They were covered in blue leather with a gold border, and the MCA seal—the music-bound globe—in the center; the covers were lined in blue silk; the pages were thick, like parchment; and the type was an elaborate calligraphy, such as might be used in a medieval book of hours. Stein had written the text in longhand, and he had had the books privately printed in New York. Opening his own copy, Stein began reading aloud: "This is perhaps the most eventful day in my life, and I believe one long to be remembered by each of you."

After reading about the distribution itself—each executive would be allotted a certain amount of stock to purchase at a price below book value—Stein called each one into the dining room to sign the papers that would make him an MCA stockholder. No one was to know what the others received. (Taft Schreiber's holding, for example, was the next highest after Wasserman's—but there was a huge gap between the two.) Following the signings, Stein continued reading from his book. He described his having formed his own orchestra in South Bend when he was twelve, and reminisced about the early years of Music Corporation. He offered homilies about the agency business, which he described as "a twenty-four-hour business." ("Unfortunately, it is not a business in which the executive can relax for any long periods of time; for while you relax, your competitor will steal your artist from you.")

He held Wasserman up as a model—someone who lived on so little sleep and worked with such concentration that even the driven Stein had, on occasion, "admonished" him to ease up a little (but to no avail). Stein had included columns of numbers to illustrate MCA's consistent growth. And he detailed how he had set up the profit-sharing trust within fifteen months after such entities were authorized by Congress, and how the change in the federal tax laws in 1947 had led him to conceive of this stock distribution plan. "May I dream for a few moments," Stein had written near the end of the book. "In my humble opinion MCA is today at the threshold of its greatest development and future. We will someday—and soon—be larger and greater than any institution ever to rise in the amusement world."

On the last page of the book was a paragraph that Stein read aloud with special emphasis. "This material and information presented to you are highly confidential. It is expected that you will keep it so and will not divulge any of these facts or figures or your individual holdings in the companies. . . . Until now MCA has proven it can keep secrets, and I am confident you as individuals will continue to help MCA justify this reputation."

Except that, at the last moment, Stein realized he was not confident enough. The idea of leaving these books in anyone else's hands proved too much, and he collected all of them before the executives left Misty Mountain that day. Even Wasserman was not allowed to keep his book; Stein only turned it over to him years later.

While this ceremony was strictly an in-house event, Stein did distribute stock to select outsiders—among them, Harry Berman, the accountant who had worked for Stein since about 1930. Berman was not an MCA employee, but he was in some ways more of an insider than anyone. He had been working out of a small office in lower Manhattan when he offered his services to Stein, for free, for a three-month period. He passed muster so well that he became Stein's personal accountant, and Music Corporation's, and also the accountant of many of Music Corporation's clients. In the early thirties, after MCA moved its New

York offices from the Paramount building to a more elegant location, the Squibb building on Fifth Avenue, Berman took over the two-story MCA penthouse office (still furnished with Stein's antiques) in the Paramount building. He prospered. He drove a red convertible Cadillac, and divided his time between his apartment a few doors off Fifth Avenue on East 67th Street, his estate in Mount Vernon, and, a little later, his horse farm in Ocala, Florida. For someone of such demonstrable affluence—and an *accountant*—it was a little strange that he was known to keep many thousands of dollars in cash in a safe-deposit box in a New York bank. In any case, Berman was (with the possible exception of Stein's sister Ruth, whom Stein brought into the company in 1946, and who handled his personal financial matters) the single person most privy to Stein's secrets from Music Corporation's early years. And Stein—who trusted virtually no one, and kept an emotional distance even from those family members closest to him—was remarkably open with Berman, confiding the most intimate matters.

For in April 1950, when Stein and his wife, Doris, were spending Easter in Zermatt, Switzerland, Stein had typed out a note to Berman.

Dear Harry,

I know how interested and concerned you are with my personal problems and therefor[e] this short message to you. Unfortunately I cannot ask you to write me since there is a chance she might open some of my mail as she often does from the offices and then I am a dead duck.

The situation is no good—in fact much worse. I plan returning around May first—Doris is remaining several weeks longer—she says two—I'll settle now for three. He is meeting her in Paris and they will spend their time together there and throughout France. To me it is most brazen—but she is really in love with this fellow and there are moments in which her mind wanders off into space and her eyes are full of tears. She has tenderness for me but little or no affection and while she is concerned about family etc. she feels many others have made the adjustments and we can as well.

She promises to come home for the summer—and hopes maybe during that time she will adjust herself but the great love she had for me these past 22 years is gone. . . .

She has lost all interest in Hollywood or the business—and seemingly is living in a new world of her own. . . . I don't know whether I shall ever be able to adjust myself. My whole world has revolved around her and I know of no other one I desire.

I hold on to my slim hopes—but am fearful my mental and physical condition will not be able to hold on much longer. I dread the approach of May first when we separate.

Stein's demeanor might have led one to suspect that he was a person of shallow emotions, but the surface only appeared imperturbable because he was so utterly *contained*. On one occasion, when he and his older daughter, Jean, had not been speaking to each other for an extended period, she received in the mail from him an envelope containing no note, just three postcards he had had made, evocative photographs of the house on Lake Arrowhead where they had spent many summers when she was a child—and, wordless as this message was, she knew that the silence between them was broken. That the taciturn Stein would have exposed his suffering to Berman so volubly was very unusual. But however much he valued Berman's friendship, aptitude (he referred to him on at least one occasion as "my brilliant tax advisor"), and longtime service, Stein did not hesitate to leave Berman behind, now that it had become more practical to do so. As the company prepared to go public, the corporate structures that Berman had helped to devise were the very ones that were to be buried; and MCA's accountants would be Price Waterhouse & Co., not Harry Berman. So Stein allotted Berman 2 percent of the company's stock, and he drew up an agreement that would phase Berman out over the next several years. Berman felt badly treated; he thought he was entitled to something more like 14 percent of the stock. "I did *so many things* for Jules," he would say repeatedly to his wife. "I made a multimillionaire out of Jules Stein."

In the meantime, Stein's crisis with Doris had passed. Richard Gully, Doris's confidant, said that he was aware of Doris's "fling" at the time, and that he was fairly certain that her lover was Count de Polignac, the father of Prince Rainier of Monaco. "He was very hot in Paris," Gully said. "There was a great glamour to Europe for Americans after the war, and there were a lot of playboys going after American women, but the only playboys that had money were Agnelli and Rothschild. Polignac didn't have money.

"Doris never would have left Jules, I feel certain—and definitely not for a man who couldn't support her," Gully added.

Stein had never fully shared his wife's social ambitions, but he seemed happy enough to indulge them. Apparently linked to Doris's ambitions was her desire not to be identified as a Jew, and not to have their children raised as Jews. Stein, for his part, made no secret of his being Jewish, but he avoided the places where most of the Jewish moguls gathered, like Temple Israel and the Hillcrest Country Club. He did contribute to Jewish charities, but he seemed almost to resent the obligation to do so. (As he wrote to his friend Charles Wrightsman, "Because I am considered an important American Jew . . . I find myself going overboard . . . in contributions to Palestine, United Jewish Welfare Fund, Federation for Jewish Charities, Cedars of Lebanon Hospital, and, thereby, leaving me very little, if any, monies for the institutions and organizations I would really like to help.") When Doris had first resolved to become the premier hostess in the movie colony, her goal had carried some business purpose; for Hollywood was a one-industry community, where social life and business tended to blend into one another. She had carved out her territory very deliberately, and was extremely proprietary. "Edie Wasserman wanted to be a hostess in her own right, but she was never allowed to by Doris," Gully said. "There was to be only one king and queen. It really was a court like Louis XIV." By the late forties, however, Hollywood had become too provincial for Doris, and she set out to conquer the world. Socializing with the Aly Khan, Prince von Thurn und Taxis of Germany, and the Duchess of Argyll did little for MCA's business, and it may have been this purposelessness that led Jules to balk. In Buenos Aires, during the reign of Evita and Juan Perón, Jules staged what Doris would later refer to, in a Schumach interview, as his "sit-down strike." It was customary in Buenos Aires society for cocktails to be served at ten in the evening, dinner at midnight. "Jules did it for a while," Doris recalled. "Finally, he said, 'I've had it.' After that he would leave after the cocktails and go home and eat alone. I'd go on to dinner and nightclubs and have a wonderful time."

Once Doris gave up her lover and returned to Jules, however, he seemed to sublimate his desires to hers; and their social life, particularly in Europe, became even more expansive. If Jules resented its demands, he gave almost no sign, other than the occasional trenchant observation. ("Doris," he once commented, "would go to the opening of a door.") But, complaisant as he was in his wife's single-minded courtship of the titled class, Jules remained his intensely mercantile self—which, on occasion, created a fissure in their facade. Doris was a committed Anglophile, and for the coronation of Queen Elizabeth II in 1953, the Steins decided to throw a party at the new MCA offices in London. The townhouse, at 139 Piccadilly, had an impressive lineage—it had once been owned by the Marquis of Queensberry, and Lord Byron had lived there, too. Connected to the townhouse was a mews apartment, which Doris turned into exquisite living quarters. (When the Steins first occupied it, Jules's sister Ruth sent a telegram to him that read: "Congratulations. Moved right back next to the store.") Most important for the coronation party, however, the MCA building would offer a perfect view of the route of the royal procession. Stein had a scaffold erected, with seating stretching across the front of 139 Piccadilly. And then an idea occurred to him. "We had all these people clamoring for seats in the stands attached to the building. . . . And the people we invited we were going to wine and dine. I decided we ought to charge for these seats. We charged, as I recall it, as much as $100 a seat. And that," Stein summed up, "paid for everything."

The apogee of the Steins' social life in this period, however, was the wedding of their elder daughter, Jean, to William vanden Heuvel, in

December 1958. It was held in New York's St. Patrick's Cathedral, and followed by a party at the St. Regis, where socialites from around the world danced to the music of Guy Lombardo and his orchestra. (Lombardo performed for free, as he and other entertainers had, also, for Jean's coming-out party seven years earlier.) To Doris and Jules, this spectacular event represented no small triumph, for Jean had seemed intent for years on defying her parents, and, certainly, denying them an occasion as much to their taste as this. Jean and her sister, Susan, had endured a bruising childhood, raised by a dour governess while Jules and Doris were abroad for extended periods. Doris was a trial as a mother—cold, alcoholic, ashamed of her origins, obsessed with her social climb, devout in her worship of style. Jules, at least, was a person of more substance, and he did seem to love his daughters, particularly Jean, his clear favorite. But he, too, was at once remote and demanding, wanting to control his daughters as fully as he did everything in his business life. He and Jean were locked in a perpetual struggle. Jules's politics were extremely conservative (during the McCarthy years, he would grow quite heated about the "Commies"), and anathema to Jean. She was repelled when his good friend Ed Weisl once took her to a courthouse in downtown Manhattan to introduce her to a young lawyer he said he was sure she'd like—and who turned out to be Roy Cohn. Jean dropped out of Wellesley College, went to live in Paris (where she became friendly with Alberto Giacometti, who painted her portrait), and had an affair with William Faulkner, who was more than thirty years her senior. Her interview with Faulkner was published in the *Paris Review*, and with that, she became features editor at the age of twenty-two. (When the journal's editor, George Plimpton, went to see Jules to ask him to invest in it, Jules asked how much money it made; upon being told that it was in the red, Jules brusquely showed Plimpton the door, saying that no one had ever before had the temerity to ask him to invest in a money-losing venture.) And so this battle of wills had gone. Until now, remarkably enough, Jean had decided to marry someone to whom her parents had introduced her—a lawyer who had gone to Cornell University on scholarship but had an aristo-cratic-sounding name—and to do it *their* way.

Nearly a year later, in October 1959, Stein achieved another milestone, one he had been planning for many years. MCA became a public company, listed on the New York Stock Exchange. Its first stock offering was highly successful—only 400,000 common shares were offered, at a price of $17.50, and the stock, heavily oversubscribed, quickly ran up to a high of $38. The chief underwriter was Lehman Brothers, the top-tier Wall Street firm where Ed Weisl, though he was a lawyer at Simpson Thacher, was so omnipresent that he was viewed as a kind of informal member. The months before the offering had been busy with preparations—first a new company, MCA, Inc., had been incorporated in Delaware, and then the entire MCA-related empire had been reorganized. It was Stein who had intended to direct all these activities; he was the one with the seat on the New York Stock Exchange and with the Wall Street relationships. But during this period he had a bout with prostate cancer, and underwent extensive surgery. Asked whether Stein, facing cancer, had thought he would die, Wasserman replied, "Jules was a pessimist. He *knew* he was going to die." As it turned out, Stein's prognosis was good. Needing time to recuperate, however, he put Wasserman in charge of the transaction.

Dealing with Wall Street was a new experience for Wasserman, and not one he cared for. He was so secretive that the analysts' questions seemed invasive, and there were some subjects in particular that he felt were none of their business. His relationship with Jimmy Hoffa was one. Hoffa had been the power behind Teamsters leader Dave Beck for years, and had become the head of the union in 1957 after Beck went to prison for corruption. Hoffa's dealings with members of organized crime were well known, and by this time, Robert F. Kennedy, as chief counsel for the Senate Select Committee on Improper Activities in the Labor or Management Field, had come to regard Hoffa and the Teamsters as "a conspiracy of evil"; he believed that they were guilty of corruption, thuggery, and murder, and yet somehow managed to elude effective prosecution. About Hoffa, Kennedy would comment, "I think it is an extremely dangerous situation at the present time, this man who has a background of corruption and dishonesty, has misused hundreds of thousands of dollars of union funds, betrayed the union membership, sold out the membership, put gangsters and racketeers in positions of power, and still heads the Teamsters Union." Not surprisingly, Wall Street analysts considered a Hoffa connection unsavory.

"I had lunch with these specialists, if that's what you call them," Wasserman said, recounting a story he had told many times. "One said, 'I understand that you know Jimmy Hoffa.' I said, 'Yes, and I'm glad I know him. We hire about fifteen thousand of his members a week. I'd rather be hiring them from someone I know than someone I don't.' "

The arrangement between Stein and Wasserman was working well. Stein could mingle with society on an ever more rarefied plane, while Wasserman—a tougher type than Stein had been, even when he was a young man in Chicago consorting with Petrillo—cultivated Jimmy Hoffa and his compatriots. It was not a bargain that really cost Wasserman, at least not at this point in his life. He was more comfortable with Moe Dalitz and Sidney Korshak, say, than he would have been at Stein's parties at Misty Mountain. Wasserman surely knew, too, that in the movie colony—in contrast to Wall Street—his associations with such men not only served a business purpose but also enhanced his aura of power. And the more power he was seen to hold, the more actually was his to wield. Power leads to more power, Mike Dann had observed about MCA, and for Wasserman that proverbial factoring was sublime. It was, in fact, all there was. Stein was a rapacious man with few outside interests, but he *was* a collector, and he would spend days driving with Doris through the English countryside to some remote hamlet in search of antiques at a steal. It was unimaginable that Wasserman would have so lent himself to an activity that did not serve to augment his reach.

But he was fully occupied, in his twenty-hour days, with those that did. Wasserman had been very much in charge of MCA's Los Angeles office, even in the early forties; but once he became president, the entire organization was in his grasp. And what he established was a more or less benevolent dictatorship. Little that involved MCA escaped him. Swifty Lazar, of course, had found this "Mafia-like" system where the soldiers were to report everything to the capo so intolerable that he had quit, but most MCA agents readily accepted Wasserman's rule. It was quite remarkable. In the space of about fifteen years, he had transformed himself from a spindly, intellectually insecure young nightclub publicist into a calibrated, coldly charismatic leader, regarded by his followers with fear and awe. His "muscle," noted by Frank Stanton, was certainly a part of his mystique, but it was derivative; it was his mental force that enabled him to devise the system in which the muscle came into play.

Information was a critical element in that system. Indeed, Wasserman had become the very personification of the maxim that information is power. His appetite was insatiable, ranging from quotas and currency restrictions and tax provisions in the overseas market to the latest merchandising revenues on *Laramie;* and to his men his retentive capacity seemed preternatural. "He had a truly photographic memory," marveled MCA agent Freddie Fields. "Therefore, he always knew where every man in the company was, what his deal was, who his clients were. He'd read lists of all this on the plane going back and forth between New York and L.A., and he'd retain it all. He was a *dominant* figure, I don't know how to explain it."

He continued, "Everybody dressed like him—"

But wasn't the uniform mandatory?

"You had to wear a white shirt and a dark tie, you didn't have to wear a black knit tie! You didn't have to wear loafers—" Fields broke off and, decades after having left MCA and its dress code behind, swung his loafer-clad foot out from beneath the table. Referring to an executive trained by Wasserman, Fields continued, "I saw him walking at the studio not long ago, and I thought at first it was Lew. He had that specific shuffle, that duck walk!

"Everyone in the company who stayed either admired or feared him. A guy like Sonny Werblin, for example. He was smart-ass, tough, competitive—but he was scared to death of Lew. He would never take him on. No one would. You might disagree about a deal or something—but you'd never take him on.

"He had an aura," Fields concluded. "He was my god."

Awestruck as some of his subordinates were, Wasserman remained down-to-earth, laconic, seemingly indifferent to the extravagant, if inchoate, feelings he inspired. Virtually everything about him was spare. He never exercised, but remained thin. He did not often exert himself to smile; while he possessed a dry sense of humor, he tended to stay poker-faced as he delivered his sallies. His clothes were so uniform he could don them thoughtlessly—dark suit, dark tie, dark raincoat, even dark bathrobe. Fueled by his work, he seemed to be otherwise self-sustaining; he appeared to require little respite, little sleep, little human connection. Though he could be very charming when necessary, he tended to mete out his words, and certainly his emotion. With those who worked for him, he was famous for never admitting that he had made a mistake—*never*—and for not dispensing praise. Sometimes, employees would think they could detect a hidden compliment in something he said, but it was so obscure they could never be sure. Hungry for any sign, they became grateful for a gesture. ("He was always cool, aloof, but he knew how to handle people—he'd put his arm on your shoulder," recalled Al Rush. "Guys lived for a pat on the back.") Wasserman's rules for his employees, too, evinced economy: tend to the client, dress appropriately, divulge no information about MCA, commit very little to paper, never leave the office without returning every call, always do your homework. Doing one's homework meant, among other things, paying close attention to detail. When advertising executives, sponsors of an MCA television series, were about to arrive for a cocktail party at Wasserman's home, Wasserman asked the MCA publicist working on the event whether he had checked which cigarette accounts the company had. He had not! Fortunately for him, he was able to find out and to change all the cigarettes in the cigarette holders in the moments before the guests arrived.

But the most important commandment by far that Wasserman gave his employees was never to attempt to mislead him. Those who did found that the only aspect of Wasserman that was not spare was his rage. His explosive tirades were legend—his removing his watch was a sure sign the storm was coming; at its peak he would scream, shake, even froth at the mouth as though he were having a seizure; some of his victims burst into tears or fainted. It was such a wild, eccentric display that one might assume it was beyond his control. That, however, seems unlikely, for these rages—like virtually everything he did—served a purpose. Discipline was enforced, certain executives were made into object lessons, and fear was kept fresh.

As Lazar had observed earlier, the culture of MCA bore no small resemblance to the Mafia's, and this likeness had become only more pronounced once Wasserman was fully in charge. Loyalty to the MCA family was a supreme value, and it was duly rewarded. An executive might be eviscerated by Wasserman time and again, but if he died while in the employ of MCA, his family would be quietly taken care of. If an agent could not afford to buy the private shares of MCA stock that were allotted to him, the company might advance the money. Mort Viner, a young agent who had started in the mailroom in 1951 and worked his way up, recalled that he told Wasserman he didn't have enough money to buy the shares available to him. It was a considerable disadvantage—while the shares might have cost, say, $700 at the time, a few months later they might be worth as much as $7,000. "Lew said, just sign this check for the amount. And at the end of the year, when I got my bonus, there was more than enough to cover the check, and he said he was finally depositing it." If someone wronged one of Wasserman's people, Wasserman would exact retribution. An MCA agent recalled a situation involving two of his then colleagues. One was only a middling employee—he worked in the nightclub area, which by the late fifties was becoming a less important venue for MCA, and he had a gambling problem besides; the other was a crackerjack TV agent. "The first agent walked into his apartment and found the TV guy screwing his wife. Lew called the TV guy and said, 'I want you out of the building *today*.' Despite the fact that he was a major piece of manpower. That was Lew," this agent declared. "His loyalty to loyalty was incredible."

Wasserman made it a habit to give credit to his troops, rather than claiming it himself; this made them more devoted to him, and also—inasmuch as it bolstered their standing with clients—freed him to do other things. "He wanted to build manpower—if he felt you were capable of representing someone he was involved with, he would gladly let you do it," declared Jay Kanter, who had started working in the MCA mailroom when he was twenty-one and eventually became a full-fledged agent, representing stars like Marlon Brando and Marilyn Monroe. "I'd hear him on the phone with studio heads—'I don't know, Marlon won't answer my phone calls, you have to call Jay Kanter.'

"We were going out to Universal one day," Kanter continued. "Lew was going to make a deal for Jimmy Stewart to do *Winchester 73*, and he was meeting with Leo Spitz and Bill Goetz, head of Universal at the time. After discussing this deal, Lew said, 'I don't know, I don't think it is going to work out.' And we left. I said, 'Lew, why? That's a great deal!' He said, 'You call them back in a few hours and tell them *you* worked it out—and you'll never have trouble getting them on the phone again.' "

Kanter was a Wasserman favorite. Mild, courteous, cautious, he had a temperate demeanor more like that of a corporate lawyer than a Hollywood agent. Wasserman no doubt liked him personally, and felt he was someone that could be trusted and would never embarrass him. That last, in any event, turned out to be wrong, in an incident that nearly derailed Kanter's career. Kanter became friendly with an older MCA agent named Jennings Lang. Lang had worked for Sam Jaffe (the agent who lamented how MCA had stolen his clients and his employees, offering them all the sweeteners that he could not) until, in 1949, Wasserman had persuaded Lang to join MCA. A big, robust character, with a keen mind and an irrepressibly amorous streak, Lang broke one of the cardinal MCA rules and had an affair with a client—the actress Joan Bennett, who was married to Walter Wanger, a serious-minded, well-regarded independent producer. One day in the fall of 1951, in the MCA parking lot in the center of Beverly Hills, Walter Wanger shot Lang in the offending part of his anatomy. Tragedy was averted—Lang recovered, and Wanger served only a four-month sentence. But it quickly emerged that the apartment used for Lang and Bennett's afternoon trysts was Jay Kanter's. Jules Stein was said to have been so infuriated by the scandal that he wanted Kanter fired on the spot, but Wasserman defended him. In the end, both Lang and Kanter were deemed too valuable to fire.

There were always a handful of young men who, encouraged by Wasserman, believed they were in line to become his successor, but in the mid-fifties Kanter seemed the most likely. He had married a spirited girl, Judy Balaban, the daughter of Stein's old friend Barney Balaban, the Paramount chief. Judy had known Doris and Jules from the time she was a little girl. Her parents had frequently invited the Steins to formal dinners in their palatial Fifth Avenue residence in New York; she was so accustomed to seeing Jules take out his violin and play with the musicians that one day she had asked her father, "Why don't the other musicians get to eat with the guests?" Now, Judy and Edie Wasserman had become fast friends, too, meeting for cocktails on weekday afternoons, organizing poolside Sunday barbecues at the Wassermans'. Edie was a tough, tightly wound, irascible woman; she took quick dislikes to people, cut them to shreds, was wont to brutalize even those she liked. Lew, it was often said, was a pussycat next to Edie, and the Cleveland connections they both had seemed more palpable in her. But she did not abuse Judy Kanter—perhaps, Judy surmised later, because Edie was impressed by her social standing as Balaban's daughter. In any event, Judy felt that this regent was grooming her, too, for Jay's eventual succession. But all the bonhomie disappeared when Jay discovered his wife with her lover, the actor Tony Franciosa. Edie exhorted Judy to stay with Kanter, but she left him for Franciosa, whom she eventually married. Wasserman reacted in his signature way; for a period of time, Franciosa is said to have had trouble finding work in Hollywood. And Edie behaved as *she* always did when someone valued chose to leave the MCA family; she refused to speak to Judy for years. Loyalty was rewarded, disloyalty treated as a capital crime; Edie severed connections to her former friends decisively and cleanly. (Mort Viner, trying to put the best face on Edie's absolutism, stressed what he saw as its positive side. "Edie is a *real* friend—the kind of friend where if you commit murder, then the other person deserved it," he declared.) When Wasserman encountered people who had left MCA, he would be more civil than his wife; but they knew that, for him, too, they had ceased to exist in any meaningful way.

It was an unforgiving system, but it served Wasserman's ends because it imposed discipline, increased efficiency, and established, in an odd way, considerable esprit de corps. Many employees felt that being part of MCA was very special; not just a job, but a sign of distinction; an elevated kind of association, to which they had consecrated themselves. What made it all work, of course, was the power of their patron—who had the wherewithal to favor or to punish, and on a large scale. But there was in this all-encompassing model one element that seemed to defy the logic of the rest—and that was the conduct of the patron's wife. Numerous people who were interviewed spoke about Edie Wasserman's philandering, something, they all maintained, that was a well-recognized if bewildering fact of life in this community. Why the most powerful man in Hollywood, who controlled so much of what transpired there, could not—or would not—control his wife was a matter of fervid speculation. Some suggested that he preferred that Edie be diverted so he was free to work. That seemed implausible; Hollywood was a very macho society, in which husbands might routinely cheat on their wives but could not be cuckolded themselves without considerable loss of face. The reason for Wasserman's forbearance, in any event, remained mysterious. He did seem to want to make a statement, in a quasi-public way, about a line drawn between them. An MCA employee recalled one occasion when Lew was showing guests around the Beverly Hills home he and Edie had bought in 1960 for $400,000. Built by the architect Harold Levitt, it was a spacious, one-story, one-bedroom home, ideal for entertaining, and situated at the top of a very long, climbing driveway. The Wassermans added a separate projection room, also designed by Levitt, which they called "the theater," and, later, a fish pond filled with koi, amid beautifully landscaped gardens, and a large Henry Moore sculpture opposite the entrance to the house. As Wasserman and his guests reached the master bedroom, Wasserman announced, "Edie sleeps here," and when they came to the den, with its three TV sets, which he watched nightly, each tuned to a different network, he declared, "And I sleep here." It was, in any event, something that also found its way into the press; a 1965 *Time* magazine profile of Wasserman mentioned the Wassermans' separate sleeping arrangements.

Wasserman's only apparent vice was a fondness for gambling, which persisted into the fifties. The combination of his extraordinarily retentive memory and his numerical wizardry made him a formidable card player, and in his early years in L.A. he had played a great deal. Many of the moguls did. Sam Goldwyn was an obsessive gambler, given to cheating—and famous for his losses (in one session, $150,000, which would be worth about $2 million today). Wasserman found it was not a bad way to test himself against these men. "There used to be big card games," Wasserman said. "It started with pinochle, then moved to bridge (that was too complicated for some people), then gin rummy, and poker. The first time I met Sam Goldwyn, it was at his house, four of us playing gin rummy for money. The next time I was there, he wanted me to play. I said, 'No, Sam, I will not play you for money, I'm going to beat you and I don't want to take your money.' He was furious, yelling. When he stopped, Frances [Goldwyn's wife] said to him, 'Listen to Lew, Sam. He's the only one who's your friend.' "

Wasserman said that in the early forties he began to visit Las Vegas, then little more than a dusty Old West desert town; Bugsy Siegel's Flamingo had not yet been built, and Wasserman gambled at the Last Frontier or the El Rancho, which by 1947 was owned by his friend Beldon Katleman. But the stakes there were smaller than in some of the Sunset Boulevard clubs—like the Clover Club, a Hollywood institution—where illegal gambling flourished. "There were very high stakes in these clubs—$100,000 in a pot, or even a half million," Wasserman said. Some of Wasserman's associates believed that it was his gambling debts that caused him to remain in such a modest house in Beverly Hills long after he was named president of the company. Harry Berman's wife, Alice, recalled his having told her in the early fifties that Wasserman had "lost big" in Las Vegas, as much as $200,000—and that Stein had had to loan him the money. Stein was surely disapproving of this weakness of Wasserman's; though Stein would play gin rummy on occasion, he limited himself to no more than 5 cents a point.

A favorite gambling anecdote of Wasserman's involved a trip he made to Cuba with Alfred Hitchcock. Of all the actors, writers, directors, and producers Wasserman cultivated, Hitchcock was probably the single most important to him. By the fifties—the decade in which Hitchcock's productions included *Strangers on a Train, Rear Window, Vertigo,* and *North by Northwest*—it was plain that he was among the most gifted directors ever to work in movies. And he was probably the best known as well—in some large part because Wasserman had persuaded him to produce and host a TV show, *Alfred Hitchcock Presents,* which went on the air in 1955 and became one of the biggest shows on television. It was a great triumph not only for Hitchcock, but for Wasserman, too. Like so many of his peers, Hitchcock had disdained television at first; but Wasserman had been so decisive that he had succumbed. One day, when he was in Wasserman's office and a passerby made some derogatory comment about TV, Hitchcock responded, "Go away and don't bother us. We're busy counting our money." There was a great deal to count. Some friends of Hitchcock's said that he had a complicated relationship with Wasserman, who he felt took advantage of him financially—but upon whom he felt quite dependent at the same time. He is said to have expressed his hostility in odd, subtle ways. One, perhaps, was the portrait of Wasserman by Bernard Buffet, which Hitchcock had commissioned and given Wasserman as a gift, and which hung in the foyer of the Wassermans' home. The portrait has a slightly sinister air; Wasserman is wearing a black suit, seated, his hands—clawlike—resting on his knees. "His hands looked like black widow spiders!" exclaimed a former MCA executive. "I said to Hitch, 'How could you do that?' And he gave me that enigmatic smile."

Wasserman rarely took a vacation, but when Hitchcock and his wife, Alma, invited Edie and Lew to spend Christmas with them at the Round Hill resort in Jamaica in 1956, Wasserman agreed. Round Hill had opened just four years earlier, but it had already become a choice winter refuge for a mix of stars and the moneyed class; guests included Clarence Dillon, Noel Coward, Grace Kelly, John and Jacqueline Kennedy (on their honeymoon), Clark Gable, the dukes of Norfolk, Bedford, and Marlborough. The day the Wassermans arrived, it was raining, and it rained the next day, and the next. "The place where you had dinner was seventy yards away, and there was so much water you had to take off your shoes and socks to get there," Wasserman said. "There were Babe and Bill Paley, carrying their shoes. Finally, I said to Hitchcock, can't we go somewhere else? And I called my friends in Havana."

Wasserman's friends were Moe Dalitz and Sam "Sambo" Tucker. Dalitz, Tucker, and other associates from the Cleveland syndicate had moved their base of operations to Las Vegas, where they had opened the Desert Inn in 1950. Now, several years later, in league with Meyer Lansky, they were expanding to Havana. Lansky had begun to focus on the prospects for a gambling empire in Cuba back in the thirties; Dalitz, Lucky Luciano, Bugsy Siegel, Lansky, and others had each put up $500,000 of their bootlegging profits to start a Havana gambling operation by paying off Fulgencio Batista, according to Lansky's longtime lieutenant, Joseph "Doc" Stacher as quoted in *Meyer Lansky* by Dennis Eisenberg, Uri Dan, and Eli Landau. By 1937, Lansky had organized one of the world's most luxurious casinos at the Hotel Nacionál, where he lived for months at a time. (The hotel was owned, nominally, by A. S. Kirkeby, the front for Lansky in whose private company Jules Stein held shares.) During the war, Lansky's gambling enterprise had become dormant. But in 1952, Batista, who had been living in exile in Florida, staged a coup to regain power, and that enabled Lansky to start rebuilding on an even more lavish scale than before. He invited Dalitz to come to Havana and invest in the hotels and casinos being built; Tucker, for a time, became the manager of the Hotel Nacionál (he had previously overseen another Lansky operation, the Beverly Hills Club in Kentucky). Referring to Dalitz, Tucker, and Lansky, Wasserman continued, "So these guys owned all the hotels. They took us to dinner in a great restaurant. We're sitting there—Hitch, Alma, Edie, Lansky, and the rest. Hitchcock at that point was the biggest TV star, with *Hitchcock Presents*. Lansky says to my wife, 'Is that *Alfred Hitchcock?*' And Hitch says to me, 'Is that *Meyer Lansky?*'

"We went to the Hotel Nacionál casino to gamble. Sambo takes out this enormous wad, it must have been tens of thousands of dollars. Hitch gives Alma fifty dollars. And she can't win a bet! They wanted her to win, but she kept losing. We were walking back to our hotel, about five in the morning, and I said to Moe, 'Why are you guys here? You own Las Vegas, and here, you risk losing it all.' Castro was already in the hills, it was reported. And he said, 'Sambo loves to fish, and this is the best fishing in the world. But then, there was nothing to do at night—so we built the casinos.' " Wasserman paused. Then, with a small smile, he added, "Do you know that when Batista bet, he *never* lost?"

Jules Stein, of course, would never have joined this group in Havana, but Wasserman was in his element. Dalitz and he seemed almost familial. Dalitz was tall, smooth, engaging, with a keen business sense and an avuncular manner, nothing hard-edged visible to a casual observer; he and Wasserman spoke the same language. And their rapport, natural as it seemed, was eminently useful for Wasserman and MCA. It was not only the narrow though lucrative business relationship in Las Vegas, but the more global one as well. For this group (Lansky, Dalitz et al.) was, in its way, a kind of highly select social club; and, as in any such organization, the connections provided could be highly beneficial.

The relationship between Dalitz and Lansky had been formed in the twenties, when they had set up a national network for bootlegging. In that same period, Dalitz had gotten to know Jimmy Hoffa, whom he introduced to Lansky. As Doc Stacher explained, "We knew Jimmy Hoffa right from the early days, because of Moe Dalitz. . . . Jimmy Hoffa met Moe when he was just a young man in a group of Jewish boys who worked for Norman Purple in the Purple Gang [in Detroit]. There was a war among the Detroit gangs, and when Dalitz's boys got the worst of it, Moe left the Purple Gang and set up on his own in Ohio." Now that Hoffa was well on his way to becoming the most powerful and feared labor boss in the country—and someone vitally important to Wasserman—it was helpful to be part of this circle.

But probably nothing was quite as helpful as Wasserman's friendship with Sidney Korshak. Since the days when Korshak had advised Willie Bioff, his power—as consigliere to the Outfit, with unions his special portfolio—had continued to grow. He still spent a good deal of his time in Chicago, where he maintained a law office with his younger brother, Marshall, and where Korshak's efficacy as a labor consultant had given him entrée into establishment circles. Many business executives were caught in a dilemma—they wanted to resist attempts by honest labor unions to organize their employees, since that would be costly; but they did not want to deal personally with mob-dominated unions. Using Korshak was one solution. In 1946, he had been retained by Joel Goldblatt, president of a chain of department stores, who had been pressured for payoffs by a number of labor officials; Korshak functioned as Goldblatt's intermediary and got him labor peace. Walter Heymann, Jules Stein's longtime banker at First National Bank, was Goldblatt's banker, too; and though Heymann (perhaps influenced by Stein's much touted distaste for Korshak) at first opposed Goldblatt's retaining Korshak, he then did an about-face, recommending him to other First National clients as well.

Soon, Korshak was ubiquitous. Herbert Siegel, later the chairman of Chris-Craft, recounted how he had first met Korshak. Siegel and his partner, Delbert Coleman, had bought the J. P. Seeburg Corporation, which manufactured jukeboxes, and the Teamsters were threatening a strike. "Someone said, hire Sidney Korshak," Siegel said. "So we called Jay Pritzker [chairman of the Hyatt chain]. 'Is Korshak the best?' 'Absolutely.' We called the chairman of Motorola. Same question. 'Absolutely.' We hired him. The problem went away immediately. And what he wanted for his fee was a new Cadillac, which then was worth about $5,000. I guess he didn't want there to be any record of it."

The Korshak magic worked because the unions with which he dealt—especially, giant organizations like the Teamsters, the laundry workers, and the hotel and restaurant unions—recognized the power behind him. Korshak operated in close league with Murray "the Camel" Humphreys, a quick-witted, charming Welshman who had organized protection rackets under Capone, and was widely viewed as the mastermind of the Outfit's infiltration of labor unions. Korshak also enjoyed a strong bond with Hoffa, forged when Hoffa was a young man trying to fight his way up in the Teamsters, and Korshak helped him, according to Chicago columnist Irving Kupcinet. "Sid was the closest person to Hoffa," asserted Leo Geffner, a lawyer in Los Angeles who dealt with Korshak in racetrack labor negotiations in later years, and became his friend. "He was close to people all the way up and down the line in the Teamsters. He made cash payoffs to business agents—$5,000 here, $3,000 there. I *know* that. That's the way it was—to keep labor peace, you'd find a corrupt business agent, and pay him off."

For Korshak to operate in the legitimate business world, it was important that his mob associations be discreet, so that those executives of major public corporations who wanted to deal with him could. Arturo Pettorino, the maître d' for many Outfit restaurants in Chicago, said that Korshak was careful not to be seated at such places with Tony Accardo or Sam Giancana (who succeeded Accardo as head of the Outfit), though Korshak was close to them both. And, according to the FBI, though Korshak and Humphreys kept in frequent touch, the two attempted to disguise their communication; when Humphreys left phone messages for Korshak, he would use the alias "Mr. Lincoln." Indeed, since Bioff had testified about Korshak's affiliation with the mob, Korshak for years had managed to escape any more damning publicity—until an article by Lester Velie, entitled "The Capone Gang Muscles into Big-Time Politics," appeared in *Collier's* in September 1950. "Legal advisor to some of the mob is Sidney Korshak," Velie wrote; he also described Korshak as "the closest man" to Jacob Arvey, then Democratic party chairman for Cook County, and the political boss who was Abraham Lincoln Marovitz's patron. Korshak charged that the Velie story was "a series of diabolical lies."

Shortly after the article appeared, Senator Estes Kefauver arrived in Chicago to hold committee hearings on organized crime, and subpoenaed Korshak to appear in a closed session. It was an unnerving time, and not only for Korshak and his underworld associates; apparently legitimate businessmen—even, for that matter, Jules Stein—had cause for concern. Just before the hearings were scheduled to begin, a former police lieutenant, William Drury, was machine-gunned at his home, and Marvin Bas, a lawyer, was shot to death on a street corner. Both had been interviewed by investigators for the Senate committee, and were about to be committee witnesses. Luis Kutner, who later wrote about his experiences with Capone as a young man, was now a practicing lawyer. His son, Tony Kutner, said, "We had been living in a not fancy place and all of a sudden, I came back from camp and we'd moved to this big house and I was Tony the rich kid—my father had gotten some big fee from the mob. And I remember the night Drury and Marvin Bas were killed. My father got a call that he was next, and we turned out all the lights and went down in the basement, where we spent the night, and there were police guarding outside."

Like many hundreds of other gang murders in Chicago in these years, the Drury and Bas killings were never solved; those who knew would not speak, and those who chanced by incriminating information understood the virtue of silence. In the late forties, Ted Raynor, a young lawyer in Chicago whose uncle had been a bartender at Colosimo's, and whose small law office was next door to the Korshak firm, began representing a trade association of mostly nightclub owners. "Sid got hold of me," Raynor began, "and he said, 'Listen, kid, you're getting involved with people that maybe you don't want to get involved with. You're a nice young man, you're doing well—'

"I said, 'It's okay, I understand, I can handle myself.'

"He said, 'Give me your word of honor that if anything disturbing happens, you'll tell me and get your ass out of there. And if I hear something, I'll tell you.' "

Raynor assented. Then one night, he continued, "I was at a meeting of nightclub owners. They were talking about some lawyer who'd been shot on a street corner. The next day, Sidney said, 'I think you have to get out of there. They should not have said what they said in front of you. You've got three kids, you can't afford to get in trouble. What if you're called to testify?' So," Raynor concluded, "I stopped representing them." Asked whether the lawyer whose murder they had been discussing was Marvin Bas, Raynor said he did not recall.

It was an illustration of the warning that Korshak would give others, too, according to his close friend Hollywood producer Robert Evans, who had received the admonition himself. "Sidney's first commandment was, the greatest insurance policy for continued breathing is continued silence," Evans said.

Korshak himself assumed a more active role vis-à-vis Kefauver, according to an article by *New York Times* reporter Seymour Hersh, which was published more than a quarter century later. "One trusted Korshak friend and business associate recalled in an interview that shortly after the committee's visit Mr. Korshak had shown him infrared photographs of Senator Kefauver in an obviously compromising position with a young woman." According to Hersh's source, the young woman had been supplied by the Chicago underworld, and the camera planted in Kefauver's room at the Drake Hotel. Kefauver left town abruptly—before the public hearings had even begun. This master stroke against Kefauver was said to have been Korshak's; and once again, in the circles where such things were common knowledge, his talents were much admired, and his power grew.

For many years, Chicago remained Korshak's home base. He had an office there, and the fact that his brother and law partner, Marshall, served for many years as a state senator and then, remarkably enough, city treasurer, lent a degree of legitimacy to the Korshak name. By the fifties, however, Sidney had established his wife, Bernice, and their two small boys in Los Angeles. There, his professional existence seemed almost chimerical. He never took the California bar exam, so he was not licensed to practice law. At first, he worked out of the Associated Booking Company office in Beverly Hills. (Ted Raynor, who visited Korshak there, recalled that "the door was *locked,* it was really hard to get in. I thought that was strange—but then I figured, that's Sidney. And he had this beautiful big office with his desk completely clear. There might just be a message on it, if it wasn't from one of the boys.") Later, Korshak would use the Beverly Hills office of Las Vegas's Riviera Casino, or, occasionally, the law offices of one of his friends. He took no notes; at most, he might scribble a number on a torn piece of paper or matchbook cover. (As he told reporters once, with lawyerly precision, "My records will show I never represented any of the hoodlums.") He was said to run his phone lines at times through friends' offices. Even so, he used the phone only guardedly. A good friend of his, who was an MCA agent, recalled, "He would never talk to you on the phone. 'C'mon, let's take a walk,' he'd say, whenever he had something to talk about. And we'd walk through the streets of Beverly Hills."

It is hard to imagine how anyone familiar with his habits could have thought he was simply "a lawyer," as Wasserman had commented. Indeed, there seems to have been among Korshak's friends little mystery about whose interests he represented. Many years later, Bernice and Sidney celebrated their fiftieth wedding anniversary at a party at the Wassermans' home. Robert Evans toasted them by reading a passage from his newly written autobiography, in which he described the Korshaks' having just returned from their honeymoon, and Bernice's scanning a batch of messages that had been left for Sidney. " 'George Washington called, everything is status quo. Thomas Jefferson called, urgent, please call ASAP. Abraham Lincoln, must speak with you, important . . .'

"She began laughing. 'Your friends sure have a strange sense of humor. Who are they?'

" 'Exactly who they said they were. Any other questions?'

"Fifty years later, Bernice has never asked another question," Evans concluded.

It was a punch line that could be appreciated by the people gathered that night at the Wassermans'. For most of Korshak's friends in Los Angeles understood that while he might on occasion volunteer (telling stories about the Capone era, for example), they were never to inquire. That was just fine; they were, by and large, incurious. Many of them—people like Tony Martin, Cyd Charisse, Dinah Shore, Robert Evans, Jill St. John—were helped by Korshak in various ways, and regarded their benefactor with a mix of gratitude and awe. But Korshak's relationship with Wasserman was different. If power was the measure, the two men were essentially peers—each wielding vast influence in companion worlds that sometimes overlapped. And though they were connected by business, several people who knew them both asserted that Korshak was Wasserman's closest friend.

Certainly Korshak was his most useful friend—which, for the profoundly utilitarian Wasserman, may have amounted to the same thing. Wasserman knew Hoffa, but Korshak knew him much better; Korshak was the most valuable intermediary to the Teamsters that Wasserman could have. And once MCA moved into TV production, the Teamsters were critical to the company's success. In the tightly scheduled television business—much more than the movie business—a strike could be devastating. And if the Teamsters were to strike, the world of production would stop. They controlled everything that had to be driven to and from a set—props, food, portable toilets, the film itself. Moreover, the Teamsters were so feared that few attempted to cross their picket lines, and their throwing in with one side or the other in a labor war could be critical (as when they sided with the IATSE against the CSU). It was almost like having a private army at your disposal. Weldon Wertz, who joined the Teamsters in 1941 and spent decades in Hollywood, said, "The Teamsters were rough. Jake Nunez was a Teamster.

He did something bad. He was crucified in a freight car here in L.A.— and they found him when the freight car was opened in Chicago." And the Teamsters pension funds (most notoriously, the Central States Pension Fund) provided pools of hundreds of millions of dollars for those with the right connections to draw on for loans. Roy Brewer said that Wasserman had used Teamsters money when MCA had started to go into TV production aggressively in the early fifties, and when he employed many of the stars, longtime contract players in the MGM stable who had just had their contracts liquidated. Asked how he knew that was so, Brewer replied, "Everyone knew it! I was very close to the Teamsters. They'd helped me in the strike. And Korshak, I believe, was the one who arranged that financing."

Korshak was famous for his sway over the Teamsters. The young MCA agent Harris Katleman had become friendly with Korshak because Korshak was close to Harris's uncle, Beldon Katleman, who owned the El Rancho. (Once, when Harris had been invited to a dinner party at Misty Mountain, Wasserman had remarked dryly to him, "Don't let Jules find out Beldon's your uncle, or he'll never invite you back.") "Sidney Korshak *controlled* the Teamsters," Harris maintained. He recalled an incident when Korshak went to Los Angeles's Hollywood Park racetrack, which was owned by Marjorie Everett, a longtime Korshak adversary from Chicago. "He went to the Turf Club, and Marge Everett threw him out—because he was a gangster! The Teamsters struck the next day and closed down Hollywood Park. She called and apologized to Sidney—and the Teamsters quit the strike."

Katleman emphasized, too, that Korshak's power was not limited to the Teamsters. In Chicago, Korshak had specialized in labor but also displayed an eclecticism—helping to win early release for the convicts in the movie industry payoffs case, for example, and allegedly blackmailing Kefauver. Furthermore, he had a reputation in Chicago for being particularly adept at making payoffs to judges in both criminal and commercial cases—a general practice that Judge Marovitz had described as almost institutionalized. Now that Korshak was operating more and more in the movie colony, he appeared to have even more wide-ranging influence; for those who enjoyed his protection, many of life's problems—some nuisances, some momentous—would simply disappear. Richard Gully got in a car accident, and the other motorist sued him; Gully told Korshak, and the suit was dropped. Performers like Tony Martin incurred big gambling debts in Las Vegas; Korshak had them cleared (as he said to Bob Evans once, after Evans had lost heavily, "I could take the markers and use 'em as toilet paper"). Mickey Rudin, Frank Sinatra's lawyer (and someone with no mean connections himself), desperately wanted to get his wife on a ship to Europe when there were no more cabins. He tried, and failed. He asked Korshak, and the next thing he knew she was on. "They gave her one of the officer's cabins," Rudin said. "And after they got her on the ship, I got a call from the travel agent—'Would you please let the person to whom it was important know that it has been done?' " Rudin added, "He was very close to Giancana"—longtime head of the Chicago Outfit—"though I always thought it was Giancana who called the shots."

For most of his friends, Korshak did the occasional favor; but with Wasserman, Korshak seemed to be almost on call—a uniquely proficient kind of chef de bureau. "Lew and Sidney were joined at the hip in the fifties," Katleman declared. "Sidney did whatever Lew needed." Given the scope of his domain, Wasserman had a range of problems that tested even Korshak's versatility. "Korshak was a fixer," declared Chet Migden, executive director of the Screen Actors Guild for many years. "The studios had a lot of money invested in actors, writers, directors. And when those people got in trouble, they needed fixers." Korshak's reach into the judicial system was not always illicit; he came to count some of L.A.'s most powerful lawyers and judges among his good friends; he would often have lunch with Superior Court Judge Laurence Rittenband, for example, who presided over both civil and criminal cases in his Santa Monica courtroom. Sometimes, though, it was Korshak's contacts in a different world that were required. MCA was shooting a movie in a Mafia-dominated neighborhood in Boston;

the script was set in the twenties, so the TV aerials were a jarring anachronism—but the producer had had no success in trying to persuade the residents to take them down. Wasserman called Korshak; within hours the aerials were down, according to an MCA executive. And there were some situations—say, a deal that was difficult for MCA—in which Korshak's mere presence might win the day. "When Sidney was brought in to negotiate, it was very powerful," Ted Raynor commented. "Dealing with him, you never knew what the consequences would be."

The SAG waiver that allowed MCA to be at once agent and TV producer had been an amazing boon, enabling MCA in the space of a few years to dominate TV production; but MCA's very success made it vulnerable, for it highlighted the waiver's brazenness. Wasserman knew that SAG would not be able to withstand much longer the criticism of its unique dispensation; and the U.S. Justice Department was beginning to scrutinize MCA's operating in tandem as well. If Wasserman was forced to choose between the agency and production businesses, his preference was unmistakable: it was for the business *he* had started. And by the late fifties—though there was no public hint that MCA might one day exit the agency business—Wasserman had begun positioning the company to do just that. He had been strongly acquisition-minded in the agency business, persuading Stein that MCA should buy up many other agencies here and also abroad. MCA had become, as Stein liked to say, "the largest agency the world has ever known." Now, Wasserman's appetite for acquisition continued unabated—but, this time, he was building a diversified entertainment company.

In 1957, Wasserman set out to acquire Paramount's pre-1948 film library. Prescient as that may seem, he was not the first to recognize the value of leasing movies to television. Two years earlier, a company called General Teleradio had bought RKO's pre-1948 library for about $18 million, and then a syndicate led by the Canadian stock promoter,

Louis "Uncle Lou" Chesler, who had ties to Meyer Lansky, had purchased Warners's pre-1948 library for about $21 million. (The talent unions were demanding residuals for any films shown on television after the Paramount Decree came into effect, so agreements involving those post-1948 films remained blocked.) At first, these deals seemed providential to the studios, still trying to cushion their losses from the forced sale of their cinema chains; but it rather quickly became clear that they had sold too cheaply. Three years after the Warners deal, with television's appetite for these movies driving up their value, company accountants figured they had underpriced their films by about $35 million. In truth, losing control of the negatives of these old movies at almost any price was shortsighted; the studios should have known from experience (and Wasserman was well aware) that the real money was in distribution. Barney Balaban somehow overlooked that fact, and became persuaded that it made sense to sell Paramount's library at a much better price than RKO and Warners had done. That price, he told Jules Stein in their discussions, was $50 million.

Stein refused, declaring that "if things went wrong I would lose everything I had spent a lifetime to acquire." Then, with Doris, he departed for a trip around the world, and left Wasserman to explore whether a deal might still be made. When it came to acquisition, Wasserman's desire was greater than Stein's, generally—and this was a deal on which he was especially keen. What he contrived, finally, was the following: MCA would make a down payment of $10 million on signing; once MCA had regained that amount from movie sales, Paramount would receive a percentage of their ongoing sales, until Paramount had received another $25 million; and the remaining $15 million would only be payable if the library's sales exceeded a certain amount.

Wasserman and Balaban shook hands on this deal, and the lawyers went to work drafting the papers. A young attorney named George Gallantz was representing Paramount; he was a protégé of Ed Weisl, who seemed to be on all sides of this transaction, as he often was in

matters involving the closely connected MCA and Paramount. Gallantz recalled that Wasserman had insisted that the deal must close in
February 1958, before the TV selling season started. "Lew walked into
the room, shut the door, and said, '*Look*—we are not leaving. This has
to be done.' He was with us a lot of the time. Any impasse, he was
there," Gallantz said. Wasserman made a very distinct impression on
Gallantz, still vivid decades later. "I saw him quite a few times, dealt
with him extensively here. There was never a conversation you would
ordinarily have over time in these situations. 'Do you live in the city or
the suburbs? Are you married? Do you have children? Do you play
golf?' There was *none* of that with Lew. He kept everyone at a distance.
I was a smart kid—I understood he did not want me to reduce the distance, and I didn't try."

For the closing, everything was transported by train to Wilmington,
Delaware, to avoid New York sales taxes; the lawyers and all their papers were given their own railway car. "At the closing, there was supposed to be a $10 million down payment," Gallantz continued. "I said
to Lew, how do you plan to transfer the $10 million? (Usually it's not
sitting somewhere in a savings account—it's out working for you somewhere, and it's transferred by wire.) So I asked him, and he said, what
do you mean? He wrote a $10 million check—and signed it himself.
The check was from a bank in Delaware—I'm sure the money got there
twenty-four hours before. I thought it was odd."

The $50 million deal was widely viewed at the time as terribly rich,
and perhaps even a serious blunder by Wasserman; but his critics may
not have known of the risk-limiting structure he had devised. Nor did
they know what an associate of Wasserman's asserted—that Wasserman had about $80 million in sales commitments before the deal
closed. With his experience in television, Wasserman no doubt had a
keener appreciation of the values in distribution than most studio executives at this time. But probably not even he could imagine just how
valuable these film libraries would become decades later, when the
original TV appetite ("like the great maw of the sperm whale," as Mil-

ton MacKaye had written) would be enlarged, many times over, by ever multiplying channels of distribution. According to Wasserman, MCA would eventually make over $1 billion on this investment of $50 million. "Not a bad return," he commented, with thinly disguised pleasure.

Wasserman quickly followed this coup with another. MCA had been leasing space at Republic Studios for Revue's TV production, but Wasserman was ready now for MCA to have a studio lot of its own. He negotiated a deal with Milton Rackmil, president of Decca Records Inc., which controlled Universal Pictures Company, Inc.

MCA would pay $11,250,000 for all the land and facilities of Universal—and then Universal would lease back studio facilities to make a number of movies for ten years, at a rental of $1 million annually to MCA. Universal was, in effect, paying the cost of being acquired by MCA. It was a remarkable deal—pronounced by Stein "one of the greatest deals Lew ever conceived and made for MCA."

"I was shocked when I found out the price," said a then executive at Universal. "Four hundred acres, all of the offices and equipment, for $11.25 million!" This executive maintained that it was Wasserman's aggressive romancing of Rackmil that had won him such an extraordinary deal. It closed in February 1959; and something that occurred then stuck in this person's mind. He knew it was customary for the buyer's bank to transfer the funds to the seller's at a closing. "But Lew wrote a check for $11.25 million! It surprised me."

Even at its bargain price, however, the Universal acquisition took some daring. MCA executive Albert Dorskind (who was fond of saying that MCA stood for Muscle, Cash, and Attorneys) worked on the Universal transaction. He pointed out that it cost $7.5 million a year just to maintain the studio (paying staff, insurance, taxes)—so MCA was taking on a responsibility to pay out $75 million over ten years. "That was a big overhead—we had to produce enough to make it worthwhile. It was very risky. Lew had guts." Dorskind also oversaw the extensive construction that was to be done at the studio after the MCA acquisition. It was that planned construction that gave him the idea of buying the Del E. Webb Corporation—made up of a construction company, large landholdings, and, according to Dorskind, interests in a number of Las Vegas casinos. Webb's construction company had built Bugsy Siegel's Flamingo, as well as the Sahara. "Lew thought it was great. We knew more about the casino business, and the talent for it than anyone—so it would make sense to own a piece of it," Dorskind said. "We were in Phoenix, negotiating, and Jules called. He said, 'Are you trying to buy that?' We said we were. 'Well, the chair says no.'

"Jules said he didn't spend his lifetime living as he had to get involved with those people," Dorskind concluded.

Moving to further solidify MCA's strength as a production company, Wasserman began aggressively adding to his store of product. In 1959, MCA had already owned about 1,650 shows outright; in addition, it owned, on the average, a 50 percent interest in about 525 additional programs, which it had co-produced with other producers. For years, MCA had been setting its clients up in corporations for tax purposes, and often MCA would finance those corporations; then they would advise the clients that their companies should back other shows. Sometimes MCA would own a piece of these companies; sometimes they would own a piece of the shows that they placed in those companies; sometimes they would distribute a piece of the shows to clients whom they especially wanted to please. It was a dizzying financial maze that no outsider could penetrate, and only MCA (or, more likely, only Wasserman) knew all its disparate parts. For example, Jack Benny had created J&M Productions at MCA's urging. Then MCA told Benny to add new properties to his corporation: *Checkmate, Ichabod and Me, The Marge and Gower Champion Show, The Gisele MacKenzie Show. Checkmate* was owned by J&M and by Revue, in a fifty-fifty split (and MCA gave 5 percent to a writer, Dick Berg, who was a favorite of Wasserman's at that time). And it was also one of the shows MCA agents demanded CBS buy, as a condition of retaining *The Jack Benny Show,* according to CBS executives.

Now, MCA was trying to buy in some of these companies, in order to gain the rights to their programs. Irving Fein, Benny's manager, who also had an interest in J&M, recalled that MCA bought J&M in 1961, in a stock-for-stock transaction that garnered Benny about $3 million. "We owned about eighty-six filmed shows at that time, and we were making twenty-seven shows a year. We had two years to go on our contract at CBS, so we could have had many more shows, and sold it for much, much more. It was a terrible mistake—but MCA convinced Jack to do it," Fein said.

Not everyone whom Wasserman targeted proved as malleable as Benny. The Goodson and Todman Company was the producer of the most popular game shows (including *What's My Line*) and Harris Katleman recalled that Wasserman had instructed him to try to develop a good relationship with its principals. "I took Goodson out a lot. Finally, I negotiated a deal for us to buy them for $12 million—which was a lot then. Lew and Jules were flying in to New York. And then Mark Goodson called me on Sunday night at ten o'clock, saying 'I want out of the deal! I don't want to work for anybody.' I met Lew at the airport—he was *destroying* me all the way in to the city. He said he wanted to meet with Goodson. We went over there and Lew said, 'Do you remember Phillips H. Lord?' (He was the Goodson-Todman of radio.) 'You know what's happened to him? He's broke! And that's what's going to happen to you!' " Katleman explained that MCA had tried to buy Lord's company, and he had refused.

Larry White, Leland Hayward's assistant before the MCA acquisition of Hayward-Deverich, said that it was hard for many people to refuse to be bought by MCA. "If you didn't sell, they'd kill you! Economically, I mean. They'd tear your guts out." But when MCA had approached him about buying his shows, he had actually been a willing seller. White had been producing a series of circus shows for television; Sonny Werblin, acting as his agent, had sold the shows to Kintner in a thirteen-show package to be aired on NBC. "The show sold for $100,000 a week, so MCA was getting $10,000. It wasn't enough for them. We were getting into our third year. They wanted to buy me out. They wanted to own all the residual rights to the programs. They were doing the Jack Benny deals at that time, it fit into that pattern. I was willing. One day, they stopped negotiating. The next thing I knew, they were selling the shows into syndication without asking me." By this time, another MCA agent, Herb Rosenthal, was handling the account. "I said to Herb, how can you do this?

" 'We got the rights.'

" 'How did you get the rights?'

" 'Lew gave your partner $100,000.' "

White's partner was a man named Joe Cates, producer of the *$64,000 Question* quiz show, which ended in a rigging scandal. "Cates never told me! They had been talking about a deal worth several million dollars—and then they got it for $100,000! I could have sued—but I wasn't capable of doing it. Lew *knew* that. He was so nice to me after that." White paused. "I feel awful, really, that I was so passive. The worst of it is that I knew what was going on and I never said anything. But you couldn't go to the government. MCA had what I call 'scare power.' It was as bad as McCarthy. Lew could put you through the wringer, and ruin your career."

———

By 1961, it was evident to Wasserman and Stein that time was running out for them in the agency business. About three years earlier, the Justice Department's antitrust division had commenced an investigation of MCA, and it was now energized by the interest of the new attorney general, Robert F. Kennedy. Stein would always insist that Kennedy's interest had been sparked by Frank Sinatra, whom Wasserman had clashed with and ultimately "fired" as a client, and who, Stein believed, was carrying out a vendetta against MCA. But one really did not have to resort to conspiracy thinking to explain why the Justice Department was focused on MCA; indeed, the more interesting question would be why no fewer than eight investigations of MCA by the antitrust division had been aborted since 1941.

During the fall and winter of 1960, a young Justice Department attorney named Leonard Posner, assigned to the MCA investigation, had begun conducting interviews in New York. Among many others, he had spoken with Pat Weaver, the former president of NBC. Weaver, who described MCA as "tough and efficient," told Posner about MCA's use of packaging, which was a version of the antitrust violation of a tie-in—that is, using one's power over one product to sell another (which is illegal because it means that others, who do not have power over the most desirable products, cannot break into the market). The situation had arisen when NBC wanted the actor Phil Silvers for a show it was producing. (Silvers had been a star on Broadway and, by the late fifties, was also enormously successful on television; he played Sergeant Bilko on the hit series *The Phil Silvers Show.*) "NBC had production facilities and was ready to go ahead with top scripts, writers, and directors and had its own facilities in Burbank, California, and merely wanted a star from MCA," Posner quoted Weaver as having told him. "MCA would agree to furnish Phil Silvers but only if it got a commission not only on Silvers but also on the salary of all producers, directors, writers, etc., employed in the show. If NBC remonstrated that it wanted the best writers, and that some of the best writers were not those in the MCA stable, MCA would simply say, 'That's the deal; that's the way it's got to be.'" Not only were such practices anti-competitive, but they could also result in MCA's serving their own interest to the detriment of their client's. An independent producer might be prepared to pay a star $10,000 for a show. But if MCA were to demand 10 percent of all the above-the-line costs—say, $25,000—despite the fact that the independent producer had already arranged for a director and other talent, then that would mean that the producer would have to pay a total cost of $35,000 for a star worth only $10,000. And that might well mean the producer could not afford to hire the star.

Weaver also told Posner that MCA's packaging in TV was an adaptation of what it had long been doing in the movie industry; if a studio wanted a top box office star, MCA would insist on furnishing all the talent for the picture. Its leverage in these situations was enormous, because the top stars were the only ones who were bankable—without at least one of them in a movie, it would be almost impossible to obtain bank financing. And MCA represented at least 70 percent of these

stars, according to Weaver's estimate. (*Fortune* magazine in 1960 esti-
mated about 60 percent.) Included in its roster were stars such as Mar-
lon Brando, Gregory Peck, Kirk Douglas, Clark Gable, Jimmy Stewart,
Marilyn Monroe, Shirley MacLaine, Tony Curtis, and Janet Leigh; and
personalities such as Jack Benny, Ed Sullivan, and Ralph Edwards.
Also immensely bankable were directors Alfred Hitchcock, Mervyn
LeRoy, Leland Hayward, and John Ford; and writers Tennessee
Williams and William Inge.

Mike Dann, who had been Weaver's assistant at NBC, was also interviewed by Posner, and elaborated on what Weaver had told him.
"General Sarnoff would frequently bellow in rage at the idea of paying
tremendous commissions to MCA for packaging the show when NBC
did its own packaging," Posner quoted Dann as having told him. But
Weaver had had considerable experience with MCA, and he knew if he
wanted its talent he had to play by its rules; so despite the General's
protests, MCA would collect a commission on all above-the-line costs.
Later, Dann told Posner, MCA extended their demands to a commission on below-the-line costs as well. (Another witness told Posner that
MCA's view of below-the-line costs was expansive; in one instance,
they had taken a percentage of what a trucking company had charged
for hauling equipment, and a cut of the truck driver's salary as well.)

Dann, who had worked for Weaver in the early fifties, had been inspired by his boss's almost messianic conviction that television, properly developed, could become a force to transform people's lives. That
it had instead become such a pedestrian, even dulling, medium, Dann
attributed in part to the pervasive influence of MCA. He argued that
creativity was being stifled because MCA had so appropriated the production business that there was a dearth of other programming
sources; and MCA was "merely interested in money, not creativity, and
hence wants only shows which are in the standard format design, to
bring in the biggest ratings by appealing to the largest mass audience."

In February 1961, Posner wrote a lengthy memorandum describing
what he believed to be MCA's antitrust violations. He acknowledged
that some of the allegations were based on hearsay but said that he

considered the overall picture "generally reliable." And he had, indeed, assembled many elements that were critical to the MCA narrative. Among them were tie-ins, exclusive contracts, packaging, demanding packaging commissions even when MCA had not done the packaging, conflicts of interest, omnibus contracts, coercive dealings, blacklists, bribes, procuring women, luring talent from other agencies with houses, cars, and huge sums of money, withholding of top talent from competitors. "Perhaps the most striking measure of MCA's power over networks," Posner wrote, "is the fact that MCA is able to insist on commission for *all* above-the-line costs (talent), even where the network supplies most of the talent, and for *all* below-the-line costs (facilities, production components), even where the network produces the show." He concluded that MCA's power was ever increasing—due to its control of a large percentage of the most sought after talent, the largest percentage of productions on network prime time, production facilities, literary works, and its unparalleled entrée to networks, advertising agencies, and sponsors. "Each dominant position feeds and reinforces MCA's control of other facets," Posner wrote. "The totality of control, through all these facets, is such that MCA wields monopoly power."

The government investigation would continue for nearly eighteen months. During that time, Bobby Kennedy repeatedly would ask in internal memoranda to be informed of the progress of the investigation, and he would urge "faster action." On one occasion early in the investigation, Posner explained that "it would be important to try to have a grand jury in the MCA matter because the witnesses were frightened to death and we wouldn't expect to be able to get any specific direct evidence without the cloak of secrecy of a grand jury." He also said that there was no likelihood of obtaining any direct evidence from MCA; he had been told that "MCA is not only cleansing its files but has actually maintained specific records in anticipation of our forthcoming antitrust suit." To that end, it had also amended its behavior, he concluded. As he wrote in a memo in August 1961, "MCA has refined its practices in television to the point where the violations are not readily perceptible, and it will require proof of a most difficult order . . . the evidence of tie-ins, once so flagrant in the band business, have become the most subtle type of practice in the television field, where the advertising agency (knowing what the facts of life are) themselves offer to buy poor shows, knowing that that is the only way they are going to get good ones." He also noted that the evidence thus far gathered on the West Coast was not quite as strong as that obtained in New York. "People on the Coast are extremely frightened and chary of talking against MCA."

On August 31, 1961, Lee Loevinger, the assistant attorney general in charge of the antitrust division, wrote a memo to J. Edgar Hoover, director of the FBI, requesting an FBI investigation of MCA. He placed particular emphasis on MCA's relationship with NBC, saying that many in the television industry believed it was a "captive market" of MCA, and that Robert Kintner may have entered into "a secret agreement (written or oral) with MCA providing for a continuous flow of programs." Summarizing the thrust of the government's investigation, he stated that MCA's drive to monopolize television production appeared to be built on two pillars: the blanket waiver from SAG, and an exclusive agreement with NBC. He was asking the FBI to look for evidence of conspiracy in both.

A few days later, the Justice Department's requests for a grand jury and FBI investigation were authorized. Almost immediately, articles appeared in the trade press stating that MCA was planning to divest its talent agency from its production business. The Screen Actors Guild, furthermore, announced that by the end of 1961, it would revoke production waivers it had given to talent agencies, with no extensions beyond June 1962; by that date, therefore, MCA would have to be out of one business or the other. SAG executives would always maintain that they took this action independently of MCA. "We told Posner we were going to shut MCA down, that it had gone too far. Posner should have been thrilled with that—but he didn't know how to accept a victory," SAG executive Chet Migden said. He added, "Lew knew it couldn't go on, it had gotten too big."

Wasserman and Stein evidently thought that the SAG move was likely to short-circuit the government's plans—and, as Migden indicated, even give the prosecutors some reward for their pains. Stein would later say that he and Wasserman had been making plans to cut away the talent agency for some time. "We wanted to do what the movie companies did with their theaters," said Stein, referring to the divestiture following the Paramount Decree, in which his friend Ed Weisl had been much involved. And Stein—in traditional MCA style—had also been active on another front. Shortly after President Kennedy took office in January 1961, Jacqueline Kennedy had decided to conduct a massive restoration program in the White House. The Steins (notwithstanding Jules's right-wing political views) volunteered to contribute. And on May 11, 1961, Jacqueline had sent them a handwritten note. "It is a wonderful thing that anyone would be so generous—and I'm so happy it is you—as all I hear from everyone is how beautiful—and perfectly arranged your collection is—and what great taste you have.

"There was never any Chippendale or Queen Anne in the White House, which breaks my heart as I love it the most. . . . There is one other place I would be so grateful for your help. . . . It is the 2nd floor hall (outside our yellow oval room—I'm sure you saw it with Tish [Letitia Baldrige, her social secretary]. It is just a sad collection of tired old mismatched stuffed chairs and department store tables and lamps. It looks like the lobby of a rather dreary hotel. . . . the reason this hall is so important is that all the important visitors the President brings upstairs pass through it and wait in it. It is where foreign dignitaries assemble before state dinners. All it has now worth keeping are 3 lovely old crystal chandeliers—and the Catlin paintings of Indians I have borrowed from the Smithsonian, which they may loan to us permanently."

In the fall of 1961, however, Justice Department officials contacted Baldrige and told her that the Steins' intended gifts could not be accepted. And Bobby Kennedy agreed with his prosecutors' decision to move aggressively with their grand jury and FBI investigation. (As Loevinger wrote in a memo, "The Attorney General has indicated a personal interest in this case and has directed that it be investigated fully and promptly.") MCA's indicated plans to divest itself voluntarily of the agency had not had the desired effect. Posner was convinced that unless the divestiture were supervised by a court, the possibility of behind-the-scenes cooperation between the talent agency and production company would remain; that the split would not be bona fide. It seemed to him, too, that the SAG ultimatum and MCA action were utterly orchestrated; he was convinced that MCA was dictating the course of events, not being acted upon.

Indeed, relations between Wasserman and the SAG officials had grown only more incestuous since they had granted him the waiver in 1952 and MCA had become the most active producer in Hollywood. For years, SAG members had been demanding that they be paid residuals when movies in which they had appeared were shown on television. A great deal hinged on how this matter was resolved for MCA—with its ownership of the Paramount pre-1948 library (and, also, some believed, Wasserman's plans to acquire the rest of Universal Pictures, now that he owned its physical plant). In 1959, Reagan—who had left the SAG presidency in 1952 after MCA got its waiver—had been asked to resume that office and lead the union's negotiations with the studios. "We needed him," Jack Dales, SAG's executive director, said. "There was no other actor like him. He could make people *believe.*" Reagan, in his autobiography *Where's the Rest of Me?*, would write that he had not really wanted to become SAG president again, since he thought it had taken a toll on his acting career. "I called my agent, (MCA's) Lew Wasserman—who else? I knew that he shared my belief that my career had suffered. To tell the truth, I was positive he'd reiterate that belief and I could say 'no' with a clear conscience. Well, I pulled the ripcord and the chute didn't open. Lew said he thought I should take the job." After a bitter six-week strike, Reagan recommended the following settlement: the studios would create a pension and welfare plan for actors—and the actors would forfeit all claims to residual payments for television showings of movies made prior to 1960. For decades to come, Reagan would be vilified for having rec-

ommended this forfeiture of pre-1960 residuals. Shortly after this settlement was made, Reagan resigned the presidency of SAG to become
a partner in a joint production venture with MCA and Revue Productions.

In February 1962, when Reagan was called before the grand jury,
he was questioned about both the 1952 waiver and also the 1960 strike
settlement. Among other things, the government was interested in
whether he had an ownership interest in films or TV productions during his tenure as SAG president. SAG tradition had long held that its
officers should not be producers, because that could pose a conflict of
interest; indeed, Reagan had first risen to the SAG presidency back in
1947 when seven of the union's top officers resigned because they had
financial interests in films in which they appeared; Reagan, the highest-
ranking officer not to resign, was elected to fill the president's un-
expired term. Rumors that Reagan had such financial interests
himself—but, unlike his colleagues, had chosen not to disclose them—
had surfaced when he was named to his sixth term as president in
1959. SAG's official publication, *Screen Actor,* had come to his defense
in an editorial in December 1959, stating that Reagan was the object of
"vile and unscrupulous tactics" and "false rumors." However, in his
grand jury testimony, which would remain secret for more than twenty
years until obtained by *Variety,* Reagan acknowledged that he had been
given a "25% ownership" interest in the reuse rights of *General Electric Theater* in the spring of 1959—so the rumors, which had been so
heatedly denied, were in fact true. Reagan testified that he had been
granted this interest in discussions with Wasserman.

What the government was looking for, however, was not just signs
of favor like Reagan's job as host of *General Electric Theater* or his financial interest in the show, but evidence of outright payola; Reagan's
tax records, and other SAG officials' as well, were examined. By this
time, the government had decided to focus its attempt to prove conspiracy on the MCA relationship with SAG, and not NBC. "The case
was twofold," said Gordon Spivack, a Justice Department lawyer who
ultimately made the recommendation to Bobby Kennedy on the dispo-

sition of this case. "Did they bribe someone to get the waiver? And did they do these tie-ins? The waiver *looked* like they must have bribed someone. But we put Reagan in front of the grand jury, and he said he got nothing—and we weren't able to find any checks," said Spivack, evincing a certain naïveté about the ways of MCA. "And as for the tie-ins (we won't give you this actor unless you take this package, or we won't give you this show unless you take these), we had a lot of smoke but no fire. People would either say it hadn't happened or, if they did feel coerced, you'd ask why, and they'd say, well, he didn't *say* you have to do x, it was more of a feeling, or 'I *understood* I had to.' Now, maybe they'd gotten to these people—I'm not going to tell you the investigation wasn't inept. They had a small staff, seven or eight people. They were putting hundreds of witnesses in front of the grand jury. They needed to locate them. So they decided to use the FBI. That in itself was okay. I said to them, so how did the FBI find these people? They said, they went to the union [SAG]. I said, the *union?* How could they go to the union? We are *investigating* the union! They were going with lists of people, turning over the lists—and, in some cases, a series of questions, too. So the union knew who was going to be called before the grand jury!"

Spivack concluded that however the investigation might have been subverted, the evidence was not strong enough to bring a criminal case. Posner and the other staff attorneys, however, disagreed; they believed MCA should be indicted, and they were afraid that it was MCA's power that would somehow prevent it from happening. In any event, at a meeting with Bobby Kennedy and a couple dozen Justice Department lawyers in June 1962, Spivack explained his recommendation that the government should bring a civil, but not a criminal, suit. "Bobby Kennedy said, 'Did you talk to Frank?' " Spivack recalled. "I said we had called him several times but he was out of the country. (Kennedy was then very tight with Sinatra, and Sinatra and Wasserman were on the outs. MCA had dumped him. And Sinatra had heard a conversation where Wasserman had said to someone about Sinatra, 'Don't bother with him. He's through.')"

While the government was weighing its options, MCA attempted to seize the initiative. On June 18, Wasserman consummated what he had begun back in 1959, with MCA's purchase of the Universal lot; now, MCA acquired Decca Records Inc. and Decca's subsidiary, Universal Pictures Company, Inc.—thus fulfilling Wasserman's goal of becoming a diversified entertainment company, dedicated to television *and* movie production, and music, too. Universal also had an international distribution system, which would be vital to MCA as it moved into movie production. At the same time, Wasserman was proceeding with his plan to spin off the talent agency, by selling it to two trusted, senior MCA agents, Larry Barnett and George Chasin, who were to pay MCA $1 million a year for ten years. (Sonny Werblin had offered to head the new agency, but Wasserman—no doubt anticipating that Werblin would be less than subordinate—declined his offer.) On July 3, Wasserman sent a notice to the Screen Actors Guild that MCA would surrender its agency franchise on July 18, and MCA lawyers informed the Justice Department of this action, too.

Meanwhile, according to Wasserman, Barnett and Chasin temporized, worrying about what the government might do to them. "Their temperament was such that when you mentioned the FBI and Justice Department they ran out of the room. Some people are that way, you know," Wasserman commented. "They could have bought a worldwide business for $10 million." But on July 13, the government intervened. "I was in New York with our lawyer, Don Rosenfeld. We had been sued Friday night, and we caught an early flight back Saturday morning. The stewardess said, 'I want your autograph.' I looked at her like she was crazy." And then, he continued, she showed him the story in the *New York Times,* with his photograph. He also said, with unmistakable satisfaction, that at this moment, when the government filed its case, "I had four folders in my files." (He had long prided himself on keeping virtually no written records, and now that policy had paid off.) The Justice Department had brought a civil antitrust suit against MCA, and named the Screen Actors Guild as a co-conspirator; it charged the company with a series of violations and asked for court orders to halt them. Most critically, the suit asked that MCA be required to divest itself of its newly acquired Decca Records and Universal Pictures. It also asked that it be ordered to dissolve—not spin off—the talent agency.

Wasserman and Stein appeared to be caught off guard by the government's action. Stein later said that he had believed until the last moment that the government would be content to let MCA carry out its voluntary spin-off. He speculated that Bobby Kennedy, in the end, had succumbed to pressure from "a famous Washington lawyer" who was representing a rival talent agency. Indeed, Herbert Siegel, who had recently acquired General Artists Corporation, said years later that he had hired Washington lawyer Abe Fortas to persuade Kennedy to break up MCA. Siegel had also hired an extraordinary New York public relations guru, Ben Sonnenberg, who often worked hand in hand with Fortas. "Sonnenberg had files on *everyone*," Siegel commented. "And Fortas was very effective. He used a rifle shot, not a cannon."

Whatever had informed Kennedy's decision-making process, its result was very threatening to MCA. "We were absolutely stymied for a while," Stein said later, "and if we hadn't made a deal or come to a consent agreement, chances are we could have been squeezed out of everything. We could have been out of business." As Wasserman had noted, Stein was a pessimist; so the situation was probably not quite that grave. But if MCA were to be cut off from the agency business *and* prohibited from becoming a full-scale entertainment company—if it were, essentially, allowed to be only a TV production company, and one whose practices were closely overseen by the government—then certainly its growth would be stunted. After the suit was filed, Stein continued, MCA's lawyers were negotiating with the government lawyers, "and they were getting noplace. And I finally said to Wasserman, 'Lew, you go to Washington and you stay there until you make a settlement.' "

Wasserman went, and stayed for four days; by the time he returned to Los Angeles, the outlines of the settlement were plain. Spivack said he vividly remembered sitting in Washington with his colleague, Harry

Sklarsky, the Justice Department's chief of field operations, and Wasserman. They told Wasserman that MCA simply could not be in a position to control both the production business and the agency, even indirectly. "And he said, 'I'll get out!'" Spivack recalled; Wasserman was altogether willing to dissolve the agency, rather than pass it along intact to Barnett and Chasin. Thus, ten days after the government had filed its suit, the Justice Department announced that MCA had agreed to the agency's dissolution. It would take two months more for the terms of MCA's consent decree to be ironed out, but the major elements had been decided during Wasserman's four-day trip. And while MCA would ultimately accept certain restrictions on its dealings (for example, it was barred from acquiring or merging with any major television, motion picture, or record company for seven years without the approval of the Justice Department), the dissolution of the agency was the only major concession it had to make. What Wasserman cared most about—the acquisition of Decca and Universal, and his ability to become a full-scale entertainment conglomerate—was preserved. Spivack said that he and Sklarsky negotiated the settlement with Wasserman. "After that, Wasserman would do little things for Sklarsky—not *money,*" Spivack said. "But Wasserman arranged some tour when Harry went to Israel. Things like that. Harry would call Wasserman."

Stein said later that he did not know what transpired in Washington. "I was satisfied with the results. I was not concerned with the conditions that produced the results. I have always believed that you let your chief executive handle affairs as they think best. Lew never told me the details of the trip to Washington and I have never asked him." Remarkable as that might seem, it was consistent with the nature of the two men's relationship as it had evolved over the years; there was no free-flowing exchange between them, and Stein did not *want* to know the details of Wasserman's dealings (and not only because of his views on business management). In this instance, Stein could not argue with the merits of what Wasserman had achieved. If they were forced to choose between the agency and production businesses, the choice was clear; in 1961, MCA's gross income was about $82 million, and the agency's was only about 10 percent of that. Stein, who would never place sentiment over dollars, had some time before acceded to the inevitable—moving away from the agency business, and further into production. But despite appearances, he was deeply emotional, and very tied to the business he had fathered. "That was the agency I loved and I wanted to see it remain in existence even if MCA got no money from it," he declared. Referring to the deal Wasserman negotiated, requiring that the agency be dissolved, Stein said, "I didn't suffer financially, I suffered mentally."

For many of his employees, too, it was a harrowing time. Daniel Welkes, an agent in the bands and acts department, recalled that in early July, simultaneous meetings had been held at MCA in New York and Los Angeles to announce what the agents knew had been brewing for about a year. "They were going to spin off the agency—it would have a new name, new address, not an ashtray left with the MCA logo. The actors who could have left the company were told about it and they said they would stay in. We were in heaven." But before the press conference to announce the spin-off could be held, the Justice Department had filed suit. After that, meetings were held at MCA twice a day, at 9:00 A.M. and 5:00 P.M., to give the agents an update. "Lew kept saying, 'We're going to work it out,' " Welkes recalled. On July 18, he and his colleagues attended the 5:00 P.M. meeting. "Lew said, 'We're still in court. We don't know what will happen. So if any of you would like to resign, it will not be treated as an act of disloyalty.' Jack Findlater [a company lawyer] had a stack of papers in his briefcase. Ronnie Leif got up and said, 'We've got to go out on our own!' He and others went up and signed the [resignation] papers. It was chaos! And then we all ran off to form splinter groups. But if we'd gone off together, the agency could have stayed intact." Later, Welkes and some of his fellow agents speculated that Wasserman had orchestrated this scene, so that the agency would more likely break up into many small pieces than reconstitute itself as a powerful and independent bloc. Leif, who had led the stampede, was Wasserman's new son-in-law; he had married Wasserman's daughter, Lynne, less than three weeks earlier.

Jules Stein, Lew Wasserman, and Ed Muhl (head of Universal Studios when it was acquired by MCA) surveying a model of MCA's black tower. *Bison Archives*

Al Rush was one of the relatively few agents who were offered the opportunity to join the production company. "In New York and California, most of the agents were let go—suddenly, overnight, they had no jobs—and they were very bitter," Rush said. Moreover, the MCA profit-sharing trust, hit by a stock market crash the previous spring, had lost as much as 30 to 40 percent of its value; so these agents did not have the cushion they otherwise would have. "They were very shaken up. The profit sharing was so low, they thought maybe Jules and Lew would give them a gift for years of service. But they didn't," Rush said. Some agents—like George Chasin, Herman Citron, Arthur Parks, and others—would do exceptionally well on their own; but many would never find their footing again.

On September 19, the consent decree was filed in a Los Angeles federal court. And at MCA's Universal lot the next day, the earth-moving equipment went into action, preparing a foundation for a fifteen-story, forbidding black sheath of a building, the largest ever constructed at a studio. Wasserman said that he had seen a black glass skyscraper in San

Francisco and liked it; also, he had visited the new Seagram tower in New York—the most refined version of the new symbol of corporate America, the modern glass skyscraper, designed by Ludwig Mies van der Rohe and Philip Johnson—and copied the silver metal braiding of the elevator walls there. There was no mistaking, in any event, that this would be Wasserman's building—a radical counterpoint to Stein's beloved "White House," now shuttered—and that this, more than ever, was now Wasserman's company. Once again, as he had done earlier when he moved into TV production, he was plotting his own rather contrarian course. While the other studios were selling off much of their property, and filming increasingly was being done abroad, Wasserman was buying, and betting that movies could be made more efficiently in a properly run Hollywood studio, as long as it was operated like a large factory, at close to full capacity—much as had been done when the studio system was at its height. In an interview with Murray Schumach in the *New York Times,* Wasserman gave his rejoinder to Selznick's words of more than a decade earlier, declaring, "Now, we will see if Hollywood will become a desert. I don't think so. But I could be wrong." Spoken with the ease of a man who knows that the record suggests otherwise.

However painful the resolution of the government's antitrust case may have been for many ex-MCA agents, and, in a way, for Stein, it was an unmitigated triumph for Wasserman. The agency had become his albatross; he had to be rid of it. To spin it off, however, carried several disadvantages. Although it was to be run by those loyal to him, they could not really do his bidding without arousing objections from the government. And if they *didn't* do his bidding, then he would find himself on the wrong side of the equation that he had created. After all, when Wasserman had come on the scene, the biggest stars were salaried employees of the studios; he had driven their salaries so high that studios finally found it more economic to give them a share in their movies; and then Wasserman had set the stars up as producers. He had changed the economy of Hollywood. But now, if he—a producer himself—had to deal with the mammoth agency he had created but which was no longer his, it could all come back to bite him. He could not, however, have dissolved the agency voluntarily; the talent that he would now want to hire for his movies would be outraged at being summarily abandoned. But if the government were forcing his hand, no one could blame him. Finally, if MCA were to have sold the agency, they would have received about $10 million. In dissolving the agency, though, Wasserman decided that MCA would demand a split commission (5 percent) on everything related to deals MCA had negotiated for its clients—which would continue for many years to come. As Wasserman commented, "If we had sold it, we would have gotten about $10 million; this way, we got about $100 million."

The outcome, then, was so sublimely advantageous that many who knew Wasserman would remain forever convinced that the government ended up doing for him what he could not do himself. Jack Dales of the Screen Actors Guild said, "Lew would most have wanted it the way it turned out—but he couldn't have just cut off the agency himself. This way, he was free and clear." For his part, Wasserman declined to shed any light on exactly how this resolution was achieved, saying, "No one but me knows how I solved it." What he did volunteer, however, was this: "Some people—even people not in the government—believed we had a monopoly . . . Well, I plead the Fifth."

The general perception that all had ended happily for MCA was underscored by a note from Jackie Kennedy to Doris and Jules in March 1963. By this time, the prohibition on gifts from the Steins had been lifted; they were contributing substantially to her White House restoration project, and they were also guests for dinner at the White House (after which they sent a gift of a whale tooth box, mounted in vermeil, which, Jackie wrote, thanking them, "is my husband's favorite thing in the world. He collects them with a passion. . . . May I also say that it is the only whale's tooth I have found beautiful, too!"). Though she rejected two of their breakfronts, she declared herself thrilled with their other offerings: two English eighteenth-century mirrors and a rare English eighteenth-century octagonal pedestal writing desk, inlaid with satinwood. "The superb eagle mirrors and the octagonal desk would be marvelous for the Long Hall. I always loved them more than any-thing," she wrote. And, referring to the antitrust case, "You know, this whole thing upset me terribly—and I felt so badly and upset for you and Mrs. Stein. In the beginning no one wanted to give anything to the White House—and you were among the very first to come forward—and give so generously of your time and offer us such beautiful things.

"Then came the anti-trust suit—and the enormous wheels of gov-ernment started to grind. I felt rather like a fly trapped in a machine and kept saying I don't care—I don't even know what an anti-trust suit is. All I care about is to behave as graciously towards the Steins as they have to me. And months went on and we all lost track. . . . As it turned out, I suppose it was best to have waited, though that never was my opinion. Because you won your suit—which I am so happy about and now nobody can tell us what we can or can't do any more."

Much as Bobby Kennedy had taken a personal interest in the MCA in-vestigation, he was more riveted in this period on other targets—his nemesis, Jimmy Hoffa, for example, and the Mafia. Shortly after he had taken office in 1961, the attorney general had declared war on or-ganized crime, calling on all government agencies to pool information on the nation's top gangsters, and to coordinate their investigations. The *Wall Street Journal* described his undertaking as "the most sweep-ing campaign against gangsters, labor racketeers and vice overlords that the country has ever seen." Las Vegas came under the government spotlight; the government knew that organized crime was well en-trenched in the lucrative hotel and gambling business that had sprung up, almost overnight, in the desert oasis—and Hoffa had now become the mob's partner, loaning massive amounts of Teamsters pension fund money to the construction of hotels there. A lucky break, moreover, had occurred in the summer of 1959, when FBI agents, tailing Murray Humphreys, realized that they had stumbled on the headquarters of the leadership of the Chicago mob—the back room of Celano's Custom Tailors on North Michigan Avenue. They had obtained permission from J. Edgar Hoover to break into the tailor shop and install a hidden microphone, in the type of covert activity known as a black-bag job. What FBI agents learned from listening in on Celano's would lead to electronic surveillance in Las Vegas as well, and ultimately they would gain considerable familiarity with the denizens of this world: Murray Humphreys, Tony Accardo, Sam Giancana, Moe Dalitz, Sidney Korshak, and many others. Obtained illegally, this information could never be used in court—but it would provide the kind of intelligence that would, some years later, help bring an end to the Vegas idyll.

A primary target in the FBI's "Top Hoodlum Program" was Wasserman's close friend Moe Dalitz, who was popularly known as "the godfather of Las Vegas." In later years, Wasserman would staunchly defend Dalitz as someone who, though admittedly a bootlegger during Prohibition, had been a legitimate businessman ever since. But these wiretaps told a different story. In January 1961, Dalitz and Morris Kleinman (Dalitz's longtime associate from the Cleveland syndicate, who had served time in the penitentiary) came to Chicago to meet with Humphreys, Accardo, and Giancana, and they worked out a deal making the Chicago group a secret partner in the Desert Inn, the Riviera, and the Fremont, as well as a bigger partner than it already was in the Stardust. Judging from Humphreys's statements in Celano's a couple days later, the relations between Dalitz and the Chicago contingent were less than cordial. "We're right at the point where we can hit him right in the head. But being a Jew guy, it's a little different," Humphreys commented about Dalitz to Gus Alex, a member of the Outfit from the Capone days who was designated to keep in close contact with Korshak. ". . . Anyway, we got harmony now. It's all worked out . . . we didn't have to go through a showdown. . . . If we ever get the gun in there, Gussie, a guy has to put his foot down. . . . Suppose somebody tries to run away on us. You think we'd let them get away with it?"

From 1961 to 1963, the FBI installed microphones in the executive suites of at least seven casinos in Las Vegas, including the Desert Inn— and from these transcribed tapes a fuller portrait of Dalitz and his activities emerged. Based on its surveillance, it was the FBI's estimate that about one third of all gambling revenues in Nevada were being skimmed—that is, unaccounted for, untaxed. At the Desert Inn, according to an FBI report, it worked this way. "Once a month, money which has been taken 'off the top' at the Desert Inn Hotel is distributed among the various owners of record and others who have an interest in the hotel. Sums in excess of $100,000 are distributed monthly. Dalitz usually receives in excess of $10,000 from each cut. Money is also designated to sources in Chicago during these distributions. Other individuals are also paid from this pool before the regular distribution is made when it is desired there be no record of these payments. This includes payments to entertainers who are in high income tax brackets. These people are frequently paid cash 'under the table' in order to induce them to appear at a particular hotel. It also includes occasional payments to public officials."

Allotting the skim wasn't easy. On one occasion in October 1962, Dalitz was meeting in his office with a longtime associate, George Gordon, a courier for the overlord of the Cleveland mob, John Scalish. Dalitz and Gordon were talking about rearranging the percentage points in the Stardust, and trying to straighten out the actual ownership in relation to the public ownership (there were seventeen individuals registered publicly as part owners, or licensees, all with varying numbers of points—but then there was the other, hidden list). The percentage points were, of course, supposed to add up to 100; but once they counted and got 96; again they counted, and came up with 110. On another occasion, two of Dalitz's employees at the Desert Inn were counting money behind locked doors for one and a half hours, trying to figure who was to receive what amount, scribbling on pieces of paper, trying to make it all balance. They never could. Payments mentioned in this episode included $2,500 to Jack Benny, $2,000 to the Catholic Church, and $30,000 to the Chicago mob.

While Dalitz was unaware of the hidden microphones, he knew that he had been named one of the top-echelon racketeers in a list compiled by Bobby Kennedy in 1961, and, also, that he had been made the subject of a crash investigation for prosecution. "If only I could get my name off that 'Top Forty,' " he lamented in July 1962. He discussed several people who he thought might be able to help him with the Kennedy administration. At a meeting held in Dalitz's office in October 1962, attended by Dalitz, Gordon, Sam Tucker, and Allard Roen, one of the publicly identified owners of the Desert Inn, Dalitz was discussing the Chicago mob. Referring to Johnny Roselli and Sam Giancana, he worried aloud, "I was seen with them. I don't think that's good. It ties the whole mob up."

Dalitz was convinced that Bobby Kennedy was the source of his troubles. Referring to a federal grand jury in Los Angeles that was investigating hidden interests in the Sands Hotel, Dalitz commented, "They feel Doc Stacher is an undisclosed partner in the Sands Hotel and that he represents the gangster element at the Sands. The government feels if they can expose that, they would cut off the money flow. . . . Bobby Kennedy is using this as a cloak to kill the industry in Nevada. He feels this is a pipeline for undisclosed interests." But he took some solace from his colleagues' solidarity. "There's less hysteria than eight months ago—at least everyone's decided to take the Fifth," he commented. Dalitz and his associates felt a considerable sense of betrayal in their relationship with the Kennedys; they knew that the mob had helped to get John Kennedy elected in 1960—and now their payback was Bobby's war on organized crime! Wilbur Clark, Dalitz's front man at the Desert Inn, commented one day that Bobby Kennedy was in Las Vegas, and he hoped Kennedy would get poisoned.

Korshak was a good friend of Dalitz's, and the two met often in Las Vegas. He agreed with Dalitz's assessment of Bobby Kennedy. Korshak had tangled with him earlier: when Korshak testified before the Senate Rackets Committee in 1957, Bobby Kennedy was his questioner. On a visit with Dalitz in February 1963, Korshak told him that "Bobby has been trying for six months to catch someone either in Las Vegas or Los Angeles who is carrying money . . . he is desperate and has now issued instructions to have narcotics agents grab any suspected money bag under the pretense that they are looking for narcotics," according to an

Sidney Korshak, who was rarely photographed, testifying before the U.S. Senate Select Committee on Improper Activities in the Labor or Management Field on October 30, 1957, in response to questions posed by the committee's chief counsel, Robert Kennedy. *Corbis-Bettmann*

FBI report. Korshak was also heard on the FBI wiretap in Dalitz's office exhorting Dalitz to take full advantage of the privilege afforded by the Fifth Amendment. "Actually, Moe, you never waive the Fifth. The rule is that you can testify and when a question is put to you, you are the judge of whether you think it will incriminate you or not. You don't have to answer." Korshak referred to a recent court case upholding this right, and added, "This in itself will stop the investigations of Bobby, you know.

"Moe, I have preached this all over the country," Korshak continued. "Do not answer anything. I have testified before Grand Juries in New York and Chicago and at that time I could do it because then I was only dealing with certain people. I tell you now, Moe, if I am called before any Grand Jury, I will take the Fifth Amendment and I am a lawyer. I will give my name and address and from that point on I will answer no questions. They can disbar me, but I will take the Fifth. Now I have to take the Fifth, because I am operating in a different atmosphere."

Korshak was preaching to the converted. "FBI agents were in here a while back, and tried to ask me some questions," Dalitz responded. "I told them to put them right back in their (obscene) pocket because I was not going to answer anything. They said, we would like you to at least hear the questions. I said, you are not going to read them because I don't want to hear them. Sam [Samuel Tucker] and Morris [Morris Kleinman] and [deleted] all told them the same thing."

During this meeting, Korshak and Dalitz discussed what they considered the happy outcome of a deal very important to Dalitz, and one that Korshak had facilitated. Since 1958, the Desert Inn had been leasing the Stardust Hotel and casino from John "Jake the Barber" Factor—though the full reality was rather more complicated. As Doc Stacher explained, when the Stardust was being built in 1957, Dalitz had feared it would be too competitive with the Desert Inn. "It looked like an old-fashioned war might break out," Stacher said, "but Meyer [Lansky] suggested a meeting and we all flew in for it. I was there with Dalitz, and his right-hand man, Kleinman, was there, and Longie [sic] Zwillman and so forth. We worked out a deal that gave each group an interlocking interest in each other's hotels, and our lawyers set it up so that nobody could really tell who owned what out there." Now, Dalitz (with other undisclosed partners) wanted to purchase the Stardust. Any transfer of ownership, obviously, had to be handled by a mob insider. And inasmuch as Korshak had known Factor for many years, and the Chicago mob also had an interest in the Stardust, Korshak was a natural intermediary.

Factor, who hailed from Chicago in the Capone era, was a notorious international swindler. In 1933, he had been about to be extradited to England to serve a long prison sentence when he was apparently kidnapped; released unharmed, he had fought extradition on the grounds that he had to remain in this country to testify against his purported kidnapper, Roger Touhy—the same Roger Touhy whom Jules Stein had speculated was behind the plan to kidnap *him*. But after Touhy had served twenty-five years in prison for the Factor kidnapping, a federal judge ruled that Touhy was innocent, and that Factor had staged his own kidnapping and, with the collusion of the state attorney's office in Chicago, framed Touhy. Touhy was ultimately paroled in November 1959, shortly after the publication of a book he wrote with a Chicago newspaperman, Ray Brennan, that detailed the whole sorry episode, and excoriated Factor, Murray "the Camel" Humphreys, and others. The book, coupled with his dramatic release, received a good deal of attention. Factor filed a libel suit; Korshak was his lawyer. Then, roughly three weeks after his release from prison, Touhy was shot-gunned to death on the doorstep of his sister's house in Chicago. Factor, who was in Chicago at the time, told the *New York Times,* "I am very broken up about it—I hope they get the killer." But Touhy's murder, in the great Chicago tradition, went unsolved.

None of this seemed to have any deleterious effect on Factor. He had served a prison sentence for another fraud in the forties, but since then he had prospered; he was a very wealthy, increasingly philanthropic member of the community in Los Angeles. He had been trying to obtain a presidential pardon for years, but had been consistently rejected. Then, on Christmas Eve 1962—only two weeks before Factor was to appear at a hearing to show cause why he should not be deported to England to face outstanding criminal charges there—President Kennedy granted him a pardon, which quashed the deportation proceedings. Among the people who had lobbied for his pardon, interestingly enough, was Senator Estes Kefauver (perhaps still under the influence of those incriminating photographs). As press stories revealed that Factor had contributed $20,000 to Kennedy's campaign in 1960, the pardon became intensely controversial—indeed, it would be compared many years later to the pardon that President Bill Clinton granted fugitive financier Marc Rich. What was especially interesting, though, was that the Justice Department's recommendation—then, as now, not disclosed—was that Factor should be pardoned. It was par-

ticularly ironic, considering Bobby Kennedy's fixation on the mob, and
Las Vegas in particular. For Factor—notwithstanding testaments to his
character from many members of the Los Angeles community—was
still deeply enmeshed with the Chicago mob through his interests in
Las Vegas.

That Bobby Kennedy was unaware of Factor's activities is hard to
imagine. These were not difficult to discover, as a letter to the attorney
general—one of a flood protesting the Factor pardon—made plain. The
writer was a Wall Street investment banker (his name was deleted before the letter was turned over in response to a Freedom of Information
Act request), who quickly said that he was a "good Democrat," and
therefore not trying to embarrass the administration—but he was troubled by the pardon for the following reasons, and felt that "responsible
citizens are entitled to some clarification." His firm had been approached to find a buyer for the Stardust Hotel. The prospective investors, however, had all come back with the same information: a
purchase was not viable because the Desert Inn, which leased and operated the Stardust, was controlled by the Cleveland Syndicate, which
was the Mafia; and the entire situation was sure to "blow up" shortly
because of the FBI investigations of mob interests in Las Vegas, and in
particular, the Desert Inn. Furthermore, these people indicated that
"Jake Factor was in some way privy to . . . Mafia control and that the
purported sale of the Stardust property in his name was merely a device
by which the Syndicate was endeavoring to bail out part of its capital
investment in the Las Vegas area."

Why Bobby Kennedy recommended to his brother that Jake Factor
be pardoned is not clear. Certainly, if he were inclined to cooperate
with the administration that pardoned him, he could have provided in-
valuable information about the mob's secret machinations in Las
Vegas. This, unsurprisingly, was something that had occurred to Korshak and his associates. But in his visit with Dalitz—about six weeks
after the Factor pardon—Korshak said, according to an FBI report,
that he was convinced that Factor's "frame of mind is such at the present time that he will not talk to the authorities about the Stardust Hotel

transaction or the parties involved." And Korshak's taped conversation with Dalitz suggests that Factor was too afraid of his confreres to brave such peril.

Dalitz was saying that he was very pleased with the deal they had made with Factor on the Stardust. "I scared the (obscene) out of him from day to day about what was going to happen," Korshak replied. "I think that was one reason he finally agreed to give us the option to purchase. Now I want to show you how scared he is. He was in Chicago last week." (Korshak referred to a situation in which "Curley"— Murray Humphreys—wanted to see if Factor, who bragged about his influence, could help a mutual friend.) "So they sat down with me and said get ahold of him [Factor] because he can do this. So I started to laugh, so . . . said to me, what are you laughing about. I said, this is the end of a friendship between John Factor and myself number one, and I said, number two, he isn't going to talk because he doesn't have that relationship, and number three, nothing is going to be able to help him. But I agreed we ought to try it, so they said fine. So John [Factor] came to town last week and came into my office. I don't even know what he came in for, but I told him a story and I said, they want to see you. He said, well I've got to run now, but I'll talk to you in about a half hour, and that was the last I saw of him. He caught the afternoon plane (laughter). . . . So this is consistent with what I was saying. He is frightened to death and that is how we were able to make this (obscene) deal."

Preparing to leave, Korshak asked Dalitz if there was any message he wanted Korshak to give to Giancana. Dalitz asked how Giancana was, and Korshak remarked that he was "still in love with Phyllis" (Phyllis McGuire, the singer). "Madly in love." Dalitz asked why they didn't get married then. "I'm not so sure that they're not married," Korshak replied. "We had dinner together four or five nights ago and I said, there are a couple of broads in town, and I asked him if he was interested. So I just have an idea they are married. I'm pretty sure." Korshak was, in fact, wrong in his intuition; but he seemed to want to underscore to Dalitz his intimacy with Giancana by relating these personal details. Regarding the question of whether Giancana had married McGuire, Korshak said, "If I had asked him, he would have told me, but I never did, you know."

"Yeah, I understand," Dalitz replied. "Thank you very much, Sidney."

In Las Vegas, Korshak appeared even more omnipotent than he did in Los Angeles. The mob's presence there was so ubiquitous that Korshak could leverage his affiliation in a variety of ways. He represented one of the largest and most corrupt unions in town, the Hotel and Restaurant Workers. He was the broker for the Teamsters Central States Pension Fund, which was pouring money into Las Vegas—to Dalitz, Factor, and many others. He spoke for the Chicago mob. And, along with them, he owned a piece of the Riviera Hotel—the Strip's first high-rise, looking more like Miami than Las Vegas, and so tall, with its nine stories, that many believed the desert soil couldn't support it. In the late fifties and early sixties, the Riviera had more cachet than any other hotel, recalled Richard Gully, whom Korshak hired as the hotel's publicist. It became part of the Korshak legend that when he arrived at the Riviera on one occasion and Jimmy Hoffa was occupying the Presidential Suite, Hoffa was moved out of it to accommodate Korshak. Something else, too, was part of the Korshak legend (though this, only whispered). For Willie Bioff—the only member of the mob to publicly identify Korshak as connected to them—had lived quietly in Arizona for years under an assumed name until he had been foolhardy enough to go to work at Korshak's Riviera in 1955. And it was not long after that that he had been murdered when his pickup truck exploded. Such incidents only added to the mystique. "When Korshak entered the room in Vegas, everything stopped," Dean Shendal, who was a debt-collector for the casino owners, said. "You'd hear people saying, '*Korshak* is here!' "

However, for all Korshak's perceived power, Humphreys, holding forth at Celano's, maintained that he had the upper hand in their relationship. For example, he had told Korshak that since he, Humphreys, had an interest in the Stardust, Korshak was not to have any, according to a 1960 FBI report. And in 1961, Humphreys recounted how he had rebuked Korshak on one occasion for not showing the mob proper fealty. He seemed to feel that Korshak was getting too self-impressed. Korshak had booked Dinah Shore at a casino in Las Vegas not controlled by the Chicago mob; Humphreys ("Mr. Lincoln") had called him, and Korshak had not responded quickly enough. Humphreys said he had ordered Korshak to book Shore at the right places in the future. "We brought you up; you're our guy," Humphreys said he had told Korshak. "Anytime we yell, you come running."

Humphreys might have offered Hoffa to Korshak as a role model. Hoffa, too, had reached an apex of power, but he didn't need to be reminded about how he got there. In a conversation with Joey Glimco, a Teamsters official in Chicago, Humphreys described Hoffa as "the best man I ever knew." And the two agreed that whenever Hoffa was asked to do something by the Chicago mob, he "just goes boom, boom, boom, he gets it done."

The microphones in Chicago and Las Vegas were a bonanza for the government, but it all came to an end in the spring of 1963 when an FBI memo on skimming, summarizing much of what had been learned through the tapes, was sent to the Justice Department. A few days later, FBI agents listened in, flabbergasted, as the casino boss of the Fremont read the memo aloud to his associates. Casinos were promptly searched, some of the devices discovered—and a hush fell on Las Vegas. News, of course, traveled east. On June 23, 1963, in Celano's, Humphreys gave his brief valedictory. "Welcome to the 11 A.M. meeting of the Chicago crime syndicate. We hope everybody is tuned in."

Before leading MCA into full-scale television production in 1952, Wasserman had already secured his edge—MCA's acting as both agent and producer. And ten years later, when he abandoned the agency business and embraced production, he apparently knew, once again, that he had a built-in advantage, albeit one that he would not want to display too soon. In the antitrust investigation, Justice Department lawyers had been very interested in the relationship between MCA and NBC; they had tried to discover not only whether Kintner had been paid off, but also whether another kind of illegal arrangement existed between him and MCA—say, whether Kintner guaranteed he would fill his prime-time schedule with nearly all MCA shows, and in return would be given first pick of their productions. Ultimately, the government lawyers had given up trying to prove that element of their case, and had focused more on the Screen Actors Guild waiver. But it would be impolitic and perhaps even rash of Wasserman, immediately after having settled the case with the government in such advantageous fashion, to flaunt his special relationship with NBC. Privately, though, Wasserman and Kintner had reached an understanding, according to attorney Billy Hunt, with whom Wasserman worked closely for years. Hunt had learned from Wasserman that when Wasserman had been deciding about the breakup of MCA's agency and production businesses, "Kintner told him that if he went into production, NBC would buy everything he made."

Operating without the engine of its agency business for the first time, MCA joined the fierce competition being waged among the major television producers in early 1963. The studios had long since overcome their aversion to producing for television, and they now depended heavily on that output; but there wasn't enough space in prime time to accommodate the volume the producers needed to thrive. Even MCA felt the press of the crowd. "Thanks to its Wasserman-Werblin-Schreiber combo, considered perhaps the hottest and shrewdest in the business, Revue again goes into '63–'64 preeminent among all the vid-film producers," stated an article in *Variety* in April 1963. "But even so it's a far cry from the 14- or 15-show status it once enjoyed and which, by virtue of its expensive facilities, are necessary to meet that kind of overhead." Just two months later, however, Wasserman and Kintner struck a deal that reestablished MCA's accustomed primacy. Remarkable in both its content and its process, it was described at the time as "the biggest and perhaps most significant deal in TV annals." MCA would produce a full season of two-hour feature films for weekly showing on NBC during the 1964–65 season; simultaneously, these films would be shown in movie theaters abroad, and later it was planned that they would have a second run, in U.S. movie theaters. It was a novel approach—it reversed the usual order, in which full feature films only made their way to television *after* their theater showings. And its genesis at NBC was unorthodox as well. Programming decisions were customarily made by a network's head of programming and then passed on to the president for approval; here, however, the deal had been negotiated between Kintner and Wasserman. It remained to be seen how successful this idea of the made-for-TV movie might be, but the immediate impact of the deal was unequivocal: it made Universal Hollywood's largest movie producer.

Others sought to follow MCA's example. In September 1965, ABC and Metro-Goldwyn-Mayer made an $8.4 million deal in which ABC was to acquire fifteen existing feature films and finance the production of six new two-hour films. CBS, too, was reported to be negotiating a similar deal with Columbia Pictures. In these deals, the networks paid less than the actual production costs of the films; the producers hoped to realize profits from distribution of the films overseas. "The appeal of the feature-length film on TV is that motion pictures have established a track record of being 'idiot proof,' " wrote television critic Jack Gould in the *New York Times* in August 1965. "A blockbuster film can register a huge rating and even an indifferent motion picture will attract enough viewers to assure the economic viability of an advertiser's investment in spot announcements, something that cannot be said for the TV show that fails to catch on."

Wasserman's earlier deal with Kintner had only been a test run. Now that the formula seemed to be working, he decided to apply it on a far larger scale—so large, in fact, that it would dwarf everything that had come before, and its true size would be kept secret. In October 1965, an NBC spokesman announced that NBC had made a deal with Universal for fifteen existing motion pictures, and "six or more" of its made-for-TV movies—thus, it seemed a virtual replica of the $8.4 million deal recently announced between ABC and MGM. No price was mentioned. Just a few days later, however, reports appeared in the trade press that MCA and NBC had actually consummated the largest single film deal in the history of television, estimated to approach $60 million. It was thought to include not fifteen but sixty Universal films for network showing at about $500,000 each; forty for showing on the network's owned-and-operated stations at about $100,000 each; and an uncertain number of made-for-TV feature films for an estimated subtotal of $15 million. Now, an MCA official responded that the press reports of a $60 million agreement were "essentially correct."

Years later, however, Wasserman said that it had been not a $60 million, but a $200 million agreement—one that included sixty first-runs, as had been reported in the later press accounts, and *two hundred* made-for-TV movies. Astronomical as this deal was, it had been negotiated directly between Kintner and Wasserman; their subordinates met later to draft the papers. The form of these two-hour TV movies was not new, but Wasserman provided a kind of inaugural fillip by coining the term "World Premiere" movies; and while the concept was not revolutionary, the deal was. "This deal was really the basis for our being able to dominate TV production," declared Frank Price, a TV executive at MCA during the years this deal was in effect. "With that contract, you could get the most important writers, directors, producers in town. That's how we were able to acquire this stable of talent. One of the things that eliminated the contract system in the old Hollywood was that no one could afford to carry all those people. So this was, in TV, a return to the old contract system. It gave you a way to pick up people whose series weren't yet on the air and carry them. No one else was able to do what MCA was, then. Because no one had gotten that kind of order before—and no one has since."

Larry White, an NBC programming executive who arrived at the network shortly after the deal was consummated, agreed that it had given MCA a hold on talent—much as it had had with the agency business—and that that was the key to its dominance in TV production. But for NBC, White said, this deal was far less salutary. Not so much because of the quality of the movies MCA delivered ("some were lousy, some were good," he said), but because of NBC's enforced dependence on MCA. "The deal was too favorable to MCA, and they had too much of a lock on NBC's time. It froze out other producers. . . . It gave MCA a semimonopoly in Hollywood."

There was considerable grousing at NBC about MCA's coup, but the man who was responsible for it wasn't there to hear the criticism. In December 1965, roughly six weeks after the NBC-MCA deal was announced, Kintner was fired. The announcement of his resignation was particularly stunning, since Kintner had been slated in late December to assume the additional post of chairman of NBC. Press reports gave no hint of the cause of his fall. But a column by the *New York Times*'s Jack Gould suggested, however obliquely, that the strains of life at the top of a TV network might have taken a strong personal toll. Television, after all, was the epicenter. As Gould wrote, "At the center of all this activity is power without a precise parallel in American life. Words can never fully describe the intoxicating sensation felt by the individual who decides that something or somebody should be seen by millions from coast to coast and then watches it happen." That had been Kintner's experience—and, thanks to Kintner, it had been Wasserman's to a degree, too.

Kintner's fate at NBC had been presaged by his firing from ABC; it was surprising in a way that the reprieve Sonny Werblin had won him at NBC had lasted so long. General Sarnoff had warned him repeatedly about his drinking; and, according to Alan Livingston, an NBC executive during the Kintner regime, it was only the intervention of Bobby Sarnoff that had prevented the General from firing Kintner earlier. Don Durgin recalled that Kintner and he were at an NBC affiliates' meeting in Acapulco in the fall of 1965. "When he was off the reservation, he would just drink as you would not believe. And at this meeting, one of the affiliates said that NBC news went on too long—it was like ABC plus thirty minutes, CBS plus forty. The affiliates wanted to cut it back for the ratings. Because of Kintner's mania for news, we knew it was a tender moment. He went into a harangue. Fifty minutes later, he was still going. He never wore undershirts, just these really expensive shirts—and the perspiration started, first the size of a dime and then bigger and bigger. He spoke intelligently, but you knew he was under the influence." Furthermore, Durgin continued, it had recently been announced that Bob Sarnoff was being moved from the chairmanship of NBC to RCA, and that Kintner would be both president and chairman of NBC—and Kintner felt free now to vent his contempt for Bob. "Kintner got this idea, born of drink, that he would no longer speak to Bob Sarnoff. There was a blackout in New York. Bob called Acapulco to say, what do we do? And Kintner refused to talk to him." Soon afterward, Kintner was fired.

It was a sad fate for Kintner, but he had utterly fulfilled his purpose for Wasserman, whose timing was impeccable; had there been a delay of even a few weeks in his negotiation with Kintner, Wasserman would have missed the deal of a lifetime. With that deal in hand, Wasserman was able to create his own version of the contract system he had once helped destroy. It was not really paradoxical. Before, he'd been on the other side, so with his innate aggression he had driven stars' incomes beyond all generally imaginable limits. When he left the agency business to become a producer, many wondered how he would deal with the soaring production expenses he had helped create, which were crippling other studios. One way was by running Universal like a factory—the most thoroughly computerized in show business—prizing efficiency, cost-effectiveness, and fully utilized facilities. His deal with Kintner helped accomplish that, with its guaranteed stream of production. These TV movies, moreover, had budgets that were said to average only about $1 million. The top twenty box office stars, therefore, who demanded the kinds of incomes Wasserman had engendered, were out of reach. But Universal was building a roster of youthful, affordable contract players and, also, loaning them out to other studios—as Wasserman's predecessors had once done in the heyday of the studio system.

"MGM *owned* this town—they had all the best actors, writers, directors," Wasserman, recalling his early years in Hollywood, once remarked, with a discernible note of admiration in his voice. Much as he had fueled the forces that had undermined MGM, it was that studio, at its height, which had long been his icon, and which he was now set to try to emulate, to a greater degree than ever before. But he would fashion his model with the financial sophistication that had always set him apart from the old moguls. For while NBC had paid $200 million for these movies, Universal retained the rights for syndication sales, foreign television, foreign theaters, and, conceivably, domestic theaters. In 1966, upon the debut of the first of these movies, *Fame Is the Name of the Game,* starring Tony Franciosa and Jill St. John, Wasserman spoke to Charles Champlin of the *Los Angeles Times.* He acknowledged that not all the World Premiere movies would be suitable for all these markets. But he was convinced the potential revenue was great. He had reason to trust his instincts; they had brought him to this high place, where, gazing out through the black glass windows of his fifteenth-story office, he could survey his four-hundred-acre domain—the humming soundstages, and the trams of the Universal City tours wending their way through the vast lot, and the places where a second black tower and two hotels were to be built. This was the city within a city that Wasserman had envisioned; MCA was spending about $110 million on a modernization program. (About a decade later, looking back on this expenditure, Wasserman would comment, "Very few companies in the industry had spent money on capital improvement programs. The theory had been don't spend any money you can't charge off to a film. I'm not going to say we can walk on water, but we were defying conventional thinking.") And the concept that had given Wasserman the confidence to go against the tide and build this elaborate landscape sounded disarmingly simple: Universal, he said, would create sources of supply in all areas of entertainment. "Every new medium has brought predictions of the death of every other," he was quoted as saying in the *Los Angeles Times* in 1966. "Radio was said to be all washed up, but stations are selling for higher prices than ever. When television came along, the studios were prepared to sell all their product, fire their people, and fold up.

"But we're only at the beginning of the beginning."

President Lyndon B. Johnson (with his back to the camera) hosting a lunch for members of the motion-picture industry on June 26, 1968. Seated at the president's left is Lew Wasserman; others at the table are Robert Benjamin, David Brown, Leo Jaffe, Arthur Krim, Benjamin Melniker, Louis Nizer, Arnold Picker, Milton Rackmil, Abraham Schneider, Jack Valenti, Edwin Weisl, and Richard Zanuck, along with White House deputy press secretary Tom Johnson. *Courtesy of the LBJ Library*

Chapter 3

POLITICAL MIGHT

On a summer morning in 1965, a young assistant to President Lyndon Johnson named Larry Levinson was passing through the gated corridor that led from the Executive Office Building to the White House. It was a private entrance, one often used by Johnson for important visitors he wanted to shield from the press. There in the waiting area was a tall, rail-thin man seated in an armchair, very upright, wearing a dark suit, dark tie. Levinson had noticed many visitors there before, but something about this one piqued his curiosity. "He was sitting there, not reading a book or a newspaper—just so composed," Levinson recalled. "I said to the guard, Sergeant Mazzoli, with whom I was friendly, 'Who's that?'

" 'That's Mr. Wasserman,' Mazzoli replied. 'He's very powerful. And, by the way, the reason he's so powerful is, *he's* Hollywood.' "

Commanding as Wasserman had been in the forties and fifties, those decades had been a mere prologue. He had transformed the agency business, and he had appropriated TV production; but in the Hollywood hierarchy, these were still substrata. Once he joined the ranks of the old moguls as chief of Universal Pictures, however, he was positioned to become industry leader. It was a new, imperial role, of his design. There had never been one individual who spoke for this industry, and who navigated its course singlehandedly. Wasserman's predecessors—L. B. Mayer, Sam Goldwyn, Jack Warner, and the rest—had reigned supreme over their own fiefdoms, but none of them had wielded authority over all of Hollywood. Wasserman was determined to do just that. In fact, he could tolerate nothing less. He had after all felt compelled to exert utter control over all aspects of his agency (though answering, ultimately, to Stein)—and the talent business had not been nearly as vulnerable to a complex array of political, social, and economic forces as this giant production business would be. And *even there,* at the old MCA, he had been caught momentarily off guard when the government filed its antitrust suit, and he had felt, for a brief time, at the mercy of the regulators. In the end the suit had been resolved most idyllically for Wasserman, but he had nonetheless taken a lesson from that experience: he meant never again to find himself without protection in Washington that was both broad and deep. So—several years before his leadership of the industry was formalized in any way—he began laying the groundwork for a Hollywood political machine that would be far more sophisticated, far richer, and far more high-powered than any that had existed before.

At the start, Wasserman worked closely with New Yorker Arthur Krim, the formidable president of United Artists. In May 1962, Krim had orchestrated the spectacular, all-star birthday gala for President John F. Kennedy at Madison Square Garden where he was serenaded by Marilyn Monroe, then went on to a dinner at the Four Seasons and an all-night party at Krim's stately Upper East Side townhouse. The event was so successful (netting $1 million, an extraordinary sum at the time) that Krim wanted to devise some way to keep these contributors engaged. In the 1960 campaign, Kennedy had gotten relatively little money from New York because it had been held back by the head of the state committee, according to Krim; most of the money Kennedy received from New York came through a citizens committee led, in part, by Robert Benjamin, Krim's partner at United Artists. Now, Krim wanted to create a money flow that would circumvent local party or-ganizations. He decided to form something called the President's Club, which would raise money that would go not to the party but directly to the president for his political use. For a membership fee of $1,000, one could join the President's Club and attend "seminars" with top people in the cabinet, as well as fund-raising dinners for the president. Of the rewards that came with membership in the President's Club, Krim said in an oral history interview for the Lyndon Baines Johnson Library "it didn't get you a favor with the government, but it got you an awful lot of fun for yourself and a feeling of being close to the charisma of power." Initially, the President's Club was based only in New York, but within a year or so Krim had enlisted Wasserman to start one in Cali-fornia, and soon there were branches nationwide.

Wasserman became a close ally of Eugene Wyman, the California Democratic party chairman. Wyman, a lawyer from Chicago, had founded a well-regarded, prosperous law firm in Beverly Hills; he was also the husband of City Councilwoman Rosalind Wyman, who played an important part in bringing the Brooklyn Dodgers to Los Angeles. "Gene had lived in the shadow of his prominent political wife," re-called Joe Cerrell, who was Wyman's political assistant. "But once he became chairman in 1961, he was like a kid in a candy store! The law firm was developed by then, so he could spend almost full-time on pol-itics. And he was willing to raise *big* bucks—something previous party chairmen had not done." Wyman had a coterie of friends and clients—many were movers and shakers on the Westside—whom he tapped for large sums. Among them were Eugene Klein, CEO of National General Corporation, owner of the Chargers football team and Wasserman's close colleague in the President's Club; Mark Taper, head of the Amer-ican Savings & Loan Association; Luis and Mark Boyar, real estate de-velopers; Alfred Hart, founder and chairman of City National Bank in Beverly Hills—and, also, a business associate of Joseph Fusco, a liquor distributor who was an apprentice in the Capone mob; and John "Jake the Barber" Factor. "Jake the Barber was an easy touch for Wyman. He gave a *lot* of money," Cerrell said. "I remember once Wyman saying,

'Get me Jake the Barber.' And his secretary (she must've been new) came back and said, 'I've looked all through the directory, there is no barber named Jake.' " Sidney Korshak was a close friend of Wyman's, and was often present at the political get-togethers at the Wyman home in Bel Air. Korshak was said to be a generous contributor ("He had to do something with all that cash!" one friend of his commented), but often not in his own name.

Wyman was famous for his pledge dinners: he would assemble his major givers at his home or in a private room of a restaurant, where every guest was expected to announce what he was going to contribute. "But they'd shil it!" Cerrell declared. "Wyman would say to one of them, ahead of time, 'You're giving $25,000—and if you can't do that much, we'll help you a little.' Then that guy would pledge $25,000. And the next one would figure, if *he's* giving $25,000, I gotta pledge $30,000!"

Though Wasserman did not attend these dinners—they were not his style—he was one of Wyman's biggest contributors, and he also raised a great deal of money from his own contacts, Cerrell said. "It was a good marriage—Wasserman would never go to party meetings, or get-out-the-vote meetings, and Gene would happily do all that stuff. And unlike so many big contributors, Wasserman never needed to sit next to the president, never needed a fancy job title. I wouldn't exactly say he was retiring—but there was no grandstanding."

In June 1963, the President's Club sponsored a $1,000-a-plate dinner for Kennedy at the Beverly Hilton Hotel, in Beverly Hills. According to Cerrell, it was Wyman and Mark Boyar who came up with the novel idea of placing eleven seats at every table; ten were filled, and the president would move from one table to the next every five minutes. "And as they were being hustled, everyone was told, 'You will be sitting with the president,' " Cerrell said. As head of the President's Club, Wasserman escorted Kennedy from one table to the next, quietly reminding him of guests' names. The day after the dinner, Wasserman received a note the president had scrawled on a few pages of the Hilton's small message pad, asking him to go on the board of the planned Na-

tional Cultural Center in Washington (Wasserman had the note framed
and displayed in his home). Wasserman had come up with a fund-
raising idea for the Center that President Kennedy liked: to designate
one night when all parts of the entertainment industry—motion picture, ballet, theater, music, nightclub—would be asked to donate the
night's proceeds to the Cultural Center. If several million dollars were
contributed, as expected, that would put the fund-raising drive over the
top. Much as Wasserman was exerting himself for Kennedy, however,
it was political, not personal. He had never been a Kennedy fan. In the
1960 election, Wasserman had strongly favored Johnson, not Kennedy,
for the Democratic nomination. And then, of course, it was Bobby
Kennedy, as attorney general, who had approved the Justice Department's suit against MCA in 1962; and Bobby, who—because of his war
on organized crime—was the bane of Moe Dalitz and Sidney Korshak,
Wasserman's close friends. So Wasserman was working for the party
more than the man.

His ambivalence was cured when Johnson became president.
Wasserman had been introduced to Johnson in the late fifties—Johnson
was then Senate majority leader—by his good friend Ed Weisl, the New
York lawyer and longtime chairman of the executive committee at
Paramount, who had been a staunch ally of Johnson's since the forties.
Johnson had made it a habit to stay with the Weisls whenever he came
to New York; Weisl, who was a close friend of Robert Lehman and
lunched so regularly at the Lehman Brothers investment firm that he
was considered almost a partner there, became the young Texas congressman's Wall Street mentor, providing him entrée to the New York
financial community. Weisl had been soliciting political contributions
to Johnson from Wasserman for some time before he introduced the
two men. Wasserman took to Johnson instantly. "He was my kind of
guy," Wasserman declared. "No sham about him." When Johnson
agreed to be Kennedy's vice presidential running mate, Weisl—who
had a long-standing animus for the Kennedy clan, dating back to a
power struggle he'd had with Joseph Kennedy, Sr., at Paramount in the
thirties—stopped speaking to Johnson for more than a year. With the

rift mended, however, they were as close as before, and after Kennedy was assassinated, Weisl was among those Johnson first called. Weisl contacted his friends in the media, urging them to suggest to the public that Johnson would be a great president, and he asked Lehman to contact leading bankers around the world with similar reassurance.

Wasserman, too, stood ready to help, in ways large and small. Jack Valenti, who joined President Johnson as one of his special assistants the day Kennedy was assassinated, recalled that Johnson was planning a trip to Los Angeles early in his 1964 campaign, and he wanted to have a trailer at a certain location. He told Valenti to call Wasserman. Wasserman recounted this story in the course of his oral history interview for the LBJ Library, conducted in December 1973. He had received a call from one of Johnson's security men the day before Johnson was to make an appearance at Los Angeles's City Hall, who said that the president needed a place to freshen up after coming in the motorcade from Long Beach. "And I said, 'Well, why are you calling me?' He said, 'I don't know. I talked to Jack Valenti, and he said if we had any problems to call you and you'd take care of them.' I said, 'All right . . . call me back in an hour.'

"I rang back to the production officer and said, 'Do we have a new dressing room?' And he said, 'We have one we're finishing.' And I think it was for Doris Day or Cary Grant, one or the other. I said, 'Where is it?' He said, 'It's back in the paint shop.' So I said, 'Okay, I'll be back to see it.' And never having been back to the paint shop before, I got in the car and went back to the paint shop. We had [these] beautiful what we now call huge mobile homes which we use on the premises for stars, with washroom facilities, sitting rooms, *et cetera*. So I said to this man, 'What do you need to connect this?' And he said, 'A four- or six-inch sewer pipe and a hundred feet of electric cord. We carry everything else.' I said, 'Well, get it ready, and I'll have it picked up in an hour.' And I left. By the time I left, the heads of production had arrived. It was quite an event for me to be in that particular department.

"I went back to my office, and the phone rang, and it was the security man. And I said, 'Get ready.' And this man came storming in, the head of the department, said, 'You don't understand, Mr. Wasserman. We can't take this off the premises. It's too wide; it's too heavy; we haven't got a license, because it's only used on the premises.' The premises are about four hundred acres. And I said, 'Don't worry about it. How heavy is it? . . . What do you need to pull it?' He said, 'But you can't take it out, you can't go out on the streets with it.'

"Well, this chap called me back. And I said, 'Have a couple of security men here, and we'll give you the rig to take it down, but I want you to know it's against the law. It's too wide and the freeway . . .' He said, 'Don't worry about that.' I couldn't tell this department head what it was going to be used for, for security reasons.

"So the next day I decided to go down and see what was going on. And, sure enough, this motorcade arrived with President and Mrs. Johnson and Governor and Mrs. [Pat] Brown. There must have been a quarter of a million people in the area; and they got out and went into this trailer, and everything was fine. The president got up and made a speech. And when it was over, I went up and said hello, and he turned to me and said, 'I understand you arranged all this.' And I said, 'Well, I helped a bit.' He turned to Jack Valenti and said, 'I want one of these at every stop' " (laughter).

But the real proof of Wasserman's resourcefulness and his whole-hearted commitment to Johnson was the money he raised. Kennedy had been scheduled to appear at a President's Club dinner in Los Angeles in early 1964; now Johnson came in his stead, and that kicked off Wasserman's campaign on his behalf. His labors evoked some praise even from his sometime adversary Jack Warner, who was a Republican. In a note to Wasserman in June 1964, Warner wrote, "I am most delighted that you are heading the fund-raising for our esteemed President Johnson's re-election campaign." Warner said he was about to leave for Europe, and thus regretted that he would not be able to visit the president with Wasserman. However, he continued, "I would like to furnish you, when I return from Europe, with a list of the big money-makers in the motion picture business who give nothing politically and a very minute amount charity-wise, and some of them give nothing." It seemed he could not resist a mild gibe: "I recollect several years back that Jules was a Republican. He being the Chairman of the Board of your company, while you are just the President, trust that you will have good fortune in receiving donations from Jules for the important task that I know you will accomplish." Wasserman—along with Wyman's and others' help—did indeed accomplish it. When the results in the November presidential election were tallied, Wasserman had recruited so many new members to the President's Club that its California roster was over five hundred, second only to Krim's New York organization. Moreover, Wasserman, Wyman, and other Democratic players had raised more money for Johnson than California had ever contributed to a Democrat.

Johnson was not the only beneficiary. Wasserman had established his credentials: within the motion picture industry, Krim was the acknowledged political power in the East, and now Wasserman was in the West. But they had achieved their political status for different reasons—and they treated it differently. Krim, a policy-minded individual with a strong interest in education and civil rights, had co-founded a prestigious law firm before going into the movie business, and, in 1951, acquiring United Artists. He had supported Adlai Stevenson at the 1960 Democratic convention; then he'd turned to helping Kennedy. He was so devastated when Kennedy was killed that he thought of leaving politics altogether, Krim's wife, Mathilde, said. Krim suggested to Johnson that he might want someone else to take over the running of the President's Club in New York (Krim was thinking of Weisl, who was known as Johnson's man in New York, and whom Johnson, in fact, named to the powerful post of Democratic national committeeman). But Johnson's aides prevailed upon Krim to continue, and soon he was working as hard for Johnson as he had for Kennedy. In May 1964, for example, he organized another hugely successful extravaganza at Madison Square Garden—preceded by a dinner at which Johnson followed Kennedy's lead, going around the room to spend some time with all of his major New York contributors, many for the first time. Johnson appreciated what Krim was accomplishing for him.

TOP: Wasserman with the president he most admired. *Courtesy of the LBJ Library*
BOTTOM: One of Lew Wasserman's signature President's Club dinners. This one
was held at the Century Plaza Hotel in Los Angeles on June 23, 1967. From left to
right: Lynda Bird Johnson, Arthur Krim, Mathilde Krim, Wasserman, President
Johnson, Edie Wasserman. *Courtesy of the LBJ Library*

Krim recalled that, at a later rally at Madison Square Garden, he was motioned to come to the stage, where the president "lifted me up and embraced me and kissed me on both cheeks."

And the more Johnson saw of Krim and his wife, Mathilde (an elegant, ethereal-looking scientist at the Sloan-Kettering Institute in New York), the more he wanted to see of them. Soon, the Krims were aloft in the Johnson whirlwind. Krim recalled that one evening in July 1965, a distinguished group of scientists (including Mathilde's boss at Sloan-Kettering, Frank Horsfall), were at the Krims' home, watching a film on Mathilde's research on cell structure. "The phone rang, and I got on, and it was the president. He said he wanted Mathilde to leave that night to go to Paris with the astronauts." (It had just been announced that the Russian astronauts were to attend the air show in Paris; Johnson decided the American astronauts should be there, too. And why Mathilde? "He was very blunt about it," Krim recalled. "He said, 'These ladies, they don't know how to dress, they don't know how to act, and Mathilde with her sophistication and her knowledge of French would be able to shepherd them.' ") "I said, 'Well, you know, she's here with the president of Sloan-Kettering—' He said, 'Put him on the phone.' Mathilde went downstairs where we were showing the film and said to Horsfall, 'The president wants to talk to you.' He said, 'President of what?' She said, 'The president of the United States.' The guy got so flustered, and he went upstairs, and Johnson twisted his arm—it didn't take much twisting. He said he wanted Mathilde to leave right away, and Horsfall said, 'But certainly, of course.' " While Mathilde packed, Johnson put Tom Dewey, the former governor of New York, on the phone with Krim, and then Hubert Humphrey. "The whole thing became a half-hour conversation on the phone between all of us. It was a very jovial night for him," Krim said. Shortly after that, Johnson invited the Krims for a weekend at Camp David in early August; and from then on, nearly every weekend that the Johnsons were able to leave Washington for their Texas ranch, Johnson invited the Krims to accompany them. Before long, Johnson had persuaded the Krims to buy a ranch, too, just a short helicopter ride from his. Johnson also asked Krim, as his personal representative, to oversee the administrative affairs at the headquarters of the Democratic National Committee. So Krim began to spend a great deal of time in Washington; he stayed overnight at the White House so often that he was given his own bedroom, Room 303. According to Krim, Johnson pressed him to join his cabinet repeatedly, but Krim always said, "I'd like to serve you the way I am, let's leave things as they are." Krim said he also declined Johnson's offers of the posts of ambassador to France and ambassador to the United Nations (the one job that tempted him).

Johnson was probably drawn to Krim for many reasons ("He was such a complete man within himself—the president *loved* to be around him," Valenti commented), but one was surely that Johnson believed Krim had no personal or business agenda. Indeed, in his oral history, Krim emphasized his sensitivity on this score. "Since a lot of people knew that I was able to see [Johnson] one-on-one, I had to carry a lot of messages to him and also get things done. I must say that of the group that came into the money aspect of politics through me, the things they wanted the president to do almost without exception had nothing to do with them or their business. It had to do with broader issues of importance, in their view, to the country. But not small, petty things. It'd have to do with health legislation, with Israel, with tax legislation. For instance, Andre Meyer would be giving me messages on the financial community, Mary Lasker would be giving them to me on health legislation, Abe Feinberg on what to do about Israel."

Krim, notably, did not mention Wasserman. And his wife, Mathilde, interviewed after Krim's death, said that while he and Wasserman collaborated, particularly in politics, Wasserman operated at a different level. "Arthur always told me that Lew was more of a lobbyist for the industry." Johnson seems to have viewed him that way, too. In January 1965, Universal Studios was celebrating its fiftieth anniversary, and President Johnson sent Wasserman a congratulatory letter, praising the studio for its "many enduring contributions to our national goals." However, Johnson's letter was accompanied by a cautionary note from his aide, Valenti.

Dear Lew:

Enclosed you will find a letter which the President was happy to send in connection with the Fiftieth Anniversary of Universal City Studios. I hope you can use it effectively in observing this milestone.

However, we do frankly have some doubts as to the wisdom of using it in the advertising supplement which you are publishing in the Sunday New York Times. It would be a marked departure from past practice to have a Presidential message of this sort used in paid company advertising.

Johnson saw Wasserman's agenda—it was plain as day—but he treated him with the solicitude appropriate to such an important fund-raiser. Wasserman was invited to White House meetings—sometimes with other business leaders, sometimes with political strategists. Wasserman recalled a meeting he had attended during the 1964 campaign—either at the White House or Camp David, he couldn't recall which. When he joined the meeting, others were discussing Proposition 14, a ballot initiative in California that would repeal a statute barring discrimination in housing. "Someone was making a speech pointing out that the president was going to lose California. I walked in at that moment, and he [Johnson] turned to me and said, 'What is this Proposition 14?' I said, 'It's a very emotional issue. It's unconstitutional, according to the advice we've all had.' And he said, 'What's going to happen with it?' And I said, 'I think it'll carry by two million votes.' At which point someone jumped up and said, 'See, you're doomed—your whole thing.' And he finally turned to me and said, 'Lew, what do you think will happen to me in California?' And I said, 'I think you'll carry by 750,000 votes.'

"At which point, someone else got up and allowed how that was ludicrous, [that] there was no way the president who was the champion of civil rights and the whole issue, [that] it was doomed, and [that] if Proposition 14 was going to carry [by] two million votes, they were going to lose California and the overflow would hit Arizona and Oregon. We were just doomed.

"So I listened to this rap patiently for about five minutes, and then stood up, which, as you know, one does not do in the company of the president, and started to leave. He said, 'Where are you going?' I said, 'I'm going back to California.' He said, 'What do you mean, you're going back to California? I thought we were going to have dinner, and you're staying for the weekend.' And I said, 'Well, I don't want to stay here.' And he said, 'Why not?' And I said, 'Well, you're getting me confused. I'm a very simple man.' He said, 'What's the matter?' I said, 'Well, you know, I live in California. I have the responsibility of some of your activity there. The only place I've heard you identified with Proposition 14 is in this room. Before you get me confused and get me thinking along those lines, I'm going to get out of here.' He laughed.

"It was quite true, which points out the difficulty of being isolated. The final result was that Proposition 14 carried by two million, seven or eight hundred thousand, and the president carried by over a million." It was counterintuitive—that a ballot initiative fueled by a backlash to civil rights legislation would win such enormous support, and that the president so largely responsible for that legislation would, too—but it did bear out Wasserman's prediction. And he had understood the situation, he was saying, because he knew California politics, and was not part of a myopic political clique in Washington.

"There was just no way [Arizona Senator Barry] Goldwater could carry California," Wasserman concluded. "I was concerned—the 'big lie' technique—if we kept talking about Proposition 14 identified with President Johnson, somebody would start to believe it, you know? I literally had never heard it until I arrived at that meeting, or heard it since."

Washington was new terrain for Wasserman, but he approached it as he did his own—with confidence, authority, self-deprecation ("I'm a very simple man") that was meant to convey the opposite, and, when necessary, a sure sense of drama (making a show of leaving a meeting was a Wasserman specialty). In this instance, his assessment turned out to be right. But he was not always so astute about what was—no matter his display of confidence—unfamiliar ground. Sometimes he seemed to be trying to focus on this new region with the lens he was accustomed to, which produced a decidedly off-kilter view. Since Wasserman was, as he put it, "in the image business," Johnson asked his advice about what he and Wasserman, too, saw as Johnson's "PR problems." By 1967 Johnson was vilified by many in the college and black communities, both groups that Johnson felt should have been in his corner. Regarding their hostility, Wasserman commented, "I believe he understood that the reason was Vietnam. I also believe that he felt that if there was a way to communicate the real issues in Vietnam, that the reasons would be answered or understood. But there was just no way to communicate."

Wasserman attributed that inability to communicate to "the fatigue factor," which he said he had learned about in his business. "A given program can be on television very successfully up to a given point and then, for some inexplicable reason, it starts to disintegrate; and research has indicated that it's called the fatigue factor. That, I believe, is the one thing that the administration failed to understand about the Vietnam War. We checked and, I believe, in the California area there was actually on television in every twenty-four-hour period over an hour of war film, seven days a week. . . . As ridiculous as it may sound, had it been possible to change the name of the war and the color of the uniforms of the enemy, it could have gone on longer. There was a total turnoff, as it were, with the mass population."

Johnson treated Wasserman to some of the special attention that he doled out so masterfully, and to such great effect. Wasserman, of course, did this himself, on a much smaller scale, and he might therefore have been expected to be cynical about Johnson's overtures; but, to the contrary, he seemed thrilled by them. Johnson, for example, had phoned Wasserman when a profile of him, entitled "Hollywood—A New Kind of King," had appeared in *Time* magazine on January 1, 1965. The cover of the magazine featured Johnson, as Man of the Year. Wasserman recalled that he was driving home from the studio. "I happen to be a telephone nut, I have telephones everywhere, my car." But he was preoccupied, and his car phone was off. "I drove in on my motor court, and my wife was standing there shouting at the top of her voice, waving her hands, saying, 'Why don't you have your car telephone on? The president's calling.' . . . And I said, 'I've only been gone twenty minutes, you know.' I went in and called the White House. . . . It was the president to tease me about the fact that there was a story on the inside of *Time* that was rather complimentary to me, about my capability and everything. He said I was stealing his thunder: here he was on the cover and there was a two-page story on the inside. And that was a call from a friend; that was not a call from the president of the United States."

Unlike Jules Stein, Wasserman had made his climb without its going to his head, at least in terms of social pretense; he seemed to pride himself on that, and he saw the same down-to-earth quality in Johnson—which was part of the attraction. "I was always very impressed by the fact that, holding the highest office in the world, he was a real person, at least with people who he considered his friends," Wasserman said. "He certainly did not put on airs or acts, or throw his clout or image about. I'm reminded of the time we were back in Washington at a private dinner about the time Luci [Johnson] and Pat [Nugent] were married, and there was an American Airlines strike. There were about ten of us at dinner, and my wife was seated on the president's right. She was complaining to him about the difficulty we were having trying to get back to California because of the strike, and he picked up the phone which was on the dining room table to call Warren Woodward [chairman of American Airlines]. And she said to him, 'Well, don't bother with that. Lew's already talked to Woody, and there's nothing he can do.' At which point, the president howled, because he was president of the United States, who certainly had more influence than her husband. He roared with it. . . . It never dawned on her, you know, that she was talking to the president of the United States. Which only proves his real quality as a friend; because she was totally at ease."

Wasserman was a guest at a number of White House functions, including state dinners, and on several occasions he and his wife, Edie, spent the night. Wasserman loved to tell the story about how once he and Edie were in Washington to attend a dinner party, and staying at a hotel. While he was at the party, he received a call from the White House, saying that the president had learned he and Edie were in town, expected them at the White House that evening, and was having their bags moved from the hotel. Still, it was certainly a qualitatively different relationship from the one that Johnson had with Krim; when Wasserman went to the White House, it was an event, and Krim all but lived there. During his presidency, Johnson taped many of his phone conversations; a log, compiled from the time Johnson became president through December 1965, shows not a single one with Wasserman. And when the Wassermans were invited to the ranch on Memorial Day weekend in 1968, along with seven other couples, Lady Bird wrote in a note to Governor John Connally's wife, Nellie, who was hosting these guests for lunch, that it was a group that "Lyndon and I think will be interested in the Library." She was referring to the Johnson Library, then in the early planning stages.

There is no question that Wasserman was very fond of Johnson. After Johnson left the White House, it seemed that Wasserman could not do enough for him. He was one of the Library's most substantial benefactors, as Lyndon and Lady Bird had anticipated; according to Jack Valenti, Wasserman donated MCA stock worth millions of dollars, which became worth hundreds of millions over the years. Wasserman contributed to Lady Bird's wildflower foundation. Once he discovered that Johnson enjoyed listening to his cassette player in his car, Wasserman continually sent him large packages of tapes. But it is also true that he traded on the currency of this relationship when Johnson was president, and, in less meaningful ways, forever after. And if Wasserman was not an intimate of Johnson's, Wasserman's business associates certainly did not know it. During the Johnson presidency, NBC executive Don Durgin recalled, "Lew would hold forth in these lunches with his stories about Lyndon and all the *inside*. He sounded more knowledgeable than our news correspondents. He was so plugged in." In later years, Wasserman would speak with great pride about his closeness to Johnson, but what seemed to be the highlight for him, as he often recounted it, was Johnson's offering him the position of secretary of commerce shortly after the 1964 election. He had refused it, he would always say, "because my wife wouldn't move to Washington." On one occasion, he said having passed up that opportunity was the one thing in his life he regretted.

Some expressed doubt that Johnson ever made such an offer, however. Harry McPherson, an aide in the Johnson White House, was quoted in the *Washington Post* in 1995 saying that Johnson did not tap Wasserman and would not have—because of concern about what might be raised in nomination hearings regarding Wasserman's connections to organized crime. Asked about his having been thus quoted, McPherson said, "Yes, I did say that, and I believe that was the case. But I was very angry with myself when I saw it in print—because I would imagine Lew would think, now why did McPherson go and say that?" Frank Stanton, the longtime president of CBS, had gotten to know Johnson in the early forties through Johnson's interests in the television business. An Austin television station that Johnson owned became a CBS affiliate, and Johnson and Stanton were soon good friends. When Johnson was president, Stanton was a close adviser, in and out of the White House regularly. Stanton said that Johnson had offered him a couple different cabinet positions—secretary of defense and secretary of health, education, and welfare, as well as undersecretary of state. He had declined, he said, because "I knew that working for him, I would have no life of my own." Stanton also said that he had never heard that Wasserman had been offered the post of secretary of commerce, and he was certain that if Johnson were seriously considering Wasserman, he would have asked Stanton what he thought. Like McPherson, he believed Johnson would have been leery of a Wasserman confirmation proceeding because of concern about his connections.

"You know, ties between the White House and Hollywood only started with JFK," Stanton remarked, pointing out that such relationships had not existed for Franklin Roosevelt, Harry Truman, or Dwight Eisenhower. "A lot of people aren't sure about the greasepaint—it's a tricky business." And despite Wasserman's fund-raising, he added, Johnson kept Hollywood at arm's length until late in his presidency. "I was never at the ranch when anyone from Hollywood was there—and *everyone* was there," Stanton commented. Of course Krim was, he acknowledged—"but I don't think of Krim as Hollywood."

One person who has repeatedly gone out of his way to assert that Johnson offered Wasserman the secretary of commerce post is Valenti. As Johnson's close aide, Valenti had become very friendly with Wasserman; Valenti and his wife stayed in the Wassermans' Palm Springs home for a long weekend following Johnson's triumphant reelection in November 1964. About two weeks later, Valenti wrote Johnson a memo, recommending nine candidates for recruitment into Johnson's administration. One was Wasserman, about whom Valenti wrote, "Ed Weisl called him 'the best business brain I have ever known.' Brilliant organizer and administrator. Tough, smart, full of common sense. Goes to the heart of problems—practitioner of the art of the possible." Valenti says that Johnson, too, was high on Wasserman by that time. "He saw in Lew much of what he had himself—drive, instinct, judgment," Valenti declared. "Johnson used to say, it's not whether you scored 1600 in your SATs, or went to Harvard or San Marcos State Teachers College. It's whether you have good judgment." And, about a week after he sent Johnson his memo, Valenti says, Johnson asked him to sound out Wasserman for the Commerce position. "That's when I talked to Lew. He was pleased but said he had just bought Universal Studios and could not depart MCA at this time." Valenti's account could not be definitively countered since, as he told it, only three people knew of the offer, and the two then-surviving ones—Wasserman and he—said it occurred. Moreover, it was only after Johnson's death that Valenti, in the course of a speech he made honoring Wasserman in November 1974, "let the secret out" that Johnson had invited Wasserman to join his cabinet, as recounted in the *Hollywood Reporter*. This much is plain: whatever the truth about the offer of a cabinet post having been made, Wasserman would certainly have appreciated that Valenti put his name in the hopper.

A little more than a year after that occurred, Wasserman had a chance to reciprocate.

The Motion Picture Association of America (MPAA), begun in 1922 and originally known as the Motion Picture Producers Association, was shaped in its early years by men like Carl Laemmle, Samuel Goldwyn, L. B. Mayer, and Adolph Zukor. In its history of more than four decades, it had had only two presidents, both with Washington experience—Will Hayes, postmaster general in the Harding administration, and his successor, Eric Johnston, president of the Chamber of Commerce, and an emissary for President Roosevelt. After Johnston retired in 1961, the job had been vacant for several years, mainly because the rivalrous, combative studio heads could not agree on a successor. It was, in fact, a vacancy that had caught the eye of President Johnson, who wanted to place one of his people there. For from the very start of his presidency in 1963—even before Wasserman brought the President's Club fund-raising to new heights—Johnson had considered Hollywood a rich money source, and the MPAA, Hollywood's Washington embassy, located just down the street from the White House, a most desirable base. In December 1963, Theodore Sorensen, who had been a speechwriter for President Kennedy, told Johnson that he was quitting the White House staff; Johnson, loath to lose Sorensen, immediately proposed that he become president of the MPAA. His procuring the job for Sorensen, Johnson figured, would not only enhance his connection to the MPAA, but enable him to keep Sorensen on call as a speechwriter. Johnson had phoned Weisl, a Paramount board member, to ask him to arrange it, saying, "I'm going to lose him [Sorensen] either to this outfit or some other outfit that I control. I'm not going to just turn him out in the pasture." In the negotiations with Sorensen that ensued, Weisl repeatedly made it plain to him that all the studio heads "expect you to serve the president first," a condition to which

Sorensen did not assent; and in the end he didn't take the job. Other names were floated, from Adlai Stevenson to Pierre Salinger, but there was no accord among the movie executives, so the limbo continued.

In the spring of 1966, however, attorney Louis Nizer, a partner in the law firm Krim had founded, became the nominee—evidently with Krim's support. The way Wasserman told the story to Steven Spielberg in an oral history interview, he was in MCA's New York office when the receptionist announced that Nizer wanted to see him. "He said, 'This is a courtesy call. I've just been hired to be head of the Association. . . . I said, 'What! You're sixty-six years old!' Well, he knew he had made a mistake by coming in. I went down and saw [Milton] Rackmil [who was still serving as Universal's representative, albeit at Wasserman's sufferance] and said, 'I want an emergency meeting of the Association by noon tomorrow.' " The president of the MPAA was Spyros Skouras, who was then board chairman of Twentieth Century-Fox; Skouras said it was too difficult to arrange a meeting, Wasserman continued. "I said, 'Look, it's very simple. I'm sending the resignation of Universal over by messenger. We're out of the Association.' He said, 'What do you mean?' I said, 'We can't get a meeting, we're out of the Association.' So we had the meeting and I *screamed* and Skouros said, 'Okay, you go find someone.' "

Wasserman quickly fastened on Valenti. He was not an immediately obvious choice. He had no Hollywood experience, and had had no Washington experience either until that day in Dallas when Johnson's life had been drastically reconfigured in an instant, and Valenti's, too. In 1962, Valenti, a Houston advertising man, had married Johnson's secretary, Mary Margaret Wiley, an attractive, svelte thirty-one-year-old blonde who had worked for Johnson since she'd graduated from college, and was a favorite of his. Mary Margaret then gave up her job with Johnson, but Johnson still tried to keep her in his ambit, persuading her to accompany him on a trip to the Far East, inviting her and her husband to the ranch—so Jack Valenti, too, became part of the Johnson circle. In November 1963, Valenti had organized a dinner in Houston for President Kennedy and his wife, Jacqueline, and Johnson and

Lady Bird; it had gone very well, so Johnson asked Valenti to accompany him to Dallas the next day, and then continue together to Austin for another dinner Valenti had arranged. Valenti was in the motorcade in Dallas, and after he rushed to Parkland Hospital, where President Kennedy had been taken, he eventually learned that the president was dead and that Johnson wanted him on Air Force One. He sped there, and for the next couple of months spent a great deal of time at Johnson's side, living with him at first in the Elms, the vice president's residence, and then in the White House. Liz Carpenter, Lady Bird's staff director and press secretary, who was also on Air Force One that day, said, "He scooped Jack up—that's so Johnsonian! Houston had been successful, so he scooped him up and took him along. Johnson was such an impromptu, impulsive, enthusiastic person—particularly when things had gone well. I don't think he would have summoned Jack otherwise. It just happened that way. Destiny. He was there, he was capable, he was a 'can-do man,' as Johnson liked to say." Valenti had a signal attribute, Carpenter added, that Johnson valued. "The Johnson expression, which came from the frontier days, was that he wanted somebody he could go to the well with. Well, Jack was certainly somebody he could go to the well with. Johnson was such a good analyst of men—that's what made him such a good majority leader. He'd use [one assistant] for completely different things than he'd use Valenti for. He could use Valenti as his eyes and ears and legs."

Valenti delivered his own self-assessment. In an undated note, apparently written after he had been with President Johnson for several weeks, Valenti wrote, "I have been pondering the question of how best I can serve you—how I can be most useful to you.

"I bring you one asset: Loyalty."

Over time, it became clear that Valenti brought Johnson more than that. The same qualities that had made him effective in the advertising world served him well in the White House, as he watched Johnson's calendar, coordinated speechwriting, and lobbied Capitol Hill. An engaging, likable individual, he prided himself on giving senators and congressmen "instant service," trying his best to return their calls within an hour or two. He made the personal touch a kind of credo; in a note to the president in February 1965, Valenti wrote, "Thought you would like to know that so far I have written 110 *letters,* personal letters, to the Congressmen and Senators I have personally talked to at the Congressional receptions." And while he was no original theorizer, he had a facility for translating abstractions into human terms. LBJ assistant Larry Levinson recalled, "The President would often say about some speech, 'I want it Valenti-ized! I want it made human!' "

Ultimately, though, what most distinguished Valenti was his worship of Lyndon Johnson. It had actually begun when he first met the then senator in 1955; Valenti had offered his impressions of Johnson in a weekly column he wrote in the *Houston Post.* "He's a tall man, tall in the cord-lean frame of a man used to being fit. There is a gentleness in his manner, but there is no disguising the taut, crackling energies that spill out of him even when he's standing still. And no mistaking either the feel of strength, unbending as a mountain crag, tough as a jungle fighter." His current proximity to Johnson had done nothing to diminish his adulation. Other Johnson aides were devoted, but none appeared as slavish as Valenti. Reporters soon noted the fatuous way Valenti spoke about LBJ, how the diminutive aide gazed up at the president as he hurried along at his side, how eagerly he leapt to perform the most menial tasks; within the first year, the press had dubbed him "the valet," and the epithet stuck. ("I hate that *Wall Street Journal,*" Valenti said to the president in a phone conversation in November 1964. "They're the ones that are always calling me 'the valet,' and I wouldn't have truck with 'em. Screw 'em!") Valenti's reputation for servility, moreover, was only underscored by the common knowledge that Johnson heaped abuse on him. He was certainly far from the only one to receive the famous Johnson treatment; but he was thought by other aides to get the worst of it. Another White House assistant said, "Jack was a hand-in-the-fire loyalist. Many of us were doubtful about Johnson because of Vietnam, among other reasons. But I don't know what Johnson could have done that would have driven Jack from his side."

Much as Valenti disliked being derided for his sycophancy, he did not temper it. In June 1965, he had delivered his famous speech to the Advertising Federation of America convention, in which he declared that there is a "curious up-soaring of mind and spirit that seems, as if by Godly osmosis, to invade the veins of a man the moment he becomes President"—and that *this* president "has extra glands I am persuaded that give him energy that ordinary men simply don't have." And he had concluded with the words that will outlive him: "I sleep each night a little better, a little more confidently because Lyndon Johnson is my President." Valenti had sent a copy of his speech to LBJ before he delivered it; neither man anticipated what ridicule would be heaped on Valenti for saying what, in their shared view, was utterly appropriate. Arthur Krim recalled a night at Camp David not long after when a couple of journalists who were present made fun of Valenti's declaration—provoking the kind of Johnson tirade Krim had not witnessed before. "He was an angry man," Krim said, "and his anger was triggered by [this remark]. . . . I don't think whoever it was that started this realized what a sensitive chord he or she was touching with the president. But the president lashed out at their failure to recognize loyalty."

Wasserman knew the value of such loyalty. And if Valenti was a worshipful subordinate, always leaping to do his boss's bidding, accepting the most harrowing abuse—well, so much the better. As he had been Johnson's man, so he would be Wasserman's. As Wasserman told it, he enlisted Weisl's support, and the two of them went to see the president to tell him they wanted to hire Valenti away. "He threw us out of his office," Wasserman claimed, "but he called me a couple days later and said, 'You can have him.' " There was at the time a fairly prevalent view that it worked the other way around; that despite the voluble protests LBJ made to Valenti about his proposed departure (according to Valenti, Johnson called him "a Benedict Arnold"), Johnson had in fact "asked Lew to take care of Valenti," as one Wasserman assistant told me. "Johnson was very pleased about Jack's going to the MPAA," Jim Jones, another White House aide, recalled, "either because he had engineered it, or because Lew Wasserman had convinced him that Jack Valenti could do more for him in fund-raising in the Hollywood community."

For Valenti, it was a remarkable opportunity. He had gone into debt collecting his $30,000 White House salary, and the MPAA annual salary of $150,000, in a seven-year contract, would solve his financial problems. It seemed, in a way, almost too easy to be true. He assumed he would have to meet the MPAA board of directors (men who for years had not been able to agree on any candidate), but Wasserman told him that would not be necessary. According to Valenti, Wasserman said, "Eddie [Weisl] and I will make sure we can elect you." At one point, someone proposed that Nizer and he be co–chief executives, Valenti continued; he called Wasserman to object, and the idea was dropped (Nizer became general counsel). "Lew was so dominant, and he was the *newest* member of that board," Valenti said. "He was the most powerful man in Hollywood. He'd commanded all the stars, and he had demonstrated he could bring the industry to a halt by denying the services of his stars." By this time, of course, Wasserman had left the talent business behind. But the fact that he no longer held that hammer didn't seem to matter. "He was respected and feared by all these moguls," Valenti said, and then added, "He never pushed anybody around unless he had to."

Wasserman and Valenti agreed that they would formally become partners at the MPAA. The MPAA's labor-negotiating arm was the Association of Motion Picture and TV Producers (AMPTP), and its longtime chairman a Paramount executive named Y. Frank Freeman. Now, Freeman would have to resign, and Wasserman take his place. Traditionally, the chairman had represented studio management in labor negotiations. "Y. Frank Freeman would have an executive committee, made up of three or four guys, to negotiate with the unions," Valenti said. "But here's the way Lew operated. Lew said, '*I* will do it—I'll come back and tell you what the deal is.' " He paused, then added admiringly, "Only Lew would have the audacity to do that."

Valenti became president of the MPAA in May 1966, and in July,

Wasserman became chairman. In one deft play—displacing Nizer and inserting Valenti—Wasserman had gained control of two critical Hollywood spheres, labor and politics. He could not countenance leaving labor negotiations in anyone else's hands. Universal, the largest motion picture and television studio, relied heavily on its television production—which was even more perishable than movie production, and thus more prone to devastating damage by a strike. Wasserman was uniquely equipped to deal with labor. His relationships on the below-the-line union side, with the Teamsters' Ralph Clare and IATSE's Dick Walsh, went back roughly twenty years; there was no one else at the studios whom these men respected as they did Wasserman. Moreover, to deal with problems that needed special handling, Wasserman had his close friend, Sidney Korshak, on call. But contacts and experience were not enough. For the kind of autonomy Wasserman had in mind—the ability to sit opposite the union representatives at the negotiating table and strike a deal for the industry, essentially on his own—he needed an assigned portfolio. Thus, the chairmanship was key. On the political side, however, he need not be so overt; the obliging (and obligated) Valenti could be his surrogate, and his cover. This suited both men perfectly. Wasserman always preferred to wield power indirectly if possible; he rarely granted press interviews unless he had some important message he wanted to publicize, and he shunned the limelight. Valenti basked in it. His White House colleagues had ribbed him about his avidity for press exposure; Bill Moyers, another Johnson aide, had once written to a newspaper editor, "I suggest you introduce Jack Valenti as the man who took Lyndon Johnson to the Far East. It seems Jack was on the front page of every newspaper where the President went on his recent trip." Now, however, when he preened for the press, he would be doing his job.

As Wasserman said later, Valenti turned out even better than he had anticipated. He had reason to be pleased with his choice. It did not hurt to have a Hollywood ambassador who was so close to the president. Valenti continued to accompany Johnson on trips, make contacts on his behalf abroad, make speeches for him on college campuses, and

write memos on political strategy. He kept in close touch with others at
the White House, too—including Bob Kintner, who after having been
fired from NBC had obtained a job as a communications adviser at the
White House. Kintner's changed circumstances had not altered the deference he showed Wasserman. Shortly after Valenti left for the MPAA,
Kintner wrote letters to all the major studio heads, congratulating them
on having landed such a talented individual. And, in August 1966,
Kintner wrote a note to Valenti, thanking him for twenty-five large
Corona cigars—and mentioning, by the by, that he had just had the opportunity to spend an hour with Wasserman ("I consider him one of
the brightest financial men in the country, as well as being an excellent
executive"). Along with Krim, Valenti urged Johnson to appoint
Wasserman to the board of the John F. Kennedy Center for the Performing Arts, and he did. Even with Valenti at the MPAA, however,
Johnson evidently wanted to keep some distance from Hollywood, as
Frank Stanton had mentioned. In August 1966, a few months after
going to the MPAA, Valenti sent a memo to the president, asking him
to schedule a lunch with the heads of the major motion picture companies. "These movie presidents can be of great usefulness to you—and
this lunch would also aid me in getting things done for you through
them," Valenti urged. But Johnson refused, appending a note to his assistant that read, "I'm afraid of this." Two years later (by which time
Johnson had decided he was not running again), he agreed to Valenti's
request, and hosted the movie men for a White House lunch.

Valenti's most important contribution in his early days at the
MPAA, however, was helping to develop a voluntary national movie
ratings system; operating under the auspices of the MPAA, a ratings
board would classify movies to give parents advance warning about
what their children would see. It was a preemptive strike. Movies had
begun to reflect the sixties' social ferment and changing mores, pushing
the boundaries in language and nudity, and in a powerful backlash, a
host of municipal and state censorship boards had sprung up. The
threat of government regulation seemed real. "There was a fire out
there," recalled Viacom chairman Sumner Redstone, who at that time

owned one of the country's biggest theater chains. "We could have taken the constitutional defense, but this was better. It was a perfect middle ground—you don't have to attack us. We'll regulate ourselves." To build support for the plan, Valenti cast a wide net—meeting with theater owners and distributors, actors, writers, directors, and producers, craft unions and religious organizations, and, not least, MPAA member companies. Most of the studio heads were opposed at first, he recalled. "I had to have a mighty force on my side to get my own companies on board—and that was Lew Wasserman. I couldn't have gotten it off the ground without Lew!" Valenti declared. But once Wasserman made his support clear, he concluded, "the other studios fell in line."

It always seemed to go that way. "We used to have a moguls' retreat, at Laguna Niguel," Valenti recalled. The famous trial lawyer Edward Bennett Williams, who was the MPAA's general counsel, and a good friend of Wasserman's, would attend these sessions also. "A subject came up—I don't recall what it was—but Lew didn't agree with it, and he started to rant. 'I am not going to listen to this—we are violating the antitrust laws!' Ed Williams said, 'No, Lew, it's okay.' Lew paid little attention to Williams. He walked to the door, put his hand on the knob—then he came back. There was a vote: Lew's way. Ed Williams said to me later, 'What a magnificent performance! What a trial lawyer he could have been!' "

With the help of Wasserman, his formidable patron, Valenti had come a long way in a short time. George Stevens, Jr., son of the famous director and chief of the Motion Picture Service of the United States Information Agency (USIA) in the early sixties, recalled that he and Edward R. Murrow, USIA head, would show films in the old mansion that was the MPAA headquarters in Washington. "I was there the night *Lilith,* with Warren Beatty and Jean Seberg, was shown," Stevens said. "It was a rather perplexing picture. When it was over, there was some applause (no one liked it much), and Jack turned to me, in a low voice, and asked, 'What do you say to somebody?' I suggested something. He strode up to the director, with his hand extended, and said, 'You've done it again, Mr. Rossen!' [Robert] Rossen was thrilled. That was probably Jack's first brush with show business, and he pulled it off well. He was a quick study." Now, just a couple years later, in September 1967, Valenti and his wife, Mary Margaret, were being feted at a sumptuous black-tie party at the Wassermans' home. Los Angeles columnist Joyce Haber reported that the event honoring the Valentis was "a glittering, galloping winner," and that Edie Wasserman was wearing "the most knockout ruby gems you've ever seen." Among the guests were Cary Grant, Alfred Hitchcock, Rock Hudson, George Stevens, James Stewart, Gregory Peck, Ross Hunter, and Jill St. John. Sidney Korshak was there, too, as he often was at Wasserman's parties. So Valenti's initiation into Hollywood life went beyond learning the ropes at the MPAA.

And while Washington had been hard on Valenti, in Hollywood he was in his element. What had seemed off-key in Washington didn't in the movie colony; his flamboyance fit right in, his flattery was appreciated, his verbal affectation much admired. He formed close, lasting friendships with Warren Beatty, Angie Dickinson, Charlton Heston, and Kirk Douglas (Valenti took to clenching his jaw like Douglas, and, one of Valenti's friends said, was delighted when told that he looked like Douglas when he did so). And he was clever enough to grasp that these stars were a great resource that, properly deployed at Hollywood fund-raisers and in congressional hearings, could help his bosses' causes on Capitol Hill in ways that had not been done before. In early 1967, he sent an article about himself in the *Los Angeles Times* to President Johnson, underlining these words: "Whatever else is true, it is clear what Lyndon Johnson saw in him. For president Valenti is fiercely energetic, enthusiastic, politic, realistic, perceptive and persuasive." Valenti attached a note, saying, "Funny, how all of a sudden I am now bright, charming, delightful—when a year ago I was a valet and a clumsy Texas oaf!" While most of the article was devoted to Valenti's role in developing the new movie ratings system, a couple of sentences, more telling, suggested that Wasserman's grand design was very nearly realized. "Valenti notes with considerable pride that 'for the first time in history, every major motion picture and television company is in the association,' with Universal's Lew Wasserman as chairman of the board.

"Indeed, there are indications that the association is on the way to becoming a forum and unifying force in the American film industry such as has not existed in recent times."

———

At the same time that Wasserman was working to bridge the gap between Hollywood and Washington, he was reaching across another divide, within Los Angeles itself. Every major city has diverse communities, but Los Angeles, because of its gigantic sprawl, was more like a collection of insular enclaves than a real metropolis. With its opulence and glamour, Hollywood naturally tended to overshadow the others in the public eye, but the entrenched power and old money were elsewhere, in the downtown business community. Many of its members lived in places like Pasadena, Hancock Park, and San Marino, and tended to view Hollywood, and its resident communities on the Westside, like Beverly Hills and Bel Air, as nouveau outposts. The two societies rarely mixed. Doris and Jules tried to break through these barriers, entertaining Norman Chandler, chairman of the Times Mirror Company, which owned the *Los Angeles Times,* with Samuel Goldwyn and Jack Benny; but the Stein parties were unusually eclectic affairs. And Wasserman, along with other MCA executives, was generally not invited.

It was Wasserman, however, whom Dorothy Buffum Chandler, Norman's wife, invited to join the board of the new Music Center for the Performing Arts in downtown Los Angeles. Dorothy, known as Buff, was determined to transform Los Angeles, long seen as a rough outpost and San Francisco's poor relation, into a city with vibrant and beautiful cultural institutions. She conceived of the Music Center—a graceful, white-columned building, designed by architect Welton Becket, on a rise above downtown L.A.—and she, almost singlehandedly, raised the money to build it. Through her fund-raising drives, she raised $18.5 million, and a county bond issue provided another $13.7

million. When the Music Center's Pavilion (later named the Dorothy Chandler Pavilion) opened in December 1964, Chandler was featured on the cover of *Time* magazine, and the accompanying story described her achievement as "perhaps the most impressive display of virtuoso money-raising and civic citizenship in the history of U.S. woman-hood."

"The first time I ever met Buffy Chandler was when she walked into my office—I think it was in 1961—and asked for a check for $25,000," Wasserman recalled. It was a surprisingly modest request for her. Charlton Heston is said to have recalled an incident in which "a very wealthy man gave her a check for $20,000 [for the Music Center], and she tore it up, said it was ridiculous, that she needed more than that." Indeed, she did not hesitate to ask friends like oilmen Edwin Pauley and Samuel Mosher for gifts of $125,000 (which she received). But Chandler evidently decided to go in easy with Wasserman, whom she did not know. And she realized, too, that he could offer her more than just money—for by bringing him onto the board of the Music Center, she was opening a door to the Hollywood community.

Wasserman, for his part, made a gesture that was sure to impress his new Music Center colleagues. Al Casey, the chief financial officer of the Times Mirror Company, recounted in his book, *Casey's Law,* that by the fall of 1963 the Center had run through the more than $30 million that had been raised, leaving no funds for pre-opening operations. It had already borrowed $350,000 from the Bank of America against advance ticket sales; now, that money was spent, and it had asked the bank for another $150,000. The bank was refusing that loan, and threatening to demand immediate repayment of the earlier $350,000. Casey convened an emergency board meeting. As he began to make his presentation to the assembled directors, Wasserman cut him short. "Wait a minute," he said. "Before you go on with your sad tale, let me just say that, following your call, I stopped in at the Bank of America on my way down to this meeting and put my personal signature on a note for a half million dollars. Your $350,000 loan has been resecured and you have $150,000 available right now." Four years later, the Music Center paid off the note.

In 1966, Buffy Chandler asked Wasserman to become the president of the Center Theatre Group, a civic organization to support drama in the two theaters of the Music Center complex, the Mark Taper Forum and the Ahmanson. "Mrs. Chandler knew that if this Music Center complex was to survive, it couldn't be just Pasadena and Orange County," explained Gordon Davidson, artistic director of the Mark Taper Forum. "It had to have the Westside, the Jewish community, the movie people. How do you get them? Get their leader." He added, "Mrs. Chandler was very comfortable crossing lines."

Davidson chose to open the Mark Taper's first season with a production of *The Devils* by Aldous Huxley—a play about a nun's sexual fantasies and a libertine priest. When the play was in rehearsal, Davidson got a call from the Los Angeles archdiocese; the cardinal understood they were about to put on a play that was anti-Catholic—and he intended to denounce it. In addition, the County Board of Supervisors, which owned the property on which the Music Center complex stood, was backing the cardinal. Buffy Chandler enlisted her newly appointed president, Wasserman, to intercede, and before long he had appeased the cardinal, who in turn de-enlisted the county supervisors, and the production went forward without incident. *The Devils,* however, was not the last play at the Mark Taper to be deemed controversial, and often by the Chandlers' friends. "If there were sex or dirty words, Mrs. Chandler's friends would beat up on her," Davidson said. "So we worked it out this way: I said, why don't I tell you what plays you should come to see? If you don't see it, you don't have to have an opinion."

Wasserman brought in his friend, Paul Ziffren, as secretary-counsel to the Center Theatre Group. Ziffren, who had been a protégé of political boss Jake Arvey's in Chicago, had moved to Los Angeles in the fifties, established an extremely successful Westside law practice, and become very active in Democratic politics. His son, Kenneth Ziffren, who would become one of the premier entertainment lawyers in L.A., was working in his father's firm at the time Paul joined Wasserman in his theater enterprise. Ken knew Wasserman socially; Paul was entertaining a lot at his Malibu beach house in those days, Ken recalled, and "Lew and Edie were the honored guests." Sidney Korshak was another. ("I knew Sidney well," Ken said. "*Charming* guy, you never felt fear around him.") But the first time he encountered Wasserman professionally was when his father assigned him to negotiate a long-term operating lease between the Center Theatre Group and the Music Center operating company. The Music Center company was represented by O'Melveny & Myers, a white-shoe, prestigious downtown law firm. "I started going downtown to meet with all the O'Melveny lawyers—at one meeting, there were eight of them and me! These negotiations went on for months, and eventually there was a manageable list of issues. My father said to prepare a memo for Mrs. Chandler, Lew, and him. I worked hard at it; he marked it up; I corrected it. I went and handed Lew the memo.

"He looked at it and said, 'Okay.' He went down each issue and told me how it should come out. He said, 'They'll say this, then you say this, this is how it should go.' He came up with answers and approaches that were totally beyond me. It was scary, *really* scary. So spectacular. It just bowled me over."

The Wasserman-Chandler connection came to extend beyond the Music Center complex. "Norman Chandler came to see me," Wasserman recalled. "He wanted me to go on the board of Caltech [California Institute of Technology]. I said, 'Why would they want me? One, I'm a Jew. Two, I'm in show business. Three, I'm from the Westside. Four, I never went to college.'

"He said, 'You've already been approved. I'm chairman of the nominating committee.' " It was a response that Wasserman (having arranged Valenti's approval by the MPAA board in a similarly seigneurial way) could appreciate. "I was on that board for fifteen years."

Wasserman was helping to bring a little ecumenism to largely segregated communities. In doing so, of course, he was also extending his personal reach across this fissured city, in a far more profound way than Stein had ever done. In the course of a decade, Wasserman had added critical segments to his network—one that was "built on power and money," as his friend, Washington attorney and Democratic eminence Robert Strauss, put it. "Lew is the only person I know who had one foot in the movie business, one foot in the business or financial community, one foot in the political community. He could call the Catholic archbishop just as easily as a rabbi, a defense contractor as easily as a studio chief, a banker as easily as a member of the *Times* editorial board. Because it was the movie colony, there was a kind of power that you couldn't have in New York or Washington," Strauss declared, and then added, sounding just a bit wistful, "No one person, in those cities, could have his power."

———

It was remarkable, really, how smooth Wasserman's assumption within the movie industry had been. Remarkable that the other studio heads just gave way, that in an instant he was able to displace Nizer and substitute his own man at the MPAA, that he could usurp total control in the labor negotiations. It was almost as though his sovereignty had become so much a recognized fact of life in Hollywood that when he claimed one or another of its prerogatives, no one thought to object. No one, that is, except his primordial rival for the presidency of MCA, Taft Schreiber, and, more importantly, Jules Stein. For when MCA stumbled in the late sixties, Stein (at Schreiber's instigation) effectively reminded Wasserman that it was *he* who still controlled the company, through his majority holdings—and that Wasserman could be deposed. That was the single fallacy in Wasserman's near-perfect assumption.

When the agency business had been shut down, Wasserman was liberated; but Stein suffered, seeing what he had built—his monument—disappear. He hated the stark black glass tower Wasserman chose for their new corporate headquarters (its offices were still filled with Stein's antiques, but they were incongruous in this ultramodern setting), and he rejected Wasserman's plan for a second tower. The idea of the tour had excited Wasserman from the start, but not Stein; he had recoiled slightly at the idea of the public's trooping through their private domain. Still, he assented. "Al Dorskind brought me a photograph—it showed the old Universal commissary, which stood right where this [tower] is," Wasserman said. "People paid a quarter, and they walked to the second floor and watched the movies being made— and they were *silent!* It was taken in 1919. I said to Dorskind, 'Do you think they would still do it?' " In Wasserman's tour, visitors rode in trams around the property, saw movies being filmed, stopped to see Doris Day's dressing room, and glimpsed the computer Wasserman had purchased to provide the kinds of cost-control studies that made factories run more efficiently. Bob Rains, a publicist at Universal, wrote in his memoir, *Beneath the Tinsel,* that on the first day of the tour, in July 1964, Stein had suddenly appeared in the doorway of Wasserman's office. He had taken the tour, he said, and he thought it would make the company money. " 'But we do have a serious problem,' Stein remarked as he took an admission ticket out of his suit coat pocket. 'Look at this! Nobody took my ticket after I purchased it. If something is not done to correct the situation, people will be giving their tickets to others once they leave the tour grounds. Think of the money we will be losing.' " Wasserman said he would take care of it right away.

Notwithstanding Wasserman's unfailing deference, there was no mistaking that Stein was more peripheral at the company than ever. He cast about for other activities, and even considered becoming a partner at the Lehman Brothers investment firm. It was Ed Weisl's suggestion— which may well have been instigated by Weisl's close cohort Wasserman. As Stein said later, "I was flattered. I mentioned the offer to Wasserman. He said that now that I had more time it might not be such a bad idea." Stein met with Bobby Lehman, who suggested that Stein might eventually succeed him as head of Lehman Brothers, and Stein asked to spend some time at the Wall Street firm in order to make up his mind. "I went there every day for a few months. I became terribly disillusioned. While they were making money, it seemed to me they were nothing but agents. They were making deals and collecting commissions. They were raising money and sometimes taking a piece of a company. They were doing the same thing we did at MCA when we were a talent agency. I thought to myself: I don't have to go to Lehman Brothers to become an agent again."

Ultimately, Stein settled on philanthropy as a consuming avocation. He had begun to think seriously about it after his bout with prostate cancer in 1959, when he had taken "inventory of my life," as he said. The next year, deciding to bring his life full circle, Stein had formed a foundation, Research to Prevent Blindness, which contributes funds to departments in ophthalmology at leading universities, and supports eye research in a variety of ways. He became a fervent promoter of his cause, and actually sought publicity. In a note to Hollywood columnist Hedda Hopper in January 1964, with his bio attached, Stein wrote, "Did you know, Hedda, that Americans spend more money on Eye Wash than Eye Research?" (He also cautioned her, "Don't get tripped up on the spelling of the word 'ophthalmology.' Note the 'h' after 'p'— most people forget that extra 'h'.") And he became galvanized by the idea that rather than leaving the choice of philanthropies to executors of his estate, he would create and control them in his lifetime.

In November 1966, the Jules Stein Eye Institute opened its doors at the University of California at Los Angeles. Its construction had cost about $5,550,000; Jules and Doris had contributed $1,250,000; Wasserman and other MCA associates and friends, $2,900,000, and the rest from the U.S. Public Health Service and the state of California. Stein had decided that *this* would be his monument; and, as he would later say, that "if I am to be remembered in the years to come, I truly believe my name will be associated more with ophthalmology and the preservation of sight than with the good fortune I have experienced in my business endeavors." Once again, Stein and his wife, Doris, made the decisions about every aspect of the Eye Institute—a stately, soft pink marble building, far more akin to the White House than the Black Tower. They commissioned a study of what pictures patients like the best: Impressionists, it turned out. So all the rooms featured large, nicely framed reproductions of a Renoir, a Monet, a Degas—but *noth-*

ing else (as in the MCA offices, pictures and personal mementos, like diplomas, were all expressly forbidden). No detail was too prosaic to rivet Stein. "Once I saw him studying a bunch of pictures of garbage cans. He was trying to decide which style, which color, was best for the Eye Institute," recalled his stepson, Gerald Oppenheimer. "And another time, he was in the hospital at UCLA, and he looked out the window of his room and saw the rooftop of the Eye Institute, which had black pebbles on it. He said, 'Get that stuff off there and put in the beige gravel!' The next day, it was done."

UCLA was suitably grateful. The university presented Stein with an honorary doctorate in 1967, and Alfred Hitchcock was one of the speakers. "You stand before us as a prime example of the maxim that a man can overcome the disadvantages of a formal education—and go on to become a success," Hitchcock began. "Of course, you started young. As I understand it, you went into the agency business immediately after receiving your medical degree. Most doctors I know fiddle around with a medical practice for years before they make good in real estate or the stock market. . . . So far as I know, though, you are the only medical man who ever made good in the movie business, with the possible exception of Vincent Edwards [the actor who starred in the TV medical series *Ben Casey*]. Anyway, I do think that your great contributions to this university are in the true spirit of forgiveness. After all, a college education delayed your marvelous career for eight long years. Congratulations."

Stein was now receiving a number of awards, and also honorary doctorates. He was pleased by these accolades. He was pleased even more by the notion, however extravagant, of what might someday be achieved through his continual funding after his death. "If it be true that blindness can be prevented—and if through my efforts we can preserve the sight of thousands, maybe millions of people—then I feel that my life has been well spent," he declared. But there was a possible hitch to this grand ambition. Since the bulk of Stein's wealth, which he intended to leave to the Eye Institute and Research to Prevent Blindness, was still in MCA stock, Stein's ability to achieve his life's ultimate goal depended to a great degree on the health of the company. And by the late sixties, that was very much in doubt.

In a strict sense, Wasserman was new to the movie production business; but he had of course been immersed in it as an agent for more than twenty years before he entered production. Having watched others struggle, he had long since determined that he would not be hostage to the inevitable volatility of movie-making. A firm believer in diversification, he had started to follow Disney's amusement park lead, with the Universal City Tour. He was determined to take advantage of the real estate potential of the four-hundred-acre Universal Studios property; he planned to build a five-hundred-room hotel, condominiums, office buildings, and also a giant entertainment center. MCA, having acquired Decca, was in the record business, too, as well as the music publishing business. It even owned a mail-order company, Spencer Gifts, and it had purchased a Colorado savings and loan. At this time, though, Wasserman's greatest hedge against the financial swings of the movie business was MCA's thriving and extraordinarily stable TV operation (thanks, especially, to the $200 million deal he had struck with Kintner).

At first, it seemed that Wasserman's talents—applied with such stunning effect in the agency and then TV production businesses—could be translated into the movie business. In January 1965, the *Time* magazine profile of Wasserman, "A New Kind of King"—the one Johnson had called to rib him about—heralded him as the savior of Hollywood. There was the usual hint of a dark side (" 'As long as I've known Lew,' says his friend Tony Curtis, 'everyone's been frightened of him' "), but the two-page piece was mainly a paean. It pointed out that "in its short existence as a major producer, MCA has made an impressive number of profitable pictures"—citing *Freud* and *To Kill a Mockingbird*, among others. And it described Wasserman as "a corporate president in show business, a modified First National City banker who has wandered through an unusual door, and he has shaped MCA into a trimly efficient manufacturing corporation, ample in size, and self-sufficient. . . . Neither a sentimental showman nor a tightwad, [Wasserman] has shown

that Hollywood can still make competent movies that are bids for quality within their own form and stay in the black, and that, as he puts it,
'if you are going to manufacture anything, you ought to have the finest
plant and facilities.' But the heavy financial investments needed to create such an entity would be for naught without a special flair for sens-
ing what is acceptable to the public—for that, ultimately, accounts for
success in the entertainment world. This, Lew Wasserman has to a
unique degree, and it has helped him bring Hollywood back from the
margin of extinction."

The encomiums were premature. For by the late sixties, even MCA's
television business was not a sufficient hedge against the ongoing losses
in movie production. In 1968, Universal Pictures lost close to $40 mil-
lion, and MCA—which had always prided itself on its strong balance
sheet—was about $90 million in debt. It turned out that MCA/Univer-
sal was not immune, after all, to a range of factors that were affecting
the motion picture industry. The American economy was entering a recession. The movie-going audience was shrinking; in 1968, about 40
million Americans were going to the movies in an average week, compared with 70 million twenty years earlier. Television was competing
for the public's attention; so many studio heads decided they could win
by offering theatergoers something they couldn't get on TV—new
blockbuster movies, often involving the highest-paid stars and thousands of extras on dazzling sets. Most of these extravaganzas failed.
Twentieth Century-Fox spent more than $30 million on *Cleopatra*.
Paramount invested about $20 million in *Paint Your Wagon*. Referring
to a string of these movies as "the gaudy, 20-million-dollar elephants,"
Vincent Canby wrote in the *New York Times* in November 1969 that
"the era of the Big Movie may be just about over." And none too soon,
Canby was saying. For these movies mainly served to highlight the gap
between those executives who green-lighted them and the public who,
in a time of social ferment and shifting values, wanted very different
fare—smaller, more idiosyncratic, culturally attuned movies, like *Midnight Cowboy*, *Easy Rider*, *I Am Curious (Yellow)*, and *The Graduate*.

Universal had not binged on $20 million movies, but neither was it producing these smaller, more evocative films. Even in MCA's thriving television business, creativity had never been its strong suit. And now that the long-derided "sausage factory" was in the movie business, its formulaic approach was even more untenable; many writers, actors, and directors viewed Universal as a place where top management exercised far too much control over the film-making process, and efficiency was the mantra. And, of course, the bar in movie-making was set so much higher than in television; the costs were far greater, and so was the risk of failure; there really *were* no formulas, as Wasserman was learning.

In 1967, Universal was pinning its hopes on the upcoming release of *Thoroughly Modern Millie*, starring Julie Andrews; its annual report said that the movie promised to be "the most successful in our history." There was some reason for optimism. Two years earlier, Andrews had starred in *The Sound of Music*, which was one of the highest-grossing films ever made, and triggered a frenzy of attempts to replicate the elements of its success. And the producer of *Thoroughly Modern Millie* was Ross Hunter, who had *Pillow Talk, Magnificent Obsession,* and other commercially successful movies to his credit. In the event, though, *Thoroughly Modern Millie* was an expensive, banal, failed spoof (described by Pauline Kael as "desperately with-it"), which produced middling results at the box office. The next movie to arouse great hope at Universal was *Isadora*, starring Vanessa Redgrave, about the free-spirited dancer Isadora Duncan—a character to whom sixties' audiences would relate, Universal executives thought. "We hadn't had a good movie for a long time," said Don Winn, an MCA executive who worked closely with Wasserman in this period. "*Isadora* was filmed entirely in Europe, and Lew went to Europe to see the rushes. The film was about halfway then. He said it was *spectacular*. He told the producers, 'This film is about a woman running around doing interesting things. Whatever you do, don't let it go over ninety minutes.' We kept waiting for the release prints—it was to be a Christmas movie. It was December, and we were still waiting! The prints came in to New York two days before the preview, which was unheard of." Wasserman,

Winn, and a couple of other MCA executives watched the movie in the New York office's screening room. "It went on and on and on and on. It was close to three hours! I fell asleep several times. Wasserman was so angry he was *speechless*. It was the maddest I've ever seen him." Redgrave was nominated for an Academy Award as Best Actress, but *Isadora* was not the hit MCA had been waiting for. It was Wasserman's longtime protégé, Jay Kanter, who was the head of European production for Universal Pictures, and who was responsible not only for *Isadora,* but other costly box office failures, including *A Countess from Hong Kong,* with Sophia Loren and Marlon Brando, directed by Charlie Chaplin.

Sustained failure was a new experience for Wasserman. And, apart from the psychic cost, it challenged the premise upon which his relationship with Stein had been built. Gerald Oppenheimer, Stein's stepson, recalled a conversation he once overheard between Stein and Cary Grant: "Jules said, 'I'm the smartest man around.' And Cary said, 'That doesn't sound like you, Jules—it's so egotistical.' Jules replied, 'I'm smart enough to know Lew Wasserman can run the business better than I can.' " For nearly twenty years, Wasserman had given Stein no reason to second-guess his own judgment. Now, Wasserman had. Alan Livingston, a veteran entertainment industry executive who was a good friend of Stein's, recalled how indignant Stein was about the quality of Universal's movies. "The movies were so terrible. Jules would say to me privately, 'I don't know what to do about Lew. He and his men are *agents*. They don't understand movies.' Lew was not in good standing with Jules at that time, and Jules was quite open about it."

In July 1968, Stein devised a rather surprising solution. He and Donald Burnham, president of the Westinghouse Electric Corporation, announced that MCA would be acquired by Westinghouse, in an exchange of stock. In return for his $102 million of MCA stock, Stein was to receive a major stake in Westinghouse—and the stock exchange would be tax-free. In the *New York Times,* reporter Eileen Shanahan questioned the rationale for the merger. She pointed out that it highlighted "the extent to which the tax laws provide a positive inducement to mergers, particularly on the part of owners of closely held or privately owned companies, whose management is getting along in years—a description that fits MCA. If the owner or owners sell the company, or their stock in it, they must pay a capital gains tax on any increase in the value of the company since they acquired it. But if the company is merged with another, through an exchange of stock that is handled just right in every detail, what also amounts to a sale, the company escapes taxation." It was a fitting coup for Stein, who had built so much of his fortune through aggressive tax maneuvers. He gave an uncharacteristically fulsome, sanguine-sounding interview to Robert Wright of the *New York Times*; asked about his motives for the merger, Stein replied, "I'm getting to the point in life when I think it would be great to become associated with this kind of company. I've always had great respect for Westinghouse since the days I attended school just south of Pittsburgh [where Westinghouse has its headquarters]. It's a delightful marriage."

The deal's architect was a young MCA executive named Daniel Ritchie, formerly at Lehman Brothers, who had joined the company in 1960. Ritchie, who came from a socially prominent family and enjoyed strong Wall Street connections, was a Stein favorite. "In the mid-sixties, he was perceived in the company as the president-to-be," said Sidney Sheinberg, then another young executive at the company. Ritchie was one of a troika of executive vice presidents appointed at this time. "There had been a lot of pressure from Wall Street that MCA was a one-man show," Sheinberg added. "Lew was never the kind to whisper and cajole in Wall Street's ear—he was respected, but perceived as too secretive." The Westinghouse deal was another sign of Ritchie's ascendance. Shortly after it had been announced, Sheinberg said, "I was in the dining room at Universal, and Don Burnham was welcoming us into the Westinghouse family. He was saying, we're going to let Lew Wasserman run the company—but there was a kind of alpha-dog dominance. I thought, he's going to be an *active* boss. This is not going to work!"

On November 1, 1968, MCA announced that its merger with Westinghouse had been delayed due to continuing discussions with the Justice Department's antitrust division. (In addition to being a manufacturer of electrical equipment, Westinghouse operated commercial radio and television stations.) Westinghouse, though, seemed caught off guard by the MCA announcement. A Westinghouse spokesman said that he had no information about it. He said the Justice Department had indeed requested information, which was furnished by both companies, and that MCA then began discussions with Justice. As far as he knew, though, Westinghouse was not engaged in any discussions. Roughly six months later, in April 1969, MCA announced what had become widely expected—the merger had been called off after prolonged discussions with Justice. There seemed little question, though, that the deal's demise had more to do with internal machinations at MCA than any overruling external force. Sheinberg, for one, believed that "the Westinghouse deal was something Wasserman had been hustled into"—and, ultimately, "Wasserman essentially put the kibosh on the deal, by deliberately not trying to cure whatever problems Justice was having." It would not have been the first time that Wasserman appeared to be *acted upon* by Justice, and yet achieved the outcome he would most have wanted.

His antagonists in the company, however, were not so easily subverted. Chief among them was Taft Schreiber. Stein was closer to Schreiber than to any other employee. Though Schreiber was ten years Stein's junior, the two men had really come up together, starting with their early, shared Chicago experience. When Schreiber, still a teenager, had come to apply for a job as an office boy at the Music Corporation, he brought his clarinet along (he had a little band, and was hoping for a possible booking, too), and the fearsome Billy Goodheart asked him to play a number. After listening, Goodheart asked what he was doing to earn money, and Schreiber responded that he was working part-time as a shoe salesman while going to school. Goodheart told him to go back to selling shoes—but Stein interceded and hired him. Schreiber set out on the course that would become the regimen at MCA for many years to come. He started in what was then called the "shipping room," opening and passing out mail, sending advertising to prospective buyers, acting as relief switchboard operator. Eventually, he progressed to helping with arrangements for one-night bookings, and then to accompanying an orchestra as a road manager. It had been Schreiber who came up with the idea of asking Western Union branch managers to send in lists of all the dance halls in their area. And he soon became known as someone with a keen financial mind who was, also, a consummate salesman. He had a rather homely countenance, but his force of personality could smooth its uneven features. He was close to Stein's brother, Bill—and this, too, probably endeared him to Jules. "Bill Stein was like an elder brother to me," Schreiber said later. "Much of the training I had came from him. Jules Stein and Goodheart gave me the formal education of contracting, railroad routing, and one-night selling, but it was Bill who instilled the excitement and enthusiasm into the daily routine. Bill was continually dinning into my inexperienced ears the simple facts of salesmanship: 'When you are with your customers, remember they are friends. If you don't have anything to sell, leave them with something—information about the business in general, what their competitors are buying, what bands are coming up. Never gossip with a band leader or buyer about another band or customer, for when you leave he will wonder what you are saying about him.' "

And Schreiber learned to operate in the same Chicago milieu that Stein did. Many years later, he would recall that when he was still just an office boy he had noticed a modest establishment, the Persian Hotel, which had a large ballroom but no band. He urged the manager to book bands for his hotel, and the manager referred him to someone at the Metropole Hotel, who, he said, had more authority to do so. Schreiber met this person, sold him on an MCA band, and then on more of them, which were placed in other hotels he evidently controlled. Months later, Schreiber received a letter from the Metropole man, expressing his pleasure in their dealings, and concluding, "If you ever need any help, let me know." It was a meaningful offer. The Metropole was well known in Chicago in those days as Capone's headquarters, and Capone took a great personal interest in obtaining bands and celebrities to appear in his locales (commitments that he expected to be honored, as Joe E. Lewis painfully found out). The way Schreiber told the story, however, he did not even realize that the Metropole was Capone's headquarters until several years after he had been doing business there—and the Metropole man, he said, turned out to be Capone's representative. Not Capone. It *seems* like a sanitized version. But Schreiber, in any event, was the single person in the company, particularly as the years wore on, who would have been most likely to know the secrets of the Chicago life that Julie Stein left behind.

Even after Schreiber had sustained the rude shock of Wasserman's being named president, he was so secure in his relationship with Stein, and so devoted to the company, that he apparently did not feel dislodged. "Taft thought he was the number two person to Jules, even after Lew was named president," asserted George Smith, who joined MCA in 1966 and became close to Schreiber. "But when the company went public, he saw that Lew had twice as much stock as he did. He was crushed by this. He spent more and more time on his art collection, and hardly came to work." By this time, Stein and Schreiber both were serious collectors; Stein, of his eighteenth-century English antiques, and Schreiber, of remarkable pieces of modern art. They inhabited one social stratum, and Wasserman another. After the acquisition of Universal, however, Schreiber once again became more involved in the business. He was the head of Universal TV, and he was also active in developing the company's real estate. And as Wasserman began to craft a political role for MCA, he relied on Schreiber for versatility; they were "covered," Wasserman said, because he was the Democrat and Schreiber the Republican. But the two men never had an easy coexistence. And in the late sixties, as the company's losses mounted, Schreiber saw opportunity, and stoked the fires of Stein's displeasure with Wasserman.

"I called Taft 'Doctor No'—whatever Lew did, he found fault with," recalled Albert Dorskind, who was an executive vice president, along with Dan Ritchie and Berle Adams. "I had a big fight with Taft. Taft said, 'Lew doesn't know what he's doing with these two-hour movies for TV, he's losing money on these!' " Schreiber had told Stein that that was the case, and he wanted the in-house accountant to compile a report. Dorskind told the accountant, instead, to hire Price Waterhouse to do an audit. "Taft stormed in, saying, 'What did you do?' " Dorskind continued.

"I said, 'The chairman is entitled to the truth.'

"He said, 'I'll never forgive you!' "

Schreiber even began fulminating to outsiders. "I went to my dentist (who was also Taft's) one day," recalled Frank Price, one of Universal's top TV producers, "and he said, 'Boy, what's going on at MCA? Taft was in here, just *steaming!*' " By this time, Jennings Lang, who had metamorphosed from agent to TV producer, was heading movie production. "Taft had called Jennings, whom he didn't like anyway, and asked him for some information about movies. Jennings, essentially, had said, 'Butt out!' " Price said. Schreiber's increasingly choleric view was that Universal would continue making terrible movies until they brought in seasoned movie producers—instead of these *agents,* as Stein had complained to Alan Livingston. Wasserman was so keen on Lang that even after the scandalous episode involving Lang, Joan Bennett, and her aggrieved husband, Walter Wanger, Wasserman had not fired him. But in Schreiber's view, Lang was unfit for his new role, and insolent besides. By mid-March 1969, it was an open secret at MCA that Schreiber was urging Stein to oust not only Lang but Wasserman, and that Stein was listening. In the new, proposed configuration, Schreiber, sixty-one, was finally to become president, to be succeeded about a year later by a younger man, Berle Adams, an agent who had started with Music Corporation in Chicago in the forties.

On March 15, the day Wasserman celebrated as his fifty-sixth birthday, he drove to South Central L.A. to meet with black community leaders and the city police chief in an attempt to forestall possible riots. (At the time of the Watts riots in 1965, Wasserman, called on by the mayor, had driven into Watts to meet with community leaders; through his political and philanthropic activities, he had become increasingly active in Los Angeles's civic life.) He would later say that tempers ran high at this meeting, on an unseasonably hot day for mid-March; he had suffered chest pains, and when he returned home, his doctor, diagnosing heart trouble, had prescribed two weeks complete bed rest, with no phone conversations, and no business conducted. Wasserman may or may not have been ill—and he did remain at home—but he was far from incommunicado. "Lew was supposed to be home sick, but we all understood he was not," said MCA executive George Smith. "He was placing calls to Hal Hoss, who was chief financial officer. It was the film division that was doing poorly, that was what was hanging around Lew's neck." Wasserman had just fired Jay Kanter, head of European production, who was responsible for a large amount of losses. "He was saying, look at the numbers in the film division. Take out the advertising, take out this movie, take out that. He's *very* numeric. When he's getting ready for combat, he will arm himself by looking at it five different ways . . . he focuses on the relationships of numbers to each other.

"I've seen him do it," Smith continued. "He takes people on, and they're not prepared, and he does the numbers one way, then another, until they don't know which side is up, or what is happening. It's not that he's fabricating anything. It's just that there are these different ways of looking at numbers, and most people can't keep up."

This corporate intrigue was taking place at an awfully awkward time for Stein. The Sheraton Universal, the first high-rise hotel to be built in the San Fernando Valley—and the first of three planned for Universal City—was ready for business. Doris and Jules had been actively involved in its design and decorating, importing chandeliers, tile, and furniture from Europe; Doris is said to have had the George V in Paris in mind as a model. To celebrate its opening, the Steins were planning a society gala more spectacular than anything they had ever done before. By this time, Doris's social striving had been rewarded, gaining her entrée to a level of international society she could barely have imagined at the start. The previous September, for example, the Steins had been invited to twin events—two Portuguese parties, two days apart,

hosted by the Antenor Patinos, and the Pierre Schlumbergers, respectively—that were considered the social events of the year, if not the
decade. The Schlumbergers entertained 1,200 guests, serving a twenty-
course dinner on silver plates. For the Patino party, their mansion was
redecorated, and the food, chefs, and hairdressers were all imported
from Paris. Among the guests were Henry Ford II, the Duke and
Duchess of Windsor, the Begun Aga Khan, the Duchess of Argyll,
Count Paolo Marinotti. It was that same titled class that Doris wanted
for her Sheraton Universal party, which was also to feature the premiere of the new Universal movie *Sweet Charity.* But how were they to
induce such people to travel such a distance? Well, by making it free.
Planes were chartered from Paris, from New York, from Palm Beach.
"It's the most amusing idea I ever heard of," said the Duke of Windsor
when he received his invitation. It ranked as "one of the country's
biggest, longest, and most opulent social extravaganzas," Charlotte
Curtis wrote in the *New York Times,* describing the guests as "extravagantly dressed princesses (including Princess Gina of Liechtenstein),
playboys, Irish aristocrats, titled Frenchmen, tycoons, interior decora-
tors from three countries, members of nice but no longer inconspicuous
old families, movie stars, and all the other odds and ends of what
passes for international society." Of course, since this was a Stein enterprise—and one that cost an estimated $250,000—there was a tax
angle. Several days after the three-day event, which began on March
26, a *New York Times* editorial, entitled ". . . and Grossness in Los Angeles," noted that at least part of the bill would be deducted as a business expense from MCA's taxes, and suggested that "the House Ways
and Means Committee, exploring tax reform as one means of combat-
ing inflation, may be a little less than overjoyed at the thought that tax
money may have helped to provide 600 members of the jet set with free
roundtrip flights from New York and Paris—to say nothing of room
and board at something a mite above relief levels."

Still homebound, Wasserman was not attending the opening gala—
but Edie was determined to. "Edie called and said, 'I want you to take
me to the party,' " declared Herbert Steinberg, an MCA publicity de-

partment executive who was very close to the Wassermans. As Steinberg escorted Edie into the Sheraton's baby-blue ballroom, lit with crystal chandeliers, "you could see the buzzing going around the room—the pro-Lew and anti-Lew factions. It was important to Edie to be there, because she didn't want people to think that he was pulling out. She wanted to be very visible." Steinberg danced with her, as did a couple of other MCA executives. "She said, 'C'mon, dance with me, kid,' " one of them recalled, and remembered, too, as they danced, what she had prophesied about the certain fate of those who were trying to overthrow her husband. "She hissed in my ear, 'We will piss on their graves!' " He paused, and added, "Remember Jimmy Westerfield, the guy who played the head of the goons in *On the Waterfront*? You'd think you were listening to his voice, coming out of her mouth."

Wasserman had been busy arming himself with numbers as usual, but in this instance his people probably provided him greater leverage. Over the years, one of Stein's favorite maxims had been that MCA's biggest asset was its manpower. (Wasserman, too, had subscribed to it, echoing L. B. Mayer's phrase, "Our assets go home every night.") Now, as sides were chosen, Wasserman had the advantage. "Berle called me into his office and told me he was going to be the next president," recalled Sheinberg, then head of TV production. "I said, in that case, I'm quitting." Lang paid Stein a visit, and told him that if Wasserman were fired, Stein would have three resignations—from himself, Sheinberg, and Price.

Shortly after Stein's festivities ended, Herb Steinberg recalled, "Jules came over to see Lew at home. Lew told him, 'I'll leave the company anytime you want me to—but your key executives are going with me. You'll have a company without people.'

"Jules said, 'Don't be silly! Nothing of that sort was contemplated.' He changed one hundred eighty degrees." A couple days later, Stein issued a public announcement that the MCA board of directors had unanimously reaffirmed Wasserman's position as president and chief executive officer, and had also taken the unprecedented action of extending the appointment for the full term of an additional year. "While

usually these elections are determined by the board following the annual stockholders meeting in June," Stein's announcement continued,
"it was determined advisable at this meeting to dispel the unfounded
and unjustified rumors regarding Lew Wasserman leaving the company."

The rapprochement, however, was halfhearted. Less than four
months later, in July, MCA announced another merger—this time, it
was to be acquired by Firestone Tire & Rubber Co., in a deal reported
in the press to have been advanced by Schreiber, a close friend of the
Firestone family. But in September, this merger, too, was called off,
without any explanation. Wasserman had won another skirmish; but
in order to regain his power, he had to improve the company's performance. Later, Wasserman would take pleasure in reviewing the history
of MCA and noting that it never had a year in which it lost money—
but 1969, with net income of only 31 cents per share, came closest to
spoiling that record. George Smith recalled that in early 1970, they re-
sorted to measures that seemed incongruous for this historically cash-
rich company. "Our cash flow was so thin. Because of tax losses, we
could get a refund of prior taxes. Usually the refund took six or eight
months. I said to Lew, I'll fly up to Sacramento and see if I can walk it
through. We got the check a week or so later. It was only a $5 million
check, but it meant a lot!"

No source was too negligible. Another MCA executive recalled
Wasserman's summoning him and showing him a list of small-time
band pianists. Since the dissolution of its talent agency, MCA had continued to collect 5 percent commissions on income from deals its agents
had negotiated. "He said, 'I want these commissions!' I said, 'I can't do
that! You want me to go to Long Beach, find these guys who make
about $100 a week, and tell them that they owe us several thousand
dollars?' He said, 'It's in the contract—I want it!' "

Finally, in 1970, Universal had a hit movie, *Airport*—the first of the
disaster movies. It was the biggest by far in the company's history. It
had cost $10 million, and by 1972 would gross over $50 million; it received ten Academy Award nominations, and Helen Hayes won an

Oscar for her performance. It was the restorative that Wasserman needed. And its success was all the more stunning, in a way, because it was so counterintuitive. As its producer, Ross Hunter, commented in an interview for an oral history in 1984, "We did *Airport* . . . when everybody in town was doing *Easy Rider* and *Five Easy Pieces,* and porno pictures, and street pictures. And they said, 'Nobody's going to the movies except young people.' And I said, 'Well, that's because there are no movies for adults. But you give them a good old-fashioned *Grand Hotel* of the air'—which *Airport* was—'and they will come out in droves.' And the picture's grossed over $200 million. . . . And, again, the studio fought me, they called it 'Hunter's Folly,' they hated it. They didn't even come to see a day's rushes. And now of course *they* are the people who were in back of it."

Hunter plainly prided himself on his knack for knowing what the public wanted. The critics might pan him (and Vincent Canby did, for *Airport*), but, he said, millions of people proved the critics wrong. He had a fairly realistic view of his product ("It may not be a great work of art, it may not give you a lesson in literature, but it will entertain you"). But he had a somewhat grandiose view of his role. "Many times I had to do a movie to save the studio, because the studio would be going under," Hunter said in the oral history. "And I could only do just so many movies, because I was only one person. For instance, the little *Tammy* movies that I did in the middle of my career—why would I do a *Tammy* movie? Because I felt there was such a need for Mom and Dad to take that child to a movie that they could really be unafraid to take it to. . . . And of course the reviews were horrendous. We were hit right smack in the face. They said it was corn—which it was; saying it was old-fashioned—which it also was; saying it was very sweet—which it was. Then the millions and millions and millions started coming into the box office, and Universal was back in business. . . . So it was exciting. It was really thrilling for me. I love the fact that I didn't want to do the movie, but I felt that I should for the industry."

Hunter's tendency to cast himself as savior, however, turned out to be his Achilles' heel. Throughout the sixties, Hunter and Wasserman were quite friendly. They were both Cleveland boys, and Hunter, like Wasserman, had worked as an usher in a movie house there as a teenager. After Wasserman took over Universal, he treated Hunter exceptionally well, lavishing on him all the perquisites due a successful producer, and Hunter was frequently invited to the Wassermans' parties. Then came *Airport,* which should have forged an even stronger tie. However, in his memoir, Universal publicist Bob Rains recalled that at the time of the movie's release, rumors about Wasserman's being fired were still prevalent. "As the *Airport* box office figures started coming in and new theatre records were being set daily, Hunter supposedly told several people he had saved Wasserman's job," Rains wrote. "Unfortunately, Hunter's claims were printed as well as repeated by Hollywood's gossip lovers. Shortly afterward, Hunter's contract came up for renewal. It was not renewed—he lost his salary, studio car, offices, and even the art on his home walls. Now normally, a producer with the successful track record Hunter had would have been at another studio immediately on a long-term basis. He was not." Hunter produced only one more theatrical film—*Lost Horizon,* for Columbia in 1973.

The newly empowered Wasserman moved deliberately to settle other scores. He dispensed with his three executive vice presidents, each in a way commensurate with the level of their disloyalty. Ritchie, who had challenged Wasserman with the Westinghouse deal, resigned in 1970, and eventually joined Westinghouse. Dorskind, who had tried to take a middle road during the coup, lost his title and was removed from the board. "Lew wanted him, in effect, to disappear," Smith said. "Lew and I would be sitting in a meeting that was pleasant, going well—and then he would say, 'Call Al Dorskind.' I would think, 'Oh no, I don't want to see this.' Al would come in. 'Sit down.' Then, 'What do you think of that?' Al would say something, and Lew would say, 'That's the dumbest idea I ever heard! Get out of here!' It was awful to watch. Like some sort of psychological need Lew had—but he wouldn't fire him."

Stein was suffering from abdominal adhesions as a result of the surgery he'd undergone for cancer in 1959, and now he had surgery to correct them. He became critically ill. As Stein was hovering near death, Wasserman summoned Adams to his office and told him he was fired. To the surprise of many, including himself, Stein recovered. He called Adams and apologized to him for what had occurred, but said there was nothing he could do, according to Adams. Commenting on Wasserman's timing in firing Adams, Herb Steinberg said, "Lew is like a home-run hitter, who waits for the right pitch." He added, though, that Adams was really not much more than "an innocent bystander—Taft was the devil, whispering in his ear. Taft *hated* Lew."

But Schreiber, Wasserman's diehard adversary, was beyond his reach. "Taft and Jules were as close as you could get," Steinberg declared. Stein would never countenance Wasserman's firing Schreiber—indeed, when Stein was so ill, he was said to have given Schreiber voting power of his stock. To some MCA employees, trying to interpret kremlinology, it appeared that Schreiber and Wasserman were now yoked in a kind of shared power. Certainly, with a Republican administration in power, it was Schreiber, more than Wasserman, who was the far more visible political player. Stuart Spencer, a Republican strategist close to Ronald Reagan, recalled that he had called Schreiber in March 1969 to ask for his help on a project, and Schreiber had demurred, saying he "had his hands full," Spencer said. "A short time later, word leaked out about what had been happening at MCA. When I saw Taft, I said, 'You sure did—trying to kill the king!' "

Schreiber's introduction to political life had begun not long after Wasserman's—unsurprisingly, since it was meant to be a tandem effort. In 1965, Schreiber joined the group of wealthy Republicans, later known as the Reagan kitchen cabinet, which was supporting Reagan in his bid to unseat Democratic governor Edmund "Pat" Brown in the 1966 election. Others in this group included Los Angeles businessmen Leonard Firestone, Holmes Tuttle, and Henry Salvatori, retired investment banker Leland Kaiser, and Reagan's lawyer, William French Smith. Schreiber was a natural addition, inasmuch as he had been Rea-

gan's agent (making the life-saving deal whereby Reagan became host
of the TV series *General Electric Theater*). Further, as the sole representative of the motion picture community in this group, Schreiber
could provide an important bridge to a moneyed world. Spencer-
Roberts, the Southern California firm that Stuart Spencer co-founded,
was managing the campaign. "Leonard Firestone brought Taft into the
Reagan kitchen cabinet early on," Spencer said. "He was smart, cun-
ning, charming as hell when he wanted to be. He was a listener. In the
beginning, I thought he was listening so much because he was on a
learning curve. Before long, he figured out there was only a slim difference between show business and politics, and then he was ready!

"Nobody in that Hollywood colony took Reagan seriously,"
Spencer continued. "Taft did, some. He saw the potential. Taft knew
everybody. He got Frank Sinatra to support Reagan. Warren Beatty admired Reagan—in that he had the guts to do what he did, crossing that
line that Warren never quite could, from actor to politician." Attempting to target Reagan's being an actor, the Democrats had produced a
half-hour TV program, entitled *Man vs. Actor*, which showed Governor Brown saying to an integrated class of small children, "I'm running
against an actor, and you know who shot Lincoln, don'tcha?" Remarkably enough, the Democrats excerpted that segment and ran it as
a one-minute spot during the campaign's final week. "*That* was a mistake," Spencer declared. "And I think Taft got on the phone to a lot of
people in Hollywood. I mean, it was not a nice thing to say about actors. I remember I asked him, did you really get out and cultivate that?
He just smiled, the way he did when he didn't want to answer."

While Schreiber was attempting to mobilize Hollywood for Reagan, Wasserman was hard at work supporting Brown. "Reagan was
disappointed in Wasserman—because he was a good friend, and Reagan expected him to support him for governor, and he didn't," Spencer
said. Nancy Reagan took it even harder than her husband; it was a
breach that would not be fully healed for many years. But if Wasserman's approach to politics discounted friendship, it was not because
Wasserman was so driven by ideology. In Spencer's view, both Wasser-

man and Schreiber had their political leanings but they were, above all, practical men, driven by their business. "If Jules woke up one morning and said, Taft, you do this on the Democratic side, and Lew, you do this on the Republican side—I think they would have done just fine," Spencer commented.

Even without Wasserman's help, Reagan won that race by a huge margin. Now that he was governor-elect, however, he had to find a way to support himself in this new incarnation. Spencer recalled the governor's dilemma. "Reagan had no savings, no investments. He had had a salary from *General Electric Theater,* and he had only two assets, his house in Pacific Palisades, and the Malibu ranch property. The idea was to create income from the sale of that ranch property. Reagan would of course be receiving his salary as governor, he wouldn't be out in the street. But [this sale] was the only way they could continue living in the style that they wanted."

As detailed by Howard Kohn and Lowell Bergman in a 1976 story in *Rolling Stone,* Reagan had bought some of the Malibu Canyon property in 1951 and continued to add to it over the decade—paying $85,000 in all. Its 290 acres were surrounded by land used by Twentieth Century-Fox to shoot movies that required an arid-looking, craggy backdrop. In December 1966, shortly after his election, Reagan sold 236 acres of his ranch to Twentieth Century for $1,930,000, or $8,178 an acre. (Reagan had paid only $275 an acre.) Twentieth Century also signed a six-year option to buy the remaining fifty-four acres, at $8,000 an acre. At the time, a movie company spokesperson said that the purchase had been made because Twentieth Century might move its corporate headquarters there. This did not occur. Then, in 1968, Reagan bought acreage from a partnership headed by Kaiser Aluminum Corp., for cash plus his remaining fifty-four-acre parcel; with the caveat that if Kaiser couldn't sell that parcel within a year, Reagan would buy it back. After a year, Kaiser said it could not sell it; and when Reagan was told he needed to repurchase it, his lawyer said it would be bought instead by a company called Fifty-Seventh Madison Corp. (which was controlled by Jules Stein). Twentieth Century, for its part, waited until

1974, and then sold the 236 acres, which it had bought for more than $8,000 an acre, along with its other property in the area, to the state of California; the movie company received $1,800 an acre overall.

Why Twentieth Century bought the land at all—and paid such a fantastic premium—was puzzling, to say the least. In 1980, when Reagan was running for president, *Wall Street Journal* reporter Jim Drinkhall asked Reagan's lawyer, William French Smith, about these transactions—the original sale, and the follow-up. Smith replied that they were "strictly arm's length" and "plain ordinary commercial transactions." At the time of the original Twentieth Century purchase from Reagan, Richard Zanuck was the young president of the company; his father, Darryl Zanuck, was the chairman, but the company at that time was mainly run by Richard. Asked recently if MCA had played a role in that purchase, Zanuck replied, "If it was anyone, it was Taft"—and then declined to say more, other than to volunteer that "it was not a payoff." Zanuck's longtime close friend and partner, David Brown (who was working for Twentieth Century at that time), told me, "It was a sweetheart deal." Asked whether company records might reflect how the decision was made, Brown said, "It wouldn't have been discussed at a board meeting, because then notes would have had to be taken." Brown added, too, that Richard Zanuck, who had a difficult relationship with his father, was very close to Schreiber. "Taft was almost like a father to Dick."

Considering the incestuous history of Reagan and MCA—especially the all-important SAG waiver, which the government had investigated in the early sixties, searching for evidence of a bribe paid Reagan—it would have been too brazen for MCA to have purchased the property outright in the original transaction. Twentieth Century, somehow, was a willing candidate. "Taft arranged it all," Spencer declared. "And Jules would be willing to do it, too, because he was pretty close to Reagan, and he was used to taking care of clients who didn't know how to handle money." Indeed, Stein had been doing just that for Reagan in the area he knew best. As Drinkhall wrote, "After his 1970 California tax return was leaked to the press, Mr. Reagan confirmed that he hadn't paid any state income taxes that year and that one of the reasons was losses in tax shelter investments"—specifically, with Oppenheimer Industries, a cattle-breeding concern whose principal shareholders were Stein, his wife, Doris, and his stepson, Harold Oppenheimer.

On a more quotidian matter, too, Reagan turned to Stein. Years later, Stein recalled that when Reagan was about to begin his first term as governor, Reagan came to see him, saying he wanted to buy a fine desk from him for his office in Sacramento. Reagan had visited the MCA offices many times over the years, and was familiar with Stein's eighteenth-century furniture; he had come to the right place for something distinctive to grace his office. "I told him to select a desk from the MCA tower," Stein said. "He went around with me and, much to my surprise, he picked a reproduction. We had grown so rapidly that I had to use some reproductions at the tower. . . . I told him he had picked a reproduction and that it would be inexpensive. He took it."

Schreiber's debut on the national political scene came with the Nixon presidential campaign in 1968. Its chief fund-raiser was Maurice Stans; and, according to Spencer, who was active in fund-raising in this campaign, Stans relied on Schreiber for the California operation. Schreiber worked closely with fellow fund-raiser Herbert Kalmbach, and the two men became social friends, often playing golf together. Following his victory, Nixon made Stans his secretary of commerce, and offered Kalmbach the position of undersecretary. (Schreiber always insisted he wanted no political appointment.) Kalmbach elected instead to build his law practice. And after Nixon asked Kalmbach to become his personal attorney in the spring of 1969, Kalmbach's practice flourished; his firm, Kalmbach, DeMarco, Knapp & Chillingworth, moved from Century City to large offices in a downtown skyscraper, and its client list expanded to include a number of major corporations, including MCA.

Schreiber also became fast friends with another key person in the

Nixon circle, Leonard Garment, who had been Nixon's law partner at the Mudge, Rose firm in New York. Garment became the president's "special consultant," a kind of freelancer involved a great deal with the arts—until everything began to disintegrate in 1973 and Garment assumed what had been John Ehrlichman's job, counsel to the president. Especially in the early months of the Nixon presidency, Garment was the one Schreiber would contact when he wanted to get something done—whether it was promoting someone for the Ninth Circuit Court of Appeals ("This man is young, conservative, a Constitutionalist, he happens to be Jewish, a USC graduate, and his record as a Judge is outstanding," Schreiber wrote to Garment), or suggesting that they do things in Texas to try to stem Nixon's losses among Jewish voters (because of Nixon's qualified support of Israel). Schreiber and Garment shared a passion for Israel. "Taft and some other prominent Jews became part of the political effort to push the Nixon administration to give to Israel until it hurt, and to build up its defense capability," Garment said. "I remember a lunch at Sans Souci, early on in the Nixon administration. Taft, Max Fisher [a Detroit businessman], Sam Rothberg [head of Israel Bonds in Los Angeles], Luis Boyar [the developer], and me. It was on Israel. The five of us met, and then we went our separate ways, to do what we had agreed to." Asked what they had done, Garment demurred, saying, "I want to be careful, even though the statute of limitations has passed."

Schreiber and Garment also shared an interest in art. Schreiber said once that he had picked up what he knew about art here and there, often from former clients—actors like Charles Laughton, Edward G. Robinson. "Taft was self-educated, yes," Garment concurred. "But as a great agent, he was intuitive about talent—and that translated to art: is this *authentic?*" Both Schreiber and Garment were friends of Joseph Hirshhorn, the chairman of Callahan Mining Corporation, who was donating his vast collection of modern art to be housed in a structure, yet to be built, that would be known as the Hirshhorn Museum and Sculpture Garden, on Washington's National Mall. There was opposition to this plan from what Garment called "the snobbish Washington arts establishment"—and from Nixon, too. "Nixon was not at all interested in the Hirshhorn," Garment said. "A guy who had made his money in penny stocks, uranium, a Jewish finagler—a museum on the Mall was to be named after *him?* But Taft wanted the museum to happen. So we cooked up a plan. The idea was to assemble a group of Republican campaign donors to Nixon (past, present, and future) who were deeply involved in museum culture, and make them the board. Taft orchestrated the whole thing—and Nixon loved it!"

Garment claims credit for having recruited Schreiber for fundraising in the 1968 campaign—"for the implicit, unstated quid pro quo of politics: you help us, we will help your agenda." Nixon was inclined to look favorably on Hollywood's agenda for a number of reasons, Garment continued. Obviously, it could be a major source of money—something Nixon's two predecessors, particularly Johnson, had appreciated full well. However, Garment, who has tended over the years to acknowledge Nixon's weaknesses but always tried to present them in the most flattering light, insisted that it was much more than money that attracted Nixon to Hollywood. "He wanted to do things for the industry—it's that simple," Garment argued. "He wanted to because he was infatuated with theater, with show business—he was an actor when he was young. And he was a Californian. He had the outsider's awe for the princes of that industry. And," he concluded, after a pause, "it was the movie industry versus the rest of the media, which he had no love for."

It was not until early 1971, in any event, that Schreiber was able to tap this presidential goodwill. Schreiber was very friendly with Robert Finch, who had been lieutenant governor of California, now was secretary of health, education, and welfare, and was probably Nixon's most long-standing political friend. Schreiber was one of Finch's great boosters; in a memo to Garment in early 1970, he had referred to Finch as "one of the great hopes of the future in our Republican Party." Now, he had enlisted Finch's help in persuading Nixon to meet with the leaders of the motion picture industry at the Western White House in San Clemente, overlooking the Pacific Ocean. It was no small thing; after

The seminal meeting between President Richard M. Nixon and Hollywood representatives at the Western White House in San Clemente on April 5, 1971. Taft
Schreiber, who organized the meeting, is seated to the president's left; Jack Valenti,
chin in hand, gazes from the far corner of the table. *Courtesy of the National Archives*

all, despite pleas from Valenti, President Johnson had declined to do it
until after he had decided not to run for reelection. And Nixon did not
finally commit to the meeting until just a few days before it took place.

For Hollywood, this audience came not a moment too soon. *Airport* may have saved Wasserman's job, and it certainly reaped staggering returns for Universal. But the landscape of the motion picture
industry was as arid and bleak as it had ever been. "If the economy is
in a recession, the motion picture production business—in terms of
films produced here rather than abroad—is in an out-and-out depression," declared an editorial in the *Los Angeles Times* in March 1971.
The paper blamed Hollywood's troubles on fiscal incentives provided
by foreign governments, and called for the U.S. government to level the
playing field by imposing import duties on foreign films. Schreiber certainly favored that. But he had many other ideas about how the gov-

ernment could help his industry as well. And the biggest, to his way of
thinking, involved tax benefits (Schreiber had, after all, been trained by
Jules Stein) and antitrust enforcement. Antitrust action was, of course,
a government weapon MCA knew something about. This time,
though, Schreiber wanted the Justice Department to set its sights on
Hollywood's current nemesis, the television networks, which had
begun producing movies themselves.

On the morning of April 5, Nixon met with about two dozen industry representatives—heads of the studios, as well as unions and
guilds, and a handful of independent producers, who took turns addressing the president. First, they described their predicament. Charlton Heston, president of the Screen Actors Guild, declared that he
represented 23,000 film actors, of whom 76 percent made less than
$3,000 in 1970. Dick Walsh, the longtime head of the IATSE, said he
represented 25,000 workers in Hollywood, and that unemployment
ranged from 40 to 85 percent. Schreiber, too, stressed the plight of the
industry (in 1970, only three companies were in the black) and the serious threat of foreign competition. He stated that 52 percent of the
gross proceeds of feature films come from abroad, for movie and TV
rights. In 1950, the industry made 383 films; in 1970, 105; and in
1971, seventy-five movies were slated—while foreign producers, he
claimed, were making 3,700 movies. Schreiber ticked off the remedies
in a kind of shorthand: changes in tax rules for the industry, more beneficial decisions from the Justice Department antitrust division, and
loans from the Export-Import Bank for movies to be exported. It fell to
Ted Ashley, the president of Warner Bros., to make the most lengthy
presentation about what the industry wanted—changes in specific FCC
rules dealing with television and, also, cable; anti-piracy legislation;
copyright protection; and a couple different forms of tax relief.

A day or two before the meeting, Schreiber had called Ashley to ask
him to participate. At that time, Ashley recalled, Schreiber was organizing the meeting meticulously, assigning each speaker his subject.
Ashley was not particularly friendly with Schreiber, and he was a committed Democrat, so he was hardly a natural candidate—"but Taft said

that they all felt I would be the most effective spokesperson, and it would be in everyone's best interest." So, after first hesitating (Ashley carried no brief for Nixon), he had decided to do it. He had boned up on his subjects and made a batch of note cards, which he studied in the back of his limousine on the way down to San Clemente. Now, when Ashley's turn came, Nixon—seated at the head of the group, with his customary yellow legal pad on the table before him—said, " 'I know I'm going to hear from you at some length and I look forward to doing so.' And he put his pad at arm's length—like, 'Look, no hands!' " Ashley recalled. After Ashley finished his presentation, he continued, "Nixon took up *all* the items, one by one"—saying they were hopeless, or he was working on them, or he had an idea how an approach should be made. "It was really a tour de force," Ashley declared.

Looking back on the meeting, Ashley would always think of it as Schreiber's set-piece. Schreiber had lobbied for it, he had cast its players, he had assigned them their parts—and when it was over, those parts were finished. At the time, Ashley was certain that Schreiber would be carrying out the follow-up with the administration behind-the-scenes. "Taft was not looking for me and the others to do anything but show up for this meeting, for stage purposes. I'm only speculating, but I think it was partly a display on Taft's part of his standing in the motion picture industry. Whatever his private strategic plan, it would be fostered if the president saw that importance was placed on it by the community."

At the press conference following the meeting, Jack Valenti, head of the MPAA, was his florid self. "As one who has had some meager knowledge about presidential meetings," began Valenti, who rarely let any group he addressed forget his stint in the Johnson White House, "I must tell you that I was quite surprised and pleased by the amount of time that the president gave to this delegation of motion picture executives. . . . We cited for him a whole catalogue of terror that is plaguing the motion picture industry today, and . . . [detailed] these problems which threaten to disfigure, if not to totally collapse, this motion picture industry as we Americans have known it for so long." Schreiber said he was impressed by the president's interest, sympathy, and grasp of the problems. Heston added a theatrical flourish. "For the first time in history," he declared, "an American chief executive has decided to take a direct personal interest in the welfare of the American film industry."

———

The meeting at San Clemente would turn out to be a watershed event for the motion picture industry, and, over time, it assumed an almost legendary quality, luminous and well etched, in the memories of some involved. Schreiber, the proud progenitor, would often recall it as something from which great benefits had come. Ashley never tired of regaling friends with stories of his role, his impressions of Nixon, and Nixon's "tour de force." Garment, who was not present but could deliver Ashley's rendition almost verbatim, and who prided himself on seeing a side of Nixon that many did not, insisted that what Nixon demonstrated that day was "as great a business performance as some political performances are." And there were other Democrats in the group, besides Ashley, who were surprised at the Nixon they had somewhat unwillingly come to San Clemente to see. David Picker, then a young producer at United Artists, still recalled how torn he felt. "I would've taken up arms against Nixon!" declared Picker, who would later see a copy of a Nixon enemies' list on which his uncle, United Artists principal Arnold Picker, was number one. "But that meeting was extraordinary. It appeared to have been scheduled as a thirty-five- to forty-minute meeting. It lasted almost two hours. People kept coming in and saying to the president, we've gotta move—and he'd say, 'I'm not finished.' He had done his homework, he was so well prepared, he gave specific answers, he was amazing. Yes, he sweated, yes, he needed a shave—but he *got* it. And he delivered things to the industry." Picker paused, then added, "It killed me that I was so impressed."

Nixon's dealings with Hollywood loomed large, of course, only to members of the motion picture industry; the aperture they provide, through which to glimpse the man, is narrow. Still, the view is slightly disarming—an image at once familiar in all its negative aspects, and yet with a couple unexpected positives as well; on balance, a somewhat more engaging Nixon than we thought we knew. Hollywood was, in a way, a kind of Rorschach for Nixon, highlighting conflicting strands of his personality. It aroused his visceral distrust, because it was made up of a great many Jews and liberal Democrats—the very people he counted his enemies, whom he felt he had to guard against and combat. But it also drew him—because of its potential for financial contributions, certainly, and celebrities' support in his 1972 campaign, too, but perhaps also for reasons more inchoate. Nixon appeared delighted on occasion to be consorting with stars, some of whom he'd first gazed at on theater screens in his dusty hometown of Yorba Linda, California; and this singularly graceless president even seemed, at these odd moments, to catch and reflect back a little of their charm. The chemistry between Nixon and Hollywood, therefore, was both delicate and volatile—and Schreiber's task was to manipulate it to his industry's best advantage.

Two days after meeting with the movie people at San Clemente, Nixon delivered a nationally televised speech in which he promised that American involvement in the Vietnam War was coming to an end—and, specifically, announced that another 100,000 U.S. troops would be withdrawn from Vietnam by December 1, 1971. At the close of his speech, he mentioned a ceremony at the White House several weeks earlier when he had awarded the Medal of Honor to a soldier's widow, and the soldier's four-year-old son had suddenly stood at attention and saluted him. He said he wanted to end the war in a way worthy of the sacrifice of that soldier, and all the others, and their families. Shortly after the speech, he returned a call to Freeman Gosden, whose *Amos 'n' Andy* was one of the most popular radio programs of all time, and also played on TV for many years. Gosden, a longtime Nixon supporter, had phoned the president to compliment him on his speech. (When Nixon became president in 1969, he ordered the removal of President Johnson's taping system. In February 1971, however, he and his chief of staff, H. R. Haldeman, had the system replaced; for a long time, only the president, Haldeman, and an aide to Haldeman, Alexander Butterfield, knew it existed.) Now, in this taped conversation, Gosden—after telling the president that "it was the most sincere job that you've ever done"—added, "At the end of that thing, I found myself, truthfully, Mr. President, crying."

NIXON: Well, actually, as a matter of fact, Freeman, I wanna tell you a little secret—you keep this between you and me?

GOSDEN: Right.

NIXON: When I presented this, I presented twelve medals of honor to next of kin, to a father, to a mother, and then to this little woman, you know—and when that little boy saluted me, that four-year-old, I broke up. Nobody saw it, because there was no press there . . .

GOSDEN: . . . You did a helluva job.

NIXON: Well, coming from a pro like you, I appreciate it. . . . Incidentally, have you got a minute?

GOSDEN: Sure, any time you want.

NIXON: I thought it was good that I met with the movie people and tried to say, by God, we're for you kids, but . . . they need to clean their own house, though. Huh?

GOSDEN: I was going to say that to you but I didn't want to get in trouble with Taft Schreiber, or any of the boys—

NIXON: I know.

GOSDEN: But here's the thing. They have got to—you say, you want something, you control this whole industry, why don't you clean your own place and get these dirty pictures off?

NIXON: That's right. Get the dirty pictures off and also get the goddam costs down, so they can compete.

GOSDEN: That's right.

NIXON: . . . I couldn't agree more. That's why, when I went out to see [Sam] Goldwyn, you know, I praised him for the fact that he didn't produce any dirty pictures. Of course, he would've, if it

hadn't been in that period, but at least he didn't while he was
there.

GOSDEN: Yeah, that's right. I tell you, the picture business is something else, and when you get in that, I hope you got your eyes
open with what you're doing there—because that is a real tricky
business.

NIXON: I know it is, I know it is.

When Nixon finished a televised speech, he had a hunger for praise
that his associates tried hard to satisfy. Alexander Butterfield, Nixon's
special assistant, recalled that before each speech Nixon would direct
him to contact cabinet members and others to find out where they
could be reached later; then, after the speech, Butterfield would call
them, write down their remarks, and report them to Nixon. Those who
did not report in promptly aroused the suspicion that was always at the
ready in Nixon, that people were against him—even those in his inner
circle. On the night of April 7, Nixon spoke to his chief of staff, H. R.
Haldeman, by phone.

NIXON: Henry [Kissinger] just told me that [Clark] MacGregor
[White House chief of congressional liaison] was disappointed in
the speech because we didn't announce more withdrawals. Now
if he's going to be that kind of guy, we have to check him off goddam fast, if he can't see this. Is that what he told you?

HALDEMAN: No, what he told me was he was very enthusiastic on
presentation and that he had hoped we could withdraw a larger
amount, but he's said that all along—

NIXON: He's shown he doesn't have much guts. Well, you haven't
heard from [Donald] Rumsfeld [then head of the Office of Economic Opportunity], haven't heard from Finch, and this is all
you've heard from MacGregor, so we've now found out who's
who, haven't we? . . . It seems to me MacGregor, Finch, Rumsfeld, they've been under great pressures, I know, but goddam it,

if they don't stand up now, I ain't gonna talk to 'em. Screw 'em!
I am not gonna do it! They're not gonna come suckin' around,
after they read the polls, understand?

Those who wanted to curry favor with the president (or, at least,
protect themselves) were fulsome—and none more than Henry
Kissinger, assistant to the president for national security affairs.
Kissinger, who enjoyed his frequent forays to Hollywood and was a
regular on the party circuit there, was a good friend of Schreiber's, and
when Kissinger saw Nixon the day after the April 5 speech, he put in a
good word for Schreiber as well.

> KISSINGER: Yesterday—I didn't tell you this—Taft Schreiber came
> in to see me and he said he had just seen Finch. He said, how can
> you be so calm when Finch is shaking all over? He said Finch
> was literally—his hands were shaking. This morning Finch is
> very happy. He thinks it was a great speech.
>
> NIXON: You know, it's a funny thing. It was nineteen minutes and
> thirty seconds, which was the right length, but beyond that—
> that little conclusion we stuck on there. That's what made it for
> Mr. Average Joe, don't you think?
>
> KISSINGER: *Absolutely!* Oh, yes.
>
> NIXON: They couldn't help but be moved by it.

> KISSINGER: I must say, [Kissinger's deputy Alexander] Haig had
> tears in his eyes, I had tears in my eyes, even though I'd heard it
> before. But, your bearing, I thought—

> NIXON: That sort of thing takes a lot out of a person—
>
> KISSINGER: Oh, God—
>
> NIXON: Just the creative thing. I didn't create too much—
>
> KISSINGER: You created the architecture. Even the parts you didn't
> write, you put it in your idiom. But also the architecture, Mr.

President, the balance of the speech—I thought it was a *really great* speech, Mr. President.

On April 9, in a wide-ranging meeting with Haldeman, Garment, Finch, and Nancy Hanks, chairman of the National Endowment for the Arts (NEA), Nixon expounded at length on his views about the motion picture industry as well as Schreiber's pet project, the Hirshhorn Museum. Nixon opened the meeting with a compliment for Hanks, an attractive, vivacious woman, so effective a spokesperson for the arts that by 1976, when she finished her second term as chairman, the federal arts budget would have grown from $8 million to almost $90 million. "In my meeting with the movie people, with all their bitching, they just spoke glowingly of you," Nixon told Hanks. Then, in an apparent reference to the "bitching," he added, "I'm not speaking of Taft Schreiber"—which was greeted by appreciative chuckles all around, from these Schreiber supporters.

When the subject of foreign competition came up, Hanks ventured that "the quality of films in this country is not as good as many of the foreign films—"

NIXON (INTERRUPTING): I think some of them are pretty lousy. I think the foreign films that are supposed to be so great . . .

HALDEMAN: What the foreigners are doing better than we are is producing family movies.

NIXON (TO HANKS): Now, now, *this* is what I want you and Leonard to get into. . . . We should start producing good movies. And the family movie is coming back, it's coming back very fast. I sense it. Do you agree?

GARMENT: Right. The romantic mood—

NIXON: My kids tell me. They, and all their friends, frankly they don't like it—the thrill of the moment. They don't like it.

GARMENT: I find my kids are fascinated by the old movies that they see on television. The nine- and ten-year-old. They find there's a strong story, strong characters. You don't have that in a lot of the contemporary—

NIXON: And they're so *offbeat!* ... Nancy, let's make a study of this damn industry, from an arts standpoint. And—is it worth saving? I don't want to subsidize a turkey! Maybe we can't get a subsidy. At the present time we sure can't get it from the Congress, the Congress will never subsidize movies, never, never—unless they improve the quality. On the other hand, the industry's hurting, and we have to do everything we can to save it.

One way to improve the quality of movies, the president continued, would be to provide better cinematography education. Hanks mentioned that the NEA was sponsoring forty interns in a program at the American Film Institute.

Nixon responded, "Remember, lean to the square side. I know your natural bent, but lean to the square side. . . . What I mean is, lean to it because . . . as a business proposition, I know we're right, and that's all Hollywood cares about, their dough. But they are on the wrong track! They are still making the weird pictures, whereas the kinds of pictures people like to see are stories, they want to see a story! . . . Like Charlton Heston, he always plays in story movies. We just gotta make some movies that do tell stories. Why is it for example that people still go see John Wayne?"

After some back-and-forth, Nixon began speaking again, very emphatically—and with an attack on one of his favorite targets. "Let me suggest this. The industry may be reflecting the national intelligentsia, and that's always wrong. What you need to tell them—I want you to talk cold turkey to them. And say, look here, you've got to clean your own houses, or we're not gonna do these things for you. We're not gonna take six steps that are going to help a sick industry. They've got to shape up. They've got to shape up their labor policies, they've got to shape up their production costs, and also, I would strongly urge, they've got to shape up in terms of what they're making . . . they damn well have got to make better movies. Isn't that a true point?"

Garment bemoaned the lack of great American movies, and Nixon remarked that the only two new movies he'd seen were *Patton* and *Love Story*. Nixon told Garment that he wanted him to "get on the phone to those movie people" and enlist their help in conducting a study in conjunction with the NEA on ways to improve the quality of American films. Finch volunteered that he thought Schreiber would help.

"Is he a decent human being?" Nixon asked. His visitors gave emphatically affirmative murmurs.

On the subject of the Hirshhorn Museum, Nixon agreed, without enthusiasm, that it should go forward—but he insisted it should not look like "that horrible Whitney thing they have in New York." Scanning a list of proposed board members, Nixon made one of his standard quips. "Is there anybody on this list that's not Jewish? Not that I'm anti-Semitic"—laughter from his visitors—"but you don't want an all-Jewish list." Garment responded, "Well, these are the art experts. I spoke to Taft about the names." "There must be at least *one*," the president objected. To which Garment replied, "There's one. He's a good friend of Johnson's. Hobart Taylor. He's black. He's not Jewish." Nixon approved of some of the proposed board members, like Schreiber, Mrs. Walter Annenberg, and producer Hal Wallis. But, he said, "Let's get the Easterners off this list." He vetoed H. J. Heinz II. "The trouble with Jack Heinz—Heinz is part of the Eastern establishment . . . he's a very nice fellow—I've had him, Eisenhower used to have him, to virtually every dinner. But he never gives! Never! Well, the hell with him." Nixon said he wanted to add Theodore Cummings to the board. Cummings, a successful developer in Los Angeles, was one of Schreiber's closest friends. "Ted Cummings is one of the wealthiest people but you'd never know it, except that he lives in a $300,000 house, right near Hillcrest, which is the most expensive golf club in America," Nixon told the group. "And he's got the best art collection."

Nixon also suggested Norton Simon, the Los Angeles industrialist, and said that he should be invited to the White House. Garment volunteered that he thought he could get a contribution from Hirshhorn, and that if Hirshhorn were shown some presidential attention, he might switch from being a Democrat to a Republican.

Schreiber's strategy, in any event, had worked nicely. Nixon had come to see the Hirshhorn—in its board of trustees, at least—as a rich resource. Referring to these prospective trustees, he spelled out his thinking. "I want to help some of those people that can help us."

Over the course of the next couple of weeks, Schreiber worked hard to exploit what Nixon had set in motion following the San Clemente meeting. He met with Peter Flanigan, the assistant to the president who was charged with directing the administration's efforts on behalf of the movie industry. Together, Schreiber and Flanigan met with Peter Peterson, director of the Council for International Economic Policy, to discuss the problem of foreign movie industry trade barriers. In Los Angeles, Dean Burch, chairman of the Federal Communications Commission, met with Schreiber and a movie industry group that Schreiber convened to discuss a number of issues, including copyright protection, in dealing with cable TV. Schreiber was sent a copy of proposed legislation dealing with piracy, and he advised Flanigan's assistant, James Loken, that the bill had unanimous industry support and "by all means we are for it." Schreiber met with Richard McLaren, the assistant attorney general in charge of antitrust, in Los Angeles to discuss, among other things, the Justice Department's suing the networks, forcing them to cease producing movies for their own exhibition. Flanigan, on Schreiber's behalf, met with Henry Kearns, head of the Export-Import Bank, to discuss how the bank might finance movies. Schreiber met with Ed Cohen, assistant secretary for tax policy in the Treasury Department, to explore how far the Treasury could go in meeting the desires of the movie industry for a couple different kinds of tax relief.

It was extraordinary to have so many different doors in Washington opened with such synchronicity. Schreiber was a tough, hard-bitten type, accustomed to the perquisites of power in the movie colony, but still his sudden ability to command attention in the nation's capital must have been rather heady. On April 26, he wrote a slightly breathless thank-you note to the president. After citing the numerous areas in which the administration was offering its help, Schreiber continued, "No President before you has shown such concern for this industry which you choose to construe as a National resource, nor could any industry have the munificent attention showered upon it that you directed for the Motion Picture and TV Film companies. . . . History will record the fact that you did all of this without any political motive, for it seems of the 20 people in attendance at San Clemente only three were Republicans. I would love to change this one-sided state in the time ahead. For all your personal intervention and help I am indebted to you to the degree that I can hardly describe. I will somehow reciprocate with my friendship, efforts and loyalty, for the benefits to accrue to my company and our industry. So too should the motion picture industry feel this enormous debt to you." And in a note to Peter Flanigan, Schreiber made his point even more clearly: "I will do whatever is within my power to help this Administration and President Nixon and expect to devote a substantial part of the coming two years to in some small part begin to repay the obligation that I feel to him and all of you."

The issue that was processed most rapidly to fulfill movie industry desires was accelerated tax depreciation. Before Nixon agreed to meet with the movie people, Treasury Secretary John Connally had assured Nixon that this could be accomplished administratively. A controversy had arisen between the movie companies and the local IRS office concerning the time frame for deducting the cost of producing a movie. The cost is deducted not when it is incurred, but over the period of anticipated revenues from its exhibition. Since so many movies were being shown on television, some IRS officials had taken the position that the costs had to be deferred against possible revenues from television showings, long after theatrical exhibitions had ended. The movie companies, naturally, wanted more liberal depreciation rules, where such deferrals did not have to be made.

What Ed Cohen quickly discovered was that there was not one apparent remedy that was optimal for all companies. Schreiber took the lead with Cohen, and adopted a rather supercilious attitude regarding his competitors. As Flanigan's assistant, Loken, wrote in a memo to his boss on April 12, just one week after San Clemente, "Schreiber advises that he has urged Jack Valenti to push the other companies to be fully responsive to Cohen. Schreiber suspects that the other companies have the notion they can get anything they want if they simply plead poverty loud enough. Schreiber and Valenti want the industry to seek practical forms of tax relief." On April 23, Loken wrote that Cohen had met with MCA executive George Smith, and that Cohen would shortly be meeting with both Smith and Schreiber. The problem was that MCA by this time was in a stronger position than most of the other companies, and the remedy they wanted was best, of course, for them. Cohen "has hit upon a scheme which will clearly help companies other than MCA, and . . . it may also be helpful to MCA," Loken wrote. About a month later, in a memo entitled, "Status of Movie Industry Efforts," Loken wrote, "Ed Cohen's office has completed development of a program which is satisfactory to MCA."

The Export-Import Bank was another area where the administration moved promptly to satisfy movie industry requests. Schreiber had been trying for some time to use the bank as a financing vehicle—something that could be hugely helpful in these cash-starved times. But his earlier proposals had been rejected by Henry Kearns, head of the bank. In a memo on April 12, 1971, Loken wrote that Schreiber had come up with a new plan: "Without blaming Kearns for the problems of last year, Schreiber commented that Kearns 'must control his people' so as to implement this new program." By early July, all previous obstacles had been overcome, and the Export-Import Bank—which had always refused to finance motion picture industry exports in the past—was ready to do so.

These were highly beneficial moves for the movie industry. But the single most desirable governmental action, certainly in Schreiber's view, would be an antitrust suit against the television networks.

Through Jack Valenti and MPAA general counsel Louis Nizer, the industry had been lobbying the Justice Department to file such a suit for nearly four years. In the fall of 1967, two of the three major national networks, CBS and ABC, announced plans to go into the movie-making business, for both theatrical and television exhibition. (NBC—which had signed its record-breaking agreement to purchase movies from MCA—remained on the sidelines.) Hollywood complained that the networks' producing movies was the same kind of vertical integration—production and exhibition—that movie producers had been found guilty of in 1948 when they had to sell their theaters. Many producers were alarmed at the prospect of the networks' buying fewer movies from Hollywood, but surely the *most* alarmed were on the fifteenth floor of the Black Tower at MCA. For while its feature film division was hemorrhaging in the late sixties, the highly profitable TV business was the engine of the company. Indeed, the World Premiere format, pioneered by MCA and NBC in 1966, had proved immensely successful, scoring consistently high audience ratings; these TV movies also served as pilots for series such as *Ironside,* and *Dragnet.* It was not surprising that ABC and CBS would decide to produce such movies for themselves; CBS even hired away the Universal executive in charge of World Premiere, which to Wasserman was tantamount to a declaration of war.

In mid-August 1970, Nizer had paid yet another visit to longtime Justice antitrust staff attorney Bernard Hollander. In a memo about his conversation with Nizer, Hollander wrote that Nizer had come "to renew his plea that the Department take some action in this matter promptly, since the situation of the motion picture industry is beyond the critical stage. Mr. Nizer stated that he was at a loss to understand why, after three years of supplying information to the Department, and with companies such as 20th Century Fox and MGM on the verge of bankruptcy, and Walter Reade and other important independents having abandoned motion picture distribution, that the Department remains quiescent in the face of what he alleges are clear antitrust violations by the networks, responsible at least in part for the dire straits in which the movie companies find themselves." About six weeks later, most of the major movie producers, evidently despairing of governmental action, decided to take matters into their own hands. They filed a civil antitrust action against the networks—in effect, demanding that CBS and ABC function strictly as exhibitors of movies made by other companies.

The San Clemente meeting, however, stirred hope that Justice might now be more compliant. There was no mistaking the importance Schreiber and other industry leaders placed on it. As Loken wrote in his notes, "Network lawsuit—biggest thing industry could get." About two weeks after San Clemente, on April 21, Attorney General John Mitchell came to see Nixon. He said he'd heard from John Ehrlichman, counsel to the president, that they were supposed to put off the network suit.

NIXON: Let me tell you the reason . . . I'm for that suit—but I don't want to have the impression, right after this "Selling of the Pentagon" [a CBS exposé of the Defense Department's public relations activities] that we are pressing this—

MITCHELL: . . . You know who's going to get all the benefit of this . . . are the motion picture industry, the people who have been after us for years.

NIXON: John, John, I'm for it, I'm for it . . . anything you can do to the networks, more power to you. . . . Under no circumstances is it to be dropped. I just don't want you to do it right now . . . but *give it to 'em*. And, incidentally, get some credit from the movie people, would ya?

MITCHELL: (inaudible)

NIXON: That's one of the reasons I'm for it . . . Taft Schreiber. . . . The main reason I'm for it though is I wanna screw the networks. In any event, they've gotta be screwed. They're terrible people. They're a bunch of bastards. But the movie people, when we were in California, with Taft Schreiber—I promised them we'd do something. Oh, no, I'm all for it! This is purely political, in timing.

Schreiber was surely disappointed by the delay. In a memo to Peter Flanigan in late May (with information from a recent phone conversation with Schreiber underlined in red), Loken wrote, "Taft Schreiber advises that what is really needed is favorable intervention by the Antitrust Division in the movie industry suit against the networks." In the margin, Flanigan wrote, "Pls. Review status of this. I had understood McLaren [antitrust division head] was contemplating this." But the political considerations continued to favor postponement. Presidential aide Charles Colson, who was dedicated to finding ways to pressure the news media to change its critical coverage of the Nixon administration, met with Nixon and Flanigan on July 2, 1971, and argued strongly against the suit's being filed. Before *The Selling of the Pentagon* had made the moment inopportune, and now the *Pentagon Papers* case was being fought. In a memo to John Ehrlichman regarding the meeting, Colson wrote that "the President made it very clear that he would like the anti-trust case proposed against the TV networks *held up* for at least several months at which point he may want to review it again. The point is that it is worth much more to us as a threat than as an accomplished fact." Or, as Nixon had expressed it in his conversation with Colson earlier that day, "If the threat of screwing them is going to help us more with their programming than doing it, then keep the threat. Don't screw them now. [Otherwise] they'll figure that we're done." And, in his memo, Colson had concluded by telling Ehrlichman, "The President told Pete Flanigan to talk to the Justice Department to be sure that this is done. I am simply advising you in the event that you would like to make the point yourself with the Attorney General."

The president and his aides were contemplating his meeting with the motion picture people for a second time, at San Clemente in July. As they weighed the pros and cons of such a meeting, however, one

concern was the network suit. In a memo to Flanigan, Loken warned
that the movie people might "inquire whether Justice will intervene in
the industry's antitrust lawsuit against the networks, and I gather
McLaren has not yet made a decision to intervene." (Loken seemed unaware that the decision was not McLaren's—nor was it the attorney
general's.) On the other hand, the accelerated depreciation rules, providing for faster write-off of production costs, were ready to be announced—but there was some sensitivity about how and when that
would be done. As Loken had written to Flanigan in June, "Treasury is
rather gun-shy of criticism that the White House is directing tax and
IRS policy. . . . If the President plans to announce the depreciation
changes in a meeting with industry leaders in California, it should be
possible to have IRS release the ruling with little fanfare that day or the
day before. This should avoid the appearance of leaving IRS no choice
but to make a decision predetermined by the President." However,
Loken added, "It should not prevent RN from taking the credit." In the
end, Nixon decided not to meet with the movie people. And the tax
changes were announced—not by Nixon but the IRS—in early September.

On September 10, *Variety* ran a banner headline across its front
page: "Tax Change Benefits Film Biz," with the subhead, "IRS Ap-
proves 'Schreiber Plan' That Will Enable Companies to Accelerate
Amortization." "The plan takes its name from Taft B. Schreiber, veepee
and director of MCA Inc.," wrote A. D. Murphy. "He was the prime
industry force in arranging for film industry's 'summit conference' last
April 5 with President Nixon at the Western White House, San
Clemente. IRS okay of the major tax computational change occurred
exactly five months after that meeting—something of a record alongside assorted current and past industry pitches for government help."
(It was surely not dubbed the "Schreiber Plan" at Treasury, but in Hollywood the name stuck. Responding to a letter of gratitude Charlton
Heston had written to the president, Flanigan struck a slightly defen-
sive note, striving to emphasize that the government action had been
taken on the merits. "I am advised by tax officials at the Treasury De-

partment that the Schreiber Plan, as you call it, is an eminently sound approach to the difficult question of film amortization.") A few days after the IRS ruling, MCA issued a press release; Wasserman stated that because of the ruling, MCA had "given the immediate go-ahead" on five additional feature films to be produced in the U.S. over the next twelve months.

All this time, Wasserman had been nearly invisible in a political scenario utterly dominated by Schreiber. That dominance, Wasserman implied, was something he had ceded to Schreiber most happily, and it went beyond the fact that Schreiber was the MCA Republican, and Wasserman the Democrat. "I never liked Nixon," he said. "In his Senate race in 1950, Ronnie Reagan and I walked precincts for Helen Gahagan Douglas"—the congresswoman whom Nixon beat by a huge margin. Interestingly, though, Wasserman may not have been as disconnected from President Nixon as he appeared to be. Herbert Klein, Nixon's director of communications and a longtime Californian, friendly with the MCA crowd, said, "We never really thought of Wasserman as being on the other side." He added, "I'm sure he gave to us—probably not in his name. But I'm sure he gave." The distance Wasserman seemed to keep, Klein insisted, was cosmetic. "We always went through Taft, whenever we wanted to get word to Wasserman." Sidney Sheinberg, the MCA executive who was Wasserman's protégé, and also a strong Democrat, recalled that Wasserman coordinated with Schreiber in this period. On the executive floors of MCA, the consensus was that there was much to be gained. "Nixon's was an imperial kind of presidency," Sheinberg said. "If you had a relationship with the White House, you *could* have an impact on what these so-called independent agencies did."

However imperceptible Wasserman's collaboration had been previously, now he came into the open in the fall of 1971. He was spearheading a bipartisan effort on the part of the motion picture industry to win passage of the president's tax package—because there was something truly momentous at stake for the motion picture industry. Investment tax credits, intended as a spur to economic growth, had been passed into law in 1962, allowing American companies to write off 7 percent of any investment made in machinery and equipment—that is, *tangible* property, which had a useful life of eight years or more. The motion picture industry could claim a credit for equipment such as cameras and projectors, but not for the full cost of making films—because while motion picture film is a depreciable asset, Treasury regulations stated that it is *intangible* property. But now, two very fortuitous things for the industry had occurred. Several months earlier, in May 1971, Walt Disney Productions, Inc., which had sued the government, arguing that it was entitled to the tax credit for the full cost of films, had won in the district court in Los Angeles. This decision could be used to bolster the industry's legislative case for inclusion in the credit. Moreover, while the investment tax credit had been repealed in 1969, Nixon wanted to reinstate it as part of his revenue package for 1971. The financial implications for Hollywood were huge.

Within the Nixon administration, Schreiber was given credit for bringing Wasserman into this joint effort, though it is doubtful Wasserman needed prompting. In a September 17 memo, Loken reported to Flanigan that Schreiber had met with Valenti, Wasserman, and Ed Weisl to discuss the tax legislation. And, he continued, "Schreiber convinced the group that the industry should push the *entire* RN tax package . . . with key Democrats in the Congress." In case the motion picture producers' influence was not sufficient, "Schreiber said the producers will enlist the aid of the distributors and exhibitors where needed to make an impact on the Democratic lawmakers." Valenti—an ardent and well-connected Democrat who performed his job better when there was a Democratic administration—had been given his marching orders. "Valenti has been instructed to work for our full tax program and to give this effort top priority," Loken wrote. And when the Revenue Act of 1971 was discussed on the floor of the House, Wilbur Mills, chairman of the Ways and Means Committee, uttered the words that would be transmuted into gold for Hollywood. Asked whether the costs of producing a film would qualify for the credit, just as the costs of acquiring a machine would qualify, Mills said, "That is correct." According to Valenti, it was Wasserman who persuaded Mills of the wisdom of that position. And, Valenti said, "In those days, Ways and Means had no subcommittees. You only had to deal with Wilbur. If he said something, then everyone else saluted and went along."

For Wasserman, his support of Nixon's revenue package was a well-defined, discrete public alliance. He would continue to leave Nixon fund-raising to Schreiber. And that suited Schreiber just fine. He had no desire to share this stage with Wasserman. Just as Wasserman had made much of his relationship with Johnson, and featured photographs of himself with the president in his home and his office, so Schreiber did with Nixon. (Ollie Atkins, the White House official photographer, enclosing a selection of prints of Schreiber with Nixon in the White House Library and the Rose Garden, wrote, "I assure you these are very rough prints but I think you look very friendly and you need not be alarmed about any strong lines or skin defects or the nose problem.") Schreiber was so grateful for all Nixon had done that he seemed almost messianic about raising money for him. In a note to Flanigan on September 9, thanking him again for all that the Nixon administration had done "so far," Schreiber wrote: "I am looking forward to the time when the President's election campaign is in full gear and in my work for him I can reemphasize what a great man he is and why he deserves the support of every good American."

Even in this pre-campaign period, Schreiber was trying to build support for Nixon in Hollywood. It was not an easy task. Frank Price, a top TV executive at MCA close to Schreiber, recalled Schreiber's asking him to have a cocktail party at his home for Nixon—not a fund-raiser, but a kind of outreach to people who had not voted for Nixon before. "I said, 'What! I've spent my adult life hating Nixon!' " Price declared. "But Taft said it was important, Nixon was doing a big favor for our industry with the investment tax credit. He also enlisted Dick Zanuck and Sammy Davis, Jr., to host a cocktail party at their homes. And, I remember, I had let people know why I was inviting them to the party—

that it was for Nixon. Word came back that I wasn't supposed to tell people why they were coming. I said, if I can't tell them why they're coming, I'm not having the party. Finally, they said okay." Schreiber also organized an event for Attorney General John Mitchell to attend a dinner in Los Angeles with people from the industry on November 9; the next morning, Mitchell met in his suite at the Beverly Hills Hotel with fourteen movie and television producers, including Schreiber.

Not all Schreiber's efforts were deemed so worthwhile. In a conversation with Haldeman in late September, Nixon complained about Kissinger's spending so much time in Hollywood.

> NIXON: I talked to him [Henry] yesterday about his over-scheduling. He was going to California to meet with Jews, with Taft Schreiber—which he does on a regular basis. Taft Schreiber was getting 500 people to a big dinner. I said, 'Henry, it's not worth it . . .'
>
> HALDEMAN: First place, Taft Schreiber can get him 500 people—I could get him *5000* people, any night of the week, in any city in the country. Henry Kissinger, right now—I'd love to be his booking agent. No trouble at all, booking a crowd for Henry. . . . Whether he gets 500 or 5000 doesn't mean much, either. He should be on TV . . . or at a university.
>
> NIXON: Meeting with Jews out there doesn't mean one goddam thing for us . . .
>
> HALDEMAN: . . . We don't need their money!
>
> NIXON: Right.
>
> HALDEMAN: We don't need it and there's a real question whether we're gonna get it—and if we're gonna get it, we're gonna get it whether Henry makes a speech to these people or not.
>
> NIXON: Right. If we're gonna get it, we're gonna get it as a payoff for Israel.
>
> HALDEMAN: . . . either a payoff or a bribe.

NIXON: . . . those people who came around with those five million dollars—where is it? Where is it? Where is those five million dollars they were gonna give?

HALDEMAN: With no strings attached. The day a Jew gives *five dollars* with no strings attached!

NIXON: That's right.

(words deleted)

Referring to Jewish supporters of Israel, Haldeman concluded, "They're a ruthless bunch. . . . They're going to turn off the instant you don't send them the signal they want and they'll stay on as long as they think you're going to. Anything they think they can pressure you into." (Haldeman's attitude toward Jews seemed both clear and consistent. In July 1970, he had written a memo to Dwight Chapin, a presidential aide, in which he said, "As a matter of general scheduling policy remember that from now through November all appointments should be weighed on the basis of their political implication. The President's time should be used at the maximum extent possible to aid in picking up Senate seats. . . . We have, for the last year and one-half, overloaded schedule activity to Blacks, youth, and Jews. From here on, until further notice, there are to be no Jewish appointments set up per se.")

Israel was another item on Schreiber's agenda, albeit not as high as Hollywood. And Nixon's comment about the $5 million apparently referred to an offer connected to Schreiber, and described in Haldeman's diaries. In an entry for May 27, 1971, Haldeman wrote that "the P" had asked him to look into a report from Len Garment, who said that "Taft Schreiber has told him that Sam Rothberg in Hollywood has committed to raising $5 million in Jewish money for the P's reelection," Haldeman wrote. "This is because of our position on Israel. The P's concerned that we are sure to have it understood with the Jewish people that we will not accept any strings at all on any contribution in this area. He doesn't want to get trapped into a situation there." Asked about this offer, Garment confirmed that it had been made, but declined to say whether the money was given. However, an entry in John Mitchell's log shows that in early January 1972—several months after Nixon was railing about the $5 million not having materialized—Mitchell had a meeting with Schreiber, Sam Rothberg, Luis Boyar, and Ted Cummings.

His lack of support among Jews was a theme that Nixon harped on repeatedly, and that seemed to eat at him. In a conversation in June 1971 with Vice President Spiro Agnew, Nixon had said, steaming, "There isn't a damn thing the Jews are gonna do for us. We have individual Jewish friends, like Bunny Lasker. You've got a few, and I've got Taft Schreiber in California. But as far as the Jewish vote, it's eighty percent the other way. *Eighty percent!*" And his resentment contributed to a deep ambivalence about support for Israel. In a conversation with Haldeman in early May 1971, Nixon had insisted that the U.S. could not continue to be such a singularly staunch friend of Israel. "Now, Henry's [Kissinger] argument will be that, well . . . the Jewish editorial writers and columnists in this country, if we're nice to Israel, will be nicer to us on Vietnam . . . *Who?* The goddam Jews are all against us! . . . There's no politics in it for me, to just be pro-Israeli. Now, godammit, there just isn't. And when they talk to the contrary, they're nuts! Now I know we've got a few friends—in California, we've got Taft Schreiber and Ted Cummings. . . . But you see the writers, half of them are Jews. You see the people who are supporting [presidential candidate Senator Edmund] Muskie and the rest, they're Jews! Frankly, if we've gotta have a political enemy, by God it'll be the Jews."

Kissinger was smack in the middle of Nixon's emotional stew. Nixon wanted his secretary of state, William Rogers (with whom Kissinger had a fierce rivalry, and whom Kissinger would ultimately replace), to take the lead on Middle East issues. "There are plenty of things wrong with Rogers, we know that, but on the other hand on this particular issue, he is squeezing the Israelis because I want him to. . . . I don't buy it, just taking the Jewish line, I don't buy it, we've gone too far," Nixon told Haldeman. "Another reason we've gotta keep Henry out of this is when he gets involved with Israel, he is totally irrational about everything else. We just gotta keep his mind on Vietnam, Soviet-American relations, and China. And it's really for his own benefit. . . . You say, what do you think the Israelis ought to do? And he won't say another goddam thing but what Mrs. Meir [Israeli Prime Minister Golda Meir] says. Nothing. Nothing. It's a strange thing, but I think if any one of us were Jewish it would be exactly the same thing. I've never met a Jew that was rational about Israel. Never one . . . and I understand it but we are just damn fools. . . . That's why [President] Johnson's appointing [Arthur] Goldberg to the U.N. was just a terrible, terrible blunder. Send Goldberg out to negotiate between the Jews and the Arabs? . . . No Jew can see the Israeli problem, just as no Irishman can see the Northern Ireland problem."

For all Nixon's remarks that sound anti-Semitic, at this moment he seemed to be attempting to put himself in a Jew's place, see through Jewish eyes—and, also, trying to enlighten Haldeman a little. Moreover, in the Yom Kippur War in the fall of 1973, when Egypt and Syria attacked Israel, Nixon would attempt, quite judiciously, to strike what he believed was the right balance. Despite his earlier tough talk about Israel, Nixon would order so many planes sent to Israel that the Israeli military advantage was quickly and definitively restored. But he also directed Kissinger to convey to Soviet leader Leonid Brezhnev that the two superpowers should seek not only to bring about a cease-fire, but to use the opportunity to impose a comprehensive peace in the Middle East. According to *Nixon: Ruin and Recovery, 1973–1990,* by Stephen Ambrose, Kissinger—knowing the Israelis' opposition to a cease-fire at this point, let alone an imposed settlement (and realizing, also, that Nixon was distracted by Watergate's "Saturday Night Massacre")—flouted the president's orders, and sought only a cease-fire.

Feeling for Israel provided some of the glue between Kissinger and Schreiber, but Kissinger's fondness for Hollywood's sybaritic pleasures probably helped encourage their friendship, too. On occasion, this proclivity of Kissinger's caused him some embarrassment. On the morning of October 15, 1972, in the midst of a substantive conversation with Nixon in the Oval Office, Kissinger suddenly digressed, declaring angrily, "That Maxine Cheshire story [in the *Washington Post*] today is an absolute outrage! I met that one girl at Taft Schreiber's house." (In the story, entitled "Problems of a Presidential Adviser," Cheshire wrote that Kissinger was dating starlet Judy Brown, best known for her role in the X-rated Danish sex film *Threesome*. "Miss Brown, a former Miss University of Missouri, said yesterday that she had decided to make public her year-long friendship with Kissinger," Cheshire continued, "because she was 'tired' of being kept in the background while he allows himself to be photographed on dates with other, better-known actresses such as Marlo Thomas and Jill St. John." After Kissinger left the Oval Office, Haldeman—who always considered Kissinger suspect, since he was a former Harvard professor with Eastern Establishment credentials, and who must therefore have been privately relishing the contretemps—delivered his commentary on the situation to the president.

HALDEMAN: It was a dirty goddam shot—but, Henry, I told him this yesterday. He came in and asked what he ought to do about it, and I said, just keep your damn mouth shut. He gave them an answer, and that gave 'em a story. [*Washington Post* editor] Ben Bradlee called him and said, there's this story about your dating this girl who plays in X-rated movies, nude movies, sex movies . . . do you want us to hold it up for the time being because of your trip? Henry said yes. Then he realized he'd fallen into a trap, so he called back, and he said it's up to you to do what you want with the story. I have nothing to say about it. That would have been fine if he just kept his mouth shut there, but then he said, *But,* for your own guidance, I want you to know that I only dated the girl three times, and as soon as I found out she was exploiting it for publicity purposes I dropped her, I never knew she was in dirty movies. . . . Poor guy. Some sexy dame, I guess, that was at a dinner party Taft Schreiber gave him, and he dated her.

NIXON: Oh, Jesus. He can do what he goddam pleases.

Kissinger was hardly the first political figure to dabble in seduction in Hollywood. There was a long tradition of powerful men (some in political life, some in business, some in the mob) courting its stars—Joseph Kennedy and Gloria Swanson, Sam Giancana and Phyllis McGuire, John F. Kennedy and Marilyn Monroe, to name a few. Sometimes, their respective paths intersected with the same woman. Judith Campbell Exner was not an actress but a glamorous Los Angeles divorcée who had simultaneous affairs with President Kennedy and Sam Giancana. And Kissinger was dating actress Jill St. John, who was also having an affair with Sidney Korshak, according to several people who knew them both. One of those people, longtime MCA agent Freddie Fields, who was a good friend of Korshak's, said, "I introduced Sidney to Jill St. John—something for which he was always grateful." Another, Andy Anderson, head of the Western Conference of Teamsters in the seventies, who was a frequent companion of Korshak's and worked closely with him for years, said that St. John was Korshak's "longtime mistress." He remembered Korshak's gifts to her—a chess set with hand-carved ivory pieces that Korshak asked Anderson to buy when he was in Hong Kong; a $50,000 diamond bracelet; and a Rolls-Royce convertible, which Korshak bought when he was in England and had shipped home. ("It was delivered to his house while he was still away, and when he got back, his wife, Bernice, said, 'Sidney, you *are* a sweet husband!' " Anderson said.)

Korshak apparently did not mind that St. John was two-timing him with the president's national security adviser; it seemed, in a way, only to enhance his own power. For the way Korshak told it to his friends, notwithstanding his competitor's elevated status, it was he, Korshak, who came first with St. John. Leo Geffner, the labor lawyer, who knew Korshak well, recounted what Korshak had told him—"Often, when Kissinger invited Jill St. John to the White House, she would say, 'Sorry, I have an invitation from someone more important.' " And Korshak seemed to get a vicarious kick out of the leverage St. John was able to exert over this high government official. "Jill St. John was seeing Kissinger *and* Sidney," Anderson said, rolling his eyes slightly. "Sidney told me that she said to Kissinger that she wouldn't sleep with him anymore unless he ended the Vietnam War."

Much as Korshak seemed to relish the odd propinquity, he was careful about public appearances. Robert Evans, the Hollywood producer who called Korshak his "consigliere and closest friend," recalled in his book, *The Kid Stays in the Picture,* that for the premiere of *The Godfather,* released by Paramount in New York in March 1972, he had called his friend Kissinger at the last moment (after the movie's star, Marlon Brando, had said he couldn't make it) and begged him to attend. Kissinger demurred; the Paris peace talks had just collapsed, he was leaving the country in the morning (on a secret mission to Moscow), he had a 7:30 breakfast with the Joint Chiefs of Staff, and there was a blizzard in Washington. As Evans tells it, he said, "Henry, I need you tonight"—and minutes later, one of Kissinger's assistants called back to say that the national security adviser would be there.

At the party after the showing of the movie, Evans spotted Korshak and his wife. It was Korshak who had made the filming of *The Godfather* possible. Evans said that he had been threatened by the mob when they tried to start shooting the picture in New York ("Get the fuck outta our town, will ya? We don't want nothin' to happen to you or your kid. Go to Kansas City or St. Louis if ya wanna, but New York ain't opening up for ya."). But, Evans continued, "One call from Korshak, suddenly, threats turned to smiles and doors, once closed, opened with an embrace." According to Evans, Korshak had also made it possible for him to get the actor he wanted, Al Pacino, for the role of Michael Corleone. Pacino had been under contract to MGM. But Korshak had placed a call to Kirk Kerkorian, who controlled MGM, and told Kerkorian that if he wanted to obtain the financing he needed to build a hotel in Las Vegas, he had better see to it that Pacino was released from his contract. He was. Now, Evans rushed over to the Korshaks and asked them to join his table.

"Not cracking a smile, he shook his head. 'No.'

" 'Why?'

" 'And give the press a fuckin' field day?'

" 'Come on, Sidney, it's your night too.'

"Like a vise, he grabbed my arm. 'Don't ever bring me and Kissinger together in public. Ever!' "

This was the dicey part of the Hollywood-Washington connection that Wasserman and Schreiber were working hard to establish. Lines blurred in Hollywood in ways that outsiders might not understand. That Korshak appeared to be Wasserman's best friend did not seem odd or inappropriate to most in that community. "They were just two powerful and important people," offered Richard Zanuck, trying to explain why he never looked askance at their closeness. "Sidney was off-cast, he didn't seem like a gangster—though we all understood what his connections were." For all his nuanced understanding of global politics, Kissinger may have been naive when it came to Hollywood mores; he may have thought that it was peccadilloes with porn starlets that posed the greatest hazard, not a much too close association with Korshak through St. John. But Korshak was well aware that the social latitude—and even eminence—he enjoyed in the movie colony existed for him nowhere else, and he conducted himself accordingly.

On the evening of December 31, 1971, President Nixon called Schreiber to wish him a happy new year. After exchanging pleasantries, Nixon said, "Well, what are you going to do tonight? I'm here in the White House, sitting in the Lincoln Room, studying for a program I am going to do with Dan Rather Sunday night. So," he concluded, with that memorable tinge of self-pity in his voice, "that's *my* New Year's Eve. What are you going to do?"

Schreiber replied that Ted Cummings and he were going to the Music Center together.

"Great! Give him my best," Nixon said. "He's a wonderful guy—and has a marvelous collection of art in his house."

Referring to the coming campaign, Schreiber said, "We'll give it all we've got."

"Well, we do appreciate good friends at a time like this, believe me."

Schreiber evidently felt he owed a great deal to Nixon, as he looked back at 1971 and forward to the election year. "Taft feels strongly that the movie/television industry is much better off now under Richard Nixon than ever before and that the top leaders in the industry, particularly those in California, are well aware of this," a White House aide had written in a memo to John Mitchell, shortly before Mitchell met with the movie people in early November 1971. Support for Schreiber's view, moreover, was lent by an article entitled, "It's the Reel Thing—Motion Picture Producers Are Making a Solid Comeback," in the January 24, 1972, issue of *Barron's*. "Few of the movie executives who drove down to San Clemente for a meeting with President Nixon last spring expected anything to come of it," writer David Loehwing began. " 'I guess most of us had been through the mill before,' says Gordon Stulberg, president of 20th Century-Fox. 'Ten years ago, I went to Washington and tried to tell people that the motion picture industry needed help then, but it was a dead end.' This time, though, was different. . . . Since the San Clemente meeting, everything has been coming up roses for the industry—at least in its dealings with the government."

Loehwing went on to cite many of the industry wins—accelerated depreciation; Export-Import Bank financing; GATT (General Agreement on Tariffs and Trade) negotiators' driving a hard bargain with countries trying to gain better access to U.S. markets by insisting that those countries remove barriers to Hollywood films; and, greatest of all, the investment tax credit. For, as Schreiber and Wasserman had hoped, Nixon's 1971 Revenue Act did indeed reinstate the investment credit, and the legislative history made it clear that films, as tangible property, were entitled to the credit. There would continue to be litigation over whether the movie industry was entitled to the credit for years prior to 1971, and, also, unsettled issues about the qualifying conditions for films, and the computation of the credit. But the foundation for what would ultimately become a bonanza worth more than a billion dollars to the movie industry had been laid, thanks to the Nixon administration's efforts.

And this was the season for gratitude. There was a big push among Nixon fund-raisers to collect contributions before a new campaign finance law with stricter reporting requirements went into effect. In his book, *Nightmare: The Underside of the Nixon Years,* Pulitzer Prize–winning journalist J. Anthony Lukas wrote that the bill was made to move more slowly through committees during the fall of 1971, because that is what the Nixon people wanted. Nixon finally signed the bill into law on February 7, 1972; since it would not take effect for sixty days, and the old law would expire on March 10, it created a month-long legal limbo, during which time contributors could be promised complete anonymity. "A CREEP [Committee for the Re-election of the President] memo to John Dean made the strategy clear: seek maximum giving during the March 10–April 7 period, during which the identity of contributors could be absolutely protected," Lukas wrote. Now, Nixon's star fund-raisers from the 1968 campaign took their respective places. Mitchell resigned as attorney general to head CREEP. Stans resigned as commerce secretary to become chairman of CREEP's Finance Committee. Kalmbach received the title of associate chairman of that finance committee (he would, however, resign on April 7). And Schreiber was a co-chairman.

Schreiber and Kalmbach had of course worked closely together in Nixon's 1968 campaign; and, according to Spencer, Schreiber had been Stans's key fund-raising contact in California. In January 1969, Stans had requested that Kalmbach take control of some surplus funds from the 1968 election—about $1,098,000 of which was in cash, in safe-deposit boxes in Washington and New York; over the next several years, much of it would be moved to safe-deposit boxes in Southern California. Kalmbach then raised about $2.8 million for the 1970 congressional campaign, where, he would later say, Haldeman had urged him to get cash whenever it was possible. (Cash contributions, in themselves, were not illegal at this time; but the law required that certain disclosures be made.) Now, before the April 7 deadline, Kalmbach raised over $8.8 million in contributions; and, after that deadline, another $1.8 million. Kalmbach said that he emphasized to potential contributors that their contributions would remain confidential if they made them before April 7. Ultimately, however, the identities of individuals solicited by him, and the size of their contributions, would be disclosed during the Watergate investigations. According to Kalmbach's list, Taft Schreiber made a pledge of $100,000, and contributed $66,101 before April 7; Jules Stein, a pledge of $150,000, and $117,822 before April 7. Other familiar names on Kalmbach's list were Ted Cummings, who pledged $50,000 to $100,000 and gave $46,406; and Jack Warner, who pledged and gave $100,000. Wasserman's name did not appear. Some additional information about Hollywood donors came to light after Common Cause successfully sued to have the identity of Nixon campaign contributors made public in 1973. Bob Hope gave $50,000; and several other studio executives and producers, $5,000 to $10,000. Considering Nixon's beneficence, one would expect to see much more flowing from the motion picture industry, but perhaps some contributions always remained undisclosed. Many records of the pre–April 7 contributions were destroyed.

It is also possible that the movie industry contributed in completely unrecorded ways. One person, then a studio executive, told me that one of his industry colleagues met with Mitchell in the months after San Clemente, and told Mitchell that the movie people realized what the administration was doing for the industry was not easy, and that they would be happy to show their gratitude by making contributions to various congressional campaigns. Mitchell was said to have replied that it would be better if this emissary were to bring him cash, since he, Mitchell, could then direct it wherever it was most needed. And he is said to have suggested that when his visitor returned for their next meeting, he should leave $300,000 to $400,000 in cash in a briefcase, checked at the coatroom.

The emissary followed Mitchell's instructions, according to this former studio executive.

Certainly, in this frenetic period, Schreiber was working hard to make good on his earlier promises to Nixon and to Flanigan. Betty Breithaupt, who became Schreiber's secretary at the start of 1972, recalled that he was mainly involved in politics at this time, "on the phone, raising money from morning to night." One person from whom he solicited a contribution was Ted Ashley, the Warner Bros. studio head whom Schreiber had tapped for the San Clemente presentation. Since Ashley was a lifelong Democrat, who even after San Clemente had had virtually no relationship with the Nixon administration, it was surprising that he would make a contribution of such size—$138,487. He made the contribution in mid-March 1972, in the period of supposedly guaranteed anonymity. Another person Schreiber solicited in this period was Joseph Hirshhorn. As Schreiber would later recount, he told Hirshhorn that "if it were not for President Nixon, his museum would not be built on the Mall and that he owed respect to this, the courage of the President, even though he, Hirshhorn, was a Democrat." Hirshhorn contributed $25,000 in cash—something that he, too, preferred not be disclosed. Schreiber said he picked up the cash and delivered it to Kalmbach, who delivered it to Stans. Evidently, this transaction was just a small part of an enormous pick-up-and-delivery operation being carried out in the last few weeks before April 7. J. Anthony Lukas quoted Hugh Sloan, treasurer of CREEP's Finance Committee, saying that the committee had a squad of four to six men collecting cash around the country, but that evidently wasn't enough manpower; the flow of cash was so abundant, Sloan said, that in one city, "we couldn't even pick up a $50,000 contribution."

On April 14, 1972—one week after the magical April 7 deadline, and the torrential flow of cash—the Justice Department filed its long-awaited answer to Hollywood's prayers: civil antitrust suits against the TV networks. These suits sought to bar the networks from either producing their own entertainment programs or participating financially in programs produced by others. Certain peculiarities about the suits were noted in the press at the time. There were reports that they had been approved many months before by Richard McLaren, the assistant attorney general for antitrust, and sent to Attorney General John Mitchell—where, for mysterious reasons, they had languished. Another oddity was that the suits relied on five-year-old data about the networks. "These [suits] strike us as being peculiar," a *Washington Post* editorial stated, "partly because the facts on which the complaints are based are outdated, partly because the cases have been dormant since 1970, and partly because the complaints seem to ignore some of the realities of the television business." A *New York Times* editorial framed the issue a little differently: "One question in particular need of an answer is why the Justice Department chose now to move on long ignored staff proposals that it challenge network financial control over TV entertainment programs. It seems clear that for more than a dozen years Democratic and Republican attorneys general have been rejecting recommendations by their aides to initiate such a challenge. . . . If resentment against past shows of independence by the networks had not been so manifest and its vigor in applying the antitrust laws had not been so erratic, the cloud over the present suit would not be so ominous." And Federal District Court Judge Edmund Palmieri, who was presiding over pretrial hearings in the motion picture studios' suit against the TV networks, told the assembled lawyers in his New York courtroom, "Now, about this prospective antitrust suit by the government, this comes as something of a bombshell to me. I had thought that the government, which knew all about this case for a long time, had decided it was going to wait and see, and then possibly get into this case by an amicus procedure in the appellate stage, and this comes to me as a surprise.

"Something must have happened in Washington," Judge Palmieri mused aloud, "some other heads must have become enthusiastic about a case that they were not enthusiastic about some time ago." The judge was suspicious, but the lawyers for the studios were jubilant. (Nizer had quietly been making his case to Justice lawyers for five years; now, he would continue to pay them visits, urging the government lawyers to move more expeditiously in their prosecution of this case. Interestingly, on one occasion when Nizer and other studio lawyers met with Justice lawyers—including Harry Sklarsky, Wasserman's old friend from *his* antitrust case—Nizer went out of his way to make a telling point. As Sklarsky duly recorded, "In colloquy with these movie firms' counsel it developed that they considered any production of movies by the networks as illegal. They however did not consider the relationship between Universal and NBC illegal, or subject to antitrust attack, even though, in practical effect, Universal makes all the movies that NBC uses or needs.")

Why the government case was brought at this moment remains a matter of speculation. Nixon had, of course, insisted that he wanted the case brought eventually, to "screw the networks." He had also said he had promised Taft Schreiber; and he had asked Mitchell, in a suggestive aside, to "get some credit from the movie people." Mitchell did meet with a group of them at an event organized by Schreiber in November 1971; and by December, he was newly focused on bringing the case. On December 14, Herbert Klein, Nixon's director of communications, who dealt with the networks a great deal, wrote a memo to Ehrlichman. "As I mentioned to you this morning," Klein began, "I am attempting to reopen with John Mitchell the question of the political merit of moving ahead at this time with the Justice Department proposal to take anti-trust action against the networks over the program production and movie production. Since this was discussed originally, there have been several events which I think would make it appear that such action lends credence to the charge of a conspiracy against the networks. . . . The proposed action against networks has been under consideration in the Justice Department for more than ten years, and even the proposal which has been drawn up is badly outdated at this time. . . . I am making one final plea for a review of this case, which I think can be gravely harmful to the President in an election year. If it has waited ten years, why not one more?"

Perhaps it was Klein's resistance that kept him out of the loop. The day the suit was filed, he was addressing a broadcasting convention. "Here I was, making a speech about their improved coverage," Klein recalled. "I was out there making peace, and after the speech, I learned the suit had been filed! They did it behind my back—I was furious! I called [Attorney General Richard] Kleindienst. I learned that Taft had called Ehrlichman just before the suit was filed." Responding to a query about Schreiber's role, Klein said, "Yes, I believe that he exerted his influence." And who had made the final decision? "Kleindienst told me it was Mitchell," Klein replied. (Kleindienst had succeeded Mitchell as attorney general after Mitchell resigned to go to CREEP on March 1. But Mitchell's authority at Justice evidently endured.)

Whatever impact Schreiber had on the final decision, he certainly had reason to celebrate, and to demonstrate his gratitude to the Nixon administration. He planned a party at his home on June 17 to honor Kissinger and Mitchell and his wife, Martha. At nearly the last moment, however, Kissinger canceled. Nixon had made his historic trip to China in mid-February 1972 (Schreiber received a green jade elephant from the president as a memento of that trip), and now, Kissinger said, Nixon was sending him back to Peking. This created a big problem for Schreiber; in Hollywood, Kissinger was a draw, but John Mitchell (now the *former* attorney general) decidedly was not. Four days before the event, presidential aide Alexander Butterfield wrote a memo to Haldeman, in which he said that he had spoken to Schreiber, and Schreiber "knows that Henry will not be there, and he understands that perfectly well. But he does not believe that we are doing all we can at this end of the line to provide an adequate substitute (or two). He says that when he calls the 150 or so people to tell them that Henry will not be there, *most* of them will drop out then and there if he cannot go on to say that the First Lady will be there . . . or the First Lady and [the Nixons' daughter] Julie . . . or some member of the First Family *and* a current member of the President's Cabinet."

Schreiber's message was heeded; Nixon's wife, Pat, attended. And the event, at Schreiber's elaborate Beverly Hills home—with a large

Henry Moore sculpture in the garden and Picassos and Giacomettis on the walls, tents decorated with pepper-tree branches, and a modest quota of the more old-time stars (Cary Grant, John Wayne, Jimmy Stewart, Charlton Heston)—appeared to be a picture-perfect Hollywood party. Mitchell was there, with a retinue of top CREEP officials—Jeb Magruder, Robert Mardian, Herbert "Bart" Porter. As the evening progressed, though, these men were increasingly distracted from the festivities—called away, one after another, to talk on a phone in the bedroom, and they remained there, consulting in low voices among themselves. Other guests, watching this surreptitious drama, were curious. "At the time, I wondered what was going on," MCA executive Frank Price recalled. "Later, of course, I put it together." The break-in of the Democratic National Committee headquarters at the Watergate complex had occurred (and the five burglars, including CREEP security chief James McCord, had been arrested) in the early hours of June 17. Mitchell had learned about it while he was having breakfast at the Beverly Hills Hotel late that morning. He and his men were trying to appear relaxed at Schreiber's party—but they could not stay off the phone. "It was fascinating to me," Price continued, "that during the Watergate hearings there was no mention of that party. I was following the coverage closely, and while there was some mention that some of the top people were out here, there was nothing saying there was a party at Taft's."

In the months following the break-in, Nixon and his close aides continued, outwardly, to be focused on the campaign, as well as affairs of state, but their concern with the details of the cover-up, and its implications, overshadowed all else. The taped conversations between Nixon and Haldeman, in which they discussed using the CIA to sabotage the FBI investigation of the break-in—which would later come to be known as the "smoking gun"—occurred on June 23, just six days after the break-in. Though an outsider, Kalmbach was drafted into the cover-up by John Dean (at Mitchell's instigation, and with Haldeman's and Ehrlichman's approval). Dean asked him to raise cash for the de-

fense of the Watergate defendants, and for their families' support—
hush money, in effect, though Dean did not describe it that way. As
Lukas wrote, Kalmbach entered what he would later describe as "a
James Bond scenario"—conspiring with a New York ex-cop named
Tony Ulasewicz to collect and deliver the money, communicating by
using aliases, public phone booths, and code (the money was the "laundry," the vault in which it was kept the "icebox"). It is extremely unlikely that Schreiber—for all his closeness to Kalmbach, and Mitchell,
and Haldeman—would have been similarly enlisted; he was independent, rich, powerful in his own right, and far too smart to have engaged
in the kinds of cloak-and-dagger operations Kalmbach was carrying
out.

Schreiber was concentrating on the campaign—especially his efforts
to bring Hollywood celebrities out in force for this Republican president, for whom he felt such fealty. It was an effort on which he had collaborated closely with Mitchell. Until now, however, the results had
been lackluster. Alexander Butterfield, in his June memo to Haldeman,
said, "Although we are not doing very well getting his [Schreiber's] top
priority celebrities to accept our social functions, we are getting invitations out to them . . . so the gestures are being made and that's what really counts. Of the 7 celebrities invited to the Echeverria [Mexican
President Luis Echeverría Alvarez] Dinner, 5 were forced to regret."
Even with this mediocre performance, however, Schreiber was unquestionably viewed by the Nixon White House as an important resource,
someone to be treated with deference. So much so, Butterfield thought,
that it was a bit overdone. In July, Butterfield wrote an "administratively confidential" memo to Gordan Strachan, a White House aide
who worked for Haldeman. "The purpose of this quick note is only to
suggest that you reissue to those of us who comprise the great army of
Taft Schreiber liaison men your earlier instructions concerning who
does what, when and to whom. . . . Mr. S. has *got* to be wondering
what kind of an organization we have here—if, in fact, we have any organization at all. . . . In accordance with my instructions from Bob

Haldeman of some 10–12 weeks ago, I talk to Taft on the telephone two or three times each week. . . . I know that Rose [Mary] Woods [Nixon's secretary] talks to Taft now and then about a variety of general subjects, that Dwight Chapin checks in with him from time to time on the subject of celebrity appearances at the Convention, that Dave Parker [a young staffer] discusses with him the Presidential schedule, that Steve Bull [another young staffer] works out with him such things as party details, that Henry Kissinger chats with him on the odd occasion about his own personal appearances at west coast gatherings, that Bart Porter is still (as recently as yesterday) in touch, and that *probably* you and Bob Haldeman call him at long intervals just to see how things are coming along."

Schreiber had become, essentially, the Nixon White House's all-purpose man in Hollywood. The fund-raising was his most important task, but he made himself useful however he could. It was Schreiber who arranged for the installation of a special TV line at the White House so that Nixon could view the Muhammad Ali–Joe Frazier fight in March 1971. (The fight promoter, a former MCA agent named Jerry Perenchio, carried out Schreiber's request.) And it was Schreiber who responded to a message of concern from the White House in January 1972, regarding a derogatory movie about the president being produced by the Smothers Brothers entitled *Another Nice Mess*. Schreiber investigated the situation, and Robert Finch relayed Schreiber's findings to John Dean. "It is a very slapstick comedy—showing the President and Vice President as Laurel and Hardy types. There is nothing dirty and it is not pornographic or violent. The President's supporters will not like it, but it is not vitriolic. It simply shows them as buffoons," Finch wrote. "Schreiber plans to get a commitment from Lew Wasserman that none of the distributors will go for it—which means that only independent distributors can buy it."

Schreiber had worked hard on the kickoff event for the fall campaign, held at San Clemente on August 27, just a couple days after the close of the Republican National Convention. Guests making their way along the path to the Spanish-style estate, La Casa Pacifica, were greeted by Mexican musicians, margaritas, and a king-size elephant (party symbolism) made of flowers. The industry's major Republicans—Jules Stein, Jack Warner, Richard Zanuck, and, of course, Schreiber—were there. There were also some Democrats. Producer David Brown, Zanuck's partner (the two were now at MCA/Universal) was a confirmed Democrat, but Zanuck had prevailed upon him to come. ("I got into what was almost mortal combat with Lillian Hellman when I got back to Martha's Vineyard," Brown recalled. "She wanted to kill me for having shown up there.") When it came to the stars, Schreiber had been intent on getting a younger crowd—the New Hollywood—rather than the stodgy old-timers who were Republican regulars. In this, he was only moderately successful. "This looks like a cocktail party at the Hollywood Wax Museum," one guest commented. Among the stars were Jack Benny, John Wayne, James Stewart, Frank Sinatra, Debbie Reynolds, Clint Eastwood, Charlton Heston, George Burns, Merv Griffin, Eva and Zsa Zsa Gabor, June Allyson, Desi Arnaz, Virginia Mayo, and Dorothy Lamour. There were also some young television actors and actresses there, probably from the MCA stable. In any event, Nixon wasn't complaining. As though to repudiate any suggestion that he had not gotten an A-list crowd, he told the assembled guests, "You are Hollywood's 400."

Frank Sinatra, who because of his mob associations had been banished from White House events by Bobby Kennedy during JFK's presidency, had made a comeback now; he flew in from his Palm Springs home with Vice President Spiro Agnew. As he shook Sinatra's hand, Rev. Billy Graham told him, "I've always admired you although we've never met." Nixon, getting into the swing of things, told the *Hollywood Reporter* that he had a movie idea. "He feels there is a film in the second volume of Carl Sandburg's work on Lincoln, about Gen. William Tecumseh Sherman," wrote Marvene Jones, "whom he describes as 'a man who had contempt for death and contempt for fame. He was a silent leader of men." One guest remarked to Governor Reagan that, although he was a Democrat, he was going to vote for Nixon. Reagan replied, "Don't forget, I was a Democrat for thirty years. You've got to go the way you believe." Kissinger was there, too, with Jill St. John. According to Marvene Jones, Kissinger told her that he'd gotten his suntan in Honolulu, where "a strange girl, bikini-clad, came up to him on the beach and flung out, 'I hear you're supposed to be a fascinating man, so fascinate me!' " St. John, perhaps tired of hearing about how many women were fascinated by her beau, offered that she had just heard that Kissinger told Nixon she was "one of the smartest girls he'd ever met." St. John also confided in Joyce Haber of the *Los Angeles Times* that she had finally become a Democrat for Nixon. "I've never accepted Henry's invitations to the White House, either here or in Washington," she told Haber, "because I figured it was wrong if I wasn't for the President." (A different explanation from her having "an invitation from someone more important.")

Nixon gave a brief speech. He said that he had remembered very well, as some of his guests came through the receiving line, that they had been at events for him in "1946, 1950, '52, '56, '60, '62, '68, and here it is '72 and you are still with us." He thanked them, and also those who had come to the convention for him. He said he enjoyed watching movies, especially on the White House projection set. Some might consider it jingoistic, he said, "But I like my movies made in Hollywood, made in America, and I don't mean that I can't appreciate a good foreign movie, or a foreign movie star or starlet, or whatever the case may be, but I think the motion picture industry, it started here, it has grown up here, this is something that is typically American and it means a lot in presenting America to the world." When he and his wife traveled, he said, "We go along streets in the cities of Africa and Asia and Latin America, and every place, on that marquee you will see the Hollywood names that we are so familiar with. It makes us feel at home as we see those names." These movies had an enormous influence both here and abroad, he continued, and he believed Hollywood had been, and would continue to be, "an influence for good."

In conclusion, Nixon told a story about how the Democratic congressman from New York, Charles Rangel, had asked him to do something about the production and export of the heroin poppy from Turkey to the United States. He worked out an agreement with Turkey where the production would be stopped within a year, Nixon continued, and he called Rangel to tell him. Rangel was appreciative, and after they spoke for a while, he said, " 'You know, Mr. President, when I was growing up in Harlem, if I had told my old man that some day I would be talking to the President of the United States, he would have told me I was crazy,' " Nixon recalled. "And I said, 'Well, Mr. Congressman, if when I was growing up, in Yorba Linda, had I told my old man that some day I would be talking to a Congressman on the phone, he would have thought I was crazy.'

"I will simply close my remarks tonight by saying if I had told my old man—and this will date us both, my old man and the man I am going to mention and me, too—if I had told my old man when I was growing up in Yorba Linda that some day I would be talking to Jack Benny, he would have said that I was crazy."

It was a nice salute to the assembled crowd. Nixon *was* divided about Hollywood. But in his sanguine mood on this evening filled with bonhomie, surrounded by many of the people whose names he had seen on those far-away marquees, what he was voicing was all he felt that was positive. The negatives, for the moment, had been shorn away. And his speech—with its glimmers of warmth, and a few personal touches, and even a certain charm—was a crowd-pleaser.

———

Almost a year to the day after that convivial event at La Casa Pacifica, Schreiber was being interviewed in his MCA tower office by a government lawyer who warned him that he had the right to refuse to answer any question if he thought it might incriminate him, and he had the right to counsel. The lawyer, Thomas McBride, was on the staff of the Watergate special prosecutor; he told Schreiber the government was investigating possible violations of federal election laws, and other federal laws. What had brought the government prosecutors to Schreiber, mainly, was their focus on the government antitrust suit against the networks. Had it been a quid pro quo, the prosecutors wanted to know, for contributions from the motion picture industry? According to a McBride memo, Daniel Margolis, a Washington lawyer who was representing ABC, said that he believed "the White House favoritism [shown in the filing of the suit] may have stemmed from the fact that major campaign contributions were made by movie industry interests and that the law firm of Kalmbach, DeMarco represented the Motion Picture Association. Mr. Margolis also mentioned Taft Schreiber as being one of the influential motion picture people in terms of White House access." In a broad discovery motion, the government sought information concerning Jules Stein, Taft Schreiber, Ted Ashley, and Herbert Kalmbach.

A great deal had unraveled in the course of the past year. In April 1973, Nixon, distraught, had fired Haldeman and Ehrlichman—notwithstanding Haldeman's having warned him, the month before, "You fire everybody now, you send them to jail." (Shortly after their firing, Nixon had a phone conversation with Haldeman in which Haldeman suggested that Ehrlichman and he could be supported through affiliations with the Nixon Foundation, as yet unformed, and that Leonard Firestone and Taft Schreiber would fund it. "Do it today—immediately," Nixon told Haldeman. "Don't announce it. Do it.") Nixon had hoped from the start to keep Mitchell protected—he would claim at one point about the cover-up, "the whole Goddamn thing, frankly, was done because it involved Mitchell"—but it was quite clear to Nixon by the spring of that year that Mitchell would be implicated. Most bitterly of all, Nixon knew that he might have to resign or face impeachment. The decisive moment came on July 13, 1973, when Alexander Butterfield, under questioning by the Senate select committee, revealed the existence of Nixon's taping system. That broke the dam.

In his interview, Schreiber gave a bare-bones, if not misleading, account of his role vis-à-vis the Nixon White House. The days of trumpeting "the Schreiber Plan" were clearly over. He mentioned the meeting at San Clemente, saying that "the industry representatives discussed what they viewed as unfair treatment by the government and an investment tax credit issue involving the Disney Corporation." On occasion after that meeting, Schreiber said, he "had talked to Mr. Flanigan and to James Loken of Mr. Flanigan's staff. . . . Schreiber said he was involved in the San Clemente meeting because of his friendship with the President and indeed had recommended to the President that he not have the meeting because he would only get complaints." Interestingly, Schreiber did manage to drop Wasserman's name twice, as someone who was involved in lobbying for the motion picture industry's interests.

Regarding his own fund-raising efforts, Schreiber said he "volunteered to assist in fund raising activities in a conversation he had with John Mitchell in mid-1971." He did so, he said, because he is "a friend of President Nixon and wanted to help him." He said he became active in fund-raising with Herbert Kalmbach, whom he knew from previous campaigns; he acknowledged having met with him in New York and Washington "a few times" in connection with fund-raising efforts for the 1972 campaign. He also acknowledged his role in soliciting the contributions from Hirshhorn and from Ashley.

Finally, Schreiber said that "on occasions" he had talked to Mitchell about the private antitrust suit the studios had brought against the networks. He made no mention now of his having lobbied for the government antitrust suit—of Nixon's having promised him the government would do something about it, of his meeting with Associate Attorney General for Antitrust Richard McLaren about it, of his having told Loken that it was the government's suit against the networks that was what was really needed, or of his allegedly having called Ehrlichman shortly before it was filed. When Mitchell was interviewed by a lawyer from the special prosecutor's team several months later, his story on the suit squared with Schreiber's. "While he may have once discussed the private suit against the networks with Schreiber, he believes this was far into 1972," the government lawyer wrote in his memorandum. And on the fund-raising, Mitchell went even further in distancing Schreiber from himself than Schreiber had. "Mitchell never discussed Schreiber's efforts to raise contributions for the President with him," the lawyer wrote.

Ashley's contribution had excited some investigative interest— because of its size, and its timing, and his being an unlikely donor. That interest sharpened in November 1973, when special prosecutor Leon Jaworski received a letter from an individual, unnamed, who claimed to be an employee of Warner Communications, urging him to investigate Ashley's contribution. "$137,000 changed hands just prior to April 7, 1972—purportedly from Ashley as an individual. A full-fledged examination will indicate that this money was actually from the Warner Communications Corporation in exchange for special consideration of the motion picture industry's interests." It was not an unlikely proposition. Political contributions out of corporate funds were prohibited; but there were so many corporate contributions masquerading as personal in the Nixon 1972 campaign that it was almost the order of the day. Among them was a $150,000 contribution, solicited by Kalmbach, from Thomas V. Jones, chairman of the Northrop Corporation. Jones, who was a member of the MCA board, made the contributions in his name with corporate funds; the corporation was fined. Many of the corporations that made these illegal contributions were in industries dependent on government regulation—like the defense industry, the airlines, and oil companies. In the past, the motion picture industry would not have fit the pattern; but in the Nixon administration it did.

The dairy industry makes a suggestive, albeit hypothetical, analogue to the motion picture industry in their respective dealings with the Nixon administration. The milk producers were focused on milk price supports; and in return for a favorable decision by Nixon, they were willing to pledge $2 million for the 1972 campaign. The Nixon White House strategy was to tell them that a favorable decision would be made, but to delay any announcement until the money commitments were firm. The White House, furthermore, wanted to disguise the contributions, for fear of their appearing to be a quid pro quo. The milk producers believed they were obligated to report their contributions, J. Anthony Lukas wrote, "but in a series of meetings, Kalmbach recalls, 'We were trying to develop a procedure . . . where they could meet their independent reporting requirements and still not result in disclosure.' " This became the procedure: the dairy industry gave its money in small amounts to a network of committees in the District of Columbia, which then passed the money to the campaign; and the committees were given names like Organization of Sensible Citizens, Committee for Political Integrity, Americans United for Objective Reporting, and so forth. Interestingly, when Ashley made his contributions, he made them through Kalmbach's partner, Frank DeMarco, as his agent, and he made them in small amounts, to thirty-one committees, with names like Effective Government Committee, Improved Government Committee, Good Government Committee, Better Society Council, Improved Society Council, Improved Society Support Group, and so forth. Jack Warner made his $100,000 contribution in a similar way. (When the government lawyers sought to question the eighty-two-year-old Warner in 1974, his doctor said that he was not "mentally or physically capable of being interviewed.")

Ashley *was* questioned, with two highly regarded lawyers in attendance. He was not charged with any crime, and over the years he has stuck to the story he gave that day in August 1974: that he made that large contribution not for the industry but for himself, with personal funds, because he wanted to raise his profile in the political world (and perhaps receive an ambassadorship, he later said); and he did it in that odd form because Schreiber had dropped by his house with Kalmbach, who told him that his partner, DeMarco, would handle the transaction; and DeMarco advised him to do it the way he did. This much is certainly true; if Ashley *had* wanted to be an ambassador, it would have been wise to contribute at that level. Ambassadorships, like much else in the Nixon White House, were for sale, and with a high price tag. One of the charges for which Kalmbach would serve time in prison was having promised federal employment in return for supporting a candidate—specifically, a pledge of $100,000 for an ambassadorship. Alexander Butterfield said that Tex Thornton, the chairman of Litton Industries (which had, coincidentally, bought Jules Stein's beloved MCA building in Beverly Hills to use as its corporate headquarters), called him one day to ask him to make a discreet inquiry for him. Thornton said he believed he was being considered for the post of U.S. ambassador to Japan, and he wanted to know if he were likely to be chosen. Butterfield promptly called Rose Mary Woods, Nixon's devoted secretary, and put the question to her. " 'Let's see,' she said, going to her lists. Then—'He gave a goddam fifty thousand!' She said it with such vitriol. I called Tex, and said, 'Looks like they're not happy, you only gave $50,000.' He said that wasn't true, that he'd actually given $89,000. Anyway," Butterfield concluded, "he didn't get it."

Viewed against the backdrop of the Nixon White House, the favors done for the motion picture industry seem unlikely to have been dispensed without some substantial consideration, even beyond the handful of large contributions from Schreiber, Stein, Warner, and Ashley. Hollywood had celebrities' support to barter, but, mainly, it had money; that was the cardinal lure for politicians. And Nixon was too ambivalent about Hollywood—and too focused on money—not to have expected to be compensated on a grand scale. As Arthur Krim commented in his oral history, "There was a kind of standing joke between President Johnson and myself because there were occasions where I would have boasted of a $10,000 contribution from somebody who subsequently gave Nixon $750,000. We were living with a different level. The president considered $10,000 a substantial contribution; Nixon thought of it as a cup of coffee."

But the government lawyers who were looking for evidence of a quid pro quo here were reminiscent of those who had tried to build a criminal antitrust case against MCA. *That* had been an intensive, high-priority investigation, which continued for years, and yet those lawyers had been badly outmaneuvered. This, on the other hand, was merely one of many Watergate-related investigations, and it seems to have been handled in a desultory, superficial manner. By February 1974, less than a year after the investigation had begun, attorney Hamilton Fox III had already reached firm conclusions. As he wrote in a memo, he was "satisfied that the antitrust suit is completely legitimate." His conviction derived mainly from interviewing the Justice Department lawyers involved in the case. Fox did think that the delay in filing might seem suspicious. However, "the explanation that has been given me for this—and I know nothing to contradict it—is that there was initially an argument within the Division over the proposed remedy in the suit." This took months to resolve, he continued, and then Mitchell asked that the suit not be filed until Herb Klein spoke to the networks' presidents; Klein delayed, and several more months went by. Fox acknowledged that Mitchell met with the movie people on several occasions during this period. "It is possible, I suppose, that Mitchell deliberately delayed the suit so that he could hold it over movie executives until they contributed. . . . But there is absolutely no evidence that Mitchell did this. I have not spoken with the major contributors from the movie industry, but I have considerable doubts that any of them are going to tell me, even if it occurred, that they made their contributions in return for Mitchell's promise to sue the networks."

Indeed. The investigation was eventually closed, and no charges brought.

The last word, really, on this episode in the MCA-Washington chronicle came, fittingly enough, from Jules Stein. His daughter Jean was visiting Los Angeles in early August 1974. Her politics were still diametrically opposed to her father's; Jules had been particularly infuriated when she'd held an event to raise money for the legal defense of Daniel Ellsberg, the former national security official who leaked the *Pentagon Papers* to the *New York Times*. Now, Jean was hosting a big party, held within a day or so of Nixon's resignation on August 9. Tom

Wicker of the *New York Times,* who had written many columns about Nixon and Watergate, was among the guests that night. So was Jules Stein—and Wicker thought that Jules might attempt to defend Nixon. Many of the guests were seated outdoors, on a big, unlit side porch, as dusk gathered and dinner was about to be served. "Watergate, of course, was very much a topic of discussion," Wicker recalled. "Suddenly, I heard Jules's voice rising above the din, out of the dark. He said, 'What I want to know is, how can I get my money back?' "

It had been quite an initiation into national politics for Schreiber. He had enjoyed access to the White House on a scale unprecedented in Hollywood, and he had been able to win nearly everything he'd wanted for his industry, and his much prized MCA. He'd been so overshadowed by Wasserman in Hollywood for decades; but now, on the political scene during the Nixon years, Schreiber had been the power broker. He had not been close to Nixon personally; but he had been to those around the president who got things done. Eventually, though, nearly all those people—Mitchell, Kalmbach, Haldeman, Ehrlichman—went to jail. And the president for whom he had expressed such full-hearted admiration resigned in disgrace.

Schreiber remained active in Republican politics. Knowing Reagan as well as he did, he had written a memo to Garment back in 1970, in which he said, "I can frankly state that somewhere in the mind of our Governor lurks the hope that if our President falters in the next few years he could be the savior of the party." Well, Nixon had certainly faltered, and Reagan was seeking the presidential nomination in 1976. Despite his long relationship with Reagan, Schreiber was unequivocally for President Gerald Ford. He was, in fact, national co-chairman of the President Ford Committee, a fund-raising group to support Ford's reelection bid. Garment recalled a lunch he had with Schreiber in late May 1976 at Schreiber's apartment at the Sherry-Netherland Hotel in New York. "I remember, there was a Monet, a Pisarro, a

Boudin—gorgeous, small paintings," Garment enthused. "Taft was certain that Ford should be nominated, that Reagan was not equipped. He said, 'This is very confidential. Ronnie is a wonderful guy. But Ford is entitled to be president. And it should be known that Mrs. Reagan gets her guidance from a fortune-teller. You can quietly let that out.' "

A few days later, Schreiber, sixty-eight, entered UCLA Medical Center for what was expected to be routine prostate surgery. During the operation, he was given a transfusion of incompatible blood— mislabeled by a hospital technician—and he died ten days later. In the last decade of his life, he had really come to prominence in the political arena; so it was not surprising that articles, following his death, focused on his political activities. While there was no mention of his closeness to Nixon's inner circle, there was the faintest suggestion of controversy. *Los Angeles Times* reporter Richard West wrote that Schreiber had been Reagan's agent since 1938, and had supported him in his political campaigns, too, but had recently defected to Ford; that he had supported candidates as diverse as the liberal Democrat Tom Bradley for mayor of Los Angeles, and the right-wing Republican candidate Max Rafferty for the U.S. Senate; and that he had served as a trustee of the Nixon Foundation. It was enough to rouse the ire of Schreiber's friends. Robert Finch wrote a letter to the editor of the *Times*. "I was more than a little distressed to see the totally inappropriate coverage and distorted characterization" of Schreiber, Finch wrote. "Instead of reciting his institutional commitments advancing the arts, health care, his church and countless eleemosynary endeavors, you inaccurately paraded a list of controversial political figures with whom he had been associated." Jules Stein, in a letter to *Times* chairman Franklin Murphy, referred to Finch's letter, saying it "affected me deeply," and added that he, too, was disturbed by the coverage. "You, yourself, were very close to Taft as head of the *Los Angeles Times* and I thought you would instruct your people to do a momentous obituary on my associate of fifty years." Stein referred to Schreiber at one point as "our beloved Taft."

It was an unusually emotional communication from the taciturn, hemmed-in Stein, and it hinted at the dramatic contrast in his relationship with Schreiber, whom he had passed over, and with Wasserman, whom he'd chosen—twice, in effect. For a corporate triangle, this one had been extraordinarily bitter and long-lived. Wasserman would have ousted Schreiber after Schreiber's attempted coup, but because of Stein, he could not; his hands were tied. Now, Wasserman was rid of his mortal antagonist—and Stein was bereft. "I have lost my oldest friend," Stein said at Schreiber's funeral.

Alfred Hitchcock and Lew Wasserman at the Academy Awards ceremony in 1974, as Wasserman received the Jean Hersholt Humanitarian Award. *Academy of Motion Picture Arts and Sciences*

Chapter 4

DOMINION

The seventies belonged to Wasserman. It was the time he had been preparing for all his life, when all his striving and positioning came to fruition in a sweetly satisfying apotheosis. He was Hollywood's leader, the company he had shaped was thriving, and there was no longer any caveat to his dominion there. On June 5, 1973, the seventy-seven-year-old Stein resigned as chairman of the board, and Wasserman, sixty, ascended to that post, while continuing to hold the title of chief executive officer (a signal that *his* chairmanship would be more activist than Stein's had been). This changing of the guard took place at the annual stockholders' meeting, still held in Chicago by decades-old custom. Sidney Sheinberg, the blunt, belligerent Texan who had joined MCA as a lawyer in 1959 and eventually become president of Universal Television, succeeded Wasserman as president—the title Wasserman had won as a young man and held on to for nearly thirty years. (As Sheinberg had prepared to travel to the board meeting in Chicago, a friend at the company who had long speculated with Sheinberg about the origins of MCA remarked, "Now you'll get to meet the *real* board of directors.") Sheinberg had never been a Stein favorite. "Would Jules have chosen Sid?" Wasserman asked, echoing the question. He considered. "Probably not. Sid was a little too tough and too brusque for Jules." But—for the first time—it did not matter.

Wasserman had long cultivated the image of someone who was inaccessible to the press, but in truth he was more press-savvy than press-shy; he had, after all, been a publicist for a Cleveland nightclub when he attracted the attention of Stein's brother, Bill. And for years, he had used the press, sparingly but deftly, meting out an interview to a favored reporter in order to publicize some message that was important for his business. Now, though—as regent—Wasserman decided it was time to step into the spotlight. He cooperated with profiles in the *Wall Street Journal* and the *Los Angeles Times Calendar* and even (with his wife, Edie) in the *Los Angeles Times Home Magazine*—all to great effect. The only one to breathe a hint of a negative was the page-one story in the *Wall Street Journal* on July 10, 1973. Reporter Earl Gottschalk wrote that some referred to MCA headquarters as the "tower of fear," and that MCA's dedication to computers and tight cost controls had led many writers to complain that its TV programs suffered from a bottom-line preoccupation, calling MCA "the factory." "A testament to the company's power," Gottschalk added, "is that no writer is willing to go on the record with specific charges about the company." These negatives, however, appeared almost incidental in a portrait of such dazzling corporate success. For Gottschalk pointed out that while the history of the entertainment industry was characterized by periodic weakness, MCA had remained strong and durable over many decades. Currently, it was the nation's leading supplier of television programs for the networks and operated the world's largest motion picture studio. It also had interests in records, music publishing, real estate, recreation, mail order gifts, and savings and loans. It had created a studio tour that was the third most popular tourist attraction in Southern California. And MCA earned a record profit in 1972 ($20.8 million on revenues of $346 million), with another record expected for 1973. MCA had achieved all this success by taking risks, Gottschalk emphasized. When the movie studios were recoiling from television, MCA had embraced it; when movie companies were trying to sell studio real estate to cut costs, MCA had bought the 440-acre Universal Studios. And now, Wasserman hoped to bring his success with television to a new level—revolutionizing the medium with MCA's Disco-Vision, a machine, still in development, that would allow movies and other material to be shown on home TV sets (the chance to sell, for yet another vehicle, the thousands of movies and TV shows MCA owned). Finally, Gottschalk wrote that while some described Wasserman as hard and intimidating, he saw no evidence of those traits. "Indeed, when he's having a drink with a visitor and showing him his Beverly Hills home (complete with a projection room), he is a gracious host with a lively wit and an easy smile."

For Wasserman, the standard of excellence against which he measured his company remained MGM, as he had known it in the late thirties and early forties. Commenting on Universal's success in the interview with the *Los Angeles Times Calendar* in September 1973, Wasserman invoked his touchstone, saying, "In its heyday, MGM—which was then probably the biggest and best of the studios—produced 100 hours of film per year. Today, the hours are, well, precious few. But here, we made 300 hours of film last year and spent more than any two or three studios spent in those heydays combined." (To arrive at his three-hundred-hour figure, however, Wasserman was combining feature films for theatrical release with TV films—a product twice the volume of the feature films.)

The *Home Magazine* piece was actually the most revealing, because the interviewer, Marshall Berges, attempted to get Wasserman to talk not only about the business but, also, himself, and the format was Q&A. It was a distinctly friendly piece. There was no mention here, as there had been in the *Wall Street Journal,* of the fact that Wasserman slept in a couch outside his wife's bedroom so as not to disturb her with his early morning rising. Here, Edie and he were photographed seated on either side of a two-seater desk that the accompanying text pointed out, "enables the Wassermans to face each other while they keep up with correspondence." Wasserman was wearing the large, dark-rimmed glasses that were so distinctive they had in the last few years become a kind of trademark—though he was not generally photographed with them on. He described his routine. Seven days a week, he would rise at 5:00 A.M. to begin his series of calls ("During high school, I worked full-time as a theatre usher, so the habit of very little sleep—maybe five hours a night—has been with me for a long time"). He would call associates to learn the previous day's grosses from the tour and MCA movies worldwide, as well as the ratings of the previous night's TV shows. By 9:00 A.M., he would arrive at his office (having driven himself there in his white Mercedes roadster, with the license plate MCA1). Throughout the day, he would meet with other MCA executives, and he would periodically receive slips of paper showing updated box office figures. In the evening, he would have dinner with his wife, and screen feature films and TV shows. Berges asked whether there was any phase of the business in which he would like to be involved if he had more time, and Wasserman replied, "I don't think so. I've been fortunate in disciplining myself so that I can focus my attention without distraction. I just blank out whatever else there might be, to achieve the benefit of concentration."

Was he ever a foolish young man? "Can I answer that?" Edie responded. "He was very mature and thoughtful at 22. He never did anything foolish. The reason, I think, was that he had to go to work at a very early age."

And what standards does he set for his executives, to help them choose stars and stories? "Rarely do I have to tell them anything," Wasserman replied. "They know I'm a very curious fellow. That I have an insatiable appetite for knowledge. That I expect them to have the answers to questions that might be asked."

Such as? "Some basic ones are Why? What? Where? How?"

Would he amplify? "Why that subject? What's the logic behind it?

What are you attempting to achieve? What's your point of view? Where is the pre-production planning? How will it be executed?"

Was he a hard and ruthless man, as some of his critics said? "If negotiating in an attempt to arrive at a favorable deal comes under the heading of being hard, I would stipulate that I'm hard. I believe all of MCA's management is ruthless in its zealousness to protect the corporation." But then, Wasserman must have recalibrated. "Actually, I don't believe the word 'ruthless' fits our time. It is outmoded. It's a carryover from robber baron days. I don't think our society today permits people to be ruthless. But as for being hard, I guess I'm guilty."

The real sticklers, however, came toward the end of the interview, when Berges's questions became more personal.

What did he do for relaxation? "Sit in the hot sun and do absolutely nothing," said the man who avoided leisure (vacations, cultural pastimes, recreation) like a scourge. "If it's a miserable weekend and there's no sun to sit in, I'm miserable."

And what did he not find time to do that he would really like to do? "I'd like to take a tour. . . . Drive across the U.S. I have flown across America more than a thousand times, but I've never seen it. I'd like to take a slow, casual, relaxing tour by auto. Just poking along and seeing the sights."

It was, perhaps, an attempt to normalize himself, to seem to be—for just this quick moment—a more regular person, who could savor life's small pleasures. But to the people who worked for him, no image could have been more incongruous. How could the man who considered his time too valuable to waste it on "hello" or "goodbye" in a phone conversation, who cut each exchange to the bone, lend himself to "just poking along"? Wasserman's mystique had only deepened with the years, his ever increasing power further enhancing his personal stature; and his associates, more than ever, were held in a thrall of reverence and fear. Perhaps no one was more acutely aware of this than Sheinberg, who was in the disconcerting position of having been uniquely elevated as heir apparent—and who felt, at the same time, diminished, because now he was always measured against Wasserman. "It was very difficult," Sheinberg said. "I had become president—but I can assure you that to convince people that anyone but Lew had authority was not easy. He *was* king of the world."

Within his domain, Wasserman was more austere and remote than ever. Few had as much opportunity to observe him up close (albeit from a narrow perspective) as his secretary, Melody Sherwood. Sherwood had joined MCA as a "floater" in the secretarial pool in the spring of 1962, when the company was still in the colonial-style mansion Stein had built. Even then, Wasserman had seemed an almost mythical presence. "A secretary would whisper, 'There goes Mr. Wasserman!' I'd run to get a look, but all I'd see was a door closing, or a shadow," Sherwood recalled. Wasserman always had two secretaries, and in 1967, his longtime secretary, Kim Bryan, was looking for a replacement for the junior secretary who had just left. "Everyone was afraid," Sherwood said; but she liked Bryan and was not so easily cowed, so she decided to apply for the job, and got it. Except for a two-year hiatus, she would work for him for the next thirty-one years.

She was trained by Bryan—a rigid taskmaster, who dealt with Wasserman's subordinates in a stern and intimidating way, as though she were an extension of her boss. It was not an easy induction. When Sherwood first started working for Wasserman, he would often leave the office in the early evening to drive to downtown Los Angeles for meetings connected with the Center Theatre Group. Since she had the late shift, it was her duty to relay messages to him when he phoned from his car. "Kim was training me as to how I was to give him these messages. 'He has no patience. Give him only the important ones. And remember, this is *not* a conversation!' I was primed. I had the messages. He called in. 'What have you got?' '*Nothing,*' I said—and hung up the phone!" Wasserman ate in the commissary nearly every day (ordering either tuna salad or fruit salad, year after year), and he wanted to be called at the phone at his table at 1:15 sharp, to be told the stock market closings. "I was nervous—it seemed rude to interrupt him at lunch, and I would blurt them out as fast as I could. In the first or second week I was there, he was having lunch with someone, and this time he did not want to be interrupted. He said, 'Don't call me with the closings. Don't call unless the place is burning down.' Well, fifteen minutes later, I saw smoke—the back lot was burning! I called security, and they said, yes, we know, call Mr. Wasserman. He answered the phone in this voice—'*Yes?*' I said, 'I'm so sorry to disturb you, sir, but the place *is* burning down!' "

Gradually, she learned what was expected, and how to do it without buckling from the strain. Her shift started at 10:00 A.M., but since she could not risk an unforeseeable traffic jam making her even a minute late, she planned to arrive at MCA by 8:30. And since her lunch break was from one to two, she was religious about being at her desk at two—never at, say, thirty seconds after two—even if Wasserman were at other MCA offices in New York or Europe, because he was likely to call then. "He was very aware of numbers—and time was a number." She of course had to have a clean desk (she would hide papers under her typewriter cover). Either she or Bryan was to pick up his phone on the first ring, and no one was ever to be left on hold. She read his mail, underlining the sentences that were important, and was prepared to tell him in few words what was the bottom line of any communication. She answered his mail, too, and perfected his signature (actually, Bryan's version of it). He never asked to see the letters she wrote for him before they went out, but she was careful to write and file every one, because it was too terrible to think of his reaction if he happened to ask to see such a letter sometime later and it did not exist. He did not like to give speeches, and would not say more than a few sentences at an event; these, too, she would generally write for him. She learned *never* to say, "I don't know," but rather, "I will find out." She learned, too, never to tell him, as she did only once, that the line was busy on a call he had asked her to place but that she would keep trying. "He yelled, 'Godammit, I don't want excuses, I want results!' " So she learned always to call the operator and ask her to break in, as it was an emergency.

She knew he wanted the tour count—the number of visitors who had entered the Universal tour—each hour. "If I hadn't given it to him at eleven, he'd buzz me at 11:05 and say, 'Well, what's wrong?' and I'd have to call over and find out why we didn't have it—maybe the machine had jammed." He kept a weekly tour count (every hour of each day, written on long graph paper) in his desk drawer. Each count was accompanied by a description of the weather, including the temperature range. In a typical exchange, she continued, "He'd say, 'What's the count?' '1412.' 'What was it last year?' 'Only 970, but there was a thunderstorm.' " Sherwood added, "It was a game. He loved numbers. And I guess if it was 10 percent over the previous year, he liked that." Wasserman kept his appointment calendar in a box on his desk, and at the end of each day she was to lock the calendar in his desk drawer; it was very important to him that no one be able to see his appointment schedule. Sometimes, Sherwood would be driving over the canyon from the San Fernando Valley to her home on the Westside, and she would suddenly wonder whether she had indeed locked away his calendar, or she would think of some other task (like writing a letter) that she had left undone. "I'd think, Omigod! I'd turn around and go back to the office and do it. I would *never* take the risk of leaving something for the next day."

Even as Wasserman's idiosyncrasies became familiar, the job was, still, peculiarly demanding. "You had to be on your toes every minute. He did not want to waste a moment. If he wanted something, he wanted it immediately. You had to know how to get it, and even if he misspoke, and said he wanted it from the wrong person, you were to know enough to realize what he *really* meant, and get it right. Kim took all this very, very seriously. It was her life; it consumed her. She would go home at the end of the day with migraine headaches."

Sherwood was a different personality—diligent, eminently capable, but also fun-loving, with an infectious laugh. It might be heresy, but she saw herself not as an acolyte but an employee in what was, after all, an entertainment company. After she had worked for Wasserman for some time, she made an effort to lighten the atmosphere slightly. She felt she had to—"otherwise it was just, 'Good morning,' 'Yes, sir,' 'No, sir,' 'Good night.' " So one day, she remarked to Wasserman, " 'That's a nice tie.' And he said, 'Don't get personal.' " She noticed that he was not that comfortable with women, and was particularly careful never to allow himself to be placed in what might be a compromising situation. When a woman was in his office, Sherwood said, there was almost always another executive there with them. "I think he didn't want to give anyone the chance to say, you know, 'Wasserman chased me around his desk.' He was very old-fashioned, the straightest person in the world—the last one to have an affair!" The door between his office and her desk was always closed, and when she entered, she would typically leave the door open. On occasion, though, if she wanted to tell him something that she did not want overheard, she would shut the door behind her as she entered. "His eyes would *pop*—either because he was thinking, what would people think—or *what is she going to say?*"

Over the years, as she got to know him a little, she became braver, and took it as her challenge to make him laugh. "I *had* to, to make him seem more real, or I couldn't have worked in that atmosphere. He'd get in the elevator and everyone would stiffen up in silence. I thought it must be very uncomfortable for him. . . . I always wanted to do something that you wouldn't think you could do with him—literally, to humanize him." For his sixty-fifth birthday, she invited about three hundred of the mid-level and lower-level executives, who would rarely have any chance to be with Wasserman, to congregate outside his office, as a surprise; she recited a poem she had written, and Ruth Cogen, Stein's sister, accompanied her on the violin. "And I would joke with the executives. Someone would be waiting to see him, and his *screams* would be coming out of the office, and I'd say, maybe you don't want to ask for that raise today." It was not unusual for men to emerge from his office in tears, she recalled.

He did not generally subject Bryan or Sherwood to this treatment. He must have realized how seriously Bryan took her job, and he evidently wanted to please her; at a labor relations dinner honoring him in 1974, Wasserman remarked, "There's a rumor around that Sid is president and I'm chairman. That's not true. There's only one person that runs MCA, fellows. It's Kim Bryan. All I hear about the company is what she tells me, and that's not a hell of a lot." One day in 1975, however, Wasserman became furious at Bryan, and eviscerated her in front of another employee—something that Bryan found particularly humiliating, Sherwood said. "Mr. Wasserman had asked her to get something from an executive, and she thought it would be easier to get it from a different person. He asked her if she'd gotten it, and she said yes, but from this other one—and he had not wanted that person to know. He *screamed*. She walked out of his office, picked up her purse, said to me, 'It's all yours'—and left."

Sherwood kept in touch with Bryan over the years, but Wasserman did not. His employees were not supposed to leave MCA; he viewed it as a kind of violation. "I'm sure her leaving upset him, but he never said a word about it," Sherwood recalled. "Once she walked out, it was as if she'd never been there."

Wasserman's imperial regime extended beyond the immediate confines of MCA, too, to the lawyers at the Beverly Hills firm of Rosenfeld, Meyer & Susman. This was the firm that Larry Beilenson had started in the early fifties with Jules Stein's encouragement and, in short order, his clients. For just as Stein had passed along many of his musician clients to his accountant, Harry Berman, so he referred his Hollywood talent to this law firm. It was, of course, a patent conflict of interest for the law firm to be representing both MCA and MCA's clients. (But, as Rosenfeld partner David Wexler commented, "Conflicts of interest don't exist here—this is show biz!") From Stein's standpoint, the arrangement was ideal; the law firm was MCA's outside counsel, so it appeared to be independent—but, in reality, it was utterly beholden to MCA. Initially, therefore, the firm's practice was mainly in entertainment law; as MCA grew into a major corporation, the firm's practice expanded, too.

Mel Ziontz, a corporate lawyer who joined the Rosenfeld firm as a young associate in 1969, recalled the first time he was summoned to a meeting with the executive his colleagues referred to, usually in hushed tones, as "LRW." Donald Rosenfeld, a tax attorney who for many years had done work for Jules Stein as well as MCA, informed Ziontz that he could not simply go to Wasserman's office; Rosenfeld would accompany him, to introduce him. "So I went there. It was full of people. Don introduced me, and I said, 'It's a pleasure to meet you.' Wasserman said, 'I hope you still feel that way at the end of this meeting.' " A junior MCA executive began his presentation, proposing that they acquire a small company that made audio consoles. "There was a project, like a jukebox; it had blank eight-tracks, and you picked a tune, and paid for your eight-track. Essentially, you could customize your own album," Ziontz continued. "Wasserman said, 'Let me get this straight. You want to manufacture equipment that would enable people to *steal our copyrights?*' " The executive committed the cardinal error of trying to defend himself, which only enraged Wasserman further. He had seen other "screamers and yellers," Ziontz said, "but they were all rank amateurs. No one else could carry it off the same way. When he was doing it, there was no profanity. It was like an out-of-body experience. His voice got very high, higher than you could imagine it could. It was so terrible. I think the guy would have jumped out the window if he could have—he was trembling, he couldn't speak. Wasserman came around his desk, *screaming* at him. Then, he turned to go back behind the desk—and it was, evidently, a signal! Everyone stood up. The meeting was over. Hal Haas [the MCA treasurer], put his arm around me, saying, 'You look a little shaken. By the way, you'd better get used to it. That was an hors d'oeuvre. Wait till you see the main course!' "

Ziontz became very close to Rosenfeld, who admired Wasserman enormously. Rosenfeld would tell and retell the story of how, during the attempted coup in 1969, he had paid a visit to his longtime client

Jules Stein. "Don told Jules he was making a big mistake in getting rid of Lew, and Lew never forgot that," Ziontz said. Rosenfeld also said that Wasserman had bailed him out financially when he became overextended in the stock market. So there was a bond between the two men that went far beyond normal business ties, and endured over decades. Nonetheless, Rosenfeld quaked before Wasserman. "Don had this big bottle of Maalox near his desk, and when he got a call from Wasserman, he'd quickly pop ten Maalox in his mouth," Ziontz said. "The first time I saw it, I asked what he was doing. And he said, 'My stomach gets so upset. It's preventative.' " And, much to his chagrin, Ziontz found himself responding as Rosenfeld did. "When Wasserman called, I got so tense—it was irrational to be so unnerved, just hearing that someone was on the line! But I did." Phones were installed in the bathrooms of the Rosenfeld firm (an anomaly in those days), so that Wasserman would never have to wait to reach a lawyer. "He wanted you to act like he was the only person in the world," Ziontz said.

Ziontz came to recognize the signal Wasserman traits—intellect, judgment, self-assurance, prodigious memory. But these qualities in themselves, he thought, did not account for what was almost a cult of idolatry that had grown up around Wasserman. Ziontz decided that Wasserman was able to encourage that worship, however subtly, because he was "a tremendous politician, and a great manipulator of people." "He would pay attention to you in small ways, to make you feel like you were important. He would remember some little thing about me; put it away in his memory bank; and toss it out to me to show he remembered my transactions. It was two-edged: I know everything about you, I'm watching you—but also, I know who you are, I recognize you as a person. He ran the gamut from being the most gracious person I dealt with at MCA to being the most severe."

For more than twenty years, Ziontz would represent MCA, dealing closely with Wasserman—who remained the firm's most important client by far. After a while, he learned how to stay on Wasserman's good side, most of the time. An extremely voluble person, master of the extended monologue, Ziontz had to suppress those instincts entirely and, instead, distill information to its essence, and convey it in a few words. He would prepare a summary of no more than one page for a meeting with Wasserman—but he suspected Wasserman only glanced at it, and threw it away. "He never took notes. He listened to what was being said, and he *got* it." Nor did Ziontz recall ever having received a memo from Wasserman. "He didn't deal with the written word." Wasserman's expectations were so high and unremitting that the job came to feel a little like a high-wire performance that had no end. "It was not just a question of conveying facts or advice. There was this whole other thing going on—you had to be *at your best*. I always thought that he wasn't getting the best advice, actually, because there was this aspect of being mortified, lest you say the wrong thing." In contentious moments, Ziontz tried to strike just the right balance— conveying that he knew his place, and yet holding his ground; Wasser- man did not like weakness. And Ziontz knew he should never, but never, violate one of the rules Wasserman had laid down.

That was what David Wexler did. Wexler, a securities lawyer at Rosenfeld, worked on MCA matters for about twenty years, beginning in 1965. He was well aware of Wasserman's prohibition against MCA's agreeing to indemnify another party; there had been an indemnification provision in some contracts involving the savings and loans MCA had acquired, and MCA eventually had to make good on those indemnifi- cation clauses, which were costly. "Wasserman said, 'I never will sign an indemnification!' He was mad and he issued a rule—and once he is- sued a rule, that was it. I am not aware of his ever changing a rule, though some rules may have just disappeared," Wexler said. In the early eighties, he was negotiating a contract between MCA and the Bass brothers, who wanted an indemnification. "They were in their rights," Wexler said. "I recommended the indemnification. I drafted the most watered-down provision I possibly could. I consulted with Don Rosenfeld and [MCA executive] Al Dorskind, who told me to go forward. Lew went ballistic! He fired me—which meant I could no longer work on MCA matters, which was three fourths of my business. It was a scary time. Now, as it happened, it changed my life for the better—I would always have been dependent on that Black Tower." Instead, he began doing securities work for a whole range of clients.

At the time, though, Wexler said, it was devastating. "I had never been angrier in my life—I'd done tender offers for them; handled their subsidiaries; wrote the scripts for their board meetings; done corporate minutes for years. Then, Lew fired me. I was expendable. I was an object lesson. It was a lesson to those around him that his orders were to be obeyed." He paused, and added, "Decent people don't *do* things like that."

It was one thing to strive to establish such control in one's immediate environment, and quite another in the outside world. Even there, though, Wasserman saw fit to punish a challenge to his authority.

George Stevens, Jr., had known Wasserman casually from the time Stevens started out in the movie business. In the mid-fifties, he had gone to work for Jack Webb, when Webb was on the Revue lot, acting in movies and, also, the immensely successful TV show *Dragnet,* which Webb produced as well. "I vividly remember Lew—lean, young, smiling—coming with Jay Kanter to see Jack," Stevens said. "He came over regularly. That was when not everyone came to Lew, he came to people. He was still on the pavement then. And I knew him around town, too." In 1967, Stevens founded the American Film Institute (AFI), which was funded by the National Endowment for the Arts, the Ford Foundation, and contributions from the movie companies. One of its first projects was dedicated to film preservation. "We found that half of the films that had been made were either missing, had been destroyed, or were deteriorating. The film companies had had no interest in preserving films because they were thinking about tomorrow." So AFI started a film rescue operation; its investigators canvassed collectors, looking for lost films, and they told the collectors that if they would turn over the film so it could be preserved, they would be given a print. And their identities would be kept confidential. Soon, ten thousand films had been recovered and were deposited in the Library of Congress.

One was *The King of Jazz,* the old movie about the former MCA client Paul Whiteman, which an AFI investigator recovered from a collector in London. It was owned by Universal. "Lew called. He was, shall I say, *intense*. 'What's this, you have this movie of ours, *The King of Jazz*?' I didn't know, I said, let me check. I called back and said, yes, good thing we found it. Lew *took off*. I'd never heard an adult speak that loudly. *'This is our movie! I want the name of the guy in London. I am going to get that print!'* Now, we were sending a print to Universal, it wasn't that they didn't have it. But I guess Lew must have felt this guy was a pirate, and he was outraged. We had an understanding with these collectors, though, that we would give them a print, and would keep their identities private, and I wasn't going to turn the guy in. I was a young guy—maybe thirty-two—and it was just very clear to me that I should do what I thought was right.

"That was the end of Universal's support of AFI. It never contributed from then on. That made it more difficult to build AFI—but we did." Wasserman, who was a trustee of the John F. Kennedy Center for the Performing Arts, would always attend the annual Kennedy Center Honors ceremony (of which Stevens was executive producer). "He was always very pleasant, avuncular—but Edie was always looking for trouble," Stevens said. "She was not happy with how she was seated, or *something*.

"He never bad-mouthed me, or bad-mouthed AFI," Stevens continued. "I never heard of him telling other companies not to support us. It wasn't like a scorched-earth policy. It was just that for him, it would always be this way. I never did fully understand it—how do you stay mad for that long? And he never referred to it except once, many years later. He said to me. 'You had your view, we had ours. It just wasn't an institution we wanted to deal with.' "

As Wasserman presided majestically over a world he had been shaping for decades, there were many things that were pleasing to him, but one seemed to outshine all the rest. For he appeared at this moment to have a good chance of attaining the only major goal that had most painfully eluded him—joining the ranks of the legendary movie producers. "Not since the heyday of Louis B. Mayer, Adolph Zukor, and Darryl F. Zanuck has Hollywood seen anything like the creative tumult of Universal City or the business success of MCA," wrote Peter Schuyten in a *Fortune* article in November 1976. Wasserman's original formula—combining inevitably volatile movie production with a stable and highly lucrative TV business—was now empirically proven. And, even more important, Wasserman had demonstrated that under his aegis, Universal—always the major studios' weak sister, prolific producer of B movies—could produce not only commercially successful movies like *Airport,* but, also, movies that made money *and* were acclaimed.

Wasserman's chief movie executive during this period was Ned Tanen, who had started out in the MCA mailroom in 1955, and was an iconoclastic, rebellious personality for the regimental MCA. Wasserman evidently liked him; for many years, Tanen was assigned the office next to Wasserman's, and Wasserman sometimes introduced him as his illegitimate son. On occasion, Tanen even stood up to Wasserman—and survived. Tanen thought that Wasserman tolerated his willfulness because he had a track record of moneymaking ideas. In the late sixties, he had started a record company, UNI, which was highly successful for a time, until it was folded into MCA Records. He also had come up with the idea of building the Universal Amphitheater, as a site for holding outdoor concerts. Apparently as a sign of his favor, Wasserman had a bust made of Tanen's head, beneath which was engraved, "The Father of the Amphitheater." There was some precedent for this at the company; a bust of Jules Stein, for example, graced the lobby of the Black Tower. But Tanen thought it was gauche. He took the small sculpture and used it as a coatrack in his office, throwing his jacket over his marble head.

Tanen's entry to the movie business came in 1969. At the time, Universal's movies were so anachronistic and mediocre that they had almost cost Wasserman his job. But the phenomenal success of Columbia Pictures' *Easy Rider* seemed to point a way to salvation. *Easy Rider* reflected the ethos of the prevailing counterculture in both its substance and costs (less than $400,000), but it was gratifyingly materialistic in its profits ($40 million in worldwide box office grosses). Wasserman put Tanen in charge of a youth movie division. His mandate was to produce films for under $1 million, offering talent a meaningful piece of the back end and even final cut—in an attempt to capture the spirit of the times with very little risk. As Tanen tells the story, Jules Stein summoned him shortly after he'd been given this assignment, and informed him that he had spent the previous evening at a dinner party with Dennis Hopper—the co-writer, co-star, and director of *Easy Rider*—and had told Hopper to come see Tanen, because Universal would do his next movie. Tanen knew how (in a word) crazy Hopper could be, and was filled with apprehension. His worst fears were realized when Hopper—after filming in Peru, and cutting the movie over an extended, binge-filled period in Taos, New Mexico—completed *The Last Movie*. Aptly titled, it was a box office failure, so panned by most critics that it sent Hopper into a decade-long retreat from directing. (Once, when Wasserman was asked if he had made any mistakes, he pointed to *The Last Movie,* saying, "At a press preview the first and last reels were mixed up. The end of the film was shown first and the beginning was shown at the end, but the film was so confusing anyway that the audience didn't know the difference.")

Other movies that came out of Tanen's unit, however, were interesting, imaginative films, notably different from Universal's conventional fare—among them, *Diary of a Mad Housewife,* directed by Frank Perry, *Taking Off,* by Milos Forman, *Minnie and Moskowitz,* by John Cassavetes. None, however, were commercial successes. Tanen argued that that was the fault of Universal's marketing and distribution people. "All they understood was Ross Hunter movies," he said. "They didn't have any idea what they were looking at in these movies—so they buried them." In any event, Tanen's unit was nearly written off as a failure. But then came the big payoff with George Lucas's *American Graffiti*—a nostalgic feature about the innocence of adolescent life on the West Coast in the early sixties, before the trauma of Vietnam. Tanen recalled that some of his fellow executives at Universal so hated the movie that they thought it should not be released; someone suggested that it might be suitable as a movie for television. Ultimately, the movie *was* released in 1973—and to the amazement of many at Universal, it was nominated for five Academy Awards. Moreover, while it cost only about $700,000, it ultimately earned about $120 million—making it one of the most profitable films in history.

As pleasant a surprise as the nominations of *American Graffiti* were, it was *The Sting*—which won the Academy Award for Best Picture in 1974—that gave Wasserman his first real movie-making triumph. "It was the first time Universal had gotten an Academy Award [for best picture] since *All Quiet on the Western Front,* and they were euphoric," declared Dick Zanuck, who co-produced *The Sting* with his partner, David Brown. "There was a *big* celebration."

Zanuck explained that like many others who had grown up in Hollywood's small-town community, he had known Wasserman since he was a youth. And when he was just starting out in the business and faced a serious crisis, he had instinctively turned to Wasserman for advice. Darryl, the longtime chief of production at Twentieth Century-Fox, had been elected president of the company in 1962, and he had made twenty-eight-year-old Dick vice president in charge of production. Since Darryl was spending nearly all his time in Paris, however, Dick was effectively running the company. And it was a failing company, reeling from the debacle of *Cleopatra,* on the verge of bankruptcy. Dick went to visit Wasserman at the Universal lot, where the Black Tower was under construction. "I told him the state of affairs at Fox. He said, "If I were you—you see this tower we're building? Why don't we make that the Twentieth Century-Fox Tower?"

Confused, Zanuck asked what he meant. Wasserman pointed out that Twentieth Century occupied immensely valuable land in West Los Angeles. " 'Get rid of that real estate and you come here. You take the tower. We'll build another tower.'

"Now, he didn't say he was proposing a merger, but he had to have been thinking that that would happen, down the line, and he would have wanted our film library, which was incredible," Zanuck continued. "I said, 'We wouldn't want to lose our identity,' and he said, 'You won't—and we could keep this big lot alive between the two of us.' " Zanuck said that he called his father in Paris, although he did not believe they should seriously consider Wasserman's proposal. "I knew it was an idea that would be great for Lew—and probably emasculate us. . . . I called him the next day. He was fine. He said, 'Well, it's always open.' "

Four years later, it would be Dick Zanuck who would make the deal for Twentieth Century to buy Reagan's Malibu ranch property. When Dick was fired in a nasty proxy fight in 1970, Wasserman offered him and David Brown a production deal at Universal. Instead, the two men went to Warner Bros. as executives, but after a year and a half there, they asked their agent, Herman Citron (formerly a longtime MCA agent) to see if Wasserman's offer was still good. That offer was $1 million for three years, to be divided between the two of them, Brown said. "Herman said it was, and that Lew and he were determined to do something on one sheet of paper," Zanuck recalled. "We'd fight out all the points of a contract later. Within a week, we were in Lew's office. He said, 'I want to take you to your office.' There was this bungalow, filled with Jules Stein's antiques, and a huge tree in the yard. And there was a little sign out front, stuck in the grass: Zanuck and Brown Company."

Zanuck and Brown immediately pitched two projects to Wasserman: *The Sting,* and *Sugarland Express,* which had been brought to them by a young director, Steven Spielberg, who was one of Universal's stable, maintained with long-term deals. Spielberg had a seven-year contract—just like in the old studio system days—and was directing TV shows. "I told Lew, 'This script, *Sugarland Express,* with Steven Spielberg—you've put it in turnaround,' " Zanuck recalled, referring to the decision not to go forward with a project. "He said, 'The kid is great. But this picture will play to empty houses.' I said, 'I think you're wrong about that. I really like it. But read *The Sting* and let me know what you think. I've got the kid down in the commissary—I'll tell him.' I turned to leave. He said, 'You really think that picture has a chance?'

'I think it has a *great* chance.' 'Well,' he said, 'I think you're totally wrong, but go ahead and make it. I didn't bring you over here to tell you what pictures to make.'

"That was such a defining moment for me with Lew," Zanuck added. "I'd never seen it before and have never seen it since—where a guy in charge says, I don't believe in this but I believe in you. *Go." Sugarland Express* was Spielberg's debut as a feature film director— heralded by critic Pauline Kael as "one of the most phenomenal directorial-debut films in the history of the movies." It did not do well at the box office, however, as Wasserman had predicted. But Zanuck and Brown were more than vindicated by the success of *The Sting*—the number one domestic box office hit of 1974.

And *The Sting* was a mere aperitif. Zanuck and Brown bought the rights to Peter Benchley's best-selling thriller *Jaws,* and they argued that Spielberg should direct the movie. "Lew said, 'The kid is great, but we need somebody tried and true—because when you get out on the water, you need somebody with real experience,' " Zanuck recalled. "I said, 'We *want* that inexperience—something fresh.' " The production, budgeted at $4 million, encountered a harrowing range of obstacles, and eventually cost about $10 million. But when it was previewed in Dallas, Texas, it seemed plain that it was worth the overages. "It was a huge hit, we had to show it three times that evening," Zanuck continued. "We made a few changes and previewed it in Long Beach. Lew was there. The audience just ate it up, *screaming.* At the end, Lew gathered the executives and we all crammed in to this little manager's office. We were euphoric. The reaction had been even bigger than in Dallas. Lew said, 'This has been an extraordinary evening.' He turned to Hy Martin, who was in charge of distribution. 'Hy, how many theaters do you have lined up?'

"Hy said, 'We have a record number of theaters. The word of mouth out of Dallas was so good. I've booked five hundred theaters.' He was beaming. 'It's never been done before.'

"Lew said, 'Hy, I want you to call up two hundred of them and tell them you're cutting back. I don't want to play Palm Springs. I want people to drive from Palm Springs to L.A. to see this. I want *lines!* I want to take this summer!'

"We were the number one picture from the beginning of the summer to the end. People were clamoring for it. Lew was so smart. He made it into a precious commodity."

Wasserman had been fixated on box office figures for many years, but he had never been as galvanized as he was by *Jaws*—which would have a first-run box office of $243 million. According to Brown, Wasserman told him that based on the opening figures for *Jaws,* he could predict within 5 percent what the ultimate numbers would be—and he did. "Lew could tell you what a picture did on Thursday night in a theater in Puerto Rico," Zanuck declared. "He would call exhibitors around the world very early in the morning. An exhibitor would tell me, 'Jesus, I got a call from Wasserman himself, and it was 3:00 A.M. his time.' He knew the theaters—when he traveled, he would go to them. And he had a photographic memory when it came to numbers. He could tell you what a particular gross was in any one of six hundred theaters, at any time. He'd say, 'Do you know we did $11,392 at the Empire Theater in Omaha?' I think he got more joy out of the figures than anything else about the whole process. He may have loved the movie, but the figures had a real fascination for him. He was captivated."

Jaws was the first in a new genre, the summer blockbuster movie. Its success ratified the notions about the movie business that had been engendered by *The Godfather* in 1972. Paramount had turned that movie into an *event*—spending heavily on advertising and marketing, booking the movie to open in a huge number of theaters across the country, and, ultimately, convincing the public that it was a moment of viewing experience they could not afford to miss. Wasserman brought the marketing approach for *The Godfather* to a new level. He had been somewhat contrarian in cutting back on the number of theaters for *Jaws*—but that, of course, had been contrived to make it even *more* of an event. Eight months before *Jaws* opened, Zanuck, Brown, and Benchley began appearing on TV and radio talk shows, promoting the story of the monster shark. Three days before the opening, on June 21, 1975, Universal began a national advertising blitz on radio and television. The campaign's poster—an image of the shark approaching the girl—was parodied in dozens of nationally syndicated cartoons. And the *Jaws* motif itself appeared on everything from beach bags to pajamas. *Jaws* became so much a feature of popular culture that summer, in so many ways, that Universal published an ad in the *Wall Street Journal* that read, "It is a movie too."

It marked a turning point in the business. Advertising and marketing budgets grew; the number of movies, overall, decreased; and a smaller number of blockbusters dominated the market. Movie critics' influence was somewhat diminished, since so much access to information was controlled by the studios through advertising and marketing. These mega-movies were used to promote a raft of other products— games, toys, T-shirts, books, records—so that each movie became a small industry. MCA excelled at these spin-off products, creating them for its television hits, too—so there were *Kojak* lollipops, and *Bionic Woman* dolls. The principle—marketing products connected to one's main attraction—was similar, in a way, to what Jules Stein had done decades earlier in his selling of confetti and liquor and party hats and souvenir ashtrays.

In the historic tension between the business and the art of moviemaking, one side had plainly won this round. Looking back at the various golden ages of film, *New York Times* critic Janet Maslin cited the early seventies not as one of the true high points, but an undeniably fertile, valuable period, in all its passion and experimentation. "The early '70s were a fine time for personal, idiosyncratic films not aimed at the lowest common denominator, the kinds of films that would be deemed much too chancy by major studios today," Maslin wrote in 1994. "Why were films that aimed to please distinct, specialized audiences so much more possible then? Maybe because the mega-mass-audience phenomenon was barely a gleam in the average studio executive's eye. If there was a single day when the era ended, it was June 21, 1975. . . . When *Jaws* made it possible for every would-be viewer in America to be targeted for a unilateral marketing blitz, it created irrevocable change. Films would now be held to a different and increasingly exacting standard, one that accepted across-the-board popularity as the ultimate sign of merit. A stellar new generation of film makers would do their best to translate personal concerns into broad, crowd-pleasing terms, and would often do so with great success. But the golden age was over. The time of the blockbuster had begun."

Much as Wasserman aspired to join the pantheon of the great movie producers, he continued to approach the business in a way that had always set him apart from his predecessors—focused on international opportunities, and searching for esoteric tax loopholes, lobbying against trade quotas, scouring for ways of cutting foreign distribution costs. Others saw romance in movies, but for Wasserman, the romance unquestionably lay in the numbers that made movies a business, and a worldwide one at that. "Numbers," he commented once, "are what make the world go round." Now, in the seventies, he instituted a system for the international distribution of Universal movies that was designed to cut costs, and, if all went well, achieve tax advantages more spectacular than any MCA had ever obtained before.

It all began in 1970, when Charles Bluhdorn, founder and chief executive of Gulf & Western, the conglomerate that had acquired control of Paramount, arranged a meeting with Wasserman. The two men knew each other only slightly; they had been introduced by Ed Weisl, who remained a power at Paramount even after the departure of Barney Balaban. Bluhdorn, an Austrian immigrant who fled Hitler and arrived in this country in 1942 as a sixteen-year-old, was a wild fount of capitalistic energy; he made his first million in the import-export business when he was twenty-one, and went on from there to acquire companies at a furious rate. By the mid-sixties, when conglomerates were the vogue (and Wasserman had begun molding his version), Bluhdorn was the ultimate conglomerateur, his creation satirized as "Engulf & Devour" in a Mel Brooks movie. Bluhdorn had many faults, but timidity was not one of them—and the idea that he brought to Wasserman was characteristically bold. The two companies should merge their feature film distribution arms overseas (they were prohibited by antitrust laws from doing so domestically). Thus, they should be able to cut the high cost of foreign distribution, strengthen their marketing clout through their dominance of the marketplace, and—if they were sufficiently clever in exploiting a loophole in the U.S. tax laws—pay no taxes on the profits of those overseas operations until that money was repatriated. Which, in effect, might mean never, if the funds were used abroad or brought back in creative ways. It could amount to billions of dollars, tax-free.

Stanley Jaffe, president of Paramount, recalled that this overseas enterprise was Bluhdorn's "economic dream," but he had brought it to Twentieth Century-Fox, MGM, and Columbia Pictures, and all had turned him down. "The impression was MCA was almost the last place you would go—this was just before *Airport,* so they were huge in TV but had no hits in feature films," Jaffe said. "A group of us met with Lew at the Essex House. We expected a long meeting, and that Lew would then say he had to think about it. Charlie told him his concept and Lew stuck out his hand and said, 'You got a deal.' Lew grasped it, and he didn't want to play games."

It was left to the subordinates to hammer out the specifics of the deal. Because of antitrust and also tax considerations, it was important that this be a new, separate entity, not a Paramount or MCA subsidiary; it was named the Cinema International Corporation (CIC). The lead negotiator for Paramount was Arthur Barron, someone Bluhdorn relied on considerably. Barron recalled that he and his colleagues discovered a big flaw in the deal as it was close to being finalized: whoever did the most business got screwed—and that, at the time, was clearly Paramount. "We called the MCA guys, George Smith and Dick Baker, and we said, we've discovered this, it can't be right," Barron said. "They said, 'That's the deal Lew made.' He'd given his marching orders. That was *it.* I called Bluhdorn—he was *fried.* He'd made a handshake deal with Lew, just wanted to sweep it up. He was shouting,

'You screw up this deal, I'm going to kill you!' Finally, I was able to calm him down enough to explain it to him. He said, 'That can't be. I'll call Lew.' Fifteen minutes later, he called back. 'I talked to Lew. That's gone.' "

The most challenging part of the deal, however, was its tax-related structuring. "CIC was largely tax-driven," explained Larry Levinson, who had left the Johnson White House to become Paramount's Washington representative. "Under the rules at the time—the famous Sub-Part F—if you intended to keep money over there, you could *defer* taxes until it was repatriated. Smart tax people took advantage of these deferral provisions. You could never pay taxes. But you had to set up this intricate latticework. I used to see these diagrams on these big boards: this entity on top of this entity on top of this entity—and the money would flow through and never be taxed. The IRS was not looking at offshore deals then (you could never get away with it today). And whenever Congress would get close to ending these deferral tax provisions, we would work to keep them away."

George Smith agreed that MCA reaped remarkable tax benefits from CIC. "I would say that, on the average, one hundred to two hundred million tax dollars were deferred every year. So it was like the government giving you a $100 to $200 million loan, interest-free, every year." He said that there were strictures on how the money could be spent overseas, however. "You couldn't make a movie with it, couldn't pay distribution costs. Generally, we put it in a bank and got interest." Smith also claimed that MCA eventually did repatriate the funds, and paid taxes at that time. But Barron and several other Paramount executives asserted that the money was indeed spent on movie production—and, despite the fact that Paramount was making the production decisions, MCA was Paramount's partner. "The MCA guys became furious, because they were in for 50 percent on these movies, and we were all getting killed on them," Barron said. Another investment was movie theaters; essentially, CIC (and its successor organization, United International Pictures) re-created in Europe the integration of production, distribution, and exhibition that movie companies in the U.S. had so enjoyed before the Paramount Decree in 1948. Barron also was unequivocal about the tax benefits. "We weren't paying foreign tax, and we weren't paying domestic tax," he stated flatly. "Taxes weren't paid even when the money was repatriated, because you could bring it back other ways." Barry Diller, who became chairman and chief executive officer of Paramount in 1974, essentially confirmed what Barron said about the tax benefits, though he differed on the question of repatriation. "The money was mainly not repatriated. Gulf & Western handled some of it differently, because it was such a worldwide company. But once MCA had the whole thing explained to them, they organized their whole business structure around it. And the end result, for both companies, was the same—the money was mainly not to be repatriated, the taxes not paid. It was a brilliant tax dodge," Diller said.

CIC's tax treaty was with the Netherlands—a locale that was uniquely favorable. "We signed the deal in Amsterdam on July 1, 1970," Barron recalled. "Technically, we were supposed to hold our meetings in Amsterdam. Soon, though, Charlie was saying, 'Let's go meet with the troops in Acapulco!' 'Let's go meet with them in Hong Kong!' Lew humored him. It got so we weren't meeting in Amsterdam at all, and the tax guys said, this has got to stop!"

Wasserman and Bluhdorn made an odd couple. Bluhdorn was in a state of constant eruption—of rapture, fury, revelation, murderous threats, apoplexy. Wasserman was composed, and generally arranged *his* volcanic moments as carefully as though they were opening scenes. Bluhdorn, who adored luxury, was one of the first corporate chiefs to indulge in a company G3 jet. Schooled by Jules Stein, Wasserman disapproved of his more flamboyant peers, and resisted that perquisite for years. Their approach to negotiation was altogether different. "Lew would say x, and if you said y, he would literally get up and leave or throw you out," Diller recalled. "Charlie was a trader—he'd be throwing in the rug, then the lamp, he'd crawl up your socks!" If Bluhdorn had a sense of the big picture, Wasserman seemed to have X-ray vision—and he was always, always prepared. "Lew would look at the financials the day before our meetings in London, and come up with five *vicious* points to trap people with—that was his management style," Diller said. "Charlie was a genius—he hardly read the papers, but he could *smell* it." Smiling at his recollection of these tempestuous CIC meetings in the mid-seventies, Diller added, "Charlie was very exasperating to Lew because they were opposite sides of the moon. Charlie tried to trick him, manipulate him—and you couldn't do that to Lew. When Lew was at his pitch (and he was still, then), it was a dazzling game to watch."

The two men had similarities, too, which in a way were even harder on the pairing than their differences. They were fiercely competitive, arrogant, accustomed to having their way, and fixated on winning the game of every negotiation. In the best of times, they were friendly rivals. Wasserman had built his fifteen-story black glass tower, which seemed much taller than it actually was, looming like a mirage over the flatness of the San Fernando Valley; Bluhdorn built his forty-four-story skyscraper on Columbus Circle, overlooking Central Park. One Paramount executive recalled accompanying Bluhdorn on a visit to the MCA tower, where the iron floor strip in the front of each elevator was engraved "MCA." "Godammit! Why don't we have 'G&W' on *our* elevators?" Bluhdorn demanded.

Their relationship became seriously fractious, however, when they decided to bring in a third partner. CIC's overhead costs had begun to rise again, and Wasserman and Bluhdorn reasoned that they could cut them by sending more product through the existing distribution system. Their prospective candidate to provide this product was Kirk Kerkorian, the wealthy Las Vegas financier who in 1969 had gained control of MGM (Wasserman's historic icon) from Edgar Bronfman, Sr. Now, under the pressure of an immense, high-interest debt load, Kerkorian was considering selling MGM's overseas theaters and real estate, as well as leasing foreign rights to its library of films. Complex three-way negotiations commenced. Wasserman, Bluhdorn, and their respective entourages were meeting, as they often did, at Paramount studio head Robert Evans's Beverly Hills home, in a screening room that bordered his pool. Evans's place was a secluded spot, situated at the end of a long, wooded drive (it had been Greta Garbo's retreat), and, according to one participant, the Paramount and MCA executives met there, rather than at either company's offices, because of antitrust concerns. Wasserman and Bluhdorn could not agree on a price for the MGM transaction. Wasserman, of course, prided himself on his ability to assess his advantage in a negotiation, and act accordingly; Bluhdorn liked to drive a hard bargain, but his excitement about the MGM deal evidently made him approach it more extravagantly than Wasserman. Frank Yablans, the president of Paramount who succeeded Stanley Jaffe, recalled, "Lew got so exasperated with Charlie. Finally, he said, 'If you're so anxious to buy something, I can sell you some of Edie's jewels.' Lew was saying Charlie was a peddler, which he was! But so was Lew. Except here, he was assuming the posture of someone with a higher calling. I had to walk Charlie around the pool for twenty minutes, just to calm him down—he was *furious!* He took it as a personal insult—which is how it was intended."

A frequent participant in these screening room meetings was Sidney Korshak, who—in a role that it is difficult to imagine anyone other than Korshak playing—was representing all three parties. Korshak had known Kerkorian for many years; and Ed Weisl, an old friend of Korshak's from Chicago, had introduced him to Bluhdorn. "We all paid him—Charlie, Lew, and Kirk," Yablans said. "He was a facilitator." While Yablans, who was close to Korshak, professed to find nothing unusual in Korshak's tripartite role, Barron said he was taken aback when he first realized it. "I knew that Sidney had represented Kirk with the unions in Las Vegas, and that he was very close to Lew," Barron said. "The first time I realized he was representing us in this, too, was when one of the guys from Paramount gave me a piece of paper and said, 'Call this number anytime, day or night, if you have a problem.' I looked at it. 'Sidney Korshak.' I said, 'Jesus, he's Kirk's lawyer!' The guy said, 'No, it's okay.' "

As the negotiations intensified, Barron continued, MGM took the position that CIC should take not just their theatrical films but also their television series for distribution. CIC, however, was structured to distribute theatrical films and, then, videocassettes—but not TV series. "It was 11:30 at night. I said to George Smith, we've gotta call Lew. George made the call. Lew got on, and George said, 'Lew, Art has something to tell you,' and passed the phone to me! I told him that MGM wanted us to take their TV series. He said, 'Art, I'm sure you'll know what to do,' and he hung up. I thought, this is worse than before! If I take them, he'll say, why did you do something so stupid? And if I don't, and the deal falls through, he'll blame me. I got out my Korshak number. I said, 'Sidney, this is where we're at.' He said, 'Hold your ground.' That was it. A half hour later, MGM took it off the table," Barron said, referring to MGM's retraction of its earlier demand. "I never knew what happened.

"I remember we got a bill," Barron concluded. "It was a piece of stationery that had 'Sidney Korshak, Counselor-at-Law' at the top. 'Fees—$50,000.' We always made attorneys give us hourly fees. I showed it to Charlie. He said, what's this? He got on the phone to Lew. 'Lew, I got this bill from Sidney Korshak, it says fees, $50,000. What should I do?' And Lew said, 'I'd pay it, because you're not getting any-thing else.' "

Korshak had other connections in the corporate world, but none had the stature of Wasserman. And the fact of their friendship served to le-gitimize Korshak to a degree, and to make him more palatable in some business circles. It also may have helped to immunize him from prose-cution; while he was investigated by federal agents for many years, no criminal charges were ever brought—perhaps because of influence brought to bear, or, too, because of the difficulty of piercing his well-fortified shield. A. O. Richards, a retired FBI official who was chief of the organized crime section in Los Angeles for many years, commented on Korshak's closeness to Wasserman, saying, "He was almost an untouchable. You couldn't go after him, he was too well protected. Who would *dare* to wiretap Korshak?"

In this singularly complaisant community, money and power tended to make almost anything acceptable; but the Wasserman-Korshak relationship still provoked comment, if not censure. "It was always the question," said veteran labor lawyer Leo Geffner. "What is Lew, a leader of the industry, powerful, so respected, doing as the intimate of someone known to be a fixer, in league with the mob?" Paradoxically, though, Wasserman's continuing to extend his mantle to Korshak—even now, when Wasserman was at the apex of his corporate life—served only to underscore his sovereignty. Both Jules Stein and Don Rosenfeld are said to have warned him repeatedly about his very public relationship with Korshak—but Wasserman did not alter it. He deemed it appropriate, so it was.

Even Wasserman would have been unable to consort with Korshak if Korshak had a criminal conviction, or if his mob associations were fully exposed in the press. The reason Korshak was such an effective emissary was that those in the legitimate world who dealt with him could pretend not to know whose interests he represented. Ever since Lester Velie's 1950 article in *Collier's,* which asserted that Korshak had mob ties, Korshak had led a charmed life, press-wise. In his hometown of Chicago, the newspapers were not interested in a piece that took a hard look at Korshak; veteran investigative journalist Sandy Smith, who worked for the *Chicago Tribune* and then the *Chicago Sun-Times* in the sixties, recalled that editors at both newspapers refused to run a Korshak piece ("I was always bucking a tide that was carrying him away from me," Smith said). Irving Kupcinet, the *Sun-Times* columnist who was something of a Chicago celebrity, was a loyal friend and booster of Korshak. And in his adopted town, Los Angeles, Korshak was given similarly deferential treatment. For years, he was mentioned only in the social columns of the *Los Angeles Times.* "If you're not invited to Sidney Korshak's Christmas party, it's a disaster," wrote his friend the columnist Joyce Haber. In 1969, the *Los Angeles Times* finally ran a feature piece on Korshak, by reporter Paul Steiger. It did mention some of the controversial elements of the Korshak biography, but the headline of the page-one story conveyed the overall tone and thrust of the piece: "Sidney Korshak: Man Who Makes Things Happen—Millionaire Lawyer's Influence and Contacts Range Over Many Fields." Korshak was said to have considered it a useful advertisement.

By the seventies, Korshak's record was not unblemished, but it seemed to carry little stigma. He did pay thousands in civil penalties to the Internal Revenue Service. And he also entered into a consent decree with the Securities and Exchange Commission in 1970, stemming from allegations of stock manipulation and fraud, in connection with the Parvin-Dohrmann company in Beverly Hills. Parvin-Dohrmann was another sixties conglomerate, and its chairman was Delbert Coleman, a wealthy Chicago businessman who had been friendly with Korshak for years. Coleman and his partner, Herbert Siegel, had owned Seeburg, the Chicago-based vending machine and jukebox company, where they had hired Korshak to handle their labor problems (and paid him, in one instance, with a Cadillac). Here, Coleman wanted to buy the Stardust Hotel and Casino from Moe Dalitz (who had earlier acquired it from Jake Factor, with Korshak's help), and Korshak introduced Coleman to Dalitz. The SEC said that Coleman authorized a secret fee of $500,000 to Korshak, which was not disclosed to shareholders, in violation of SEC rules; and, moreover, that Coleman, aided by Korshak and others, manipulated the price of Parvin-Dohrmann stock. (Among those who profited were Korshak's brother, Marshall, and the actress Jill St. John.) In the end, Korshak had to disgorge most of his profit, and both he and Coleman had to sever their ties with Parvin-Dohrmann. It evidently caused a strain in their friendship as well. The SEC case triggered a Justice Department inquiry, and Korshak may have worried about what Coleman was willing to say to the investigators to protect himself. Herbert Siegel recalled that during this period, "Sidney came up to me at '21,' and he said, 'If your ex-partner isn't careful, he's going to be wearing cement shoes.' "

It probably did not sound like an empty threat, coming from someone with Korshak's bona fides. Many remembered that years after Willie Bioff had testified that Korshak was a mob affiliate—testimony that dogged Korshak always—Bioff finally received his comeuppance. Korshak had a view of informants that was catholic in his particular world. A friend of Korshak's recalled a conversation the two had one day in the seventies. Korshak told him that a man whom the mob considered a "rat fink," and whom they had been searching for, had finally been located. "That's great," this friend said. "Where is he?"

"In Arizona, Nevada, and New Mexico," Korshak replied.

It was not a persona that most of his Hollywood friends ever saw. By the seventies, Korshak, a graying man in his signature Pucci dark silk suits, had become a fixture in this community, with many of the trappings of respectability. The Hillcrest Country Club prided itself on its selectivity. Yet Korshak was a long-standing member, and he frequently lunched there, often in the company of a prominent lawyer or a judge. Leo Geffner, who became very friendly with Korshak during their racetrack negotiations in the early seventies, recalled meeting him for lunch one day at the Luau, a Beverly Hills restaurant. "This guy sits down with us—I didn't catch his name. He was *very* friendly with Sid. After he left, I asked who he was. The Beverly Hills chief of police!" Geffner exclaimed. Reagan was governor at this time. (Korshak had been a major contributor to his campaign, according to Korshak's friend Tony Martin.) Korshak told Geffner that he and Reagan had been friends for a very long time. "Sidney would say, 'Ronnie says he's so pure, he's really phony with this big moralistic platform—he and I used to be with hookers in the same bedroom!' He said they went out screwing together in between Reagan's two marriages." Their relationship, in any event, was still strong, according to Korshak. "Sid would often say, 'I talked to Ron last night'—not bragging, just factual," Geffner said. And Korshak had acquired an extensive art collection. "You'd go to the bathroom in his house, and you'd see a small Degas— a Cézanne—a Matisse! He didn't know anything about art—I think it was more, this is what you do when you're rich, you have art. He had a curator for the collection in his house."

At the same time, there was no pretense about his other life. "He was the fixer, the moneyman, the consigliere to the real big boys," Geffner declared. "I can't tell you how many times I'd be sitting at the racetrack with him, and someone would bring him a note, and he'd say, I'm sorry, I have to go—and later I'd find out that there had been a private plane waiting for him to take him to Las Vegas, or Chicago, or Miami." And Korshak's view of the mobsters who summoned him, Geffner added, was "that they were great guys, getting a bum rap."

To his friends in the show business world, Korshak continued to be a magnanimous patron. And the fact that these people saw only beneficence from someone who they knew had a darker side made his generosity seem all the more noteworthy, if not positively redemptive. Korshak no doubt enjoyed helping his friends, but he also plainly relished each opportunity to demonstrate his clout and, perhaps, insure a sense of indebtedness in his friends. He disdained the small favor. Warren Beatty, who knew Korshak quite well, recalled that he wanted to go to the Democratic National Convention in Chicago in 1968, but he had waited too long to make reservations. He was told that every hotel in the city was fully booked. "I called Sidney. 'Can you find me a room?'

" 'Where would you like to stay, Warren?'

" 'The Ambassador East would be nice—but, really, *anywhere.*'

" 'How many suites would you like?'

" 'A *room,* Sidney—I really don't need a suite. A room would be great.'

"Three minutes later, the phone rang," Beatty continued. " 'You have three suites at the Ambassador East.' "

Korshak negotiated contracts for many of his friends—among them, Frank Yablans and Robert Evans—for free. "I'd say I wanted to pay him, and he'd say, 'Give me $1 million'—or, 'Buy me a hot dog,' " Yablans recalled. Yablans, a street-wise, tough-talking type from

Brooklyn, who described some of the CIC negotiations in which he was involved as "sit-downs," was quite impressed with his friend's credentials. "Sidney was in the mob, but the way a Jew is in the mob. They wanted him to handle Hollywood, the Teamsters, Las Vegas—but not to *kill* people in Hollywood." Korshak's primary allegiance, however, resulted in his having some strange habits for someone who was now dealing at the level of major corporations like MCA and Gulf & Western. "I'd get a call at the Gulf & Western Building, in New York. 'Francis, meet me on the corner.' I'd come down there, and we'd start talking. I remember once I said, 'Sidney, why are you making me walk to the corner and stand on Columbus Circle, on this cold day, to tell me something that could be *taped,* and it would not matter?' But that was Sidney," Yablans said fondly. "It was so ingrained in him."

No one in this show business circle, though, was more infatuated with Korshak than Evans, and Korshak seems to have been very fond of Evans, too (Evans reminded Korshak of Bugsy Siegel, according to Yablans). Evans and Korshak were close companions for many years, and the older man was the godfather of Evans's son with actress Ali MacGraw. "He said he was my godfather, too," Evans declared. Korshak had told him that he had indeed started out as Capone's lawyer, Evans said, and that by the mid-thirties he was fully ensconced in the mob. He had proceeded to move up from there. For Evans, proximity to Korshak was a heady thing; every swagger seemed to thrill him. "We were at '21' one night," he recounted. "Sidney used to stay at the Carlyle, and he said, 'Let's walk.' He had two hundred thousand-dollar bills in his pocket. I said, 'Are you *crazy?* How can you walk with all that money?' And he said, 'Who's gonna take it?' "

Korshak's long run of scant press attention finally ended in June 1976, when the *New York Times* published a four-part series about him by Seymour Hersh, in collaboration with Jeff Gerth, which appeared each day on the newspaper's front page. "To his associates in Los Angeles, Sidney R. Korshak is a highly successful labor lawyer, an astute business adviser to major corporations, a multi-millionaire with immense influence and many connections, a friend of top Hollywood stars and executives," Hersh wrote. Among those, he continued, were Wasserman and Bluhdorn. "But Sidney Korshak leads a double life. To scores of Federal, state and local law enforcement officials, Mr. Korshak is the most important link between organized crime and legitimate business." Those officials contended that he had been involved in bribery, kickbacks, extortion, fraud, and labor racketeering, and had also given illegal advice to members of organized crime—but, by and large, they said they had been unable to mount successful prosecutions because of the reluctance of witnesses to testify.

Hersh described Korshak's role as a "mediator" in the CIC transaction, and wrote that all three participants—Wasserman, Bluhdorn, and Kerkorian—"said they knew of no evidence linking Mr. Korshak to organized crime and labor racketeering." Wasserman was quoted, saying that Korshak was a "very good personal friend . . . a very well-respected lawyer . . . a man of his word and good company."

"Told of some of Mr. Korshak's connections with organized crime," Hersh continued, "Mr. Wasserman said: 'I don't believe them. I've never seen him with so-called syndicate members or organization members.' "

Korshak did not cast *this* article as a good advertisement. Over the years, his friends would tend to minimize it, as a piece that tried hard to indict Korshak but did not prove a case. Still, it drew a picture of the man in a way that had not been done before—and that would make it impossible, from then on, for the business executives with whom he dealt to claim they knew nothing about his ties. In Korshak's life, it was a defining moment. It was certainly far less onerous for Wasserman, but he must have been mightily displeased—and it was Wasserman who had a good deal of sway with the Chandler family, publishers of the *Los Angeles Times*. It was the practice of that newspaper to publish syndicated articles of interest that appeared in the *New York Times*, particularly if the articles were about Los Angeles. Ruth Hirschman, the program director of KPFK, a public radio station in Los Angeles, recalled that that Sunday in late June, she read the article in the *New York Times*—and was amazed not to see it in the *Los Angeles Times*.

"A front-page story, the first of four parts, about this man who was so influential in Los Angeles—*and they weren't running it?*" She immediately called Hersh and asked for permission to have the piece read aloud on KPFK each day, as the next three installments appeared in the *New York Times*. He agreed. Her show caused a sensation, she said.

At the time, she was reminded of something that had occurred in about 1962, when KPFK was just starting out, in offices on the street across from where the new Universal tower was being built. She was told that Wasserman had offered the new station space in the tower. "I thought, 'Wow!' But our manager said, 'Uh-uh. The day will come when Wasserman does not like what we put on the air, and you know what? We will come to work the next morning, and we will not be able to get on the elevator.' "

The CIC negotiations were unusual in many respects, but none more so than that Korshak was openly representing MCA. For despite the fact that dozens of people who dealt with Wasserman over the years attested to his closeness to Korshak—and Wasserman himself acknowledged it, as a relationship that had begun in 1939, when Wasserman first arrived in Los Angeles—the specifics of Korshak's role vis-à-vis MCA had always been veiled. It is true, of course, that what Korshak as the consummate fixer did for Wasserman in some areas would of necessity be secret. But his much surmised role in labor relations at MCA could have been public, as it was at other companies. The 1969 *Los Angeles Times* profile of Korshak listed various clients that employed him as a labor consultant, for example, including Schenley Industries, the Dodgers, the California horse-racing association—but not MCA. Participants in the labor negotiations held between the studios and the unions—where Wasserman played a storied role—said that Korshak never appeared. Invisible though he was, however, he was a critical player. *The* critical player, according to Andy Anderson, who was head of the Western Conference of Teamsters for ten years, beginning in

1974. "The Teamsters never struck Lew," Anderson declared. "And it was because of Sidney."

Anderson, a big, burly man from Oregon, had come to Southern California to organize workers for the Teamsters in 1954. He had known Dave Beck, Hoffa's predecessor, and grasped early the potential for mutuality that existed between the Hollywood studios and the Teamsters leadership. "When Dave Beck retired in Seattle," Anderson said, "he had a screening room built in his house, and the studios used to send him movies before they were released." As Anderson rose in the Teamsters hierarchy, Korshak became his ubiquitous contact. "We'd negotiate with Sidney on the parking lot at the baseball stadium, the racetracks, the liquor industry, the breweries, the food industry, the motion picture industry." They had lunch together at Hillcrest dozens of times, and at the Bistro, the Beverly Hills restaurant in which Korshak owned an interest, and where he held court at his special table in the back. Anderson said that until Hoffa went to prison in 1967, he was always in close touch with Korshak ("he checked with Sidney on everything he did, and he *still* got in trouble"). Korshak evidently felt he could trust Anderson. When they were together, Anderson said, they would sometimes be joined by "these characters. Sidney would introduce me, and he'd say about me, 'He's okay, we can talk in front of him.' Then, after they left, he'd say, 'You never met them.' " Korshak took his precautions, Anderson noted. "Sidney always used new money, usually hundred-dollar bills, fresh from the bank, so the money from the boys couldn't be traced to him." Anderson was awed at how much money Korshak was able to collect from clients who bought labor peace from him. "By February of each year, he told me he'd have more than $1 million in retainers, already paid up," Anderson said. (The IRS investigation of Korshak found no more than $50,000 a year in retainers.) He recalled a meeting between Korshak and Mickey Rudin, where Rudin was representing his major client, Frank Sinatra, who owned a large beer company. "Sidney said, 'Mickey, I get $10,000 for this, $20,000 for this, $40,000 for this.' "

But Korshak had to pay *his* dues, too. "On Christmas Eve or Christmas Day, he'd have to go to Chicago to see the boys. I always understood it was something he had to do, to go meet with the boys, as a way of expressing his loyalty. If he had said, 'No, I have something else to do'—well, that would not have been what they expected of him."

When Anderson became head of the Western Conference, Korshak introduced him to Wasserman. Wasserman was friendly, attentive, solicitous. Anderson recalled that Wasserman asked him where his favorite lunch place was—the Cove, at the Ambassador Hotel—and whether they might go there together. "I said, 'I'd love to show you off!'" Anderson replied. After that, Wasserman suggested that they make it an annual tradition to have lunch together at the Cove, just before Christmas. When Wasserman had a fund-raiser for Edmund "Jerry" Brown, son of former Governor Pat Brown, who was now running for governor himself, Korshak invited Anderson and his wife as his guests. "And Lew took my wife and showed her the whole house. There were a hundred people there, but he took the time to do that himself."

Wasserman and he established a smooth working relationship, but Korshak was always the connector. "Whenever there was a problem, Sid would call me. 'Come to my house.' And Lew would come there. I would meet with them, then I would meet with the local. We were never that far apart." In these sessions, he said, "Lew never wrote any note—he told me never to take any notes. Sidney wouldn't either. Or, if he had to write something, he would write on the back of a matchbook cover, and then throw it away." Anderson remembered that once, in the mid-seventies, the union was having a lot of problems at the studios (he refused to be more specific) and Korshak and he agreed on a resolution. Korshak told him to come to his house. "Lew was there. Sid said, 'I told Lew what you said, but he wants to hear it from you directly. So I told him, and Lew said, 'You're my friend forever.'" Wasserman was the only studio head with whom Korshak had such a close relationship, Anderson added—but he was the only one that mattered. "Lew would tell the other studios, 'Guys, this is how it is.'"

Wasserman could dictate to his fellows because he had made labor relations his metier, in a way that no other studio head ever had. "In the early seventies, Lew was first among equals, the leader in labor relations," Leo Geffner said. "He was a strong Democrat, very pro-labor, very close to the unions." Contrasting Wasserman with men like Jack Warner and Harry Cohn, who had fought the unions bitterly, Geffner said, "With Lew, it was different. He knew that he could work with them and still make a lot of money." And Wasserman's relations were as strong with the above-the-line unions (the Screen Actors Guild, the Writers Guild of America, and the Directors Guild of America), as the Teamsters and the IA. "The stories are legion of hard times, an impasse reached, and Lew being called in. Often, he'd be there all night. The unions trusted him. They knew that when Lew came, the hard-liners would take a back seat," Geffner said.

Moreover, though Wasserman's meetings with Korshak and Anderson were secret—Korshak never appeared in negotiating sessions with the MPAA, or played any visible part—it was an *open* secret that Wasserman, through Korshak, could insure labor peace with the Teamsters. And the Teamsters were the most powerful union by far, as well as the most feared. Anderson emphasized that other unions' picket lines might be crossed without incurring mortal peril, but not the Teamsters'. Also, the IA negotiated jointly with the Teamsters in this period; so there was general unity among all the below-the-line unions. While Korshak was key to Wasserman's success, however, Wasserman did not rely solely on him. Just as Wasserman courted Anderson in the seventies, so he had others for many years. Among his close associates were those union men who had enormously benefited the studios in the 1946 strike, and helped in the destruction of the CSU—the IA's Roy Brewer and Dick Walsh, and the Teamsters' Ralph Clare. Wasserman said that when MCA took over the Universal back lot in 1962, he fired the existing security guards and put in his own. "The Teamsters didn't like it and they were going to strike," Wasserman recalled. "But they didn't." This he attributed to his friendship with Clare. When Clare retired in 1971, Wasserman threw him a big party on a stage set at Universal; Clare was said to have received a new Cadillac, too. And it was fitting, in a way, that the emcee of the party for Clare was the actor Walter Pidgeon—someone who, at the most critical moment in Wasserman's labor relations history, had tipped the scales in Wasserman's favor by urging his fellow SAG board members to vote to give MCA the all-important waiver in 1952.

"People misuse the word power," Wasserman commented once. "They think it implies an abuse. I don't consider I have *power*. I have relationships."

By the time Wasserman assumed full title to MCA, his political influence had grown enormously. It had been roughly a decade since he had decided to extend his reach to Washington, and he had come a long way from the Hollywood heavyweight who managed to make the star's dressing room available to Lyndon Johnson. Since then, he had become the president's friend, if not his intimate, and had been his guest quite a few times at the White House. It evidently meant a great deal to Wasserman, who never forgot his meager beginnings. In his oral history interview at the LBJ Library, Wasserman—a man who seemed generally to forswear emotion—remarked, "I have yet to enter the White House where I don't tear up." He was proud of the fact that he was one of the participants in the earliest planning meeting for the LBJ Library, and he was a major donor. In the final days of the 1968 campaign, when the Republicans were spending what was, at the time, the largest sum ever to elect a president, the Democrats were borrowing frantically. The two largest loans came from Wasserman and Jake Factor, each of whom lent the party $240,000. Wasserman commented later that he believed it was the shortage of cash, caused by diminished contributions after the violence of the 1968 Democratic National Convention in Chicago, that probably cost Hubert Humphrey that election. "It's my personal belief that, to this day, if Senator Humphrey had

been on NBC television the night before the election instead of ABC—
ABC being the least expensive of the networks, which is the only reason Senator Humphrey bought it—it could have made a difference in
the election."

Wasserman had standing as a major Democratic contributor and,
also, a savvy observer of the political scene, particularly regarding television, that powerful new campaign medium. But what really set him
apart was that he had harnessed everything Hollywood had to offer—
money, stars, glamour—to create a smoothly functioning, high-powered
apparatus, the likes of which had not existed before. And while it was
unquestionably of his design and under his control, Wasserman's vehicle
was the MPAA, headed by Valenti. That provided the illusion of an independent entity that represented the entire industry—though Wasserman's peers knew the reality. Regarding Valenti's role at the MPAA,
Frank Yablans of Paramount remarked, "We were all his bosses, but
Lew was his *chief* boss." And Valenti was proving to be an extremely capable functionary, someone who grasped the power of Hollywood
celebrity in Washington (perhaps because he was so affected by it himself) and was adept at manipulating it. While every lobbyist tries to court
the congressmen and senators whose votes he covets, Valenti, a born
courtier, raised it to an art.

In its old headquarters, the MPAA had a modest screening room;
now, a large new building had been constructed, featuring a massive
office for Valenti, an underground parking garage, and a state-of-the-
art screening room with red carpet, red velvet curtains, and well-
cushioned, reclining leather seats. This screening room became a
Washington institution. Valenti would regularly invite an assortment of
power brokers, senators, congressmen, other government officials,
lawyers, and journalists for dinner and a movie. Not surprisingly, great
care was taken to cater to the sensibilities of the guests. Wasserman
said, "Jack had the pick of the pictures, and he'd match the guests to
the pictures. He wouldn't invite far-right congressmen to see half-
naked women." These invitations soon became among the most sought

after in town. It was a bit of Hollywood transplanted in Washington— or, as Jim Jones, who had worked in the Johnson White House and later was elected to Congress, put it, "It was the pizzazz of coming down there, being treated so royally, seeing movies before everyone else." Larry Levinson thought Valenti was tapping into something more fundamental. "Movies and power in this town go together," he declared. And that axiom was nowhere truer than at the apex of power. "One thing all presidents love is screening movies. Nixon would sit alone and watch *Patton* again and again. He watched it the night before they bombed Cambodia," Levinson continued. "Jack was able to use the power and glamour and mystique of Hollywood—a new president came in, and he'd put himself in the center of the process of getting movies to the president. He'd get so excited. He'd call Sid Sheinberg and say, 'Sid! The president is going to Camp David! We've got to get him *Jaws*!'"

The combination of movies and power was pleasing, no doubt, but the real glue in this Hollywood-Washington nexus that Wasserman was soldering was, of course, money. The President's Club had been Wasserman's apprenticeship; by the seventies, he had made fundraising into a science. He organized dinners at hotels, as he had begun doing in the early sixties, but now these events were for a thousand guests, or more. When too much time had passed without a response after invitations had been sent, Wasserman's social affairs assistant, Ann O'Connor, would call the foot-draggers. "She'd say, 'Are you taking a table? May I report to Mr. Wasserman that you will be doing so?' " recalled Levinson. Wasserman and his wife, Edie, had also begun hosting frequent fund-raisers at their home—for the president, for the Democratic National Committee, for senators and congressmen (particularly if they were on committees important to Hollywood, like Finance, Commerce, or Judiciary). Wasserman devoted almost as much attention to cultivating politicians as he once had his stars. "Lew worked at it carefully, day in and day out," said George Smith, who worked closely with Wasserman on legislative affairs. "He would send a note or make a phone call, if there was bad news or good news, people would get calls out of nowhere from Lew. He helped people on the way up when they couldn't get *arrested*—and, ten years later, they'd be on an important committee, and they'd remember."

The events at Wasserman's home were a great prize for the beneficiary. "In Hollywood, an invitation to Lew's house was like an invitation to the president's house—a command performance," declared Lloyd Hand, a lawyer from Texas, active in Johnson's 1964 campaign in California, who became his chief of protocol. But Wasserman's rules were strict. He would brook no interference; the Democratic National Committee people might have their ideas about a guest list, but only those approved by Wasserman would be invited. Wasserman's friend Bob Strauss, the former chairman of the DNC, came to refer to Wasserman's events as "turnkey" operations—because all the recipient had to do was show up and collect the precise amount Wasserman had said would be raised. MCA had developed a computerized list of contributors, as closely guarded as Music Corporation of America's list of band-booking locales had once been. "It was *gold,*" declared Smith. And Wasserman brought his characteristic fixation on detail to these events—reminiscent of the dinner at his home for advertising executives years earlier, when he'd ordered that the cigarettes from a competitor be replaced by those made by his guests' client. "Lew watched every detail," Smith continued. "He would do the table seating himself—because he knew who hated whom, who would be outraged at not being near the honored guest, how to handle the fifteen egomaniacs who all had to be at the main table for ten." He always added a sprinkling of stars, too—like Jill St. John and Angie Dickinson—to lend events the requisite glamour.

It was probably futile to try to sabotage a Wasserman political event. The Jewish Federation Council tried to do just that, at a huge, $1,000-a-plate dinner Wasserman organized for President Jimmy Carter at the Century Plaza Hotel in 1978. Angered by the joint U.S.-Soviet declaration on the Mideast, and the president's support for a Palestinian homeland, the federation sponsored a demonstration outside the hotel. To no avail—Wasserman later told *Los Angeles Times* reporter Robert Scheer that the event was the most successful fund-raiser in California history. Wasserman also told Scheer that he supported Carter completely in his peace initiatives, and felt it was necessary to include the Palestinians in the negotiation process. "How you gonna convince anyone without talking to them? I never made a deal with an empty chair. I made deals with Harry Cohn and Jack Warner, Louis B. Mayer; I could give you thousands of people. Billions of dollars worth of contracts I made. Never made one with an empty chair. . . . Well, there are a million Palestinian people, aren't there? You gonna pretend they're not there?"

It was a somewhat belligerent-sounding outburst from the smooth Wasserman. He evidently wanted to make it clear that he took marching orders from no one—including, and perhaps most particularly, the Jewish organizations that wanted to claim him as a giant political asset. When Scheer, who was writing a story about the Los Angeles Jewish community, told Wasserman that scores of people had identified him as the most powerful Jew in Los Angeles, Wasserman took umbrage at this narrow description. He responded that MCA was not in any way a "Jewish company," and he also said, "I feel first I'm an American." He pointed out that MCA had produced the movie *Jesus Christ Superstar*—incurring the wrath of the American Jewish Committee, which protested the movie's suggestion that the Jews had killed Christ. Referring to the AJC, Wasserman said, "They're not in my life. Period." He objected to the notion, even, that there *was* a Jewish community. "I must tell you in all candor, in my judgment, under oath, pentothal—whatever you like—I would testify with my last breath that I don't know of a Jewish community if you're talking about a structured community. It is nonexistent. Are there Jews who share the same concerns? Yes. There are also many Irish. . . . And this bugaboo about the American Jewish Committee speaking for all the Jews in America, well, I know one Jew they don't speak for—they don't speak for Lew Wasserman."

His position of influence, hard-earned, was not to be appropriated by anyone else. Moreover, it was increasingly important to Wasserman that he not be viewed merely as someone beholden to parochial interests, but, rather as someone whose only agenda was the commonweal as he, and he alone, saw it. This was the image that Wasserman sought to create, as he flew back and forth between Los Angeles and Washington in the seventies and eighties, paying social calls, consulting with politicians on issues that were important to *them.* Thus, over an extended period of time, he came to seem a rarity in political life, a major, powerful benefactor who wanted nothing in return for his financial support, and political acumen, and friendship. Bob Daly, the former co-head of Warner Bros. movie studio, referring to Wasserman's peripatetic Washington schedule, commented, "He built up a lot of goodwill with these people, and was not just there with his hand out. But when it *counted,*" Daly added, "he put his hand out strongly."

The investment tax credit was one instance where it counted— where, by Wasserman's estimate, it meant billions in tax savings to the motion picture industry, and about a billion to MCA alone. This was the legislation that had been passed in 1962, allowing American companies to write off 7 percent of any investment in machinery and equipment—"tangible" property—which had a useful life of eight years or more. According to Treasury regulations, film was not a "tangible" property. Although it was Disney that had sued the government, arguing that it was entitled to the tax credit for the full cost of films, Wasserman had been behind that suit, according to Valenti. "It was Lew's idea," Valenti said, "and Lew's idea that Disney should be the plaintiff. Disney was the *perfect* plaintiff." Indeed, according to George Smith, MCA considered contributing to Disney's legal expenses, but then decided that if its support were to become known that would compromise Disney's position as a lone plaintiff. "We figured Disney was the best-qualified plaintiff, because its product had such longevity, more than any company's," said John Baity, the lawyer at the firm of Donovan, Leisure, who represented Disney in the suit. "I asked the other studios to stand down, and they were happy to do it." MCA and

Disney, too, had been close historically. Jules Stein and Walt Disney were good friends. MCA had been the agent for Disney's TV shows and, although it was little known, MCA had helped to fund Disneyland at its inception in the mid-fifties.

In May 1971, Disney won, before Federal District Court Judge Manuel Real in Los Angeles. It evidently came as something of a surprise to the winning side. "Many of us thought there were some defects to our argument," acknowledged George Smith. But the victory was so important that it was almost the sine qua non for the MCA-driven strategy that followed. For with that court decision in hand, Wasserman was able to give Ways and Means Committee Chairman Wilbur Mills a rationale for the position Wasserman was urging him to take. Mills did so in the House debate, and his committee report stated, "Questions have arisen . . . whether motion picture and television films are tangible . . . personal property eligible for the credit. A court case decided the question in favor of the taxpayer. The committee agrees with the court that motion picture and TV films are tangible personal property eligible for the investment credit." That was another major advance for MCA's case, but Smith and his associates thought the chances of that critical district court decision's being reversed on appeal in the Ninth Circuit were high—because of the weaknesses in their argument, combined with the reputation of the judge who had decided in their favor. "The Ninth Circuit had overturned Manny Real many, many times. We got this sentence in the committee report, hoping it would help—figuring maybe it would make them think Manny was not *that* wrong this time. Committee reports," Smith added, "are loaded with oddities." And then, amazingly, it worked! "In its decision, the Ninth Circuit said the committee report showed what Congress had intended [in the original statute]. For the Ninth Circuit to rely on a committee report and not on a trial court was really a bootstrap. It was kind of crazy," Smith concluded, shaking his head.

There were still many unresolved issues, however, and the litigation continued for a number of years. Eventually, MCA—with Baity as its lawyer—took the lead. He said he retained one image, years later, from his meetings with Wasserman. "Lew had this perfectly clear desk, and this was his habit: he would take his letter-opener, long, like a stiletto, out of his desk drawer, and turn its point on the desk, as he talked to you," Baity said. In the mid-seventies, the television networks entered the fray, arguing that they, not the motion picture studios, were entitled to the investment tax credit; and Baity made a motion for summary judgment, trying to knock out ABC as a litigant. He lost. "Lew called, and said, 'I guess you've lost your touch,' " Baity recalled. "This was after *years,* and all the successes. He had never called to say, 'Great!' when we won."

By the summer of 1976, the long saga of the investment tax credit seemed about to have an idyllic ending for the motion picture industry. A section of the Tax Reform Act of 1976 had been drafted to resolve the unsettled issues—and, after much suasion, it had been done in such a way that was altogether pleasing to Wasserman. But then he learned that Senator Edward Kennedy was offering an amendment to the bill that would allow all these hard-won provisions in regard to the past—but would disallow the investment tax credit to the motion picture industry for the future. The investment tax credit had been passed as part of legislation during his late brother's administration, and Kennedy was convinced that it had not been intended for movies.

That was when Senator John Tunney, the junior senator from California, heard from Wasserman. "I had a car phone (one of the few that was available then), and I got a call from Lew. He said Ted Kennedy was offering this amendment, to take the investment tax credit away from the movie industry. 'Jack Valenti says you're the only one who can beat Kennedy.' Wasserman and Valenti felt my taking on Teddy was important, because we were known to be close—and they knew I was close to a number of freshmen senators, too, whom I could probably bring along. I said, 'Lew, I am in San Francisco for this big fundraising dinner. I *can't* not show for it. I am campaigning very hard! I need my dinner!' He said, 'We need you. We need you to go to bat for us.' I made a decision I would not go back—but then, ten minutes later, I turned around and took a plane back to Washington." He would have netted $40,000 to $50,000 from his fund-raising dinner, he added. "That was a lot of money then—I only spent $2 million on my whole campaign."

Kennedy opened the debate on the Senate floor on August 4. "The investment credit has traditionally, historically, and for sound reasons, been targeted on machinery and equipment, in order to increase competition within capital-intensive industries like manufacturing. It was never conceived as a means or device to apply in the area of personal services." Moreover, he argued, "since a large part of the costs of motion picture and television films result from personal efforts of actors, directors, and producers, it is inequitable to allow the investment credit for this particular result of personal efforts, when it is not available for other personal efforts, such as books, stage plays, paintings, records, or other works of art. . . . Why should there be an investment credit for John Wayne's salary in a movie, but not for John Denver's work when he makes a record?"

Tunney did not attempt to address Kennedy's points. Instead, he relied on the staples of motion picture industry defense. He stressed the importance of the industry to the American economy ("We were able to bring into this country $400 million as a result of the showing of American films overseas . . . [an] extraordinary benefit to our balance of payments"). He described the high unemployment within the industry. And he tried to counter its members' image as a particularly moneyed, privileged class. "I might further say that to some the motion picture industry is a whipping boy, and I am afraid this has frequently been the case here on the floor of the Senate. . . . It is so obvious to me that some people who do not understand this industry believe that all the screen technicians somehow live the life of Riley, sitting around swimming pools drinking martinis all day. The great bulk of the people who make up the motion picture industry are average hardworking men and women trying to earn a living."

A senator from Alabama, James Allen, tried to cut to the bottom line. "Is it correct that a picture like *Jaws* that made tens of millions of dollars in profits should cost, say, $10 million to produce, that . . . 7 percent of that [$10 million] be treated as investment tax credit, and that $700,000 should be stricken from the tax liability; is that correct?" Tunney gave a somewhat waffling answer, and Allen said he would support Kennedy's amendment.

Kennedy, for his part, tried to make the big picture vivid. "We are basically talking about a $30 million item in this tax bill. If we were to have an appropriation before the Senate this evening that said, 'We are going to spend $30 million of American taxpayers' money on movies,' I wonder how many votes there would be on the floor of the U.S. Senate for a direct subsidy like that. Yet we are providing the same amount of subsidy through the tax laws."

The vote was thirty-three in favor of Kennedy's amendment, and forty-nine opposed. George Smith, who was watching the vote, raced to the phone to report to Wasserman. "Mine was the second call he got. Alan Cranston [California's other senator] had called Lew from the floor—'Done!' " And Tunney, who had led the opposition to the amendment, had played an extremely important, if not definitive, role. He said that after he had returned to Washington, he persuaded about five freshmen senators who were going to vote in favor of Kennedy's amendment to change their vote.

Wasserman was a very important backer of Tunney's. He had been one of his top twenty supporters when Tunney first ran for the Senate in 1970, and he was one of his top ten in 1976. Indeed, that year he gave Tunney the use of the Universal Amphitheater for a fund-raising event where Diana Ross performed and Warren Beatty was the master of ceremonies; Tunney raised $350,000. But until the moment that Wasserman reached him in his car in San Francisco, Wasserman had not asked anything of him, Tunney said. "We'd go to dinner, the three of us—Lew, Edie, and me. He was always a perfect host, did things with a lot of style. Always appropriate in the way he handled the situation, as related to raising money, to handling the relationships with a senator. He'd go out of his way and help me with little things—I'd want my children to go to Universal Studios, for example, and he'd make sure his people handled it. He was so attentive—I thought it went back to his days as an agent. With me, he was always operating on a very high level, and on a very friendly basis. I remember once he called me at night and said, why don't you come over for breakfast? I did. Edie came by, but it was just the two of us. He had this wonderful butler. Lew was gracious, hospitable, friendly—and never talked in a heavy-duty way about the issues. He would question me about education, civil rights, foreign policy—but not his specific business interests. He had people who did that—George Smith, Valenti, others. But even then, it was never something just for MCA, but for the industry as a whole.

"And he never put the muscle on, until that time," Tunney continued. He added that it was not as if Wasserman was asking him to compromise his principles. "Lew and I had discussed the investment tax credit, and I'd told him I was in favor of it—I'd probably even said it at a fund-raiser at Lew's house!" When Wasserman called, in any event, the reality was inescapable. "I *needed* the entertainment industry. And when Lew wanted to, he could exert enormous power." Tunney paused, seeming to reflect on that—and then summed it up: "The truth is, I didn't have a choice."

———

Long after Stein had turned the company completely over to Wasserman, he would still come to work most days, taking the small private elevator from the tower's fifteenth floor, where the executive offices were, to his penthouse office just above; he had had French doors constructed for his office in an effort to counter the starkness of Wasserman's building. And Wasserman, to whom every second counted, would generally take the time to go upstairs and consult with Stein—who still, after all, owned nearly 20 percent of the company stock. Considering how Wasserman felt about any failure of allegiance (leaving the company was a violation, challenging one of his rules a capital offense), it seems likely that he never forgave Stein for almost firing him, after Wasserman had worked for him for more than thirty years. Even before that near-betrayal, there had evidently been the strains that are almost inevitable in a relationship between founder and putative successor that continues for several decades. "Jules and Lew always seemed proper to each other in front of me," said David Wexler, echoing what many others who observed the rather formal pair had indicated. "But what I understood from Don Rosenfeld was that Jules had given Lew the power to run the company, but when there were big decisions, Lew had to come to him. And for Lew, this went on for so many years, and Jules *would not die.*"

In old age, Stein continued to read the same five newspapers every morning. (He read the obituary page first, to see whom he had succeeded in outliving.) He was peremptory as ever. Amanda Dunne, the lovely wife of screenwriter Philip Dunne, recalled being seated next to Stein at a luncheon. "We were chatting, and finally he said, 'You've had three cigarettes in less than two hours.' 'Yes.' 'Well, I want you to give up smoking.' I thought—! And who are you? But he was substantial; he paid attention; he was at ease in his skin. Not Doris," Dunne added. "We were sometimes her designated drivers home at the end of a dinner. Jules would leave early, and Doris would always have drunk too much to drive." Jules seemed to have finally lost patience with Doris's pretensions ("you and your anti-Semitic friends!" he once rebuked her), but he did not return to the observant Judaism of his youth; he sometimes remarked that his sister Ruth Cogen went to synagogue for him. He was concerned enough with posterity that he granted numerous interviews about his life to former *New York Times* reporter Murray Schumach—but, characteristically, he retained control over this material, and it was never published. The imprint of his early experience with inflation in Germany never left him, and in the seventies he became convinced that this country was on the verge of a terrible depression. Stein's frugality (which somehow coexisted with his extravagance in certain areas) never diminished. He would only fly tourist class. (When he was critically ill, he was booking a flight home to Los Angeles from New York. He refused to fly first class but instead booked three seats in economy, so that he could lie down—with the proviso that if the plane was not sold out, the airline would refund him the cost of the two extra seats.) He instructed family members away from home to call collect; he would refuse the call, and return it on his corporate WATS line. He was very proud of the fact that his granddaughter Katrina vanden Heuvel attended Princeton University; but when she sent him a bill for her books, he returned it, saying that she should be paying for such things herself. And he tried to impose his will on his grandchildren, as he had on his daughters. He was very concerned with how they dressed; when Katrina, as a teenager, chose hippie-style flowered skirts and platform shoes, he took her to the illustrious costume designer Edith Head, who had an office on the Universal lot, and asked her to design Katrina's wardrobe. "I know my grandparents hoped to marry me off to a prince," said Katrina. "They made my sister, Wendy, and me practice curtsying for days before Prince Charles came."

Stein continued to have a deep reservoir of emotion, generally well guarded, but there was an occasional rupture. His daughter Susan was critically injured in a motorbike accident, and all his self-control evaporated. "This is the worst thing that has ever happened to me," he murmured. "*Jules!* Get ahold of yourself," Doris remonstrated. And with his daughter Jean—his favorite, who flouted him—he continued to find ways to express his disapproval. She loved the Middle European music box with revolving instrumentalists that he always kept near his desk, and she would ask him on occasion if he would leave it to her. "It's going into inventory!" he would reply brusquely. But on MCA's fiftieth anniversary, in 1974, he gave her a copy of the company's annual report, with the following inscription: "To my daughter Jean, with whom I disagree politically, socially, financially, economically, and otherwise, but still love very much. Devotedly, Father."

He never stopped keeping count—of clear financial wins and losses, and of the maddening what-might-have-been of a missed opportunity. In 1962, shortly after MCA had acquired the Columbia Savings and Loan Association in Colorado, Jules and Doris attended the opening of a branch in Fort Collins, Colorado. Jules had commandeered Jack Benny as the featured speaker; he was also doing TV commercials for the S&L. As Stein was leaving the event, a man appeared at his elbow carrying a large box; he said it was his invention, and he was presenting it as a gift in the hope that Stein might become his business partner. "I felt like throwing the carton at this fellow," Stein said. "I wanted no part of the thing. I had had a long day and was carrying two heavy briefcases, and the last thing I wanted was a big box to carry on the airplane. Well, anyway, I got it home and the directions said to open it in the bathroom, plug it in, and follow the directions. So I took it to our upstairs bathroom. It has mirrored walls and a mirrored ceiling. I scanned the directions. I did not read them too carefully. I filled the container with water and I plugged the contraption into the electrical outlet.

"The next thing I knew there was water squirting all over the place; all over the mirrored walls and even the mirrored ceiling. It was a mess. I guess I must have made a lot of noise while this contraption was squirting water. . . . Next thing I knew Doris was there. She was very angry. So I just shoved everything back into the box and forgot about it.

"This contraption that I decided to forget about later became famous as the Water Pik, one of the most successful items on the international market in years. The man who handed me the carton was Gene Rouse, for many years the president of the company. Many years later, when I was thinking what a fool I had been, I got in touch with Mr. Rouse just to find out exactly how much our company lost by my failure to pay attention to the directions on this device. It made me feel worse than ever." Rouse told him that when he had approached Stein, the company he had formed the year before to market this device was almost broke, and he was desperate. "For an investment of $100,000 or much less, I would have gotten down on the ground and kissed your feet," Rouse said. Shortly thereafter, Rouse managed to find a backer who invested $17,000, and in 1963 the company turned around. By 1966, Stein learned, it had made $2,616,483 before taxes; then it merged into Teledyne in a tax-free stock exchange for $16 million of Teledyne stock.

These numbers did not allow Stein to make his desired calculation with precision. "I was still curious about how much we lost by not going into Water Pik at that time, so I called Rouse again," Stein continued. He learned that if MCA had put in $100,000, it would have been worth $50 million by 1967 (and substantially more by 1975, when Stein called Rouse for the second time). "Since that day when I turned down the chance to get into Water Pik in a big way, I've visited dentists because of my teeth. All of them tell me to use Water Pik. This advice upsets me as much as my teeth."

But Stein comforted himself with this observation: "Counting up all my mistakes, I'm still millions ahead."

His interest in the market and the daily fluctuations of MCA stock did not abate. In the early seventies, he met a young Wall Street research analyst and broker named Laura Sloate, who was blind. While Stein may have first become interested in her because of her handicap and her ability to overcome it—she founded her own firm in 1974—he quickly came to value her acumen. She advised him on investments for the MCA profit-sharing plan ("Mr. Stein was *giddy* when the MCA stock ran up after *Jaws*—the plan became really big then," Sloate recalled), and he introduced her to people like Billy Wilder and Richard Rodgers, the composer. She was somewhat in awe of Stein—"I thought he had become so successful because he had a genius capability of seeing opportunity before others did"—and, perhaps for this reason, was never able to relax in his presence. "It was rare that I would ask him a question; my function was to answer his questions. I found him scary—but he was very generous and kind to me." Not long before he died, he gave her something he said was to remember him by: a $20 gold coin from 1923 (the year he graduated from medical school), split, with a watch placed inside.

Stein had been focused on his estate planning for decades. As the avatar of creating ingenious schemes to reduce or avoid taxes at MCA, it must have galled Stein not to be able to find any way around a high estate tax. He estimated that under the prevailing tax structure, estates of wealthy individuals were subject to a federal tax of 70 percent—and, after adding various other costs, the figure would reach 75 to 80 percent. "I find no single method of passing on substantial wealth to beneficiaries," he concluded. In addition, though, Stein by this time may have preferred to leave the bulk of his wealth to the institutions for which he held such high hopes. In any event, it was decided: Doris and he would be leaving approximately 75 percent of their wealth to be divided equally between Research to Prevent Blindness and the Jules Stein Eye Institute.

In April 1981, when Stein was quite ill, he wrote a letter to the trustees of the Jules Stein Eye Institute. He was worried about what might occur when a substantial block of MCA stock came under the trustees' control. "Because I am the founder of MCA, and have been so long associated with it, and because so large a part of my prospective estate is likely to consist of shares in that Company, I am deeply concerned with its welfare," Stein wrote. He exhorted the trustees, in deciding how to vote or dispose of the MCA shares, to consult with Wasserman (providing he was still the chairman, or still held a substantial stock interest in MCA). "I have great admiration for Mr. Wasserman's extraordinary intelligence and soundness of judgment. Moreover, he himself is a major shareholder in MCA and our interest in the treatment of MCA holdings would, I am sure, be alike. . . . I ask that you consult with him . . . even if a situation may arise in which he may appear to have a conflict of interest. I have utter confidence in his integrity."

Having said that, Stein, characteristically, went on to say what *his* preference would be, if it became necessary to sell shares: they should be offered first to MCA itself, and if that offer were not accepted, they should be sold through some wide form of public distribution. What he urged them to avoid, with the greatest care, was selling the shares in such a way as to endanger the management of the company and enable an outside interest to acquire control of MCA. It was a prospect that was evidently painful for Stein to contemplate, as he considered what might happen to the company after his death. He felt it was safest left in Wasserman's hands—but, in truth, it was hard for him to leave it in anyone's. "While this memorandum is necessarily precatory," Stein concluded, "I hope you will be guided by it, as it expresses a position of the greatest importance to me."

A few weeks later, Stein died. He was eighty-five. About a year before, he had asked Wasserman and Herb Steinberg, who organized many MCA social events, to lunch at the commissary. "Jules started out by saying that he didn't want his funeral to be an unhappy event," Steinberg recalled. "He said he wanted people to celebrate his life, because he'd led a good, long life. He had written down what he wanted. It was to be at the Eye Institute, in the open space outdoors. He wanted Benny Goodman and his band, and Dinah Shore. He wanted Chancellor Frank Murphy to give the eulogy. Lew and I looked at each other. What can you say? 'Okay.' "

After Stein died, Steinberg and Wasserman were both given envelopes Stein had left for them, with all the instructions, typed out, that Stein had issued at their lunch. Steinberg carried them out as best he could. "I called Benny Goodman in Connecticut. He said, 'I'm not coming in for a damn funeral!' " Dinah Shore also declined. The performers, in the end, were Henry Mancini and Helen O'Connell. One of the eulogists was Stein's granddaughter Katrina, who commented, "This occasion, like all the important events in his life, was produced by my grandfather." Indeed, it recalled his elaborate staging of the handing out of MCA shares at Misty Mountain in 1954. Once again, nothing had been left to chance—not even the hors d'oeuvres, or the songs (among his selections were "Life Is Just a Bowl of Cherries" and "I'll See You Again"). She also said, "My grandfather was a very private person. He gave neither his love nor his friendship easily, but once he did you knew that you had it forever." However ambivalent Wasserman probably was about his patron, he did "tear up," as he might have put it, in the pallbearers' procession (which included President Reagan, Jimmy Stewart, Cary Grant, and Jimmy Petrillo). But Edie—sporting a large diamond pin, its letters spelling the word LOVE, and seated near the Stein family—was heard to say in a loud stage whisper, "It's *about time!*"

Lew Wasserman, 1983. *Gunther/MPTV*

Chapter 5

WASSERMAN & SON

W asserman had been so dominant for so long that his power had become ingrained in the psyche of the Hollywood community and, certainly, in his own. It should not have been surprising, therefore, that even after cracks in his hegemony began to appear, not many took note of them, and Wasserman continued to comport himself in as magisterial a way as he had before. It was of course only human to resist any diminution of one's long-held power, even though that very resistance is apt to accelerate its loss—just as the moguls, decades earlier, had resisted the forces of change, only to be engulfed by them. But it was Wasserman who had marshaled those forces, besting the moguls, and who moreover had always been seen by his followers as preternatural. The fact that he was just human, in the end, came as a rude shock to those who had deified him for decades.

The first signs of insurgency came in the area of labor relations, where Wasserman had carefully cultivated supremacy. He had inserted himself into the chairmanship of the Association of Motion Picture and Television Producers (AMPTP), the labor arm of the MPAA. It was a role for which he was uniquely equipped—since he alone had the rela-

tionship with Korshak and the union leaders, the historical experience
and memory, the willingness and stamina to endure all-night sessions
at the negotiating table. All in all, it was a privilege his colleagues in the
industry had been quite happy to cede to him for a number of years.
But by the early seventies, suspicion of Wasserman had begun to fester.
Dan Slusser was a labor relations employee at Twentieth Century-Fox
before he joined MCA in 1973. "I was in many meetings when I was at
Fox where people said, 'Watch out for Wasserman.' They did all think
he was getting the advantage," Slusser said. He pointed out that Universal was strongest in television, whereas the other studios were primarily producing movies for theatrical distribution. "Everybody
thought that Lew had this vision of taking care of himself by taking
care of television, not theatrical. They thought that when Lew came
into the room and said, 'Good morning,' he was picking their pocket.
He was so smart. They were afraid. They all knew that he could do the
math in his head quicker than they could do it on a calculator." And
while a strike would be damaging to theatrical motion picture production, it would be even more devastating to television production, with
its fixed schedule. So there was more at stake for Wasserman.

It was inevitable that other studios' executives would come to resent Wasserman's control. Norman Samnick, Warner Communications' head of labor relations, who was based in New York, recalled
that one of his colleagues at the Warner studio told him that Wasserman "treated him like a ribbon clerk." "Lew was so in command, and
the others so subservient," Samnick continued. "I called Frank Wells
[president of the studio] one day, and I said, 'How did you vote?' Frank
said, 'You don't *vote* with Lew. He tells you what the deal is.' And
when Samnick was in Wasserman's ambit, he found himself bowing,
too. "I remember once I said, 'An 8 percent increase, no more.' And
Lew came in and said, 'I just made a deal for 10 percent.' I said, 'Ten
percent is the right number. That's what I was just saying!' " Given that
the deals Wasserman struck were often richer than his industry colleagues thought justified, his dominance was even more galling. "I
think he bought labor peace at any cost," Samnick declared. And even

his rich deals seemed more to his advantage than others, since for many years the costs of these deals that involved television were passed on to the networks—and Universal, of course, was the biggest TV producer by far.

Wasserman had resigned the chairmanship of the AMPTP in the fall of 1974—a move meant to suggest, perhaps, that this system was in fact a democracy. He was succeeded by Gordon Stulberg, the president of Twentieth Century-Fox. But when Stulberg left Fox a few months later, Sheinberg ascended to the chairmanship. Moreover, the AMPTP continued to be run by Billy Hunt, the lawyer whom Wasserman had placed in the job. The changes, therefore, were nominal. Describing how intimately involved Wasserman was in labor relations, Hunt said that most mornings Wasserman would meet with him at the AMPTP offices at about 8:30 before going to MCA. "None of the company presidents participated in the negotiations, except for Lew," Hunt said. "You could always count on Lew. If you called him at any hour and said, can you come down, we have a problem, he was never too busy. He'd get in his car and be there. I knew he had ego and vanity—but he'd get in the ditch and start digging with you." Hunt acknowledged that the industry viewed him as "Lew's boy."

Ultimately, the challenge to Wasserman was fueled by Steve Ross. A onetime funeral home operator who had gained control of Warner Bros. in 1969, Ross had built the failing studio into a major entertainment conglomerate, renamed Warner Communications, with its main properties movies, a record company, and cable. Ross's passion for cable set him apart from his entertainment industry peers; they viewed it as a threat, and were fighting for government regulation that would hobble it. Ross was playing a role analogous to that played by Wasserman decades earlier, when he had embraced television while the studio chiefs tried to destroy it. If Wasserman saw the similarity, it did not sway him; he didn't believe in cable, and he did not care for Ross. Ross was decidedly not Wasserman's type—too brash, too bold, too flamboyant, and, perhaps, insufficiently deferential. Indeed, Ross hoped to succeed Wasserman as industry leader, and he was beginning to posi-

384 WHEN HOLLYWOOD HAD A KING

tion himself in the national political scene. It was not surprising that Ross would tire of deferring to Wasserman in the labor decisions so critical to his movie business.

In the summer of 1975, the producers had begun negotiations with the IATSE for a three-year contract that would take effect the following year. The two sides were very far apart. Three years earlier, the union had accepted a deal with slight increases, subsequently made even more meager by inflation; and the new president of the IATSE, Walter Diehl, who had succeeded veteran Richard Walsh, was determined to make up for the IATSE's earlier concessions. Moreover, Walsh had really not believed in the utility of strikes; Diehl let it be known that he believed differently. Wasserman, his producer-side colleagues knew, essentially agreed with the union that this deal needed to make up for the last. The question was, would they follow Wasserman's lead, as they always had before? "The real story started on a plane with Steve Ross and Alan Hirschfield, in June 1975," Samnick said. Hirschfield was then the president and chief executive officer of Columbia Pictures Industries; Columbia had been nearly bankrupt when Hirschfield took over in 1973, but by now it was regaining its financial health and Hirschfield was being hailed in the press as a wunderkind. "Hirschfield had been an investment banker at Allen & Co., involved in Steve's decision to buy Atlantic Records, so he had credibility with Steve. And together, they started second-guessing Lew," Samnick continued. Frank Wells, head of the Warner studio, became Ross's agent, and Wells found an ally in Dennis Stanfill, chairman and chief executive officer of Twentieth Century-Fox. Formerly an investment banker at Lehman Brothers, Stanfill had come to Los Angeles in 1965 to be vice president in charge of finance for the Times Mirror Company, and he had joined Twentieth Century-Fox in 1969. These three CEOs, then—Ross, Hirschfield, and Stanfill—were all relative newcomers to the industry; but they were also self-assured, successful, and ambitious men, to whom obeisance did not come naturally.

Stanfill had had the opportunity to observe Wasserman from different vantage points since he'd arrived in Los Angeles. When he was working for Times Mirror, he saw Wasserman's efforts on behalf of Buffy Chandler and also her husband, Norman. Stanfill pointed out that those relationships had not only enabled Wasserman to broaden his base, but also gave him the opportunity to exert considerable influence on the *Los Angeles Times*. Once Stanfill joined the motion picture industry as a novice, he understood Wasserman's advantage there. "One of Lew's great strengths was he had continuity in his job over so many years," Stanfill remarked. "He had a strong base, he had control of his company. He could afford to take the long view." And his closeness to the unions provided many benefits. For, as Stanfill learned on the job, "It's not just the big agreement you make with the unions, but the day-to-day workings with them. There can be a dispute about something—say, Teamsters on a location say we should have seven drivers, and the producer says, we need only three. Well, if you don't work it out, you can have a strike. But if you—like Lew—have the power buttons to push, then you don't *have* these disputes."

The confrontation finally came in early September, when Billy Hunt made a staggering offer to the union. He did so, he said, after having had lunch with Wasserman and Sheinberg, who approved his proposal: a 15 percent increase the first year, followed by 12 percent the second, and 12 percent the third. Ordinarily, increases were in the 3 to 5 percent range. "It may have been the most expensive contract the industry had ever negotiated—though I know it was seen as a catch-up," said Nick Counter, the attorney who would succeed Hunt at the AMPTP.

At an emergency meeting of the studio presidents, the other companies argued that Hunt had had no authority to make the offer. Wells and Stanfill were Wasserman's most vocal adversaries. "Frank Wells and I thought it was just too rich," Stanfill said. "Lew by and large had run the AMPTP, and Frank and I felt we wanted to have a strong voice in this, because we wanted to get the costs of the industry under control. We were *demanding* to have some participation in these industry decisions." The only studio to side with MCA in supporting the deal Hunt had offered was Paramount. (MCA and Paramount were partners in CIC, of course; and some thought that Barry Diller, head of the

Paramount studio, saw political benefit in casting his lot with Wasserman—or, also, aspired someday to *be* Wasserman.) Faced with this open revolt, Wasserman told the group that Hunt had been authorized and, therefore, they were "reneging"—and since he would not be party to that, he was resigning from the association.

It was a stunning turn of events. It is true that in the Wasserman code, reneging was an unpardonable sin. He had built his relations with the unions on the foundation that his word was his bond. Robert Gilbert, the labor lawyer who negotiated with Wasserman for many years, said, "On occasion, I would work something out with Wasserman over the phone. Some of his subalterns would try to make a hit with the boss, trying to welch on what Wasserman had agreed to. I would pick up the phone and call Wasserman, and tell him that so-and-so was not living up to our agreement. He'd say, I will talk to him and the check will be on your desk this afternoon." But it was surely not only the issue of "reneging" that prompted Wasserman's dramatic exit. For just as the seeds of the rebellion had been planted months before in the conversation between Ross and Hirschfield, so Wasserman's response, too, must have been at least as deliberate. (Regarding Wasserman's resignation, Hunt remarked, with wry understatement, "Lew was not an impulsive person.") Why Wasserman did what he did would remain a matter of some debate; but what he had done was plain. Aware of his colleagues' growing restiveness, Wasserman had decided to make sure an offer was extended that was so rich that it was virtually guaranteed to provoke the rejection it did.

Wasserman and Sheinberg arranged to meet with Diehl the next day in a suite at the Hollywood Roosevelt Hotel. No longer bound by membership in the AMPTP, Wasserman wanted to strike a separate deal—similar to the one that Hunt, with Wasserman's approval, had already offered. According to an IA member who was working closely with Diehl and attended the meeting, Diehl laid out his demands, and Wasserman and Sheinberg walked down the hall to confer. "Walter felt we had asked for so much that they'd never do it," this IA member recalled. "He said to me, we'll compromise on this. And when they walked into the room, he started to offer it. They said, no, we'll take it." Universal and Paramount both agreed to this deal—a 39 percent wage increase over a forty-two-month period; with benefits included, some estimated that it represented as much as a 57 percent increase. "Afterward, we were told that the union was shocked to be able to get that much," said Marshall Wortman, a labor relations executive at MCA, echoing what Diehl's associate had said.

The fate of the other studios remained uncertain. Diehl is said to have offered to Wasserman to drive an even harder bargain with them. Faced with the prospect of a strike—while Universal and Paramount remained open for business—the others were helpless. "They *begged* to make the same deal," Wasserman said, smiling at the recollection. "I could have kept them from making it, but I don't play that kind of pool." So they made the deal Wasserman had authored—and were punished for their challenge, just as Wasserman had punished past challengers. Of course, Universal, too, had to pay these huge increases (though some would be passed on to the networks). But as Chuck Weiss, a corporate vice president at Twentieth Century-Fox, pointed out, "Universal could well afford it. The other studios didn't have much in the pipeline. At the time, we were struggling at Fox." They believed they were paying the price, he said, "for crossing Lew."

Wasserman's revenge, however, was costly. Universal and Paramount formed a separate organization, the Alliance, to deal with labor issues. Over the next few years, the unions and guilds had the advantage of being able to play the AMPTP off the Alliance, and vice versa. In 1980, there was a long, bitter Screen Actors Guild strike, and in early 1981, a Writers Guild strike. "Those strikes happened in part because there was no cohesive unit for bargaining on the producers' side," said Nick Counter, then a labor lawyer in private practice. When he was asked to head the AMPTP in 1981, Counter said, "My condition for taking the job was that they would solidify the association. I told them, you can't be in this position where the unions and guilds can whipsaw you." The two groups then rejoined in what was named the Alliance (instead of the Association) of Motion Picture and Television Producers.

Even for the unions, the mega-deal was a mixed blessing. Leo Geffner, the lawyer who represented the IATSE, said, "Walter Diehl was very unhappy about the settlement. He said, it's *too rich*. He thought it was a dumb thing to do personally, but politically he had to deliver or lose his job. He said at the time, it's going to push too many producers into going nonunion—and his prophecy turned out to be true." Geffner explained that independent producers began to use more nonunion labor. And, in a covert way, by making deals with so-called independent producers that were really studio-financed, some major studios did, too.

"That was the beginning of Lew's losing his power," Geffner continued. "He was not the star after that. There was such resentment of him among the other studio heads for what he'd done."

In times of crisis, Wasserman would still play a decisive role—for example, in helping to avert what seemed about to become the first strike ever by the Directors Guild, and to settle the Writers Guild strike in the summer of 1981. But these were cameo appearances. "Lew started getting out of the labor stuff in the late seventies," recalled Dan Slusser, who had worked closely with Wasserman in this area. "It was hard for him. He had devoted all his spare time to it. And then there was all this talk about how it had been to his advantage."

———

Once Wasserman was no longer intimately involved in relations with the unions, he had less need of Korshak and, not surprisingly, he began to draw away from his close friend of about forty years. But his distancing was also an indication of the degree to which the world had begun to impinge on the two men. Before, when associates had warned Wasserman about his closeness to Korshak, he had been impervious. Now, he evidently did not feel so immune. Moreover, the Hersh article in the *New York Times* seemed to have pierced Korshak's magic shield;

Korshak was becoming an ever more popular target for law enforcement, the media, even a *cartoonist*, Garry Trudeau, who had sport with the relationship between Korshak and Wasserman. Wasserman prided himself on his loyalty—it ranked high in the Wasserman code—and he never publicly turned his back on Korshak. But, to Korshak, the rupture was unmistakable, and unforgivable.

In April 1978, Korshak attended a fund-raiser for Governor Jerry Brown at Wasserman's home. There was nothing unusual about this—he had attended numerous political events there, including Wasserman's huge fund-raiser for Jimmy Carter during his 1976 presidential campaign. But Korshak's presence now caused comment in a way it had not before. Asked by reporters whether he was made uncomfortable by Korshak's attendance, Brown (who had accepted a $1,000 contribution to his 1974 election campaign from Korshak), said he was not. The next year, in a *Doonesbury* cartoon, Trudeau featured Gray Davis, Governor Brown's chief of staff, describing the public relations problem caused by the relationship between the governor and Korshak, "the local low-life, an alumnus from the Capone mob." In the next day's cartoon, the beleaguered governor was protesting that he barely knew Korshak, having only "run into him a few times at Lew Wasserman's parties"—and then explained that "Wasserman has to deal with Korshak to get his movies made." The *Chicago Tribune* was among the newspapers that ran the series—but the *Los Angeles Times* did not.

Just a few weeks after Korshak attended the fund-raiser for Brown, California Attorney General Evelle Younger released a list of reputed organized crime figures with ties in California. Korshak was included. Next to his picture, the text read: "His name has been linked with organized crime for more than 30 years, and he has been the subject of several organized crime investigations." The report also stated that he was a senior adviser to organized crime groups in Chicago, California, Las Vegas, and New York. Korshak responded that he had contributed $3,000 to Younger's two campaigns for attorney general and had been asked to serve on Younger's advisory committee for his 1978 gubernatorial bid. "The damage this has caused me is irreparable because what can I do to combat it?" Korshak said in a rare, brief interview.

Much as Korshak loathed such exposure, it affected his reputation and his ability to operate in the legitimate business world—but not his freedom. The FBI, despite its years of investigating Korshak, had not succeeded in gathering enough evidence to win an indictment. But in 1979, an FBI agent named Michael Wacks thought there was a chance. Joseph Hauser, a corrupt insurance company executive who had been indicted for making payoffs to various labor unions to gain insurance contracts, had begun cooperating with the government. He took part in an undercover sting operation known as Brilab, short for bribery-labor, in which he posed as a representative of a fictitious Beverly Hills insurance firm. Wacks and others in the bureau saw great potential in Hauser, a wealthy Beverly Hills resident who had moved in Korshak's circles, and who, according to Wacks, had also dealt directly with Andy Anderson of the Teamsters. "Anderson and Korshak were the ones we were going for," Wacks said. "It was rare to get someone like Hauser. The FBI gets somebody like him once in a hundred years— someone at that level, with those contacts. He got so jammed, we made him an offer he felt he couldn't refuse. Otherwise, he'd spend the rest of his life in prison."

Posing as insurance men, Wacks and another undercover agent would often accompany Hauser to the Bistro in Beverly Hills, where they sought to be seated at a table near Korshak's; but they usually couldn't overhear much. One day in mid-April 1979, however, they learned through a wiretap on Chicago insurance executive Allen Dorfman's phone that Dorfman, Korshak, and Anderson had arranged to have lunch at the Bistro the following day. (Dorfman, a close Korshak associate and a mob liaison to the Teamsters Central States Pension Fund, was being investigated by the FBI; he would be indicted on racketeering charges in 1983, and murdered two weeks after his indictment.) Wacks and his confederates were there, at an adjacent table, when Korshak and Anderson arrived before Dorfman. And, according to Wacks, he heard Korshak say to Anderson, "Have you got the money for Lou [phonetic]? I'm going to have dinner with him tonight." Then, Wacks saw Anderson hand Korshak a large envelope, which Korshak put in an inside pocket of his jacket. The exchange was suggestive; Wacks immediately thought of Lew Wasserman, but it was pure speculation. He tried to get a court order to allow him to have a hidden microphone placed at Korshak's table, but he failed. And Hauser, he finally realized, was "too hot" to be able to entrap Korshak or Anderson. "Korshak would see him at the Bistro, say hello, and keep going," Wacks said. They made one more effort; the following month, Hauser approached a close associate of Korshak's about getting the Teamsters to buy insurance from him, and the associate suggested meeting with Korshak's brother, Marshall, in Chicago. Hauser and an undercover agent had lunch with Marshall at the Covenant Club, and Marshall agreed to arrange a meeting with Teamsters officials. But then Dorfman heard about the planned meeting and he evidently suspected Hauser was working for the government. "Don't walk away from Hauser," Dorfman said. "Run from him." Hauser's handlers turned his attention away from the Korshaks. The Brilab operation moved to Louisiana, Texas, Oklahoma, and Arkansas. Eventually, more than a dozen individuals (union officials, organized crime figures, and public officials) would be convicted.

In April 1983, Hauser testified before the Senate Permanent Subcommittee on Investigations about the control of organized crime over the health plans, pension plans, and life insurance coverage of the Teamsters, laborers, and hotel workers unions. At one point in his testimony, he said, "Organized crime leader Tony Accardo, whom I have known for many years . . . told me on several occasions that he had sent Korshak to Los Angeles to represent the mob there. Since then, Mr. Korshak has become well known as a labor consultant in Las Vegas and Los Angeles. I don't need to tell this Subcommittee who Sidney Korshak is." Hauser's statement was consistent with that made two years earlier by Jimmy "the Weasel" Fratianno, a Mafia member who became a government informant and testified in a deposition that Korshak was not a member of La Cosa Nostra but was controlled by "the Chicago family."

What had always been known in a general way about Korshak—the stuff of his mystique, titillating to his friends, half hidden in shadow—was now repeatedly being brought to light. Those who had done business with Korshak for years found it was no longer tenable to plead ignorance. In 1985, the New Jersey Casino Control Commission rejected Hilton Corp.'s bid for a casino license on the grounds that it had used Korshak as an attorney for more than a decade. The commission found him to be "a key actor in organized crime's unholy alliances with corrupt union officers." Under prolonged questioning by the commission, Hilton chairman Barron Hilton had finally said he'd seen the error of his ways. Regarding Korshak, he said, "I wish to hell we would never have hired him, because I can see it's a distinct problem here in the minds of you gentlemen about this fellow's integrity." After hearing of Hilton's testimony, Korshak wrote to him, saying, "You have caused me irreparable harm, and as long as I live I will never forget that. When did I become a shady character? I imagine when you were having difficulty getting a license in Atlantic City."

"What Barron Hilton did pained Sidney so," said Frank Yablans, who remained close to Korshak until Korshak's death in 1996. "He couldn't accept the idea that people were distancing themselves. Lew and Sidney had been very close. But eventually they became estranged. Earlier, it was easier, there was some kind of acceptance—the newspapers wouldn't write about Sidney. But what you once controlled, you couldn't control anymore. So Lew moved to get some distance. And Sidney was old-school—he couldn't accept that in this new reality, it brought Lew too much heat."

Korshak had also outlived his usefulness for Wasserman, Yablans added. In the mid-seventies, Hoffa, Giancana, and Roselli were all murdered. "After they were gone, Sidney started to lose his power. He still had influence in Chicago and Vegas, but he lost it in Hollywood. In

Chicago and Vegas, people respected him for what he'd done. But not in Hollywood—Hollywood only respects you for what you can do.

"At the end of his life," he continued, "Sidney was very bitter—bitter about Lew, bitter about everything."

Because, in the end, he regretted the life he'd lived?

"No! Not because he regretted the life he'd lived," said Yablans, rolling his eyes at such obtuseness. "Because he couldn't *live* the life anymore."

———

When Wasserman had shuttered the agency and gone fully into production at Universal Studios, one question had hovered most insistently over the sprawling enterprise: would the production business prove to be his Frankenstein? In the previous two decades, after all, he had done more than any other individual to shift the balance of power from the studios to the star, and, even more, the agent. He had driven stars' salaries up, encouraged them to free themselves of the studios' fetters, transposed Jules Stein's packaging from bands to movies, revolutionized the business by obtaining a percentage of movies' profits for his star clients—and mortally weakened the studio system. Now that *he* was the studio head, would he not be bedeviled by the very forces he had earlier set in motion—taking on a life of their own, out of his control? One way Wasserman had attempted to inoculate himself against them was with his mammoth TV movie deal with Kintner, which had enabled him to re-create his own version of the old studio system, with a stable of actors, actresses, writers, and directors under long-term contracts. Eventually, though, the forces he had set in motion when he was an agent began to win out.

Just as Wasserman had redefined the relationship of the star and the studio, so others were now seeking to redefine the relationship of the film-maker and the studio. George Lucas was one of the first to chart this new terrain. When he made *American Graffiti,* he had no leverage at all. Earning less than a schoolteacher's salary, he had devoted himself for about three years to that mostly autobiographical project—and he had been angry at the way it was treated at the end. He knew that some Universal executives were reluctant to release the film, and he was opposed to the changes they demanded when it was recut. He held these putative movie executives in low esteem, as unworthy successors to a Darryl Zanuck or Jack Warner. "They're people who have never made a movie in their lives, agents and lawyers with no idea of dramatic flow," Lucas said in an interview in the mid-seventies. "But they can come in, see a movie twice, and in those few hours they can tell you to take this out or shorten that. The movie industry was built by independent entrepreneurs, dictators who had a very strong feeling about movies. They knew what they wanted and they made it happen."

After the unexpected success of *American Graffiti,* Lucas had more clout. And he struck a deal with Twentieth Century-Fox for the movie that would become *Star Wars*—a deal that was truly portentous, guarding against any future studio interference and giving him extraordinary financial advantages. In return for taking a low fee as a director, Lucas retained exclusive rights to sequels, music, profits from the soundtrack albums, and, ultimately, merchandising—after a period of time, he owned the rights to every toy, game, book, and cartoon. Just how almost unimaginably meaningful that was began to become apparent when *Star Wars* was completed in 1977. Ned Tanen recalled that he attended a screening with his wife and daughter. He had more than his usual competitor's interest, because it was a movie that he thought should have been Universal's. Following *American Graffiti,* Universal had had the chance to buy this next Lucas project in an embryonic form. "It was just maybe a fourteen-page outline, and you could hardly read it—it was like hieroglyphics—R2D2!" exclaimed Tanen. "Still, this guy had just made *American Graffiti*—and we could buy it for $25,000. So I brought it to Lew, three times—and three times he threw me out of his office." Now, Tanen continued, the screening began. "I watched the first two minutes," he said. "I couldn't stay. I knew this was going to be huge. I went out and sat on the curb like a bum for the next two hours. Monday morning, Lew walked into my office. 'I heard you went to the screening of *Star Wars*. What did you think?' I said, 'It's going to go by *Jaws* like it never happened.' (*Jaws* was everything to him at that time.) He walked out and slammed the door. I counted the seconds: 1-2-3-4-5. The door opened, and he said, '*You* put that in turnaround.'

"What was I going to say? He ran the company, he paid my salary, he could say whatever he wanted. If I didn't like it, I could stop picking up my checks. But for years, I carried that around. People would say, 'Tanen put *Star Wars* in turnaround.' " In some quarters there was apparently some skepticism, though, about whether the responsibility was truly Tanen's. One person who knew Jules Stein well recalled him saying, repeatedly, "I want to find out who in this company rejected *Star Wars!*" Tanen said that Stein quizzed him, but he did not divulge what had occurred. "I was Lew's guy," Tanen said.

After *Star Wars,* Tanen was offered the script for *Raiders of the Lost Ark.* Lucas was the producer, and his friend Steven Spielberg was attached as the director. Lucas's lawyer was Tom Pollock, a noted entertainment attorney, and he had structured the deal in a way that was groundbreaking at the time. Lucas was asking for a straight partnership with the studio, Pollock explained—without the studio's first taking credit for "distribution fees," "overhead," and other charges that, traditionally, reduced the net profits to be shared—and mutual approval over everything, in terms of sequels. "No one else had made a deal like this before," Pollock said. "George was very much into the idea that the studio and he should be dealing as equals. He was saying, 'I'm making the movie, they're putting up the money and doing the marketing. We're fifty-fifty partners.' It was a radical concept, to be as simple and fair as that. But Lew hadn't been confronted with it before, and he felt, if we start doing this, then what's left for the way we do business? His attitude was, we don't *want* to be fair, we're taking all these risks.' " Wasserman's immediate response was actually less reasoned, as Tanen recalled it. "I showed the deal to Lew. He threw the papers across the room. He said, 'Nobody runs my business but me!' He was so angry—because of what they were trying to do and, also, because of his frustration. He knew it was changing and he couldn't control it anymore."

The deal had been offered to five studios, and Paramount finally accepted it. "Michael Eisner [president of the Paramount studio] went out on a limb for this movie in a big way," Pollock said. "I was in a room with Eisner, Diller [the studio's chairman], and Bluhdorn. And in front of me, an outsider, Diller said, 'Michael, are you sure you want to make this ridiculous deal?' Eisner said, 'Yes.' It was positioned publicly by Diller in that room: 'This one is yours, not mine.' " Someone in the movie division at Universal recalled the day they learned that Eisner had indeed made the *Raiders* deal. "I remember Sid [Sheinberg] *screaming*, 'Eisner made it! It's going to break the business!' " Released in 1981, *Raiders* was a gigantic box office hit.

Increasingly, agents and lawyers were crafting the kinds of deals that denied the studios their accustomed power—much as Wasserman had done decades earlier. When Wasserman had reached his agreement with the Kennedy Justice Department that the agency business would not be sold but shut down, many close observers had counted that one of Wasserman's craftiest manipulations. Thanks to the government, he would not have to deal as studio head with a mainly intact, still powerful, supremely aggressive agency on the other side of the table from him. Indeed, he had enjoyed its absence for close to two decades. But in 1975, a young agent named Michael Ovitz and several of his colleagues left William Morris to start their own company, Creative Artists Association (CAA). And by the early eighties, Ovitz was a new kind of force to be reckoned with. He idolized Wasserman, and though he barely knew him, behaved as though he were a disciple. He studied Wasserman's old methods of operation at the MCA agency as though they were canonical, and he tried to bring them to new life at CAA. He became such an aggressive practitioner of packaging, for example, that before long it was almost an industry-wide phenomenon, and—in this town with a notably short memory—many forgot that it had been carried out even more boldly (with MCA's collecting commissions for *virtual* packaging) decades earlier. Wasserman no doubt privately appreciated the irony, but it must have been small comfort for being on the disadvantaged side.

For all their latent power, these currents created mere ripples on the surface. There was some public murmuring in 1981 that Wasserman's control was less complete than it had been, and his company less strong (its earnings dropped precipitously that year, and Wasserman instituted a round of cost cutting). But the criticism was quieted for a time by the greatest movie triumph ever—*E.T. the Extra-Terrestrial,* which Universal released in 1982. Sean Daniel, who had joined the company as a young executive assistant in the movie division in 1976, and achieved early success two years later with a very *un*-Universal kind of movie, *National Lampoon's Animal House,* recalled the preview of *E.T.* Spielberg, Edie and Lew Wasserman, Lorraine and Sid Sheinberg, Daniel, and a few other people traveled to Texas. "Lew didn't believe in corporate jets, but he had leased one for that occasion," Daniel said. "Steven had wanted the preview to be in his lucky theater, in Dallas—the *Jaws* theater—but it wasn't available that night, so we went to Houston. No one in that group had ever seen a preview like that. The audience could not believe a movie was making them feel this way. There was such a level of cheering and exhilaration! I remember Lew smiling—*beaming* is the word—as he walked out to the lobby. It was a happy plane ride back."

E.T. broke all previous box office records, and retained its standing as the biggest movie ever for many years. The young director Wasserman had thought too untested for *Jaws* had become a phenomenon. And, though Spielberg would on occasion make a movie at another studio, he was, by and large, Universal's phenomenon. Because Spielberg was grateful—not so much for the chance he'd been given on *Jaws,* but, more, for the one given him earlier by Sid Sheinberg. When he was head of television for MCA/Universal, Sheinberg had seen a prize-winning short film Spielberg had made and, on the strength of that, brought him into the MCA-TV stable with the seven-year contract. It was 1969, and Spielberg was just twenty-one. Now Sheinberg (not the head of the movie division) oversaw all Spielberg movies at

Steven Spielberg, with Amy Irving and Warner Communications CEO Steve Ross—who was trying to woo Spielberg from MCA. *James Smeal/Ron Galella Ltd.*

Universal. Some in the Hollywood community, however, did not believe that Spielberg would continue to be undyingly loyal to Sheinberg and Universal. Hadn't he already repaid his debt many times over, they wondered, and might he not switch his allegiance to another studio or, at least, play the field?

One who was desperate to win Spielberg away from his base at Universal was Steve Ross. Ross's hopes of succeeding Wasserman as industry leader had been crushed by the government investigation of Warner Communications' ties to the mob-run Westchester Premier Theatre. That investigation had resulted in a guilty plea from Ross's closest associate at the company and the conviction of an assistant treasurer; and Ross himself had come perilously close to being indicted. Ross knew that Wasserman disdained him—which would have made his stealing Spielberg away from MCA all the sweeter. Terry Semel, president of the

Warner Bros. studio and a good friend of Spielberg's, arranged a four-day weekend for Ross and Spielberg at the Warner villa in Acapulco in early 1982. Interviewed in 1993, Spielberg recalled the encounter that gave rise to his long, close relationship with Ross: "I had typecast what a CEO was . . . and in my mind, they looked like J. C. Penney. And suddenly here was this older movie star. We quickly found out what we had in common: my favorite movies were made between 1932 and 1952 and those were his favorites, too. Steve to me was a blast from the past. He had silver-screen charisma, much like an older Cary Grant, or a Walter Pidgeon. He had style in a tradition that seemed to have bred itself out of society. He had flash. He was a magnetic host—eventually, that became his calling card. And at Acapulco, he *was* the weekend."

Sheinberg could not compete; few would describe this abrasive, often bad-tempered executive as having "silver-screen charisma" or "flash." But Spielberg evidently did not view it as a competition. He was devoted to both men. Spielberg—who for many years had a difficult relationship with his father and was fond of casting friendships in familial terms—once tried to differentiate his relationships with Ross and Sheinberg by saying that Ross was "a surrogate father," while Sheinberg was "an older-brother figure." In any event, he did not believe that Ross was courting him with any business purpose; Spielberg insisted that Ross's had been a "friendship without agenda." And for Spielberg, the issue of his loyalty was apparently as uncomplicated as his view of Ross; his first allegiance was to Universal. While he did make a number of movies at the Warner Bros. studio, Universal remained his home. That was made official for the first time in 1983, when Universal provided him a permanent office, built and decorated at his direction, for his independent production company, Amblin. A two-story adobe mansion, with cedar beams, Mexican tile floors, Navajo pottery, and Tiffany lamps, it featured a forty-five-seat screening room, outfitted with George Lucas's THX sound system and Dolby stereo, and two cutting rooms. There was also a full kitchen, presided over by a permanent chef, and a game room filled with the latest video games. Perhaps it was a kind of Walter Mitty fantasy of Spielberg's when he was wandering around the lot in 1969, often with not very much to do, that he would someday have such a studio castle.

It was something MCA now was only too happy to provide. MCA was a strong company, with substantial assets in movies, records, and books, theme parks and real estate. But Spielberg was arguably the biggest asset of all. "There are very few things Steven could ask of us that he would not get," Sheinberg said in an interview in 1984. "There is no one we are more anxious to please."

Perhaps the strongest sign of that desire was the deal that Sheinberg made with Spielberg after the triumph of *E.T.* It was to apply not just to his next movie at Universal but to all subsequent ones as well (it would, indeed, remain constant over the next twenty years). And it was a fifty-fifty partnership—essentially, the *Raiders* deal, reincarnated.

Wasserman had entered the movie business with no illusions. He knew that movie production, with its endemic overruns in time and costs, and the unpredictability of box office success, was inimical to control. It was, therefore, a business for which Wasserman was temperamentally unsuited, but he was drawn to it nonetheless—how rule Hollywood, and not be in the movie business? So, while doing everything imaginable to exercise as much control as he could, he suffered its failures and deeply savored its triumphs. But television was his safe harbor. He had been there at its inception, had shaped its nascent form according to his desires, and had dominated it, with ease, essentially unchallenged, for decades. It was not a dominion he was prepared to lose.

Through the seventies, the strength of Universal Television was undiminished. No other TV producer came close to MCA. In the fall of 1976, Norman Lear was MCA's closest competitor—he supplied four hours of shows a week on prime-time network programming, and MCA supplied fourteen. Among MCA's were *The Bionic Woman, The Six Million Dollar Man, Emergency, Baretta, Kojak, The Rockford Files,* and *Columbo.* Several of these had started out as World Premiere movies—illustrating yet another benefit to MCA in that historic deal with NBC. Selling a new series to a network ordinarily involved many time-consuming stages, but these movies essentially served as "back-door pilots" for series, thus performing a dual function and dramatically accelerating the sales process.

Long after Kintner had made that deal with Wasserman and then abruptly left his job in late 1965, MCA's relationship with NBC had remained intact. The players changed, but the dynamics did not, and MCA continued to court key NBC executives aggressively. NBC executive Don Durgin recalled that after Sonny Werblin left MCA, it was the inimitable Jennings Lang who worked his wiles on NBC. "Jennings had this beautiful house," Durgin said. "MCA had bought him the house—or, to put it more exactly, the company had given him an interest-free loan, never expected to be repaid. And all the art! He had the paintings like postage stamps on the wall. In the living room, the chairs swiveled and leaned back, the paintings would suddenly be lifted up on chains, and a screen came down—and then there would be an MCA projectionist, to show the movies." At NBC, Kintner had been succeeded by Walter Scott. "Walter was a very sensible man, but he was captivated by Jennings and his shameless schmoozing. Jennings was a great combination of Jewish Hollywood and street smarts, but with such warmth and generosity that you couldn't resist," Durgin continued. "One day at the Bel Air Hotel, Walter opened his door—and there was a live peacock [NBC's logo], strutting about on his patio!"

Oddly—inasmuch as this was, after all, a business—such courtship was a meaningful part of the process. Larry White, who had been a TV executive at CBS, arrived at NBC in 1966, when the Wasserman-Kintner deal was still young; it would be renewed many times, he recalled. "The individual personal relationships between suppliers and buyers was a strong determining factor," White said. "The quality of the material was almost secondary. If you weren't in the loop and weren't personally involved, you wouldn't get the business. It's very strange—there's no other business like this that I can think of." When White became head of programming at NBC, he decided to try to take a more rational approach. He believed that while the MCA movies delivered to NBC were by no means all bad, the MCA-NBC relationship was heavily weighted in MCA's favor, and it effectively froze out other movie producers. "I went to Hollywood and had dinner with Frank Price [head of Universal Television]," White said. "I told him I was going to look at everybody's submissions on an equal basis." Shortly after that, Sid Sheinberg complained about White to Sheinberg's good friend Herbert Schlosser, the president of NBC. Life at NBC was difficult for him from then on, White said, and he left in 1975.

Even after Sheinberg was elevated to the MCA presidency, he continued to cast a proprietary eye on Universal Television, where he had been president, and where he probably spent his happiest years at the company. He had reported to Wasserman, of course, but the hugely successful division seemed more *his,* in a way that the larger company never fully would. Sheinberg had first come to Wasserman's attention as a company lawyer—Wasserman said he brought the young attorney with him to a negotiating session and thought he was "brilliant." Sheinberg had his early, sustained exposure to Wasserman, however, when he was an executive in the TV division. He recalled the time when Wasserman and Schlosser were negotiating one of the big TV movie deals, and they were stuck on a point that Sheinberg thought not nearly critical enough to be a deal-breaker. When Schlosser continued to balk, Sheinberg recalled, "Lew said, 'You've just blown this deal, and you go tell them at NBC that you have no deal!' Herb Schlosser fell backward into his chair. Afterward, Lew was driving me home, in his Bentley coupé (a gift from Jules Stein), and he said to me, 'You look shaky.' I said, 'I'm troubled.' He said, 'I learned a long time ago that in every negotiation you have to decide whether you have the power to control it or you don't. If you don't, make the best deal you can and get out. If you think you do, then exploit that.' A couple hours later, he called me at home. 'They caved.' And after that, in the course of Lew's negotiations with NBC," Sheinberg concluded, "it was, 'Whatever you want.' "

Frank Price succeeded Sheinberg as head of the television division, and remained in that post for five years. He sought to find new forms for MCA TV—for example, the serialized novel. *Rich Man, Poor Man,* based on Irwin Shaw's novel, was a great hit as a twelve-part series on ABC. He also tried to break into the half-hour comedy business—but MCA's efforts under his regime were no more successful than they had been before. "One of the things I did was develop some terrific young producers—Steve Cannell, Steve Bochco," Price said. "It was an apprentice system that was working really well." Price, who had a fractious relationship with Sheinberg, left MCA in 1978, eventually to head Columbia Pictures. After Price's departure, a number of top TV writers and producers left as well. One of them, the producer Glen Larson, told *Business Week* in 1981, "Price was a real innovator and knew how to handle people."

The exodus was about more than personal chemistry, though, according to the entertainment lawyer Kenneth Ziffren, who was representing many writers and producers in television. Just as the economic relationships between the talent and the studios in motion pictures were being redefined (thanks to the efforts of aggressive agents and lawyers), they were in television, too. "What happened was Lew and Sid were unwilling to make the back-ended deals I was able to make all over town," Ziffren said. Universal insisted on a net profit definition so expansive in its application of costs and fees that there was little defined *profit,* in the end, to share with the talent. "My clients were getting nothing on the back end. Plus, Universal was getting an investment tax credit! I said, my guy wants to see some of the upside, and if you're not going to give him any, we're leaving." Ziffren said he did this with a number of the writers and producers who had been Universal Television's strongest performers. The result of their departure was not manifested immediately, but by the late eighties Universal Television had started to weaken noticeably.

Ziffren was awed by Wasserman when he had first started practicing law, with his father, Paul, and he had dealt with Wasserman on the lease for the Center Theatre Group. But that had been more than a decade earlier, in a very different venue. Now, he said, "The rules of this game had started to change, and my major critique of Lew and

Sid is that they were too rigid, and they did not keep up with the times."

One business opportunity MCA missed was pay television. By the late seventies, pay television—through which revenues came from showing theatrical movies, uninterrupted, on special channels—was becoming so popular that some believed it might be the prime method for viewing motion pictures by the end of the century. Its pioneer, however, was not MCA, king of TV, but Home Box Office, Inc., a fledgling subsidiary of Time, Inc. In 1976, the rather fusty Time, Inc. had invested $7.5 million to lease satellite time to transmit HBO's signal to cable systems. That move had revolutionized the cable industry. There were other entrants to this new market of providing movies to be shown over local cable systems, like Showtime and the Movie Channel. But HBO was the dominant player by a large margin.

Wasserman had always been alert to the nexus between movies and television—in his buying of the Paramount library of films, in his introduction of the made-for-TV movie, in his efforts to develop the Disco-Vision machine. (That last must have been a sore disappointment for Wasserman. He prided himself on seeing the future, as he had in television, and Disco-Vision would have been a great sequel. "I think its potential is literally mind-boggling," he told *Fortune* magazine in 1976. But MCA withdrew from its manufacturing in 1982, after investing about $100 million in laser beam video technology.) Perhaps Wasserman had missed this opportunity for cable programming because of his shunning of the cable business itself. It was plain by 1979, in any event, that pay television was too big a phenomenon to ignore. Motion picture distributors were not happy with the gross revenues they were receiving from pay TV, as opposed to theatrical exhibition, and HBO was considered a particularly tough negotiator. Most of the major movie studios participated in discussions about starting a pay TV network, but it was MCA/Universal, Paramount, Columbia, and Fox, along with Getty Oil Company, that decided, in early 1980, to go forward. They formed a joint venture to start a network known as Premiere. And Premiere was to have a giant advantage, in that certain films distributed by the venture partners would be made available exclusively to Premiere for a nine-month period before being made available to other programming services, such as HBO.

The U.S. Justice Department promptly filed an antitrust suit, charging the five defendants with price fixing and a group boycott. In December 1980, after extensive discovery, Federal District Court Judge Gerhard Goettel ruled on the government's motion for a preliminary injunction. Essentially, the defendants were arguing that the (anticompetitive) steps they were taking were required to combat HBO's monopoly power. It was an interesting argument for MCA, especially in light of its lifelong history of seeking and embracing such power. Indeed, Judge Goettel, acknowledging that some HBO practices suggested monopoly power, described them in a way that was reminiscent of MCA. "Undoubtedly . . . HBO, by its pioneering efforts, has achieved a very substantial portion of the existing market. It has already obtained a substantial profit margin and a high return on investment, which it probably will be able to continue for some years to come. Its use of volume discounts has assisted it in obtaining affiliations with large cable systems. Certain of its practices, such as the obtaining of exclusive licenses, which it refuses to share with other networks, and its selective tactics in purchasing from motion picture producers, do suggest the exercise of monopoly . . . power. However, it is to be expected that the first entrant in the industry would have a substantial head start and that new entrants would have some catching up to do."

The judge seemed offended by the defendants' rationale, and the conduct they sought to justify. "The construction of the Premiere venture is concededly very clever and would, almost certainly, gain the defendants a successful entry into the market. In structuring their venture, however, the defendants are arrogating to themselves one-half of the essential product of the industry." And, he also wrote, "There are a number of ways of achieving product differentiation without cornering the market on one-half of the hit motion pictures being produced in Hollywood." The government won its motion, and that was the end of Premiere.

Michael Fuchs, an HBO executive who became its CEO in 1984, recalled that MCA and Paramount were the leaders of the Premiere initiative. "MCA, especially, was very eager to go to war with us," Fuchs said. "They had been hostile from the beginning. They were so angry that this WASP company had come into *their* business and built something the movie business should have built." Through the eighties, Fuchs dealt with MCA a great deal. Universal licensed its movies to HBO. And, also, in 1981, MCA did finally enter the pay-TV programming business, as a partner with Time, Inc. and Paramount in a cable TV service, USA Network. But, whether he was dealing with MCA as a partner or as a supplier, Fuchs said, it was never easy. "They were infused with the idea that they were leaders of the industry. Sometimes they didn't even have to get the best deal—as long as they were the acknowledged leader. They were the most arrogant studio to deal with, by far. And they were so rooted in the past. Everything was precedent-oriented. This was the entertainment business—and Lew was in his seventies!" Fuchs exclaimed. When he would visit MCA's Black Tower and see Jules Stein's antique furniture, he added, "that always symbolized to me where they were."

———

Universal Television was no longer invincible, but it did continue through the mid-eighties to be MCA's most lucrative division. A large proportion of its steady flow of earnings came from syndicating hit series to independent TV stations; and as the number of these stations grew in the eighties, so did the demand for reruns. It was of the greatest moment to Wasserman, therefore, when the Federal Communications Commission in 1983 proposed changing its rules governing the ownership and syndication of TV programs—rules that had restricted the networks and, conversely, empowered the motion picture studios for the past thirteen years. And when it came to waging this critical battle in Washington, the other studio heads put aside past resentments and were only too glad for Wasserman to try to work his political legerdemain.

In 1970, the three main networks—ABC, CBS, and NBC—were capturing about 90 percent of the television audience, and the FCC wanted to curb their control over the distribution of programming, here and overseas. It instituted the financial interest and syndication rules, quickly known as "fin-syn"; among other things, these rules prevented the networks from selling their programming to independent stations in this country, or *syndicating* them, and also from acquiring a financial interest in programming they had not produced themselves. Fin-syn was a boon to the Hollywood studios; it gave them carte blanche to increase their TV production and strengthen their distribution, here and abroad. It also encouraged the growth of diversified entertainment conglomerates—like MCA—with interests in movies, television, music, and other media. Before, the studios and the networks had been contenders; now, the networks had one hand tied behind their back. Not surprisingly, Wasserman had been a progenitor of these rules. Leonard Goldenson, the longtime chairman of ABC, later said that Wasserman "was in the forefront of those who, in the late sixties, pressured the FCC into barring networks from syndication and from more than token production of programming."

By the early eighties, the balance had shifted dramatically. The networks were weakened, facing increased competition from new technologies, including cable television. Indeed, an FCC study of the situation, completed in the late seventies, concluded that the fin-syn rules should be abolished. And in early August 1983, the FCC proposed gutting much of its fin-syn rules. "I was in Hawaii when Lew, Sid Sheinberg, and Barry Diller called me," Valenti recalled. " 'We have a big problem. We want to go to war, and you are our commander-in-chief.' " Soon, the Commerce and Justice departments filed a series of comments with the FCC supporting the repeal. Valenti was orchestrating furious machinations in Congress—the Senate Appropriations Committee attached an amendment to a bill prohibiting the FCC from spending any funds on repeal of the fin-syn rules. And a group of independent producers testified in Washington about how the repeal of fin-syn would mean far less diversity in TV fare, and likely put them out of business—an argument with considerable merit, though these independents' effort was quietly organized and financed by the major studios, which stayed in the background. But the most meaningful action took place elsewhere. Larry Levinson, then Paramount's Washington representative, recalled that the studios were deathly afraid the networks were about to be unbound. "The studios developed a huge war chest—it was the most important of Hollywood issues, ever. But Mark Fowler [chairman of the FCC] was saying, 'Nuts to Hollywood! We have to have a free market for TV programs.' Now, Jack Valenti, a Democrat, didn't really have the access to the Reagan White House—he'd go over there and see Ed Meese [counselor to the president], bring him videotapes—but he wasn't really getting anywhere. The only way was to have Ronnie contacted (Lew referred to Reagan not as 'Mr. President,' but 'Ronnie'). So there was this conversation between Lew and Reagan. Suddenly, the chairman of the FCC was summoned to the White House, lectured by Ed Meese . . . and the rule was put back. But to give us cover—it couldn't be that transparent—Jack worked out this prohibition against the FCC using any funds to rescind the fin-syn rules."

Michael Deaver, deputy chief of staff to President Reagan, confirmed that Wasserman had come to see Reagan to ask that the rules not be repealed, and Reagan had done as he asked. Explaining Reagan's willingness, Deaver pointed out that Wasserman had been Reagan's agent, starting in the late thirties, so it was a relationship with a history. "They were friendly, and Lew was very powerful, and he spoke for the industry. And Reagan *loved* that industry," Deaver emphasized. "He would talk about it, much more than about the presidency." Deaver also confirmed that it was Meese who delivered the message to Fowler about "what Reagan wanted." (Fowler denied that he had acted under orders.)

Asked about his having persuaded Reagan, Wasserman replied, not so obliquely, "Most things in Washington that are done are done quietly—because if you do it publicly, in the House or in the Senate, it can be very difficult."

The Justice and Commerce departments reversed their positions, to favor the retention of the rules; this was done, admittedly, at Reagan's instruction. It was, of course, one thing for Reagan to order his cabinet appointments at Justice and Commerce to reverse themselves; and another to interfere with an independent agency. Charles Ferris, the FCC chairman who preceded Fowler, said, "Reagan took Mark to the woodshed, and that was that. It was improper—the FCC is an independent regulatory agency, a creature of Congress." About Reagan, Ferris commented, "I'm sure he was as casual as could be. He didn't have distinct boundaries. He probably thought it was okay. Mark Fowler had worked on his campaign in 1976 and in 1980, so he had a preexisting relationship with Reagan."

Hollywood had averted disaster. It would only be a matter of time before the rules were abolished, but time was money. The FCC was persuaded that the movie studios and the television networks should settle the matter themselves, as Valenti had argued. Bob Daly, then co-head of Warner Bros., who became Hollywood's chief negotiator in these settlement talks, recalled that the status quo was so favorable to Hollywood that "the object was delay, delay, delay, never make a deal." Eventually, in 1994, the rules were repealed. "The relationship between Lew and Reagan was really the thing," Daly commented. "I remember this meeting," he continued, pointing to a framed photograph of President Reagan with Wasserman, Valenti, Daly himself, and three other studio heads. "It wasn't to discuss the issue of the financial interest-syndication rules, it was to bless it. And Reagan had a great line. He said, 'If I had this much attention from so many studio heads, I never would have run for office!'"

It must have been a particularly satisfying coup for Wasserman. His world was changing in ways he had not chosen, and some of his industry colleagues had balked at his dominance in the labor arena. But this had been a hard test of his political prowess, and he had passed it brilliantly—for which those colleagues would owe him a debt of gratitude. Moreover, he had secured an enormous, continuing advantage in television production, his medium, which had enabled him to control so much of his destiny from the start. That had been possible, thanks to

Reagan—as this was now. But even the far-seeing Wasserman could not have imagined, back in 1952, that the complaisant Screen Actors Guild president who was doing his bidding would one day be president of the United States, and doing it again.

Now that Reagan *was* president, Wasserman seemed to find it a little dislocating; he knew his old client too well. Harry McPherson, who had become friendly with Wasserman when he was an aide in the Johnson White House, recalled an evening at the Reagan White House in early December 1983, at a reception for the Kennedy Center Honors. "Lew and I were standing in the back of the East Room—there weren't enough seats for everybody. And Reagan started talking in his genial way, reading what had been written for him about the performing arts. I whispered to Lew, 'I have a feeling this guy isn't going to run again.' He said, 'What makes you say that?' 'He doesn't belong here—look at him! He shouldn't be president. And I think he's done the things that are fun for him—he cut taxes, built up the Defense Department, what else is he going to do? I think he's going to give it up.' Lew said, 'You don't understand anything. This guy's an actor! This is the best role he's ever had! He's not walking off *this* stage—he'd have to be carried off.' "

Several years later, Wasserman had the opportunity to do a favor for Reagan, continuing the pattern of reciprocity that had served both men so well over decades. The Reagan presidential library was to be built at Stanford University, but, after continuing student protests and faculty opposition (on the grounds that the library, dedicated to this arch-conservative president, would compromise the university's independence), the Reagans in 1987 decided to look for a new site. According to Wasserman, he and Walter Annenberg managed to find a new location, in Simi Valley, north of Los Angeles. When the Reagan Library opened in 1991, it was the largest and most expensive of presidential libraries, and Wasserman was a generous contributor.

By the mid-eighties, on Wall Street and in Hollywood, speculation about the future of MCA was rampant. It was not only that Wasser-

Edie and Lew Wasserman in 1986—the year that marked their fiftieth wedding anniversary. *Ron Galella/Gamma Presse*

man was in his seventies, and that the merger-and-acquisition boom
was at its height, but, also, that there was a distinct fin de siècle air at
the company. It was still powerful, still reaping occasional bonanzas
from Spielberg's films (in 1985, *Back to the Future,* which Spielberg
produced, was the year's top box office hit). But at a time when the
media entertainment business was increasingly turbulent, reconfigur-
ing for the future at an ever more rapid pace, MCA seemed to be missing the beat. For some time, Wall Street analysts had been contrasting
MCA with Warner Communications, which had of course invested in
cable systems in the early seventies, and, also, the video game business,
in Atari (that eventually turned out much less well). Then there was
Rupert Murdoch, who had acquired Twentieth Century-Fox and
started the Fox network, and who—with publications all over the
world and direct broadcast satellite services—was attempting to build
a global communications giant. While Murdoch was building an empire and Warner diversified adventurously, MCA stuck to its knitting.
Wasserman would respond to this criticism (occasionally voiced even
by one of his own executives) by saying, "I subscribe to the Rothschild
theory. There is nothing wrong with keeping your eggs in one basket,
providing you watch that basket like hell."

MCA did make some effort to diversify—it acquired Putnam
Books, the publishing company, for about $13 million in 1976—but its
more major initiatives were unsuccessful. Frank Price, who after heading Columbia Pictures returned as the president of the motion picture
division at Universal in 1984, echoed Wall Street's comparison of MCA
and Warner Communications. "MCA's approach was, what can we get
at a bargain-basement sale? Rather than saying, the way Steve Ross
did, this is our future, we will *get* it!" In 1976, for example, MCA had
set its sights on SeaWorld, Inc., the owner of three marine parks.
Adding SeaWorld to the Universal Tour (which was eventually transformed from an industrial tour to movie-theme attractions) would
have established MCA as a major force in the theme park business.
After MCA made a hostile bid for SeaWorld in October 1976, Harcourt Brace made a slightly higher offer. Mel Ziontz, who represented

MCA in its acquisition efforts through the seventies and eighties, beginning with this deal, recalled the debate at MCA about whether to top the Harcourt bid. "When some of Lew's people said MCA should make a higher offer, Lew started *screaming!* He said he wasn't going to get in a bidding war and be made to look like a fool and pay more than the company was worth. His view was that we had to go significantly higher than Harcourt Brace had." MCA dropped out, and Harcourt Brace acquired SeaWorld. Ziontz said he later ascertained from the SeaWorld side that if MCA had raised its bid slightly, it would have won the company. Jay Stein, the head of MCA's theme park division during this period, had argued strongly that MCA should raise its bid. Wasserman, of course, was famous for not acknowledging mistakes. Stein commented, "I only knew Lew to indirectly acknowledge a mistake one time, ten years after the fact—but it was huge. He said, 'Maybe we *should* have bought SeaWorld.' "

In 1977, MCA had tried to buy Coca-Cola Bottling Co. of Los Angeles. MCA made a low offer—$140 million—that was topped by one from Northwest Industries for $200 million. Four years later, Northwest sold Coca-Cola of L.A. to Beatrice Foods for $600 million. In this instance, Arthur MacDonald, the chairman of the bottling company, was offended not only by MCA's low-ball offer, but also by the phone call he received, in which an imperious Wasserman announced his intention to take over his company. MacDonald and his board fought MCA, and encouraged Northwest.

It was odd, in a way, that the man who had built MCA through his aggressive acquisitions of other agencies should prove to be such an inept acquirer. But MCA had been a private company, making cash deals for other private companies; Wasserman had been able to strike those deals quickly and quietly, making offers that—with the force of MCA behind him—some small companies felt they could not refuse. Now, there were myriad disclosure requirements, and strict protocols for the very public process of making a bid—which generally provoked other bids. For the intensely secretive Wasserman, it was like trying to operate in a fishbowl, and it must have brought back to mind the reasons he had *not* wanted to take MCA public many years before. "Lew Wasserman did not like tender offers," Ziontz stated, flatly. "He liked to negotiate in a controlled environment."

It was partly because of MCA's failure to make any major acquisitions that it became a more tempting target itself. Hollywood's largest movie and television production company, MCA also had interests in music, theme parks, publishing, extensive real estate, and a valuable film library; *and* it was cash-rich and debt-free. Moreover, the company's breakup value was close to double the price of its shares (at least in part because of the market's perception that MCA was not being aggressively managed). Jay Stein recalled the first appearance of a predator. MCA planned to build a $175 million theme park in Orlando, Florida, which would replicate its studio tour at Universal. In 1984, Stein recalled, "I made a big presentation to Michael Milken—with all the numbers and concepts. It was one of those early morning meetings with Milken, who was then the prince of princes, and attended by Lew and Sid. Milken was going to give us the money to do the Florida park." Not long after, Wasserman learned that Steve Wynn, the chairman and CEO of Golden Nugget, had acquired over 5 percent of MCA stock. Milken, the wizard of Drexel Burnham Lambert, who orchestrated and financed with junk bonds many of the takeovers of the eighties, was a close friend of Wynn's. He had financed Wynn's acquisition of Golden Nugget, and Wynn was a big buyer of Milken's junk bonds. "Lew was furious! We had turned over confidential information to Milken," Stein said, adding that Wasserman believed Milken had activated Wynn.

MCA hired investigators to prepare a dossier on Wynn, and alerted its lawyers to prepare to sue him. But those were evidently only backup defenses in case Wasserman's own rather idiosyncratic approach failed. "Lew called up Steve Wynn," said Dan Slusser, who worked closely with Wasserman for many years, and said he was present for Wasserman's call. "Lew said, 'If you're buying the stock because you think this is a good company, welcome. If you're buying it for any other reason—I wouldn't.' "

And that was all it took?

"He stopped buying the stock," Slusser replied. And, a short time later, Wynn sold it.

An unfriendly takeover of MCA would not be simple, because Wasserman owned about 7 percent of the stock, and he was a trustee of various company trusts established by Stein, which held close to 13 percent; but it was still possible. And Wasserman was worrying, as Stein had before him, about what would befall the company when he became ill or died. While Stein had entertained doubts about Wasserman's aegis back in 1969, he seemed to feel by the time of his death that he was leaving the company in capable hands. It was clear that Wasserman meant Sheinberg to be his successor, and wanted to protect his ability to carry out that role. What was less clear was whether he felt Sheinberg would be able to keep the company intact on his own.

In 1984, MCA held talks about acquiring Walt Disney Studios when that company was trying to repel the advances of investor Saul Steinberg. "All the terms were done," said Barry Diller, who had learned what happened from one of the principals. "But the Disney family said that Ron Miller [a Disney executive] had to be president. Sid [Sheinberg] said to Lew, 'It's fine.' Felix [Rohatyn, the investment banker advising MCA] said to Lew, '*Do* it—a year from now, you'll get rid of Miller, and make Sid president.' But Lew said, 'No. Sidney is president.'

"It was Lew's inflexibility that caused him to blow deals he should not have blown," Diller added. "He and Jules had built the best company—they should have owned the world. And had they made this deal with Disney, *everything* would have been different."

In 1984 and again in 1985, Wasserman held merger talks with the electronics giant RCA, the owner of NBC. Recalling these talks, Sheinberg said that the RCA chairman, Thornton Bradshaw, had been eager for the merger. A management structure had been worked out in which Wasserman would be chairman of the executive committee of the merged companies, and Sheinberg would report to him. Then, after many meetings, Sheinberg continued, the RCA head took out of his pocket a table of organization that showed Sheinberg reporting through him. The sudden shift, Sheinberg felt, did not augur well for his future. "Lew put his arm around me," Sheinberg said, remembering what was a somewhat rare physical gesture. 'This isn't going to happen,' he said." The merger talks ended. So, the template seemed to be set: Wasserman would make no deal where Sheinberg's position was not protected.

Despite the fact that MCA had been a public company for roughly thirty years, it had so much the ethos of a family business that some who were close to it referred to it at times as Wasserman & Son. This old-fashioned sense of a company handed down was strong in Wasserman. "Who's minding the store?" he would sometimes ask. And if Sheinberg was away, Wasserman made sure he was there. Still, the relationship between the two men was hardly uncomplicated. Wasserman knew that his choice of Sheinberg was not a widely popular one—beginning, of course, with Jules Stein. There were a number of MCA executives who thought of themselves as Wasserman people, and for most of them, Sheinberg would always be an inadequate student of the master. While Wasserman was smooth and polished, Sheinberg was rough and prickly. He leavened his acerbity with a remarkable candor, and sometimes odd, amusing behavior (in the late afternoon, if he was in a particularly good mood, he might open his office door and howl into the corridor). Few disputed his intellect, or his understanding of the business, or his fundamental decency. Still, none of his positive traits made Wasserman's diehard followers warm to him. They even disparaged Sheinberg's rages as a rank imitation—and they did not accept them as his rightful province. "It was one thing to be screamed at by the god of this company, another, by the pretender," Ziontz commented. In the seventies, especially, some MCA executives believed that Wasserman realized he had made a mistake in his choice of a successor, and would rectify it. Wasserman heard the critics—they were numerous—but he never wavered in his support of Sheinberg.

For his part, Sheinberg seemed to revere Wasserman, and he certainly understood why people might view him in a different light.

"There is only one Lew Wasserman," Sheinberg would sometimes comment, with a trace of ruefulness. He also said, "Anyone who tries to measure up to him is destined to failure—as I, for one, can certainly tell you." He suggested that there was a reservoir of deep affection beneath the cool, businesslike surface of their relationship, and he referred to Wasserman on more than one occasion as his "surrogate father." Still, Sheinberg had considerable ego, and—as he *was* president, after all—he wanted to come into his own. Ziontz, who dealt a great deal with both men through the seventies and eighties, recalled that Sheinberg was extremely deferential to Wasserman in his early years as president. He tried so hard to emulate Wasserman that he went for several years without taking a single vacation. But, little by little, he began to assert himself. "My reporting lines were always to Lew," Ziontz said. "With Lew, knowledge was power, and you would never run the risk that Lew would find out from a third party something that he could have found out from you sooner. But now Sid wanted me to report to him as well." This posed a dilemma for Ziontz. On one occasion, he recalled, he had phoned Wasserman with important news about an acquisition they were attempting, and was relieved to find that Wasserman and Sheinberg were having lunch together in the commissary, as they did most days. Great! he thought. And when Wasserman picked up the phone at his table, he delivered the news, and—hearing Sheinberg's voice in the background—was satisfied that he had met his dual obligation. But when he returned to his office, he received a call from Sheinberg, who upbraided him at length for not having communicated with him directly.

Naturally, Wasserman gave no public hint of any jealous retention of power. "Sid runs the company; the only time he will discuss an idea with me is if he wants my opinion," Wasserman pointedly told reporter Geraldine Fabrikant of the *New York Times* in October 1985. But the fact that he never ceded the title of chief executive officer—Sheinberg remained, always, chief operating officer—revealed Wasserman's unwillingness to relinquish control, and the tensions, however subliminal, that must have existed between the two men. And the titles reflected the reality at MCA; Sheinberg might have the operating responsibility, day to day, but when it came to any major strategic move, Wasserman had the decisive vote. "Sid seemed always so agitated and so frustrated for a guy who was one of the biggest in the business," Michael Fuchs said. "Lew kept him down. Sid was the chained dog, Lew, the emperor, in the background behind those big glasses—every bit as nasty as Sid, but you didn't see it."

By the mid-eighties, though, Sheinberg began to exercise his operating powers more ambitiously. He changed the way divisions accounted for their profits, so that each one had a clear bottom line (before, their profits were sometimes intermingled, and only Wasserman could penetrate the corporate thicket). He hired several new division heads— among them, Tom Pollock, the lawyer whose deal papers had so enraged Wasserman that he'd hurled them across his office. Pollock was to run the Universal studio, and he said later that he believed that his job, among other things, was "to bring the film division into the modern world from an economic standpoint. Which meant, you attract the film-makers to make the movies—and if you have to make unusual deals, you do." (Even after he joined the company, Pollock said, Wasserman and he never discussed the *Raiders* deal. "I mean, why would I want to have *that* conversation with Lew?") During the next few years, Pollock brought Ron Howard, Brian Grazer, Martin Scorsese, and Ivan Reitman to Universal. And Sheinberg made a very public, pronounced change in the company's approach to acquisitions. In February 1987, he told Fabrikant in the *New York Times,* "Our view of acquisitions was not necessarily a proper one. I think we recognize that the price of passing on all deals is that history is likely to pass you by. In a sense, I think the world around us changed." MCA acquired WOR-TV, a New York area independent television station; a toymaker, LJN Toys; and a 50 percent stake in Cineplex Odeon Corporation, a Canadian theater chain with many theaters in the U.S.

However, its most aggressive acquisition by far was in the music business. MCA Records historically had been a weak division, but it became profitable in the mid-eighties under the leadership of Irving

Azoff—though it was also plagued by scandal in a mob-related investigation by the U.S. Attorney's Office in Los Angeles. In 1989, Azoff resigned. And in early 1990, Sheinberg was negotiating with his friend David Geffen, the legendary music producer, to acquire Geffen Records. The terms were set, Geffen recalled, and he was meeting with Wasserman and Sheinberg at the offices of MCA's lawyers, Rosenfeld, Meyer & Susman. Now, all of a sudden, Geffen continued, "there were seventeen new things we had never discussed before. Lew screamed and got up and walked around, like he was going to leave the room. My lawyer was going through the roof. I said to Lew, 'Let me understand this. Every one of these points is take it or leave it?' He said yes.

"I went out to the corridor. I said to my chief financial officer, what does it mean in terms of dollars? He said he thought, at the most, $1 million. I went back in. I said to Lew, 'Every single one of these is important to you?'

" 'Every single one.'

" 'And if I say yes, we've got a deal?'

" 'Yes.'

" 'Okay. I say yes.' "

In March 1990, MCA acquired Geffen Records, for 10 million shares of MCA stock, valued at the time at about $545 million. Geffen was willing to do a deal for stock, not cash, because he was convinced that the status quo at MCA would not be maintained for long. In the meantime, Geffen said, he felt comfortable being with MCA. "I thought, I'll be safe here—Lew and Sid would not do anything dishonest. That company was run honestly and decently." Pleased as he was with the deal, he was convinced that if he had not made every concession at the very end, it would never have happened—and that Wasserman's performance that day was emblematic. Pointing to all MCA's abortive deals, Geffen said, "Sid wanted to make acquisitions, but he had to go to dad. And Lew was stuck in time. If you buy all of Decca-Universal, with some 400 acres, for $11 million, how do you buy anything else? Lew could say he didn't do these deals out of loyalty to Sid—but he didn't let Sid be CEO. I think he didn't do them because of his unwillingness to be wrong. As long as he didn't do these things, he wouldn't be wrong."

Now, MCA had done a major deal, finally—but that still did not resolve the existential questions hovering about the company. Geffen was hardly alone in his assessment that change at MCA was overdue. The market's view had been illustrated quite dramatically in June 1987, when Wasserman was hospitalized for colon surgery—and the stock rose from $48 a share to more than $60 on the speculation that he might die or be forced to retire. (Though it did not become public at the time, Wasserman nearly did die; a nurse inserted a thermometer in his mouth when he was groggy, and he bit down so hard that he broke it, ingesting shards of glass.) Several corporate raiders were rumored then to be buying the stock—among them, Ronald Perelman, who had accomplished his hostile takeover of Revlon with the help of Milken's financing; Nelson Peltz, another Milken protégé, who had taken over Triangle Industries; and Denver oilman Marvin Davis, former owner of Twentieth Century-Fox. Even after Wasserman had recovered and returned to work, heavy trading in MCA's stock continued, causing some observers to predict that a battle for control was inevitable. In *U.S. News & World Report* in September 1987, Harold Vogel, entertainment analyst for Merrill Lynch, predicted that skirmishes over control of MCA would continue until some major change occurred. He also remarked that if Wasserman wanted to avoid MCA's being taken over by a raider (who would find it more profitable to break it up than keep it whole), he might "place it in long-term hands the same way Leonard Goldenson did when he merged ABC with Capital Cities."

For Wasserman, the idea of MCA being raided was anathema. MCA had adopted the usual takeover defenses; but even after that, MCA stock rose another 13 percent. Over the next couple of years, however, the takeover mania cooled somewhat; Milken, its preeminent financier, went off to jail, the over-leveraged acquisitions he and others had backed began to take their toll, and the poor economic climate made it more difficult to finance transactions of size. So the threat of a hostile takeover of MCA was not as serious for the moment; but it would probably become so again upon Wasserman's death. Wasserman continued to explore his options. One prospective partner with whom he had discussions was Capital Cities/ABC. And in the summer of 1990, he had merger talks with the company that had been MCA's longtime ally and partner, Gulf & Western, now renamed Paramount Communications. Paramount was a recently spurned suitor, having tried and failed to break up the Time Warner merger and win Time, Inc., the year before—and it was eagerly on the rebound.

Paramount's CEO was Martin Davis, who had succeeded Bluhdorn after he died in 1983. Davis had joined Paramount as a publicity man in 1958, and Eddie Weisl had shepherded his rise. Weisl had introduced Davis to Wasserman; Davis recalled accompanying Weisl to late-night, high-stakes poker games in Los Angeles with Wasserman, prominent attorney Martin Gang, and tax expert Sylvan Oestreicher—all so numerically inclined that Davis could not hope to compete. "They gave me a pad, and my job was to keep score," Davis said. By the time Davis and Wasserman began their merger talks, they had been friendly for decades; that long familiarity, in Davis's view, made it easier for the two of them to forge an agreement for a stock-for-stock merger of the two companies. "I had an understanding with Lew," Davis said. "We would share MCA and Paramount. There was no documentation of these talks, because we were afraid of antitrust. But the plan was that I would have dropped the Paramount studio. And we would use the construct of CIC as the model for the domestic entity." They were to be co-CEOs, Davis said, which suited him—"I felt I could only learn from Lew." They were ready to bring in the teams of investment bankers and lawyers. "But then—it wasn't just the eleventh hour, but *after* the eleventh hour—Lew said that he would be chairman of the executive committee, and Sidney [Sheinberg] and I would be sharing power, under him, as co-CEOs. He thought it was so late that I would just agree. But I knew it was a way to get me in there and then slice my head off. I would have been gone in six months.

"Lew had awesome power," Davis continued. "He'd draw this cloak of superiority around him and you'd bow to him—I don't know if out of respect or fear, it's hard to draw a line between the two." Reflecting on the merger agreement that he thought he had with Wasserman, Davis added, "You think you're close, but that was because he was one of the great manipulators of all time. We were all his toys."

———

While Wasserman was negotiating with Davis in 1990, he knew that there was an interested suitor in the wings—the Matsushita Electric Industrial Company, one of the world's largest consumer electronics manufacturers. Like its sometime rival Sony, which had acquired Columbia Pictures a year before, Matsushita was interested in making a "software" (film, television, and music) acquisition to complement its consumer electronic "hardware" products. To that end, Matsushita had engaged Michael Ovitz, the agent, to initiate its executives in the mysteries of Hollywood and to broker a suitable match. Considering Ovitz's longtime fixation on Wasserman and MCA, it was not surprising that he would steer his Japanese clients in its direction. What was surprising, though, was that Wasserman, industry leader, would seriously consider selling his company to a foreign owner. It was a highly sensitive issue; five of the seven major Hollywood studios had been sold or merged into larger companies in the last several years, and four of the new owners had come from abroad. And as it had become increasingly clear that Japanese companies were prospecting in the entertainment industry, the conventional wisdom in Hollywood was that Wasserman, of all people, would never sell to the Japanese—because he saw the industry as a national asset, whose control and profits, especially at a time of declining United States competitiveness, ought not to be surrendered to foreign hands. Indeed, it may well have been Wasserman's discomfort on this score that encouraged him, rather, to seek the deal with Paramount. But when that foundered—once again, apparently, on the issue of Sheinberg's role—the path was cleared for Matsushita.

It was so fitting and ironic that it was Ovitz who was attempting to engineer the acquisition of MCA that it seemed almost a literary conceit. Ovitz had sought to create his agency, CAA, in the likeness of the old MCA. He had built a highly disciplined, intensely motivated work-force, young agents who were imbued with a sense of larger purpose, and who tended to worship their leader. He enforced a rigid dress code of somber suits, and forbade his agents to speak to the press. For many years, he had kept a very low profile in the press himself. He was intensely secretive. He planned long-range, and he planned big; in 1975, when he was starting his small breakaway from William Morris, he told the New York literary agent Morton Janklow, "I'm going to build the biggest agency the world has ever known in ten years." By the mid-eighties, right on schedule, CAA had emerged as the dominant Hollywood agency. Ovitz commissioned I. M. Pei to design its headquarters—a landmark with a domed exterior and a soaring atrium—in the center of Beverly Hills (a building as overstated for what it housed as Jules Stein's "White House" had been fifty years earlier). With a stable of about six hundred clients, including many of the most sought-after actors, actresses, writers, and directors, CAA had established considerable dominance. It controlled much of the best story material. It packaged these elements, in all-or-nothing deals, for movies as well as for television projects. And, since it controlled so much of the product, its agents were able to demand record-breaking contracts from the buyers—the networks and the studios. For Wasserman, it was like watching a rerun. Except that now, he was the aging studio head, and Ovitz the agent who was driving the deals that diminished Wasserman's profits, and his control.

Wasserman, of course, had made it up as he went along, building on the foundation established by Stein. There was no mistaking now that Wasserman was the original, and Ovitz the knockoff. Indeed, there was an almost cartoonish quality to Ovitz as he mimicked Wasserman's ruthlessness (according to the screenwriter Joe Eszterhas, when he told Ovitz he wanted to leave CAA, Ovitz said, "My foot soldiers who go up and down Wilshire Boulevard each day will blow your brains out"). Still, Ovitz had followed the blueprint and, thus far, achieved quite remarkable success. The next step was to transcend his role as a talent agent, as Wasserman had done many years before. Ovitz had begun to do that by operating as a corporate deal-maker; Sony had hired him as its Hollywood consultant when it made its acquisition of Columbia Pictures. He was quite focused, though, on moving from the agency business into production—like Wasserman. And Sony had ultimately given him the chance to do this, offering him the job of running Columbia Pictures. But Ovitz had found that insufficient. He had wanted to run not only Columbia Pictures, but Sony's record division, too—and with a corporate structure that would have given him near autonomy. Sony had rejected his counterproposal.

Now, with Matsushita, Ovitz had the chance to achieve what he had not with Sony. He had tried, for example, to lead Sony to MCA. Other Sony advisers argued that MCA had been living on its legend in the last fifteen years or so—having not only missed opportunities in cable but, also, having blundered badly with its recently acquired toy unit, LJN, and its interest in the Cineplex Odeon theater chain—and that its value was not nearly the roughly $8 billion that Wasserman and its board thought it was. Ovitz, though, had been adamant. "Mike was in love with MCA," one of the advisers recalled. "He said, 'You have got to be able to see the potential. It has this great film library. It has mystique and magic. Wasserman is like royalty in Los Angeles—you don't understand what that kind of clout and prestige is worth. And you can resuscitate the company." Ovitz, in any event, had not prevailed—in part because he had just been one member of a team. Now he persuaded Matsushita that he alone should guide them through the treacherous shoals of Hollywood. He tutored the Matsushita executives, and led them successfully to the selection of MCA. And he persuaded them that they should invest him with the powers to hire the team of lawyers, investment bankers, and public relations specialists to represent the company in this transaction; and—most important—that Matsushita should communicate with MCA, and MCA with Matsushita, through him. Finally—though the stated premise of the deal was that MCA management should remain in place—there was certainly the possibility (amply foreshadowed) that Ovitz might end up running MCA. That he might, in effect, *become* Wasserman.

From the start, Ovitz set out to make Sheinberg his ally; he wanted to transform the perennial deal-breaker into this deal's crucial facilitator. He first began talking to Sheinberg in early 1990 about the possibility of his having a buyer for MCA, and he continued to court him attentively in the following months. "At the beginning, Michael wanted to know whether it would be possible to make a deal, what would be important, how we would go about it," Sheinberg said. "He indicated that he was representing a Japanese company, but he did not name it." Sheinberg added that from the start he had believed it to be Matsushita. "I told him I thought a deal was possible, assuming it was one we believed was in the best interests of the employees and the shareholders. I felt that a straightforward approach was the best one, that it was really not mysterious. He said, 'But I want to be sure that I do the right thing.' He wanted, I think, to be sure he didn't turn left when he should have turned right—especially with regard to Lew Wasserman."

Sheinberg said that the Time Warner merger in 1989—which had created a behemoth, the world's largest media entertainment company—had had a strong impact on both Wasserman and him. They had become more convinced than ever that MCA needed greater size and more financial power in the increasingly agglomerated and global world of media entertainment companies. Sheinberg did not mention any more personal concern; but he certainly knew that if Wasserman died, the company would likely be put into play, and he would not survive. Matsushita seemed to be offering the best possible outcome for Sheinberg; he would both be cashed out of his substantial stock position and—if the Matsushita executives meant what they said—assured of continuing to run MCA. Moreover, Ovitz had emphasized to Sheinberg from the start that Matsushita not only wanted management to remain in place but that the managers would retain their autonomy—far more autonomy than if they were acquired by another American company, or even a European one. Matsushita's ignorance about the business would, in effect, be a blessing.

Several people who had conversations with Wasserman in this period said that his worry about the weakened economy also contributed to his willingness to seriously contemplate selling the company. Like Jules Stein in the seventies, Wasserman was grimly pessimistic. "Lew vividly recalled the Depression, and he *really* believed that it was coming," said Kerry McCluggage, recalling lunchtime conversations with Wasserman in 1989 and 1990, when McCluggage was head of Universal TV. Wasserman's apprehension about a depression exacerbated his sense of the company's vulnerability. "He was very worried about the legacy of the company that he had built with Jules Stein. He was convinced that it needed to be a nine-hundred-pound gorilla—and it was only a four-hundred-pound gorilla."

It was not until late August 1990 that Ovitz made his formal approach. He called Felix Rohatyn, of Lazard Frères, to express Matsushita's interest in MCA. Rohatyn had been MCA's investment banker and a member of its board since the mid-seventies. When MCA had made its bid for SeaWorld, Rohatyn had been representing the marine park company—and Wasserman decided he should hire the banker who had handed him one of his biggest losses. Over the next couple of weeks, Ovitz had a number of meetings with Sheinberg and Wasserman, at which he evaded any mention of what Matsushita might be willing to pay.

Finally, on September 19, at a meeting with Rohatyn and Sheinberg at Lazard Frères, Ovitz said that Matsushita was contemplating a price somewhere between $75 and $90 per share, and MCA decided to go forward. The stock was then trading at only $36 a share—the market had plunged after Saddam Hussein invaded Kuwait on August 2—but Rohatyn had warned Ovitz in their initial conversation that MCA would not negotiate on the basis of the present, weakened market values.

Perhaps thanks to Ovitz's mania for secrecy, no hint of the transaction had yet become public. But on September 25, a story in the *Wall Street Journal* by Laura Landro and Richard Turner reported the crucial elements of the negotiations—including a price ranging from $80 to $90 a share—and cited as its source "individuals with knowledge of the talks." Over the ensuing months, the identity of the primary source for this story was a point of sharp interest among the participants in the deal. One magazine story in February 1991, which adhered in most respects to the chronology of the transaction provided to the press by CAA's publicist, Stephen Rivers, strongly implied that David Geffen was the source—since Geffen, loquacious with the press, owned 10 million shares of MCA stock and stood to profit mightily from the sale. However, a widely held view among many of the people involved in the deal was that it was Ovitz who had engineered the leak.

One could see why he might have done so, for the leak increased the likelihood that the deal would be made. Ovitz had seen how Sony had deliberated in a distinctly Japanese fashion before deciding to go ahead with the Columbia acquisition; ten months elapsed between Sony's first conversations with Columbia executives and the consummation of the deal. Wasserman and Sheinberg, Ovitz knew, would never tolerate such a wait. And in mid-September, there was reportedly still discord in the upper levels of Matsushita's management about whether to proceed with this bold move into alien territory. A participant said that Matsushita was greatly upset by the leak, because the executives felt that "it made it sound as though things were so much farther ahead than they really were." One of the leak's benefits, then, was to remove any illusion of open-endedness from the process, and to insure that there would be constant pressure on Matsushita to act.

Probably most significant, though, the leak also put pressure on Wasserman.

He had seemed in the last year or so, especially, to be signaling a greater readiness to make a deal, but his ability to walk away from one was never in doubt. He had always done it before. Once the story had leaked, however, MCA's stock price ran up from $36 a share to $61, and Wasserman was well aware that if the deal fell through the price would sink back into the low 30s, perhaps even into the 20s. That would likely prompt an attack from a raider, shareholder suits—and it would mean that the responsibility for his shareholders' loss would be his. Many believed that Wasserman's often expressed concern for his shareholders was not platitudinous but real—a carryover, perhaps, from when the company had been closely held. Several people involved in the deal speculated that Ovitz, who had studied Wasserman for years, had made an astute calculation. One said, "He figured that the best way to insure against Lew's walking away was to put him in a moral dilemma—to make the decision to do it so invidious to his share-holders that it would be very difficult for him."

The leak had other, corollary benefits. It served as a political barom-eter. The Sony-Columbia deal had triggered criticism in Washington that had resulted in congressional hearings. Now MCA's lobbyists could begin massaging any potentially troublesome members of Congress, so that by the time the deal was concluded there would be no real opposi-tion. It also allowed the Matsushita executives to gauge U.S. public opinion, something to which they were very sensitive. As the *Yomiuri Shimbun* reported on October 6, "A manager of the Ministry of Inter-national Trade and Industry (MITI) said, 'At present the reaction in the American press is fifty per cent favorable, thirty per cent neutral, and twenty per cent adverse.' . . . The release of information before the agreement has . . . been a blessing." And, finally, the price range that was reported in the *Wall Street Journal*—from $80 to $90 a share—was high enough that it would probably discourage other bidders.

Ovitz's team denied responsibility for the leak. They pointed out that it could well have damaged them, in that it would predictably drive the stock price up and, also, would be so traumatic for Mat-sushita that the company might have backed away from the deal. It ap-parently was traumatic; the *Mainichi Shimbun* quoted one Matsushita executive as saying that news coming out during negotiations was like "being suddenly caught putting on makeup backstage." However, after a couple of days of damage control, one person in the deal said, Ovitz persuaded the top Matsushita executives to proceed. He was remark-ably well positioned to do that, inasmuch as he had been in a meeting with the senior Matsushita executives in Japan when the faxes of the *Wall Street Journal* story were handed to them.

From the early days of the negotiations, MCA executives and their advisers found Ovitz's centrality peculiar. His role—that of a kind of *über*-consultant who was commanding the deal team of investment bankers and lawyers—was one they had never encountered before. Even stranger, they thought, was the nonappearance of his client. One person involved in the deal recalls asking Sheinberg, only half in jest, "Sid, does he really represent these people?" And Felix Rohatyn, recalling a Matsushita request—through Ovitz—for confidential information, said he had told Sheinberg, "You've got to look these people in the eye. You can't give them any information without even seeing who they are." But that was exactly what was happening. MCA's investment bankers compiled information and turned it over to Ovitz, who gave it to Matsushita. An MCA executive recalled a discussion with his colleagues in which they were struggling to understand the plot they were all involved in. "I said, 'Ovitz is in the middle. All we know about what they are saying is what he tells us, and all they know about what we are saying is what he tells them—and he may be telling both of us things that the other has never said.' "

For Ovitz, the matchmaker, there was an advantage in keeping the parties apart that went beyond the control of information. Had the Matsushita and MCA executives met and talked to one another at length, they would surely have realized that they were separated by a cultural gulf that dwarfed the one that existed between Sony and Columbia. Sony, which was founded after the Second World War and based in Tokyo, was the most cosmopolitan and Western of all Japanese companies. Nonetheless, it only gradually ventured into the world of American entertainment—participating in an extremely lucrative joint venture with CBS Records for nearly twenty years before buying that company in 1987, and then, in 1989, acquiring Columbia Pictures. Matsushita, based not in Tokyo but in the more hidebound, old-money city of Osaka, was a conservative company, steeped in the philosophy of its legendary founder, Konosuke Matsushita, who is worshipped by Japanese workers as "the god of business management." He started the company in 1918, and eventually became messianic about his goal: providing as many electric fans, light bulbs, radios, and other household appliances as possible at as low a price as possible, not only to make a profit but also to achieve a social good. Konosuke Matsushita's philosophy has since been codified into a company creed and in the Seven Spirits of Matsushita, which are generally recited at morning assemblies, and "spiritual training" (a study of that philosophy) is a part of the corporate regimen. While Sony put a heavy premium on creativity and cultivated an environment that encourages a degree of outspokenness unusual in a Japanese company, Matsushita favored homogeneity, and its executives were known for their modesty. ("The higher you climb in the hierarchy, the more modest you become," a middle-level Matsushita executive once told the writer James Lardner.)

Ovitz was anxious about the chemistry between the Matsushita and MCA executives—Sheinberg, in particular. An aficionado of Oriental culture, Ovitz felt that he had a rapport with his Japanese clients, and could project what their reactions to a person or situation might be. He had found certain passages in Edwin O. Reischauer's 1988 book *The Japanese Today* particularly relevant in preparing for this transaction. In one passage, Reischauer describes the difference between Western and Japanese personality types. The Japanese type is "at least superficially smooth, affable, mild, and formally correct," he writes. "Westerners seem to them by contrast a little rough, unpredictable, and immature in their frankness and ready display of emotions. In the West unpredictability in a person may be seen as amusing or spirited, but to the Japanese it is a particularly reprehensible trait." Reischauer seemed to have been writing with Sheinberg in mind. One person involved in the transaction said, "There were egos to be handled here—and there was nothing to be gained from putting them together, except for that one time. There's no rushing Matsushita Electric Industrial—no rushing a company that is that old and that rich. And there's no telling Lew and Sid how to run their company. You want to control the two sides, control how you put them together—you have to immerse them slowly in the bathwater. It's like sculpting—you need a base to work from, then you can knead and play with it. But if it is thrown together too quickly it could have an ugly face."

Some of the principals finally met on October 7, at a dinner at Wasserman's home—and even then it was not Matsushita's president, Akio Tanii, but its executive vice president, Masahiko Hirata, and its senior managing director, Keiya Toyonaga, who attended. When Ovitz introduced Hirata to Sheinberg, Sheinberg told Hirata, "You probably don't know this, but I am responsible, in part, for your VHS system's having become as successful as it did." Sheinberg was referring to the bruising battle Sony and Matsushita had fought in the late seventies over their competing videocassette recorder systems. Initially, Matsushita's VHS system, introduced after Sony's Betamax, had captured the market by underselling the Betamax. Then, with the rise of the prerecorded movie cassette, the VHS victory became self-sustaining; more video stores carried VHS cassettes than carried Betamax because there were more VHS machines on the market; and because there were more VHS cassettes available, more people bought VHS machines.

Just how Sheinberg came into this scenario was not immediately apparent, but he went on to explain. An extremely litigious person, Sheinberg had been the progenitor of a lawsuit (he often referred to it, in fact, as "my personal lawsuit") that Universal and Walt Disney Productions filed against Sony in 1976, in which they sought to block Sony's sales of the Betamax—arguing that the machines, which were used to record movies and programs from television sets, violated copyright law. Ultimately, Universal and Disney lost their battle in the United States Supreme Court in 1984. The litigation, moreover, appears to have been not only quixotic but—insofar as it was prompted by a fear that the VCR would hurt the entertainment industry— profoundly wrongheaded. (And reminiscent, too, of the moguls' fear of television—a fear that Wasserman, of course, had not shared, and which in later years he gently ridiculed.) One ancillary effect of the lawsuit was to make it more difficult for Sony to license, for prerecorded cassettes, movies from most major Hollywood studios—a handicap that had then fired Sony's desire to own software. The slowdown of Sony, Sheinberg claimed, had worked to the advantage of VHS, the late starter.

After Sheinberg finished describing at some length his inadvertent contribution to Matsushita in the hard-fought Betamax-VHS battle—a battle that had been crucial to Hirata, who was heavily involved in the development of the VHS—Hirata responded by shaking Sheinberg's hand and saying, simply, "Thank you."

About six weeks later, the parties met again, this time to negotiate their deal. They gathered with their advisers for dinner at New York's Plaza Athénée hotel, in the rococo-style restaurant, La Régence, and Wasserman rose to toast his companions and welcome the Japanese. Then, referring to the process they would all be embarking on the next morning, he declared, "We've come here to make a deal. If we do, that's fine—and if we don't, that's fine, too."

Whether he had been in the role of buyer or seller, it had always been his stance. It had, of course, provided him a psychological advantage vis-à-vis his opponent. But it had not just been tactical posturing—Wasserman had demonstrated his professed equanimity by walking away from many deals over the course of what he liked to refer to as his "long and checkered career." And doing so had become a signal trait, a kind of assertion of his preeminence—it somehow seemed demeaning to him to betray eagerness for a deal, or to return to a negotiating table, or to make a higher bid after an offer had been rejected. In the role he had painstakingly crafted for himself, he had decided that such behavior was beneath him. One of his lawyers attending this dinner said later, "For fifty-nine years, Lew Wasserman has been doing deals, and he doesn't ever show his cards. I have been in many sessions with Lew where he stands up, politely says goodbye, and the other side never sees him again." So Wasserman's words served to remind everyone at this long, formal dining table of the possibility—even the likelihood—that he might do that again.

Such an outcome seemed almost preordained when the negotiations began the next day. Two months earlier, Ovitz had spoken to Rohatyn and Sheinberg of a price range of $75 to $90. Now, he announced that Matsushita was prepared to pay $60 a share in cash, plus an equity stake worth about $3 a share in WWOR, the MCA-owned television station that was to be spun off to shareholders. (United States laws forbids majority foreign ownership of a broadcast property.) Seeking to explain the dramatic discrepancy, Ovitz pointed to changed world conditions—an increasing likelihood of war in the Persian Gulf, a weakening economy. And in private conversations with Sheinberg he swore that he had learned the amount of Matsushita's offer only an hour before he presented it, and that he had exhorted the company to offer $65 a share instead.

It was a stunning blow. Some MCA executives concluded that Ovitz had indicated his initial price range simply in order to bring Wasserman to the table. "If he had said their range was in the 60s, no meetings would ever have taken place," one executive said. In fact, there had been some indication earlier that the range Ovitz had conveyed might be wrong—but that suggestion had gone generally unheeded. In the first week of October, stories had begun to appear in the Japanese press stating that Matsushita might pay about $6 billion for the company (roughly $60 a share), while MCA was seeking a purchase price of between $7.4 and $8.5 billion (roughly between $80 and $95 a share). But the MCA executives, who were following the Japanese press, did not put much credence in these figures. "When we saw that $60 to $65 a share, we were laughing," one of them said. "We were sitting here with our calculators, multiplying the number of shares we owned by $100. But then we said, 'No, let's not be pigs—multiply by $90. Lew will never take less than $90."

It is possible that the Matsushita executives had not trusted Ovitz sufficiently to confide what they were willing to pay. For while they certainly relied on him for the human elements of the deal—and they allowed him to hire investment bankers for the transaction—they had a second, secret team of advisers working on the numbers. Someone who has advised Sony says, "The Japanese never rely on just one adviser. There are always second and third tracks." In the early summer of 1990, Hirata had engaged the mergers-and-acquisitions partnership of Nomura Wasserstein Perella, with offices in Osaka and Tokyo, to work on the deal. Matsushita "hired Nomura Wasserstein Perella as advisers because they're Japanese and the client trusts Japanese people," one person explained. "The client was coming into Hollywood blind, and therefore hired a Seeing Eye dog—Ovitz—but didn't trust him. He's a white American." Matsushita had studied the Sony transaction under a microscope, determined not to repeat its mistakes—among them, having badly overpaid for Columbia. And the Matsushita executives were leery of Ovitz when it came to price. "They realized that for him what counted was getting the deal done—that he wouldn't care what price they paid. They didn't want to look like fools." Although Japanese bankers at Nomura Wasserstein Perella were assisted by American colleagues, only the Japanese dealt with Matsushita directly. They did not attend the negotiating sessions, but they had rooms in the Waldorf-Astoria, as did the Matsushita executives, and were in close contact with them. According to one person, they counseled the Matsushita executives, "Don't be in a hurry. It's not a competitive situation. Remember who you are."

After MCA flatly rejected Matsushita's offer of $60 in cash, Matsushita came back the following day with an offer of $64 in cash, but that, too, MCA rejected. MCA was unwilling to make a counterproposal. "We were not going to name a price," Rohatyn said. "Either they were going to make a proposal or not, but we were not going to have the price end up in the *Mainichi Shimbun* as part of a deal that didn't happen." Rohatyn and the other MCA advisers did not know what Wasserman would ultimately be willing to accept; as usual, he was keeping his own counsel. By the Wednesday night before Thanksgiving—three days after the discussions began—most, if not all, of the advisers concluded that the deal was dead. Ovitz left to spend the holiday in Los Angeles. And an MCA board meeting was called for Thanksgiving, at which the advisers planned to recommend against accepting Matsushita's offer of $64 in cash.

Wasserman's old friend Bob Strauss was one of the advisers, and wearing a dizzying array of hats; an MCA board member who frequently represented the company, and who had also represented Matsushita, he had been hired here as counselor to the transaction—representing both sides. (Strauss thought his role was unprecedented, but he evidently did not know about Sidney Korshak and CIC.) Now, Wasserman and Strauss and their wives went to dinner at "21." Recalling that dinner, Strauss said, "The deal had shut down. We didn't discuss it. We discussed whether to have the chicken or the fish. Edie Wasserman drank water and Helen Strauss had three scotches, as usual. It was an evening of nostalgia and reminiscences. And then, in the car, I said, 'Well, Lew, I guess it wasn't meant to be—you can't have a damn stroke over losing a deal.' He said, 'You're right. The only thing that troubles me—we can't eat any better, how many more dinners at "21" can we have?—is the management, and the shareholders.' And he said, 'You have to make up your mind before you go into negotiations what the parameters are, or you get carried away with the momentum of the negotiations—you know that as well as anyone. And it's just a shame—when two or three bucks more would have done it.' "

Over the next fifteen hours, Strauss labored with Matsushita's other advisers to bring the deal back. On Thanksgiving morning, Ovitz, after talking by phone with Hirata, called Sheinberg and told him that Hirata wanted to meet with him and Wasserman, and that Matsushita would raise its offer by $2. "I said, 'Let's find a small room for this meeting,' " Sheinberg said later. "The whole process had been done in these enormous rooms, in the most abstract, inhuman way. I think one of my greatest contributions to this deal was finding a small room." When they met, Hirata said, " 'It has taken us a long time to come this short distance,' " Sheinberg continued. "We were touched by that. That convinced us that psychologically he wanted to make this deal. At that moment, there was some human connection that hadn't been there before."

About the discrepancy between Ovitz's initial statement and the final offer, Sheinberg, referring to the opening overture, said, "We did

believe it to be in the realm—it would be dishonest to say otherwise.
We did go through a period of sitting there, asking ourselves, 'Why are
we here?' " Despite such recriminations, Sheinberg had remained surprisingly calm. Ovitz had warned him that one explosion of temper
could destroy the deal, and he had evidently taken it to heart. Strauss
said, "This deal never would have been made without Sid. If being
abrasive, mercurial, and emotional are his weaknesses, they never
showed here. He was as calm, unemotional, and objective as a person
could be. He had spent a lot of time with Ovitz, and developed the confidence that Ovitz could deliver what he said he could." Rohatyn remarked that he had "never seen Sid so conciliatory."

After the two sides reached an agreement in principle on price—
Matsushita would raise its offer $2 a share, to $66 in cash, plus the eq-
uity stake in WWOR—there were myriad other issues still unresolved,
and those were fought over bitterly in the next three days. Questions
that the MCA advisers thought had already been settled were re-
opened. Even on Monday morning, an hour before the contract was
scheduled for signing, a new batch of minor issues surfaced. The signing was set for 8:00 A.M. in New York; at that moment, Matsushita's
president, Tanii, in Osaka, was to go on Japanese television. His appearance had to be put off for over an hour.

Commenting on the arduousness of the negotiation, Rohatyn said,
"This was completely contrary to their culture. The Japanese are accustomed to negotiating for two weeks, then going home for several
months, then coming back—it can take a year. Here Ovitz had pushed
them to understand that it had to be done in one week. And yet it was
clear in negotiating sessions that their party didn't have negotiating authority—they had to be calling Japan constantly. And the time change
made that difficult. So it was a combination of culture differences, language differences, time differences. Their philosophy of negotiation is
war by other means, with an open-ended time frame. Here a negotiation has a certain human element, which is much more sentimental.
People recognize that they are buying not only a business but something that involves people, and that there are emotions that can be

traumatic. You make allowances for them in the way you negotiate. But in this deal—and in deals with other Japanese companies that I've seen—the human side was not a factor. Here I never saw the side of the negotiations that I've seen in nine out of ten situations as they near the end, where people generally sit down and try to work things out. Instead, to the end we were lobbing Scuds at each other, firing Patriot missiles."

This was a deal that apparently would not have happened if Matsushita had not agreed to raise its offer by $2 a share. That $2 was not insignificant—it amounted to an additional $200 million. But the reason that the deal had hinged on it, Rohatyn emphasized, was not strictly financial; rather, the $2 had come to symbolize in the minds of the MCA executives and their advisers a broader issue—"whether we could really talk to these people or not." That was a question, of course, that might have been more reasonably answered in a period of communication and mutual assessment in the months leading up to the deal. But Ovitz, the marriage broker, had made sure that the parties were utter strangers when they made their leap of faith.

There was a hint of the magnitude of the cultural divide that MCA and Matsushita executives would be attempting to bridge in the first words that Tanii uttered publicly upon the deal's signing. While Wasserman, Sheinberg, and Hirata were offering champagne toasts to one another in New York, Tanii began his televised press conference in Osaka—a proceeding for which he had been drilled with more than a hundred prepared questions and answers. Probably the most predictable question was the one that had been asked of Akio Morita, the co-founder of Sony, when Sony acquired Columbia. Would his company be willing to produce a movie about the wartime role of the late Emperor Hirohito? Morita had said he would never interfere with such a production, though he could not guarantee that theaters in Japan would be willing to show it. However, according to an article in the *Mainichi Shimbun*, when Tanii was asked, "What would you do if MCA produces a picture in which the Emperor of Japan appears as a war criminal?" he replied, "MCA is a company with a good history and tradition, and will exercise appropriate judgment." Pressed on this and other questions about the making of films critical of Japan, Tanii was more unequivocal, according to the *Asahi Shimbun*. "Since this acquisition is itself aimed at the cooperation of two countries, I am sure that such movies will never be produced," Tanii declared. Several days later—after a flurry of articles in the United States and some expressions of concern from Congress—he issued a statement saying that Matsushita "has no intention of becoming involved in decisions regarding the subject or content of creative products at MCA." Upon reflection, he surely realized that that was not only more diplomatic but, also, true; it would be foolish to endanger the value of Matsushita's investment by overt censorship. Still, Tanii's initial, instinctive response illustrated just how radical and wild this foray into Hollywood was for the sober Matsushita.

And for Wasserman, it was quite an introduction to Tanii, whom he had never met—but who was now his boss. After the signing ceremony, Wasserman, accompanied by his wife and a group of MCA executives, headed for the MCA plane to go home. He had asked Mel Ziontz to come to New York for the signing—Ziontz had not been involved in this transaction, since MCA had been represented by its New York lawyers, but Ziontz had worked for Wasserman for about twenty years. Like many others, Ziontz was perplexed by what had happened in this odd deal, from beginning to end. Initially, he had been shocked to learn that Wasserman, whom he knew as "a super-patriot," was considering selling MCA to a Japanese company. Then, after Matsushita had made its two surprisingly low offers, and Wasserman had rejected them, he was sure the deal was dead, and that Wasserman would walk away. Ziontz was stunned that he had come back. "Lew had *never* done that," he said. Despite the fact that the price was so much lower than MCA executives had anticipated, Ziontz expected to find his old friends in a celebratory mood; most of them had, by their lights, become wealthy overnight. Instead, they were commiserating with one another. "They kept repeating that Lew had said it would be in the 80s, and *never* less than 75. How could this be? And it wasn't

about the money—they were going to get a gezillion dollars, anyway—
it was, how could he have been *had?* Could he be sick? Was it his fear
of a worldwide depression? Was it that he thought Sid wasn't up to it?
They were desperate to find the explanation," Ziontz recalled. "Their
idol had let them down."

The possibility that he could have been *had*—by the brash, upstart
talent agent who had studied how Wasserman had had his way with
people over decades—was for Wasserman's followers the most painful
possibility of all. It was also the most plausible: Wasserman had indeed
been lured by Ovitz's naming of a price range that squared with his
own thinking, and once the story leaked and the stock price shot up, he
had been placed in a very difficult position. Had he been younger, he
would surely have extricated himself, endured the plummeting stock
price, and dealt with the fallout. But he was seventy-seven years old,
and the world he had fashioned was no longer his. This notion—that
Wasserman had been outmaneuvered by Ovitz—was given some credence on the MCA plane coming back to Los Angeles, Ziontz recalled.
"No one wanted to sit next to Edie, and there was a lot of shuffling
around. I ended up in that seat. And I remember her taking off on the
subject of Ovitz—it was like he had horns and a forked tail! She was
saying he was *so deceitful.* I thought it was indiscreet. Ovitz had been
the instrumentality of the deal—and her saying these things made it
look like Lew got taken. Then Edie fell asleep. And Lew talked to me
the whole way back. I was trying to find out why he had done it, without being enough of a jerk to ask outright."

But Wasserman did not say. "All I can tell you is, he was not a guy
who was ecstatic about what he'd just done," Ziontz concluded. "He
was nostalgic, reminiscing about the old days, about all the people he'd
known, about how he had built the company."

Lew Wasserman and Sidney Sheinberg. *Steve Granitz/Retna Ltd.*

Chapter 6

LOST EMPIRE

The strange union began with some sense of foreboding in the Black Tower, and perhaps in Osaka as well. Sheinberg, who had been the most heavily courted by Ovitz, and the most susceptible to the romance of the deal, seemed hardest hit by reality—even though he had by some measures come out of it awfully well. He was contractually guaranteed to succeed Wasserman; he had received roughly $113 million (for his stock holdings, plus a signing bonus on a new five-year contract), and he was being paid a salary of $8.6 million a year. However, in March 1991, about three months after the deal's signing, he and Wasserman had traveled to Osaka, where, for the first time in their new incarnation as subordinates, they had undergone a budget review. According to one friend of Sheinberg's, the process left him convinced that Matsushita was frightened by the acquisition, and was uncertain how to proceed. Friends said, too, that he was finding his day-to-day tasks, now involving the integration of the two companies, more onerous, and that he was disturbed by the persistent press speculation that, sooner or later, Ovitz would run MCA.

Interviewed after his return from Osaka, Sheinberg was plainly troubled, and made no attempt to disguise it. He emphasized, repeatedly, that the deal had been unlike any other, and seemed mystified by the process that had taken place. "It was so odd not to meet with the principals. We didn't meet Tanii until he came and visited in January. The chairman, who is the son-in-law of the founder, we just met two weeks ago in Osaka. I don't know why people met so little. The structuring was admittedly being done by Mr. Ovitz. It was a very traumatic experience for us—it *is* a traumatic experience, and will last a long time. Because there's a lot that's unknown. Only a fool cannot recognize that. Everyone gets married thinking it's forever—and 50 percent of the time, or something like that, it doesn't work. And the lack of human contact made it more traumatic. As did their lack of understanding of the business—an understanding that can only come through human interchange." The Matsushita executives had supposedly been educated by Ovitz, Sheinberg added. "The future will show if that education was adequate."

Several times in the course of the conversation, he wondered if he was "naive," as he said those close to him were now telling him. He repeated that he was finding the transition difficult. "Someone said recently that since this deal was made, Wasserman looks younger and Sheinberg looks older," he declared ruefully.

Wasserman did appear much more sanguine than Sheinberg when he was visited in his corner office down the hall. That was to be expected—in terms of revealing what they were really thinking, the two men were polar opposites: Wasserman had long been hermetically sealed, and Sheinberg a fairly open book. But they were, too, at such diametrically different points in their careers; Sheinberg felt he still had much to prove, while Wasserman had proved all he'd needed to—he had only to put his house in order and see his company safe. He had accomplished the former. Many years before, Wasserman had acquired five million shares of MCA stock at an average price of 3 cents per share; if he had sold his stock to Matsushita for cash—for about $327 million—he would have had to pay a capital gains tax of about $110 million. Instead, Matsushita had obliged him by giving him preferred stock in exchange for his common, and had thus cured his capital gains problem; shareholder suits had been filed, challenging his special treatment, and were eventually settled. Wasserman collected dividends of $28.6 million annually at a rate of 8.75 percent. (Geffen, MCA's largest shareholder, and Sheinberg had also been offered the preferred, but both had opted for cash. "I took the after-tax results of that sale and turned it into billions of dollars," said Geffen, adding that the market boom of the nineties had offered almost infinite opportunity. "Lew and I discussed it. He saw disaster coming. He wanted a fixed return. If he had the money available, he could have made a greater fortune.") Wasserman, however, had always owned bonds, not stocks (except for MCA's). As he once remarked, "Money is too hard to make to risk losing it in the stock market."

Whether Wasserman had succeeded in securing what he still thought of as his company was far less settled. But if he was harboring doubts about the long-term viability of this union, he gave no sign. Rather, he seemed to be preoccupied with the links between this present and the past. He remarked that the night before he accepted Matsushita's offer, he had spent a great deal of time thinking about Jules Stein, and decided that Jules would have been in favor of the deal. And he was voluble on the similarities he saw between Jules and Konosuke Matsushita.

The only time in the course of this conversation that Wasserman betrayed any unease was when the subject of foreign ownership was raised. Many in Hollywood felt disillusioned by his sale to the Japanese, as he was well aware. Not surprisingly, Hollywood takes its culture quite seriously; to some, the transfer of these assets signaled the loss of a cultural patrimony. One industry executive remarked, "It's the equivalent of France selling the Louvre, even though the French can still be the curators." Asked what his thoughts were about foreign ownership of such a large portion of the American entertainment industry, Wasserman replied, tersely, "None." On being pressed, he added, "It's going to be one world—though I'm not going to live to see it." Acknowledging that it would have been inconceivable twenty years ago for this quintessentially American industry not to be American-owned, Wasserman said, with a note of resignation, "They have the money. Isn't that what we're talking about? It's impossible to have a savings rate of 14 percent in Japan and 3 percent here and for us to be competitive. If those people are going to work the way they do—students in Japan go to school forty-six weeks a year, six days a week. My grandson is always on holiday."

Over the course of the next three and a half years, the Japanese financial insuperability Wasserman was describing that day proved to be illusory; the financial bubble, inflated by the easy-money mania of the eighties, finally collapsed, plunging the country into a severe recession. Matsushita itself was beset with falling sales and internal scandals; its president, Akio Tanii, and executive vice president for financial affairs, Masahiko Hirata—the two men most responsible for the acquisition of MCA—resigned. Whether things might have gone differently if the Japanese economy had not gone into this downward spiral can only be conjectured. As it was, Wasserman and Sheinberg were forced to realize that a central premise upon which they had made the deal was flawed. Reasonably or not—but with Ovitz's encouragement—they had believed that Matsushita would be at once a passive and yet free-spending investor, a kind of corporate sugar daddy. Thus, they thought, they would be free not only to continue to run the company as they saw fit but, also, to make the acquisitions that would enable them to compete in the global media entertainment world. They wanted to make a $600 million bid for Britain's Virgin Records; while it would likely have proven unsuccessful, since Virgin went to British conglomerate Thorn EMI for $973 million, Matsushita vetoed it, according to Wasserman and Sheinberg. They wanted to build a theme park in Osaka, and their plans were curtailed. They wanted to buy a stake in a broadcast network (FCC rules prohibited majority foreign ownership). Sheinberg said that they first broached a possible deal for NBC, and then CBS—and Matsushita rejected their proposals.

They took the veto of the CBS proposal especially hard. Wasserman had long wanted to own a network; it was the kind of control, through vertical integration, that he had *almost* succeeded in establishing, in a way, when NBC had been such a captive of MCA's in the sixties. According to Leonard Goldenson, the founder of ABC, Wasserman had approached him about a merger in the early eighties—shortly after President Reagan had ordered his FCC chairman *not* to revoke the fin-syn rules. In his book, *Beating the Odds,* Goldenson wrote that he told Wasserman a merger made no sense as long as fin-syn was in place; for ABC was prohibited from syndicating its shows, while syndication was one of MCA's most profitable businesses. Nonetheless, he said, Wasserman came back several times. "There is only one reason I can think of which might have prompted Lew to seek a merger with ABC," Goldenson wrote. "He must have thought that, since he got his pal Ronald Reagan to keep the Financial Interest and Syndication Rules in effect, then he could also get him to scrap the rules when it served Wasserman's interest." And Wasserman had, of course, engaged in extensive merger negotiations with RCA, which owned NBC, in the mid-eighties. Inasmuch as Wasserman had not succeeded in making a deal with a network during this time, however, he had wanted the fin-syn rules to continue in effect. And so they had—while Bob Daly, of Warner Bros., who was representing the studios, followed his strategy of "delay, delay, delay" in settlement discussions with the networks. A decade had been bought.

By the early nineties, though, it was clear that fin-syn's days were numbered. Difficult as it had been to make the economic case that the rules should be retained in 1983, it was even harder now. When the rules were instituted in 1970, the three networks had more than 90 percent of the television viewing audience; now, cable television, independent stations, the Fox fourth network, and other video choices had reduced the three networks' audience to roughly 60 percent. In 1991, the FCC loosened the restrictions slightly; two years later, it loosened them further—and provided for the networks to enjoy complete freedom by 1995. Hollywood's independent producers were unhappy, but the real powers—the major studios—were crying crocodile tears. They no longer wanted the restrictions on the networks, because they wanted to *own* the networks. Rupert Murdoch had established the model to which others aspired, by using his network to create value for shows Fox owned. It became a gold rush. By the summer of 1995, Disney would announce its plans to acquire ABC, and Time Warner, Turner. CBS—which Wasserman had so coveted—was to be acquired by Westinghouse Electric Corp.

CBS would have been a kind of capstone for Wasserman. It was the beloved creation of Bill Paley, who had disdained him personally, and who had not wanted to play by MCA rules, and who had not bought MCA shows for a very long time—so it would be quite gratifying now to acquire a stake in that once high-handed network. More important, the television business, which Wasserman had shaped and dominated, had finally changed in ways that severely tested MCA's prowess; by the late eighties, costs were rising, and networks were holding their license fees constant. Also MCA had at long last achieved success in the lucrative half-hour comedy business; but then the president of Universal Television, Kerry McCluggage, who had brought in a stable of comedy writers, left the company for Paramount about a year after the Matsushita acquisition—and much of Universal's television talent went with him. So the television division was struggling now as it never had in its history. But owning a meaningful interest in a network, Wasserman and Sheinberg believed, would help them to revive it, and restore it to its rightful place of honor within the company. When they brought the CBS proposal to Matsushita in 1994, they felt there was an undeniable urgency. Already, in a world where the movie, television, music, and publishing businesses were being consolidated into a few giant conglomerates, they felt they had missed vital opportunities—and fallen far behind Sumner Redstone's Viacom (which had acquired Paramount Communications), Steve Ross's Time Warner, and Rupert Murdoch's News Corp.

Except that it was no longer, even figuratively, Wasserman's MCA. "It was crazy, this idea that they didn't own the company anymore and they believed they should be able to make fundamental decisions—and they were so angry when they found out they couldn't," commented

Mel Ziontz. "Only in the entertainment industry could something like this happen: you sell the company for billions of dollars, take hundreds of millions out yourself, and then you expect to be making all the decisions!"

In mid-October 1994, Wasserman and Sheinberg threw down the gauntlet to Matsushita—declaring that they would refuse to sign new five-year contracts (to take effect in 1995) unless Matsushita allowed them to wield more authority, particularly in terms of strategic acquisitions. The two sides agreed to meet to discuss the conflict. The day before the meeting, the story appeared in the press that the MCA executives were threatening to walk away from the company when their contracts expired unless they were given autonomy, and, also, that they had a powerful bargaining chip. Just the week before, Steven Spielberg, David Geffen, and former Walt Disney Studios chairman Jeffrey Katzenberg had announced that they intended to launch a new studio. There was press speculation that if Wasserman and Sheinberg left MCA, Geffen and Spielberg (who was still the engine of the Universal movie business) would go, too.

This was hardly what the conservative, regimental Matsushita executives could have envisioned when Ovitz had shepherded them to MCA about four and a half years earlier. They were said to be aghast at the public airing of what they considered to be private troubles between them and their subsidiary. And they had now had ample exposure to the man whom Ovitz had carefully shielded them from prior to their signing of the deal—and who was no longer on his best behavior. "The Japanese don't like Sid. They find him irritating," one person was quoted as saying in a *Los Angeles Times* story on October 18 with the headline, "Will Japanese Bend to Lew and Sid?" The next day, during a four-hour heated meeting held in San Francisco, the Japanese gave the answer that might have been predicted: they said they would not cede greater control to Wasserman and Sheinberg. "To hand over complete management control is contrary to established business practice," a Matsushita statement read.

About five months later, Matsushita delivered its fuller response to the MCA ultimatum. In the end of March 1995, the news broke that Matsushita was engaged in talks to sell MCA—something the Japanese had chosen not to convey to Wasserman and Sheinberg. And, it quickly developed, Matsushita was selling MCA to Seagram, the company controlled by the Bronfmans—a Canadian family that made its fortune in the liquor business in the twenties and thirties and then, in the sixties, expanded into oil and chemicals. Edgar Bronfman, Jr., a forty-two-year-old member of the family's third generation, had always been infatuated with show business. He had tried his hand at songwriting and scriptwriting instead of going to college, and had pursued these interests well into his twenties, but then in 1982 his father, Edgar Sr., had persuaded him to join the family business. It was seven years later, when his father promoted him to president and formally anointed him to be his successor as chairman, that Edgar Jr. decided he wanted to move Seagram into entertainment. He had bought a stake in Time Warner; Edgar was quite mesmerized by Steve Ross, whom he took for a kind of role model. And—inasmuch as Ross was a superlative deal-maker, who relied on his facility with numbers, his intuition about people, and his considerable charm to achieve his ends—Bronfman seemed to have tried to follow a Ross-like script in his approach to Matsushita.

It had been critical to Seagram's plan that an agreement be reached with Matsushita before an auction could take place, driving up the price. Someone involved in this transaction said that Matsushita clearly could have gotten more money for MCA, but the Japanese owners had been so traumatized by their public battles with Wasserman and Sheinberg that what they wanted was a quiet, decorous way out. Thus it was decided that Bronfman would go to Osaka to meet with the Matsushita president, Yoichi Morishita, and that he would go alone, armed only with his "winning personality," an adviser said. After about four weeks and one more secret trip to Osaka, a deal was reached. Regarding the purchase price of $5.7 billion for more than 80 percent of MCA (Matsushita kept almost 20 percent), Bronfman later remarked with a smile that seemed to belie his words, "We didn't steal the company, but we certainly succeeded in buying it below auction value."

One of Bronfman's advisers in this clandestine operation was the ubiquitous Michael Ovitz. At the time, Ovitz did not publicly acknowledge advising Bronfman on this purchase. Even Edgar Sr. was not fully aware of Ovitz's role. He said that at the meeting to close the deal he was surprised to see Ovitz take a seat on Seagram's side of the table rather than on Matsushita's side, since he knew Ovitz had advised Matsushita on their purchase of MCA. Edgar Sr. said he had asked Ovitz why he had so placed himself, and Ovitz had responded, "Come on, Edgar, you *know.*" Despite the secrecy, Wasserman and Sheinberg also figured out what Ovitz had done, and they were outraged at what they felt was his betrayal. Sheinberg stopped speaking to Ovitz, and he berated the Bronfmans for going behind their backs. Wasserman let Sheinberg vent ("Sid's emotional," he said later); he chose the dignity of the high road, uttering no reproof and accepting the Bronfmans' invitation to stay on as chairman emeritus of the company, and to join the Seagram board. But when he learned that the Bronfmans were negotiating with Ovitz to make him the new CEO of MCA—*that* goal, to be realized, after all!—Wasserman called Edgar Sr. and threatened to resign.

There was a time when such a move by Wasserman would have killed the negotiations, and when Wasserman would have found a way to make Ovitz pay even more dearly for what Sheinberg called his "treachery." That time was past. The Bronfmans did not make a deal with Ovitz—but only because he so over-reached (as he had earlier with Sony) that he doomed it himself. Ovitz was pushing for a compensation package that could have been one of the largest in American corporate history—roughly $240 million. Edgar Jr. was remarkably unfazed—perhaps recalling Steve Ross's central tenet, which was to find the right people and pay them so well that it would be impossible to lure them away. But Charles Bronfman, Edgar Jr.'s uncle, who had had deep reservations about his nephew's moving Seagram into the entertainment business, finally told him that Ovitz's price could not be met. In early June 1995, at a meeting of MCA senior executives the day after these protracted negotiations broke down, one executive recalled Edgar Jr. saying, "Frankly, Ovitz was Plan A. I don't have a Plan B."

Hardly an admission one might expect from the man who was, in effect, the Wasserman understudy, now positioned to run MCA. But Bronfman, born to great wealth, did not seem daunted by the fact that Seagram, at his behest, had spent almost $6 billion to get into the entertainment business and now had no guide to this new territory. He asked David Geffen to help him find someone to run the company while a search for a CEO was undertaken (about a year later, Frank Biondi would be hired); and Geffen suggested an old friend, Ron Meyer, Ovitz's second-in-command at CAA. Meyer—a high school dropout and former Marine whose warm geniality made him very popular in the Hollywood community—assumed Sheinberg's old post, as president and chief operating officer. Even Meyer's friends rolled their eyes at the unprepossessing agent's ascension. Meyer himself said, "I know these people looked at me like Cinderella's stepsisters looked at her." Meyer then began to select people for his team; Edgar Jr. contributed a couple of his choices, too. In the new group that emerged in MCA's top corporate ranks there was a marked preponderance of people who had either no experience in managing a giant corporation, or no experience in running any facet of the entertainment business. But whatever Bronfman and his people lacked in experience, they made up for in conviction—and contempt for the past.

Bronfman made it plain that he felt he was *not* a Wasserman understudy but, rather, a lead player in his own right. He would often refer to the deplorable state of affairs at MCA when Seagram took it over, calling it a "truly broken company." Asked whether he thought the company had fallen into that state during the Matsushita years, when MCA had been stymied in its acquisition attempts, Bronfman replied that that period is "used as a convenient excuse." He went on to say, "I don't think the Matsushita ownership materially affected what was a company in long-term decline. I think Lew fifteen years ago took the position that these businesses were not going to grow, so he was going to manage risk." And he added, pointedly, "One is an investor's perspective, one is a business-leadership perspective. You can't grow a company where managing risk is your first, second, and third priority."

Bronfman set out to demonstrate what business leadership was. He undertook a major corporate overhaul, aimed at changing everything from MCA's culture to its organizational systems to its top-level executives. A former MCA executive said, "It was their agenda to replace not only the creative people—that usually happens—but the infrastructure, the institutional memory of the company: legal, pension, human relations, accounting. . . . They felt everyone had to go, because everyone was tainted with this disease. The disease was the way Lew did it." Bronfman seemed, in fact, to want to replace the way Lew had done it not so much with his original imprint, but with the way Steve Ross had—showering his people with gifts and money, creating a talent-friendly environment, and carrying it all out with great style. Meyer was no Steve Ross, but he was outgoing and likable, and he had Seagram's resources at his disposal. He spent millions to change Universal's stern public face into a smiling one, extending lavish deals to many producers, directors, and actors. "As a young agent, I found this a very intimidating environment," Meyer declared. Brian Grazer, who with Ron Howard runs Imagine Entertainment, Universal's major movie supplier, and who worked with both regimes, confirmed this. "Under Sid and Tom"—that is, Sheinberg and Pollock—"the culture was about fear. You'd want to be successful because you feared them so much," Grazer said. "One wants to succeed for Edgar and Ron Meyer because they give you love."

To Bronfman, Meyer, and their colleagues, the very architecture of the Universal lot embodied all that was wrong with the old MCA culture—uncaring, rigid, fearsome—and the Black Tower was its ultimate symbol. Bronfman banished the Jules Stein antiques and had the offices redone in a muted, California-contemporary decor. Shortly after buying the company, Bronfman had decided to change its name to "Universal." And he ordered the "MCA" that had been engraved on the elevator floor plates expunged. Apparently eager to erect his own landmark—much as his grandfather Sam Bronfman had had Ludwig Mies van der Rohe design the Seagram Building in New York City—Bronfman chose the Dutch architect Rem Koolhaas to design Univer-

Lew Wasserman and Edgar Bronfman, Jr., in 1996. *Ron Galella/Gamma Presse*

sal's new corporate headquarters as part of its planned expansion. One person close to the Universal team said that an aspect of Koolhaas's assignment was to deal with the tower: "How do you flatten that building, without, maybe, having to do it literally?" It was not surprising then—considering Bronfman's almost reflexive impulse to denigrate his predecessors, while at the same time making a show of deference—that to celebrate the anniversary of Wasserman's sixtieth year at the company, in 1996, Bronfman named the tower the Lew R. Wasserman Building.

It may well be that the more difficult Bronfman found his job (and the worse his reviews became), the more compelled he was to belittle his predecessors; it was their fault, he was saying, that he could find no quick fix to the company's problems. But his wholesale indictment, while it had elements of truth, was insupportable. It was simply not so, for example, that MCA was a "truly broken company" when it had come into Bronfman's hands. It had solid core assets—in music, in movie and television production, in recreation, in publishing—which needed to be galvanized. It had been churning out steady, if somewhat flat, earnings through the early nineties, and in 1995, the year of the Seagram acquisition, the music and recreation divisions were especially strong. In fact, television was the only Universal division that was losing money and probably deserved to be called "broken"—yet another painful irony for Wasserman, in a season full of them. Bronfman had tried to bring Universal TV into the comedy business by making a deal with Brillstein-Grey Entertainment, the TV production company; but he had paid $75 million for something that by many estimates was worth only a fraction of that—and that seemed unlikely to resuscitate the TV business in any event. So in October 1997, about two and a half years after taking over the company, Bronfman decided to make a bold move. It had become his pattern: faced with a crisis or a challenge, he would reach for a high-profile (if dubious) deal as a remedy. Now—tired of trying to find a cure for this ailing TV business, which he didn't like anyway—he sold it.

It was a startling and unprecedented transaction: Universal sold most of its cable and domestic television assets, including the USA cable network, a pay TV programming service, to Barry Diller's HSN, Inc., which would be renamed USA Networks. The deal did give Universal a stake in the company—and the possibility of regaining control of its assets in the future, though Diller said, at the time, that that day might be thirty years away. Diller, meanwhile, won a remarkable prize—USA had one of the five biggest cable network subscriber bases in the country. One entertainment executive said, "This is a great deal for Barry. How could he have got access to 73 million homes? It could have taken him the rest of his career." Bronfman admired Diller intensely; Diller had been his friend and mentor since the two first met in the mid-seventies, when Diller was an executive at Paramount and Bronfman was a twenty-year-old youth, looking for a toehold in Hollywood. So it was not surprising, in a way, that Bronfman would decide to bet on Diller to make more of the business than he could have himself. Still, it seemed so inescapably lopsided—as though Bronfman had amputated a limb, while Diller had vastly extended his reach. It was plain, though, that Bronfman did not see it that way, and that he had expected accolades for the deal he and Diller had cooked up together. As Bronfman said, "It breaks the paradigm, it's out of the box, it's innovative, no one's ever done it before."

In Hollywood, however, there was a popular view that the reason no one had ever done it before was not an earlier lack of ingenuity. Universal was now the only major studio with almost no domestic television operation of its own. One studio head commented, "It is not pure happenstance that all majors are in both the motion picture and the TV production businesses. There is a reason. It has evolved over the past fifty years. After all, TV and motion pictures are similar creative processes at heart, and the distribution is intermeshed." Perhaps Bronfman's worst sin in the eyes of Hollywood, though, was that he had been taken in a deal (just how badly taken would be illustrated three years later, when Diller's USA would essentially get $11.7 billion of value in return for assets it bought for $4.1 billion). And it was not the first time Bronfman had been bested since he took over MCA from the

man who, according to legend, *never* was. Indeed, while Hollywood
denizens chortled at Edgar Jr.'s combination of arrogance and pratfalls,
the more sober question they asked one another was whether Wasserman had really miscalculated and lost control, as it seemed, or whether
he had executed some grand, quintessentially inscrutable design, in
what was actually his deal of all deals. In a piece in the *Los Angeles
Times Magazine* in May 1995, after the Seagram acquisition, Frank
Rose reviewed what had happened since Wasserman had decided to
make the Matsushita deal, and asked: "Would Wasserman really make
a deal to sell the company and come away with less than he wanted?"
For the answer, Rose quoted "an old Hollywood hand" who told him,
"Put your money on Wasserman. Not Sheinberg, Wasserman. Wasserman is brilliant. And he never loses."

The Wasserman mystique died hard. The defining characteristics of the
persona he had created were that he never lost in a deal, never made a
mistake, could see around corners into tomorrow, and that his reach,
from the underworld to the White House, gave him a matchless control. But Wasserman lived so long that he outlasted his myth. It was
hard to see in the Wasserman of the Seagram era the monumental, intimidating figure he had been. Shorn of his corporate power, deprived
of the work that had consumed him and lent meaning to his life, his
long stride painfully hobbled by age's infirmities, Wasserman seemed
remarkably life-size—eager for company, nostalgic, vulnerable.

While the company he had built was being overhauled and dis-
membered, Wasserman stuck stubbornly to his routine: leaving the
house for Universal every day at 8:15, working on the approximately
$2 billion in trusts that he was managing (including five Jules Stein
trusts), generally eating lunch at his table in the commissary. He
eschewed the extensive redecoration being done in the rest of the building; his corner office, alone, was still furnished with Stein's antiques—
even Stein's desk, which Doris Stein had offered to Wasserman after
Jules died. Sometimes he would complain wryly to visitors about the

fact that even though he had a contract as a consultant, his advice was never sought; or about the silliness of building a bathroom for every executive office; or the pettiness of removing "MCA" from the elevator floor plate. Some friends felt it was unseemly for Wasserman to remain while his world was taken apart, piece by piece, all around him. Sheinberg had started an independent production company, financed by a generous deal from Seagram (facilitated by Spielberg). He had brought his two sons into the company, and taken office space in a building in Beverly Hills. He tried to persuade Wasserman to join him there. Sheinberg argued that Wasserman, by remaining at Universal— and not publicly criticizing the Bronfman regime—was lending legitimacy to the damage that was being done to the company, and was letting his former employees down. (Sheinberg, for his part, was characteristically unrestrained, referring to Bronfman's firing of MCA executives as "ethnic cleansing.") Wasserman bought a building in Beverly Hills for his grandson Casey, and he acknowledged that he could, obviously, have his office there. But the truth, evidently, was that he *had* to be here. "They named the building for me, how can I leave?" he said with a slight smile.

His secretary of many years, Melody Sherwood, now found him far more approachable. He would often regale her with the stories he'd long loved to tell, but which she had never before heard firsthand. One of his stories bore an uncanny similarity to the one Jules Stein had recounted: of his having been summoned to Bette Davis's home, finding her in bed, being certain it was an invitation, but, as Stein put it, leaving the way he came. Except that in Wasserman's version, it was *he* who was summoned to *Joan Crawford's* home, and found *her* in bed— but had not responded to her implicit invitation. Since Sherwood had not known the story Stein had told many years earlier, she had no reason to wonder about the veracity of Wasserman's at the time. Sherwood loved his stories, which he told and retold; and she was so emboldened by his talkativeness that she tried to draw him out in less programmed ways. Since she had started working for him, she had been curious about what lay beneath the implacable facade. "In my

conversations with him, I was always trying to find out how he *felt*,"
Sherwood said. "One day, I said to him, 'Everyone in the industry
wants to be you. Who would you want to be?' And, without a moment's hesitation, he said, 'Clark Gable.' "

She was momentarily speechless. It was hardly what one might have
anticipated—that Wasserman, in his private fantasy, was as starstruck
as the masses of fans, and wished he could have been the devastatingly
handsome, dashing Gable? "Then," Sherwood continued, "I said, 'If
you weren't married' (because I knew he would only approach it that
way), 'what star would you have wanted?' And, again without a moment's hesitation, he said, 'Bette Davis.' I thought, well, she was a very
strong, opinionated woman, just like Mrs. W."—that is, Edie Wasserman. "I thought he really was crazy about Mrs. W., and I told her later
that I took what he said about Bette Davis as a great compliment to
her."

Wasserman had time now for the preoccupations of ordinary life—
family, in particular. Friends had long disagreed about what happiness
Wasserman derived from his marriage. Certainly, the marriage had endured. In a *Vanity Fair* piece in 1996, writer Dominick Dunne wrote
that they were "unmistakably a couple, and a devoted one at that, although in her amazingly forthright way [Edie] said to me, 'There were
some bad times between the 10th and 20th years. He never stopped
working, and I felt neglected, but we weathered it." (Edie Wasserman
did not respond to a request for an interview for this book.) There was
no debate, though, about how much Wasserman's relationship with his
grandson added to his life. It had been a delayed gratification. In 1970,
the Wassermans' daughter, Lynne, had made a second marriage, to a
stockbroker named Jack Meyrowitz (he subsequently changed his
name to Myers), of whom her parents severely disapproved. Lynne had
had a daughter, Carol, with her first husband, Ron Lief, and now, a
son, Casey, with Myers. Lynne, who has told friends that her childhood
was exceedingly difficult, broke off relations with her parents in the
seventies. According to Ned Tanen, who worked closely with Wasserman for many years, Lynne would not allow Edie to see the children

but she did occasionally drop her little girl off at a friend's house where Lew stopped to see her on his way home from work. It was during this period that Wasserman commented, in a *New West* magazine story in 1978, that "I was unfortunate not to have a son, only a daughter."

In the early eighties, though, Lynne separated from Myers, and the estrangement from her parents began to ease. Wasserman soon became a doting grandfather—fixated, in particular, on his grandson, Casey, who was then about eight years old. The two became regulars, every weekend, at Nate 'n Al's, Beverly Hills's landmark delicatessen; when Casey became a teenager, Wasserman would rearrange his schedule to attend Casey's after-school tennis matches. It was just the stuff of family life—but it caused great comment among those who knew Wasserman, because he had not lent himself to such pastimes before. Some who listened to the habitually spare Wasserman rhapsodizing about Casey over the years have wondered about such concentration on the male grandchild. What seemed plain, in any event, was that Wasserman counted himself unfortunate no longer, because he'd finally gotten a son. When Casey turned twenty-one in 1995, he changed his name to Wasserman. In a recent article in the *Los Angeles Times,* Casey described his name change as a rejection of his father, who had been convicted in a money-laundering deal, and with whom he had long had a poor relationship—and an acknowledgment of his "real" family. Wasserman made Casey, at twenty-one, president of the family's charitable foundation—which contributes primarily to education, health and welfare, and Jewish culture.

He devoted more time to his philanthropy, too. Wasserman had established a scholarship fund at the California Institute of Technology in the seventies; since then, he had continued to fund hundreds of scholarships at various colleges, including Brandeis University, New York University, and the University of California at Los Angeles. ("All because I couldn't get a scholarship to college," Wasserman said.) He and Edie gave large amounts to the $40 million Edie and Lew Wasserman Eye Research Center building, which will be the third building in the complex of the Jules Stein Eye Institute at UCLA. (The second building was named for Doris Stein; at its dedication ceremony, one Stein family friend remarked, "They're making Doris sound like Madame Curie!") For many years, Jules Stein and Wasserman had contributed to the Motion Picture & Television Fund, which supports the Country House, a retirement place in Woodland Hills for people who have worked in the film and television industry. Wasserman would often describe how Jules walked into his office one day, quite upset, and said he'd been out to the home and found the grounds in terrible condition. "Jules said, 'I've taken care of it. I'm giving them a million dollars; you'll give them a million—and we'll put it in trust for the maintenance of the grounds.' A couple years went by. We were trying to build a hospital out there, and money was tight. Finally, I walked into his office, and said, 'I've solved the problem. You're going to give $1.5 million, I'm going to give $1.5 million, and we'll build a hospital.' " When Edie Wasserman paid a visit to the home in 1978, she later told *Variety* reporter Army Archerd, "I flipped over the place." She joined its board, and raising money for it became her consuming avocation. She worked at that fund-raising, Wasserman once said, as though it meant life or death to her. Each year, she had her birthday dinner there; Wasserman said he had established a fund so that a dinner would be held in her honor at the home, on November 4, in perpetuity. Friends said that he deplored the fact that in recent years the major studios were less generous in their contributions to the fund for the home—shirking their obligation, in his view. "We all got rich off these people!" he would say, with some heat. And it was not only the Motion Picture & Television Fund that was suffering from a relative paucity in giving by contemporary Hollywood. The Walt Disney Concert Hall, Los Angeles's new performing arts center, also had trouble tapping Hollywood support in the post-Wasserman era. When Wasserman ruled this world—and mobilized its charitable giving—he was deeply rooted in the Los Angeles community; his successors, heads of the media entertainment behemoths—Sumner Redstone, Rupert Murdoch, Gerald Levin—were not.

Wasserman was ecumenical in his donations. Historically, the mo-

tion picture industry leaders had cultivated good relations with the
Catholic Church. It was useful to have the church on their side, and it
generally was. After the CSU was crushed, when Father Dunne was in
great disfavor with the Hollywood producers, his superiors had, of
course, obligingly transferred him to Arizona—and Louis B. Mayer
had been an honorary pallbearer at Archbishop Cantwell's funeral. So
it was not surprising that Wasserman, like his predecessors, would establish close relations with the archdiocese. When Pope John Paul II
visited Los Angeles in 1987, Wasserman had hosted him at the Universal Amphitheater, where he had introduced him to a crowd of thousands. He contributed generously in the nineties to the construction of
the Cathedral of Our Lady of the Angels, in downtown Los Angeles. A
good friend of Cardinal Roger Mahony's, Wasserman was the only
non-Catholic recipient of the Cardinal's Award, an honor bestowed on
those who are outstanding for their good works.

His relationship with Jewish charities—and the Jewish community
generally—had been more complicated. Wasserman certainly had
never tried to disown his Jewishness—the Steins' high-society aspirations were not his—but he resisted the conventions (the tyranny, he
seemed to feel) of organized Jewish life. He had, of course, declined to
join Hillcrest—the club that had been founded by Jews, for Jews, in the
early twenties, in reaction to the policies of other country clubs in Los
Angeles barring Jews. One might question exactly when, in Wasserman's twenty-hour days of devout purposefulness, he would have
found time to go to the club. But the reason he gave for his refusal to
join, in any event, was that it was restricted to Jews. He had persis-
tently refused the demands of many Jewish charities, though he said he
had contributed to Israel even before its founding. He had had his run-
ins with the American Jewish Committee, and the Jewish Federation
Council. Now, though, Wasserman had softened toward the Jewish bu-
reaucratic world. He gave many millions to Jewish causes such as the
United Jewish Fund, the World Jewish Congress—and, yes, the American Jewish Committee. He was a major supporter of Steven Spielberg's

Shoah Foundation, and of Charles Bronfman's Birthright Israel initiative. He also gave $1 million toward the creation of the Yitzhak Rabin Hillel Center for Jewish Life at UCLA. (This was not surprising; Wasserman had been a strong supporter of Rabin's, and of the Oslo peace accords.) The UCLA Hillel director, Rabbi Chaim Seidler-Feller, would later comment that Wasserman "was not an intensely involved Jew," but that his contributions to various Jewish causes represented a renewed commitment to this community late in life. And Wasserman even joined Hillcrest! He emphasized that he had done so only because his grandson, Casey, wanted to join and could not satisfy Hillcrest's charitable-giving requirement on his own (contributions were made through the Wasserman family foundation). Wasserman enjoyed recounting how when he had received Hillcrest's voluminous application (and financial disclosure) forms, he had written "Nuts!" across the top, and returned them. He was promptly invited to join.

Some who had been excommunicated from Wasserman's world for years found they were now welcome. Ned Tanen had told Wasserman he wanted to leave MCA in 1982, but Wasserman would not let him out of his contract; in 1984, he went to work for Paramount. He knew that by leaving he was committing the cardinal sin—but he may have thought that Wasserman would make an exception in his case, since they had a reasonably close, if tempestuous, relationship, and Wasserman had always given him a leeway he did not allow most others. Tanen recalled that when he had been badly injured in a motorcycle accident, confined to bed for weeks, "these people were *there* for me. Lew and Edie came to see me every day. Lew said, 'If you ever get on a motorcycle again, I will cancel your goddamn insurance!' Now, I don't know if that was showing affection—but that was Lew." Once Tanen left, however, "the curtain came down." He realized that he was to be no exception. "The minute you leave Lew Wasserman, it's revisionist history. It's not that you died. It's that you were never there. If he didn't need you, you didn't exist." What shook him the most, however, was that when his ex-wife (who was the mother of his children, and someone the Wassermans had known well) committed suicide, he never heard from Lew or Edie—no call, no note. After that, he considered the rupture final.

When the Seagram acquisition of MCA was announced, a *Los Angeles Times* reporter called Tanen and asked what he thought of the fact that the company had been sold without Wasserman's knowledge. "I think it's disgraceful and stupid on their part," Tanen was quoted as saying. "I certainly wouldn't have dealt in Mr. Wasserman's company without discussing it with him. . . . Obviously the Japanese have a totally different way of operating. . . . I was under the impression that they venerated their elders." A couple nights later, he was meeting a friend for dinner at Drai's, a Beverly Hills restaurant popular with the entertainment crowd. "I got there, my friend was late as usual, and I heard this *voice,* saying, 'The only goddamn man in the place! I always told him—the rest were *piss-ants!* They were all *piss-ants!*' There is Edie, across the room, saying all this at the top of her voice. A relative from Cleveland was with them, and their granddaughter. Lew was sitting with his back to me. And she came across, and pulled me over there, still carrying on. Lew stood up, and he said, 'Thank you for what you said [in the newspaper]. You never should've retired. You were the best movie executive I ever worked with.'

"I started to laugh, almost hysterically. I said, I worked for you for twenty-eight years, and you never told me once!" Tanen added that not long before he left MCA, a trade publication had compiled a list of the one hundred highest-grossing films ever. He sent Wasserman a memo with the list enclosed, saying that he thought Wasserman might be interested to see that sixteen or so of the hundred were MCA/Universal's films. "I must have had twenty people tell me he carried that damn memo around and showed it to them. But he never said a word to me— and twelve or thirteen of those movies were mine." Tanen paused, and then said, "It was very tough for him to acknowledge anyone else— especially in the movie business." In any event, after the exchange at Drai's, Tanen would sometimes go to Universal to have lunch with Wasserman.

Even in this period of relative clemency, however, some violations were not forgiven. Don Hewitt, executive producer of CBS's *60 Minutes,* had been a good friend of Wasserman's for many years. In 1984, Lowell Bergman, a highly regarded investigative reporter and *60 Minutes* producer, was working on a piece about Senator Paul Laxalt, who was chairman of the Committee for the Re-election of the President. A major figure in the piece was Wasserman's old friend Moe Dalitz; he and his business associates had been important backers of Laxalt from the early days of Laxalt's political career. About a week before the show was to air, Bergman recalled, Hewitt told him he had had dinner with Wasserman the night before and that Wasserman had insisted that Dalitz was not part of the mob—as Bergman was asserting—but, rather, had been a legitimate businessman ever since Prohibition. The piece did not air, for reasons that Bergman said were complicated, but he was upset with Hewitt for divulging the facts of a show in progress to an outsider—and one, moreover, with close ties to one of the program's subjects.

Five years later, Hewitt and Wasserman had an exchange about another upcoming piece. Once again Bergman was the producer, but this time it was about Hollywood and the mob, and Hewitt, at Bergman's request, was calling Wasserman to ask him if he would cooperate. The piece focused on two recent Justice Department–FBI investigations of MCA, involving its record and home video divisions. These investigations had resulted in very bad publicity for MCA—the record division had been in business with someone in the mob, and the vice president of the home video division had boasted of his mob ties on FBI wiretaps. Prosecutors, however, had not succeeded in proving that more senior MCA executives were aware of these activities and associations. Marvin Rudnick, an assistant U.S. attorney in Los Angeles, who had been trying to prove it, had been targeted by MCA's battalion of well-connected lawyers and, ultimately, fired by the Justice Department.

Hewitt said that he called Wasserman. "I said, 'Lew, Ed Bradley [the on-camera producer] is doing this story about mob influence in Hollywood. Do you want to participate?'

"He said, 'No.'

"Then he said, 'You're not going to do it, are you?'

"I said, 'Yes, we're going to do it. I can't tell our producer not to do a story.' Well, the minute the show aired, our friendship ended abruptly. Edie, especially, was apoplectic. I was at the Four Seasons one day and Nick Dunne was at the next table, waiting for his guest, who turned out to be Edie. She turned her back, wouldn't even say hello. And Lew and I never talked to each other again."

For a number of years after MCA was sold to Matsushita, the political world had remained Wasserman's proud bailiwick. In 1992, Bill Clinton—who knew Wasserman only casually—called him from his campaign bus and asked him to do a fund-raiser for him; Wasserman was happy to comply. He liked to point out later that the $10,000-a-couple dinner at his home raised $1.7 million—"the most successful dinner in a private home in American political history," he said. And it was the start of an extremely warm relationship between Clinton and Wasserman ("I am crazy about him," Wasserman once remarked. "If you get me going on the subject of Bill Clinton, I'll sound like a love-struck teenager.") Active as he was, though, there seemed to be a subtle shift in his political life. When he had started out, he had been the industry lobbyist, while his East Coast counterpart, Arthur Krim, forswore lobbying, at least in his relationship with Johnson. Over the years, however, Wasserman had become far more polished and urbane, customarily expressing his concerns to politicians about issues unrelated to Hollywood; and he only operated as the overt industry lobbyist in matters of the greatest moment—for example, the investment tax credit, and the fin-syn rules. In December 1993, he was placed in a position where he had to choose—industry lobbyist or statesman—and he made the quite predictable choice.

Negotiations for a world trade agreement—known as the Uruguay Round, to modify the General Agreement on Tariffs and Trade (GATT)—had gotten close to the deadline in Geneva, without reaching any agreement from the Europeans to allow greater access for American films, television programs, and music. What the Europeans were

arguing for was the "cultural exception": excluding audiovisual products from the agreement. After three days of intense, round-the-clock
negotiations, U.S. trade representative Mickey Kantor recalled that if
the U.S. agreed to the cultural exception, "it was clear we could get impressive trade-offs, benefits for the U.S. I called the president and I explained the situation. He said, 'My tendency is to say, make the
deal—but you've gotta call Lew Wasserman, and see what he says.' I
called Lew in California, told him what had been going on, and explained what I thought the choices were. He wanted me to confirm that
this was the largest trade deal in history—which it was. He said, 'Our
industry is just fine. We have a huge percentage of the European market and we always will. New technology will overrun whatever they try
to do to us. You do what's right for the country.' " It was not a response that drew universal acclaim in Hollywood; Valenti, who was
blamed for the defeat, was said to have expressed the view privately
that if Wasserman had advised Clinton differently, Hollywood might
well have prevailed.

Kantor was pleased that Wasserman had risen above parochial interests. But he also meant to underscore just how singular Wasserman's
authority was. "When it came down to crunch time, the president of the
United States knew who to call. There was no debate about who it
should be, it was *only* Wasserman. And President Clinton understood
that if Lew Wasserman was satisfied with what we thought we had to
do, it was okay," Kantor said. "It wasn't just that he had power and was
the head of a major studio and was shrewd and smart. He was a very
thoughtful, impressive human being. You know, sometimes you ask big
contributors for advice to feed their egos. But people actually wanted to
hear from Lew." In 1995, President Clinton awarded Wasserman the
Presidential Medal of Freedom; after that, Wasserman wore its small
pin on his lapel.

By the late nineties, Wasserman was limiting his political activities.
He would still host an occasional event, or talk to a particular senator
at Valenti's request, but he had withdrawn from the fund-raising apparatus that he had created. Valenti tried manfully to run the machine,

but the drastic consolidation in the entertainment world meant that the MPAA was radically changed, too. Many of the studios were now small parts of giant conglomerates, all with diverse interests and agendas—and all with their own Washington lobbying offices. The straight lines that once delineated MPAA member interests now looked like a crazy grid; the studios' common enemy, for example, used to be the networks, but now some studios (or their parent companies) owned the networks. Indeed, in this reconfigured world, the only "enemies" that all MPAA members had in common were piracy and copyright infringement. Some entertainment executives wondered aloud if the lobbying organization that had been founded in the early days of the motion picture industry—and transformed by Wasserman—had outlived its usefulness. And there was considerable speculation that whenever Valenti finally retired, yielding the post he had held on to tenaciously for more than three decades, the MPAA might cease to exist.

As the MPAA seemed to have become an anachronism, so did the role that Wasserman had created for himself. "Even Lew couldn't be *Lew* today," commented Jonathan Dolgen, the chairman of the Viacom Entertainment Group, pointing out that contemporary studio heads, small players in giant corporations, could not simply follow the lead of one of their studio peers. The way they relate to one another is a throwback, Dolgen continued. "In the early days, none of the moguls deferred to any other. Then came Lew's era, when all of them deferred to him. And now it is, again, the way it was in earlier times."

All the constructs Wasserman had so painstakingly built—his company, his role as industry leader, his political machine—were being either dismantled or transmuted. His persona, no less a construct, had been bound up with the rest; now it had lost its purpose. He still wanted to adhere to the rules he'd lived by—he seemed to feel it was a weakness not to—but he was pulled by other impulses. He had generally refused testimonial dinners in his honor; now, he sometimes accepted—allowing himself the pleasure of being feted. "I must be slipping," he remarked about having agreed to be honored at an AFL-

CIO dinner. He had, of course, forsworn revealing how he *felt* about anything, certainly in a public context. However, after MCA (now Universal) had changed hands a third time, Wasserman volunteered, "It's sad for me." For in 2000, following Bronfman's failed tenure, Universal and Seagram were bought by Vivendi, a French water utility whose CEO, Jean-Marie Messier, aimed to transform it into a global media giant. (Only two years later, Messier was fired and the company began trying to sell off assets, making Universal's future uncertain yet again.) And Wasserman had always insisted that he would not cooperate with any book written about him, at least in part because he would not betray the confidences of the stars that were his former clients. But, like Stein toward the end of his life, Wasserman was not immune to the appeal of having his story told. And as he saw it, he was not fully "cooperating"—his parameters were that he would talk mainly about the business, not himself, and would certainly divulge no client secrets.

He permitted himself, though, to reminisce. He had met Grace Kelly when she was eighteen, "the most beautiful thing I'd ever seen." He told MCA's head theatrical agent, Edith Van Cleve, to put her in a play. What can she do? Van Cleve wanted to know. "She can't *do* anything, I just want her to walk across the stage!" Wasserman said. They put her in a play, Stanley Kramer saw her, and he hired her for *High Noon,* opposite Gary Cooper. When she decided to marry Prince Rainier, Wasserman continued, he asked her why she was giving up her career. "She said, 'Lew, I've never been a princess.' I kissed her on the forehead and wished her well. She gave up the biggest female acting career—I think she could have been bigger than Greta Garbo, Bette Davis, Betty Grable, Joan Crawford."

Hitchcock, he said, was a genius, and also a great practical joker. There was a party at Chasen's, and when the waiter brought Wasserman his drink (vodka), it was blue. "I said, 'This must be somebody else's drink.' And then we sat down to eat, and everything was blue! The *potatoes* were blue! Hitch says, 'I'm in a blue mood.' "

Jimmy Stewart, he said, was a good friend. In 1949, when Stewart was getting married, Wasserman suggested that the two of them have a

quiet dinner at Chasen's the night before his wedding. He agreed—his fi-
ancée had been nervous about his having some wild Hollywood stag
party. As Wasserman and Stewart drove up together to Chasen's, Spencer
Tracy, Jack Benny, and Dave Chasen were sitting on the curb, and a fifty-
foot sign was hung across the entrance of the distinctive green and white
building: "James Stewart's Final Performance Tonight." "I had life-size
cutouts made of all his roles in movies that were failures, and covered the
front of Chasen's with them," Wasserman recalled. He had employed a
liveried British manservant to wait on Stewart—every time Stewart took
a drink, the servant wiped his mouth. And when they sat down to dinner, Wasserman continued, "Chasen's had this enormous serving platter.
People lifted the giant top off and inside were two midgets, with syringes,
squirting yellow liquid at him. He thought it was urine!" Wasserman
also recalled that in 1962, when the Justice Department brought its antitrust charges against MCA (and Wasserman's picture was in the *New
York Times*), Stewart had immediately come to see him. "Jimmy Stewart
came in to my office, threw his checkbook down on my desk, and said,
'Take as much as you want.' He had no idea what was going to happen
to me."

Wasserman was most comfortable, though, talking about his business exploits—and, especially, the deals that had become Hollywood
legend. The purchase of the Paramount film library was a favorite. It
had the elements he found gratifying—he had seen the future, he had
acted upon his conviction, critics had said he'd overpaid, and hinted
gleefully that it might be his undoing. But he had proven them oh so
wrong—by more than a billion dollars, over the years. *Content,* he had
understood then, long before the word was in vogue, would have in-
calculable value in the expanding universe of television. There were
other profitable aspects to the deal, though they were much smaller; he
had realized there was money to be made in releasing the old movies
theatrically as well—*For Whom the Bell Tolls,* for example. "We took
in $5 million just in Spain, post-Franco," he recalled.

"I knew I could do well with the Paramount pictures, I just didn't
know *how* well," Wasserman continued. He paused. The silence grew.

Seated at his perfectly clear desk, peering from behind his giant black-rimmed glasses, he grimaced slightly. Then he said, "Those are the smart things. Now, do you want to know the *dumb* thing I did?"

Those were not words that Lew Wasserman was ever supposed to utter, and his visitor tried to demur, but he went on. "Sold the company to the Japanese," he said, with some force. "It wasn't the price that was wrong, but the sale itself."

In death, Wasserman's mythic personality was brought back to life. He died at home on the morning of June 3, 2002—he was eighty-nine—after having suffered a stroke about two weeks earlier; and, in accordance with his directive, he was buried in a private family ceremony that very afternoon, before many people even knew he had died. Jules Stein had choreographed his funeral, but Wasserman was intent on escaping the major event that his would have been. Still, at Universal—where Wasserman had continued to go to his office each day until he had his stroke—some executives were said to be fearful of being criticized if they did nothing to mark his death. Moreover, Barry Diller—who had become the head of Vivendi Universal Entertainment—had known Wasserman nearly all his life, admired him, and wanted to hold a memorial service. After some initial hesitation—Wasserman's family was unhappy with the way he had been treated at Universal—they agreed.

The service was held on the afternoon of July 15 at the Universal Amphitheater. VIP guests left their cars at the entrance, but everyone else—including busloads of Universal employees, who were given the afternoon off—made their way through the Universal City street of shops and restaurants known as CityWalk. It was a surreal approach to a memorial service—music blaring from Sam Goody's, a huge King Kong suspended overhead, crowds of tourists, and occasional signs that said, "Memorial," with arrows pointing in the right direction. But Wasserman probably would have liked it. He had been very proud of CityWalk; built in the early nineties, it was hugely successful, earning about $100 million a year—and just as Wasserman often used to pull box office figures out of his pocket for a visitor, so he would, too, tallies of the lunches and dinners served at CityWalk restaurants. Inside the Amphitheater, as people settled in their seats, "Whatever Will Be, Will Be (Que Sera, Sera)" and songs from the soundtrack of *Pillow Talk* were playing. There were hundreds of Hollywood people, of course, and quite a few politicians—among them, Bill Clinton, Al Gore, California Governor Gray Davis, and Los Angeles Mayor James Hahn.

Diller set the tone. "At a time when the general image of business executives is not sterling, Lew Wasserman is the gold standard. No one who worked for Lew ever thought any decision was made on any basis other than what was right and honest and in the best and safe interest of them or the company. . . . He was the one who invented a profit-sharing trust that made secretaries and senior executives alike very wealthy if they gave the same loyalty and trust to the company that it was prepared to give to them.

"He was tough and spare except when there was need, and then he was neither. I remember when calling him he didn't say hello—he didn't do 'how ya doing'—he answered the phone with courteous impatience. 'Yes, Barry.' But when I asked for something charitable, he never failed to simply say, 'You have my proxy.'

"I never worked in his company until he was chairman emeritus," Diller continued. "But along my own way, I learned so many lessons from him. I was this twenty-four-year-old executive at ABC when I first approached him in some close to adult position. I was purchasing films for ABC from Universal, and I went to his office, and I asked him—I said, given that we were buying sixty-four units at $600,000 each, couldn't you just cut one little unit from that sixty-four? Two beats. He stared. He said, 'No.' Nothing more. Just, no. Silence. The stare. And I folded like the cheapest tent." The audience laughed, hard. "But as I got up to go, dejectedly, knowing the fool that I was, he walked me out, and in that very quiet voice of his, he said, 'Next time you try this, be prepared to call it off if you don't get what you want. Because, otherwise, you never will.' And the door closed behind him."

Steven Spielberg—who said that when he first met Wasserman, he thought his glasses looked like two giant movie screens—pointed out that while it is well known that Sid Sheinberg gave him his first directing job, it is not so well known that Wasserman saved him from being fired on that job. The television pilot was *Night Gallery,* and its star was Joan Crawford. "I could tell from the very first day we met that the minute the meeting was over, Joan was going to get on the telephone and raise hell. Lew had been her manager, he was the one who got the call. And she said, 'Who's this kid they have directing me?' Lew replied, 'Joan, if you're unhappy, don't mention it because they won't replace him, they'll replace you.' From that day on, Joan Crawford treated me like King Vidor." That was the beginning of his long friendship with Wasserman, Spielberg said; he had been his "guardian angel."

Bill Clinton described how he first met Wasserman. It was the mideighties, he was governor, and Arkansas's economy was in the doldrums. He had the idea of trying to attract Hollywood to make movies in Arkansas, and asked to make an appointment with Wasserman. To his surprise, he said, Wasserman agreed. "At that time, only my mother thought I would ever become president, so there was nothing in it for Lew to spend forty-five minutes talking to a politician from a state which for all I know he had never even visited—but he did. Furthermore, he was brutally honest with me. When I asked what I could do to get more movies made in Arkansas, he said in very elegant and brief language, 'Not much.' And to compound the irony, he actually made me like it—I mean, I actually enjoyed this meeting. So from time to time our paths would cross. He helped me become president, he helped me stay president, he helped me be a better president. When I left the White House, he helped me build a library and a foundation, so I could continue my public service—as he had helped other presidents, of both parties. He never asked me for anything. *Not anything.*"

Several speakers made it plain how thoroughly they idolized

Wasserman. Sid Sheinberg said that his heroes when he was a boy were the Knights of the Round Table, and he had fantasized being a page, training to be a knight, becoming a knight himself. Well, it had come true. "It is said that in those days of King Arthur, knights lived by the old code, the code of honor. My dear friend Lew Wasserman lived his life by the code. I was privileged to ride close beside him for some thirty years, and observe and learn from him for over forty years. We who aspired to sit at his Round Table were expected to know the code and live by it." In closing, Sheinberg said, "I loved my king and I miss him. And I will miss him forever." Suzanne Pleshette, a close friend of Edie's and Lew's, talked about how uncomfortable Lew was around women, all women, except of course Edie—"This was not an arrangement," she said emphatically. "This was a love story!" She said that Lew had loved talent, and always looked after their interests. She recounted the story about his having been barred from the Warner lot and taken the stars to lunch—a longer and longer lunch, with Bette Davis leading the mutiny. In closing, she declared, "Lew should have been president—but he didn't want to give up his day job." And Valenti—speaking without notes, choking up at times, striding about the stage, microphone in hand, more like an evangelical preacher than a lobbyist for the motion picture industry—acknowledged as he had many times before that "whatever I am and whatever role I play in this industry, I owe it all to Lew." And he repeated what he had told a journalist earlier. "If Hollywood was Mount Olympus, Lew Wasserman is Zeus."

Much of what was said in the Amphitheater that day was true, as far as it went. In Hollywood, certainly, Lew Wasserman *was* the gold standard, and it is unimaginable that he would have defrauded what he thought of as his company, robbing employees and shareholders, in the way that has become almost commonplace in today's corporate world. Indeed, his secretary, Melody Sherwood, said that when the company's profit-sharing trust converted to a 401(k), he worried a great deal that employees might make unwise decisions about their investment allocations and lose their retirement funds. "He was very paternalistic," she commented. The profit-sharing trust did make employees richer than they might have imagined—MCA events coordinator Herb Steinberg said that when he retired and saw that he was worth over a million dollars, he could hardly believe his eyes. Wasserman clearly did live by a code, and expected his associates to adhere to it as well. It is almost certainly true, as Clinton said, that Wasserman never asked him for anything. And—inflated as Valenti's verbiage is—it is also true that if Hollywood were Mount Olympus, Wasserman was indeed Zeus.

But getting to be "Zeus" had entailed a course of conduct rather different from anything that was evoked that afternoon. Wasserman was Hollywood's gold standard—but he had extended his mantle to Sidney Korshak, who was the mob's proxy in the industry Wasserman ruled, and who, when displeased, credibly threatened that someone might soon be "wearing cement shoes." The profit-sharing trust was a boon to employees, but it was devised, initially, as a means of restraining valuable executives from leaving, in a way that a contract could not legally do. Wasserman probably did not ask Clinton for anything, but he certainly did ask—and receive—from Reagan. Wasserman did live by a code; in doing so, he provided his own, unique interpretations of the culture's most fundamental concepts. "Loyalty," which was central to his code, meant that he would always protect those who were loyal to him—unless they decided to leave MCA, in which case they ceased to exist. "Integrity" meant that when he gave his word, especially in a labor context, it was all one needed. But it was somehow not inconsistent with his creating a monopoly through the use of illegal tactics and what Larry White called "scare power," or using Korshak as a fixer, or threatening a reluctant seller that his business would be destroyed, or stealing clients with all kinds of lucre, or destroying someone's career out of personal pique.

Jules Stein, of course, had set the pattern. There was little Wasserman carried out that did not have an antecedent in some practice of Stein's in the earlier era. But Stein was less ambitious than Wasserman. Stein was so intent on building his financial empire that he was willing to do whatever it required; then, he wanted to erase that unsavory past and enjoy legitimacy (and the fruits of empire). Wasserman did not care as much about building a financial empire—his net worth after the Matsushita sale was estimated at about $500 million, which was not that remarkable in an age that was spawning billionaires. But his appetite for power was far, far greater. It was actually fortuitous for Wasserman that he clashed with Billy Goodheart in MCA's New York office, because if he had remained in New York he could not have become the ruling figure he did. When he arrived in Hollywood, he found a small, insular community, insubstantial, built on fiction, trafficking in illusion, dominated by a single enterprise—and populated with many who, like him, had come from places they wanted to leave behind, to reinvent themselves. Far from Cleveland's Woodland Avenue, Wasserman *did* reinvent himself, developing a persona that was utterly commanding, glacial, charming when necessary, expert, ruthless, frightening, charismatic—in sum, one fit for a ruler. Unlike Stein, he did not attempt to erase his past or, more, disguise his present. In Hollywood, his ties to the underworld only served to augment his standing. And it was the juxtaposition of high and low, White House and Korshak, that elevated him even higher.

It was one thing to have been a guest at the White House, and another to have been offered—and declined—a cabinet position. That offer, by President Johnson, became the keystone in Wasserman's rendition of his political life. Wasserman's surrogate, Valenti, only "let the secret out" in 1974, after Johnson had died. From then on, Wasserman referred to it freely, and often. Wasserman had been interviewed for an oral history at the LBJ Library in December 1973—an interview that he stipulated was to remain sealed until after his death.

At one point during the fairly lengthy interview, Wasserman was asked, "Did you ever consider taking any post with the government?"

"No. No," Wasserman replied. "As a matter of fact, in, I think it was, December of 1963, Ed Weisl and I went up to the Hotel Carlyle to visit the president. It was after Dallas, and we sat around for a few hours. . . . At the end of the discussion, I turned to him and said, 'I'd like to ask you a very important favor.' I had the feeling that the president bristled at the remark, and said, 'Yes, Lew, what is it?' And I said, 'I want you to promise me that I never have to work for the government.' He laughed, and he promised it to me; and that was the end of it."

Wasserman went on to say that he subsequently asked not to be appointed to any commissions either. But this request, he said, was not heeded. Because one day he got a call from Roger Stevens, who was founding chairman of the Kennedy Center for the Performing Arts, saying that he was appointing Wasserman to the Kennedy Center's executive committee. Wasserman said he replied that he was not a director of the Kennedy Center—at which point Stevens read him an article in that day's *Washington Post,* which mentioned his appointment. Wasserman said he called Johnson to object—but Johnson, essentially, would have none of it. Wasserman's claimed protestations ring a little hollow, considering that both Valenti and Krim had lobbied for his appointment. In any event, Wasserman remained on the board of the Kennedy Center for many years.

There was no mention of the cabinet post. Surely, had it been offered, Wasserman would have said so then—and described how it was done despite his protests, as he did in the instance of the Kennedy Center appointment. Instead, he said, Johnson promised he wouldn't have to serve—"and that was the end of it."

It seems virtually certain that that *was* the end of it. Valenti did include Wasserman's name, with many others, in a memo to President Johnson. But, as several friends of Johnson's suggested, he would not have taken the risk of a Wasserman confirmation proceeding—where Wasserman could be interrogated about his association with Korshak, Hoffa, and Dalitz; not to mention the very recent settlement of the government's mammoth antitrust case against MCA, in which Wasserman was a named defendant. It was an odd résumé for a secretary of commerce. And, on another level, it was fanciful, really, to think that this intensely secretive man—who prided himself on keeping almost no

files, who rarely took a note, and who counseled others, like Andy Anderson, to take no notes—could have functioned within the government bureaucracy.

Some who knew Wasserman well believed that quite a few of his famous stories were concoctions, heady brews that started with some
truth and added half-truth and a dose of fiction. Like virtually everything else in Wasserman's life, his stories served a purpose. They established him as one of the cognoscenti, enhanced his aura, and enabled
him to control the moment—for he didn't freely converse with people
so much as tell stories. They were part of the elaborate facade Wasserman constructed, which kept others from glimpsing what was within
and projected what he chose. Like anyone from hardscrabble beginnings who came to enjoy such an iron-fisted dominion, Wasserman
probably was afraid, sometimes, that it might all be taken away—but
that was not something that those who worked closely with him for
decades ever saw. Instead, in a movie colony roiled with insecurity,
where one day's success foretold nothing about the next, where nearly
everything was transient and chimerical, Wasserman was a counter-
vailing force—supremely confident, professedly infallible, rock-solid,
enduring.

For roughly fifty years, his legend grew. Wasserman benefited most
of all, but his community did, too, in many ways. He helped to free
stars from the studios' bonds, and made them much wealthier than
they had been before. He may have helped to keep television from fulfilling the potential that Pat Weaver envisioned for that medium—but
he did provide myriad job opportunities to the men and women who
worked in it. He helped to keep general labor peace in the industry for
decades, and he *was* someone who had a bond with the unions that
was unique on the producers' side. He established the standard for
charitable and political giving and civic participation in an industry
that had not had such a model—and he enforced it. He made Hollywood more powerful in Washington than it had ever been, and
achieved benefits worth billions of dollars—good things to have done
from a parochial standpoint, though not for the public at large. But,

despite his having assumed the role of a statesman in his last years, Wasserman was profoundly parochial. He had found a place—the *only* place, really—where he could be king, and his allegiance was always there.

At Wasserman's memorial service, a drawing on a huge screen faced the audience. It showed a bleak, desert landscape, with "Hollywood" written across the background in small letters, nothing but a pair of oversize black-rimmed glasses on the sandy ground—and, alongside them, a small figure, dwarfed by the giant glasses, gazing at them. As though centuries from now, when all else has been swept away, those glasses—indestructible—will be the telltale artifact, clue to the singular time when Hollywood was his.

Acknowledgments

When I decided to write this book, I had no idea whether the voices of my two protagonists, Lew Wasserman and Jules Stein, would be heard in any fresh way. I was immensely heartened, therefore, when Wasserman decided to talk to me (ambivalent though he was). I warmed to him over the course of our interviews; he was a pale reflection of the commanding, ruthless figure he had been, and I found myself sometimes straining to align the two. I often thought that I would have preferred to write about him when he was *Lew Wasserman*—rather than now, at the end of his remarkable life, when he was old, ailing, and dispossessed, and an infinitely softer, more sympathetic subject. I did my best, in any event, to get him right, earlier and later, and I wrote always believing that he would read the book (most of it was written before he died) and looking forward, more or less, to his review. I remain very grateful to him. As for Stein, it was his daughter, Jean Stein, who made it possible for her father to speak in these pages. She was so unstintingly generous (while never breathing a syllable of a query about how her father's story was turning out) that it is difficult for me to express the depth of my gratitude to her. I know that Jean, a biographer, respected the process; but she might have respected it and still not been nearly as magnanimous as she was.

From the start, my partner in this undertaking was my editor, Ann Godoff, the former president, publisher, and editor-in-chief of Random House. It was her instinctive enthusiasm for this book (I sometimes thought she grasped its scope better than I did) that brought me to Random House. She had promised me she would give the manuscript her close attention, despite the press of her other duties, and she was as good as her word. She read with alacrity the sections I submitted. When I was at a complete loss for a title, she made it her mission to find it— calling with one idea after another, for weeks on end, as though it were her most important task, until finally she had the right one. She edited the manuscript closely at the end. She was extravagant in her praise, but she also told me flat out that my first attempt at an introduction was not usable—and by that time I trusted her so implicitly that all I wanted was to be able to write one she liked. This happy collaboration came to an abrupt end when Ann was fired in late January 2003. The book, on the verge of moving into production, seemed orphaned. However, within days of Ann's departure, Jonathan Karp stepped into the breach. He read the manuscript promptly and offered valuable suggestions, which I scrambled to implement. I am singularly lucky he was there, I admire his talents, and I appreciate enormously everything he's done; but he would be the first to say that this is Ann's book.

I am grateful to my friend and formidable agent, Binky Urban, who was very much there when I needed her, in the aftermath of Ann's departure, and who consistently extended herself for me—seeming to ingest sections of the book whole when I sent them, never leaving me in suspense about her reaction for longer than a weekend. At Random House, I am grateful, too, to Meredith Blum, who as Ann Godoff's assistant was attentively shepherding the book, and to Jonathan Jao, who took over when Meredith left, and displayed such care, taste, and efficiency that I came to rely on him enormously. Thanks to Libby McGuire, the associate publisher; to Steve Messina, in charge of production, for his hard work and outstanding patience; to Dan Rembert, who designed the book's cover; to Casey Hampton, who did its interior design; and to Elizabeth Fogarty, the book's talented publicist. Thanks also to Laura Goldin, for her legal advice and good judgment. My photo researcher, Larry Schwartz, did an outstanding job on a tight time schedule, and photographer Stephanie Diani, while a perfectionist, made sitting for my picture not so onerous.

I especially want to thank my friends at *The New Yorker.* Its editor, David Remnick, has been extraordinarily patient with my extended leave—and I *owe* him. Pieces I wrote for the magazine have found their way into this book, albeit in altered form, and it has been excerpted, too, in *The New Yorker.* So, as always, I am in the debt of my longtime, cherished friends and editors, John Bennett and Dorothy Wickenden. Thanks, also, to my numerous other colleagues at the magazine who have helped to make my pieces better, and life more enjoyable. I hope the many will forgive me for mentioning just the few: Martin Baron, Virginia Cannon, Perri Dorset, Henry Finder, Ann Goldstein, Dana Goodyear, Eleanor Gould, Mary Hawthorne, Pamela McCarthy, Erin Overbey, Elizabeth Pearson-Griffiths, Maurie Perl, Lauren Porcaro, Nandi Rodrigo, and Amy Tubke-Davidson. I am also grateful to the magazine's former editor, Robert Gottlieb, who brought me to *The New Yorker,* and who assigned me to write about the sale of MCA to Matsushita, back in 1991 (my introduction to Lew Wasserman). I owe a great deal, in addition, to Tina Brown; among a host of other things, it was under her aegis that I wrote about the metamorphosis of MCA, headed by Edgar Bronfman, Jr.

I am extremely indebted to my research assistants. Quite a few came and went, over the five-year course of this project: John Dietrick, Lisa Fingeret, Jennifer Hamm, Todd Hurvitz, and Katy O'Connell. They were all diligent and provided valuable help. It was Kathryn Beaumont, however, who worked for me for the longest period of time, and—because of her curiosity, acumen, sound judgment, and commitment to the project—I came to rely on her the most.

I was fortunate to encounter a number of dedicated and generous archivists. Linda Seelke, at the Lyndon Baines Johnson Library, in

Austin, consistently went out of her way to respond to my myriad requests. Her colleagues, Claudia Anderson and Kyla Wilson, were also very helpful. At the Margaret Herrick Library at the Academy of Motion Picture Arts and Sciences in Los Angeles, Barbara Hall guided me to illuminating material, very important to the book; and she was a pleasure to work with as I returned to the library again and again. At the National Archives, John Powers led me through the maze of the Nixon Presidential Materials Project, and David Paynter also lent considerable assistance; without their help, my research there would have taken much longer, and been far less rewarding. Megan De Noyer, at the Kennedy Library in Boston, took an interest in this project, too, as did Steven Plotkin. I am indebted to the Columbia University Oral History Project in New York, where Alexander Freund, Gregory Culler, and Kate Foster lent their assistance. Thanks, too, to Ann Sindelar, of the Western Reserve Historical Society, in Cleveland, Ohio; to Ned Comstock, at the University of Southern California Cinema-Television Library, in Los Angeles; to Russell L. Martin III at the Degolyer Library at Southern Methodist University, in Dallas; and to Jeanie Child, on the archives staff of the Office of the Circuit Court Clerk of Cook County, in Chicago. I am grateful to Valerie Yaros, at the Screen Actors Guild, for providing long-ago photos from the Guild's archives.

Thanks to Wayne Johnson, at the Chicago Crime Commission. And, also, to Linda Colton of the Federal Bureau of Investigation, Sam Morrison of the U.S. Justice Department, and Hannah Hall and Reba Freeman of the Securities and Exchange Commission, all of whom responded to my Freedom of Information requests at their respective agencies.

I am singularly grateful to Alice Berman, who spent an inordinate amount of time and energy to help me with research materials that were absolutely vital to the telling of this story.

Among the friends whose advice I sought on portions of the manuscript were Peter Baumbusch, Lucy Eisenberg, Ken Goldman, Bill Kilberg, and Nick Nicholas. Another friend, Ken Mate, gave me the benefit of his investigative skills. John Schulman of Warner Bros. was especially helpful in handling my permissions request when time was short. And I also owe special thanks to a number of fellow journalists who shared insights and, in some cases, files with me: Lowell Bergman, Gary Cohen, Jim Drinkhall, Pat McGilligan, Warren Olney, Maurice Posseley, Dave Robb, Robert Scheer, Murray Schumach, and Sandy Smith. I am especially indebted to Sandy—for his recollections, and the *carton* of documents he sent.

Family members generally come last in these lists, but they are of course the most important. To begin, I want to thank my aunt, Doris Bornstein, who has been my devoted reader all my life, and who—though she is very ill—swore to me that she would not miss the publication of this book.

As ever, I am immensely grateful to my son, Ari Schlossberg. Much as he suffered the writing life involuntarily when he was a child, now that he is an adult he has chosen that life for himself, and his extraordinary talent and accomplishments have buoyed my spirits on the most dismal of writing days. For his balanced judgment, keen insight, leavening humor, and innate generosity, I cannot thank him enough. My three stepchildren, Adam, Jake, and Cara Levine, have also learned now what it is like to live with someone writing a book; it was not always easy, but they generally remained their good-natured, highly engaging, lovable selves, and I appreciate their forbearance. I am grateful, too, to Dena and Irv Schechter, and Shirley Levine, for welcoming me so wholeheartedly into their family, and overlooking my being derelict in countless ways as I struggled to finish this book. It was my husband, Mel Levine, however, who bore the brunt of the process, as he witnessed my absorption and travails, close up. It still amazes me—he's not a *saint*—that he remained consistently steady, cheerful, sympathetic, encouraging, and (perhaps most important) interested in this project over its long life. My beloved companion, he was also my mainstay, my trusted sounding board, my counselor, my first reader, my proofreader at the end (and the best chapter titles were his). I always believed writing a book had to be a fundamentally solitary pursuit for me; but he has proven me wrong, to my unending delight.

Source Notes

Because this story spanned most of the last century, the nature of my research changed as the book's chronological narrative progressed. For the early years, I was able to cull a great deal of material from oral histories, memoirs, private letters, confidential company records, and personal financial records, as well as newspaper and magazine articles, court filings, and transcripts of court testimony and congressional hearings. I tried hard to locate people to interview who had known Jules Stein in the company's early days, and who were familiar with the Chicago scene in the twenties and thirties; I was lucky to find a few. For the middle and later years, there was a multitude of articles about MCA in the trade and general press, as well as many thousands of pages of relevant government documents; but the backbone of my research for this, the largest portion of the book, was the interviewing process. I was fortunate that Lew Wasserman not only agreed to talk to me but also told many friends who called to ask whether or not they should see me that it was all right with him if they did. I interviewed about 250 people; many of them had worked for MCA over the years, or had been MCA clients, or were Wasserman's business partners, or his competitors. I spoke, too, with those who were knowledgeable about the parallel universes in which Wasserman operated—labor, politics, Las Vegas.

The following is a list of those whom I interviewed. In addition, I spoke with dozens of people who agreed to be interviewed only on a basis of confidentiality.

Robert Abboud

Berle Adams

Gene Allen

Andy Anderson

Edward Anhalt

Ted Ashley

John Baity

Bill Baker

Judy Balaban

Art Barron

Martin Baum

Warren Beatty

Lowell Bergman

Alice Berman

Betty Breithaupt

Roy Brewer

Frank Brill

Charles Bronfman

Edgar Bronfman, Sr.

Edgar Bronfman, Jr.

David Brown

Helen Gurley Brown

Harry Busch

Alexander Butterfield

Liz Carpenter

Bob Carruthers

Joe Cerrell

Edwin Cohen

Jim Corman

Pierre Cossette

Nick Counter

Kenneth Cox

Jack Dales

Robert Daly

Sean Daniel

Michael Dann

Gordon Davidson

Martin Davis

Michael Deaver

Irene Diamond

Barry Diller

Jonathan Dolgen

Albert Dorskind

Kirk Douglas

Corydon Dunham

Don Durgin

Ed Edelman

Robert Evans

Irving Fein

Charles Ferris

Freddy Fields

Jack Findlater

Arthur Fleischer

Bill Fleming

Mike Franklin

George French

Michael Fuchs

George Gallantz

Michael Gardner

Leonard Garment

David Geffen

Leo Geffner

Henry Geller

Robert Gilbert

Brian Grazer

Richard Gully

Ed Guthman

Lloyd Hand

Richard Heffner

Charlton Heston

Mark Heter

Don Hewitt

Leonard Hill

Jean Howard

Billy Hunt

Salvatore Ianucci

Stanley Jaffe

Joel Jankowski

Jim Jones

Max Kampelman

Jay Kanter

Mickey Kantor

Harris Katleman

Barry Kemp

Herbert Klein
Boris Kostelanetz
Mathilde Krim
Irving Kupcinet
Tony Kutner
Sol Leon
Larry Levinson
Chuck Lewis
Harriet Lewis
Tom Lewyn
Martin Lipton
Alan Livingston
Charles Manatt
Stuart Mandel
Dan Margolis
Abraham Lincoln Marovitz
Tony Martin
Kerry McCluggage
Harry McPherson
Sue Mengers
Howard Metzenbaum
Marvin Meyer
Ron Meyer
Gene Meyers
Chester Migden
Howard Monderer
Charles Morgan
Jim Murray
Lyn Nofziger
Bill O'Connor
Gerald Oppenheimer
Ruby Petersdorf
Arturo Pettorino
David Picker
Tom Pollock
Frank Price
Bob Rains
Lou Ratener
Ted Raynor
Sumner Redstone
A. O. Richards
Fred Richman

Felix Rohatyn
Herbert Rosenthal
Mickey Rudin
Al Rush
Herman Rush
Norman Samnick
Gunther Schiff
Herbert Schlosser
Shelly Schultz
Murray Schumach
Daniel Selznick
Ruth Seymour
Bob Shapiro
Sidney Sheinberg
Dean Shendal
Melody Sherwood
Tom Short
George Sidney
Herbert Siegel
Leonard Silverstein
Don Sipes
Laura Sloate
Dan Slusser
George Smith
Ben Sonnenberg
Stuart Spencer
Gordon Spivack
Dennis Stanfil
Frank Stanton
Jay Stein
Jean Stein
Herbert Steinberg
George Stevens, Jr.
Senator Ted Stevens
Robert Strauss
Steve Tallent
Ned Tanen
John Tunney
Jack Valenti
Katrina van den Heuvel
Mort Viner
Michael Wacks

Lew Wasserman	Don Winn
Daniel Welkes	Marshall Wortman
Weldon Wertz	Frank Yablans
David Wexler	Richard Zanuck
Larry White	Kenneth Ziffren
Tom Wicker	Mel Ziontz
Pete Wilson	

The following is a selective compilation, made up of the sources I found most useful. I have omitted references to many hundreds of daily newspaper stories and magazine articles—I relied most on the *New York Times,* the *Wall Street Journal,* the *Washington Post,* and the *Los Angeles Times*—and included only those from which I quoted, or which were especially interesting.

CHAPTER 1: THE TWO CAESARS

Documents

Finley v. MCA et al., U.S. District Court, Southern District of California, Central Division, 1946.

Frank Rizzo and Nicholas Belcaster et al. v. James C. Petrillo et al., Circuit Court, Cook County, Illinois, 1933.

James C. Petrillo v. Maurice O. Wells, Circuit Court, Cook County, Illinois, 1929.

People of the State of Illinois v. Max Caldwell et al., Criminal Court of Cook County, Illinois, 1934.

Petrillo, James. Documents obtained through a Freedom of Information Act request to the U.S. Department of Justice.

United States of America v. Louis Campagna et al., U.S. District Court, Southern District of New York, October 1943.

Books

Cohen, Michael Mickey. *Mickey Cohen: In My Own Words.* Englewood Cliffs, New Jersey: Prentice-Hall, 1975.

Demaris, Ovid. *Captive City.* New York: Lyle Stuart, 1969.

Gilbert, Edith. *Summer Resort Life: Tango Teas and All!* Charlevoix, Michigan: Jet'iquette, 1976.

Hayward, Brooke. *Haywire.* New York: Alfred A. Knopf, 1977.

McDougal, Dennis. *The Last Mogul.* New York: Crown, 1998.

Pye, Michael. *Moguls.* New York: Holt, Rinehart & Winston, 1980.

Vincent, Sidney Z., and Judah Rubinstein. *Merging Traditions: Jewish Life in Cleveland.* Cleveland: Western Reserve Historical Society, 1978.

Zorach, William. *Art Is My Life.* New York: Harper & Row, 1967.

Articles

"Beckerman Indicted." Editorial. Cleveland *Plain Dealer,* Dec. 7, 1933.

"Bioff Says Gang Made Him Keep His Job." *New York Times*, Oct. 9, 1943.

Coughlan, Robert. "Petrillo." *Life*, Aug. 3, 1942.

Davenport, Walter. "Heat Wave." *Collier's*, Mar. 10, 1934.

Frazier, George. "Santa Claus with a Horn." *Collier's*, Mar. 8, 1947.

"Free Beckerman in Arson Trial." Cleveland *Plain Dealer,* June 28, 1936.

Gould, Jack. "Portrait of the Unpredictable Petrillo." *New York Times Magazine,* Dec. 28, 1947.

Hatch, Harold E. "Seize Beckerman As Arson Plotter." Cleveland *Plain Dealer,* Dec. 7, 1933.

Hopper, Hedda. "Hollywood." *Chicago Tribune*, Oct. 21, 1943.

Liebling, A. J. "Second City." *New Yorker*, Jan. 12, Jan. 19, Jan. 26, 1952.

McWilliams, Carey. "Racketeers and Movie Magnates." *New Republic,* Oct. 27, 1941.

"Paramount." *Fortune,* Mar. 1937.

"Paramount: Oscar for Profits." *Fortune,* June 1947.

Stein, Jean. "West of Eden," *New Yorker,* Feb. 23 and Mar. 2, 1998.

Winkler, Joseph. "A Statement from Executive Officer Winkler." *International Musician,* Mar. 22, 1922.

Wittels, David G. "Star-Spangled Octopus." *Saturday Evening Post,* Aug. 10, 1946.

Miscellaneous

Jaffe, Sam. "An Oral History with Sam Jaffe." Interviewed by Barbara Hall. Academy of Motion Picture Arts and Sciences Oral History Program. Beverly Hills, California: Academy Foundation, 1992.

Kramer, Karl. Unpublished memoir.

Kutner, Luis. "My Years with Capone." Interview by Neil Elliot with "Mr. X." Chicago Historical Society.

Rush, Herman. "Uncle Manie." Unpublished memoir about Manie Sacks.

Sosnik, Harry. "A View from the Podium." Drafts and research materials for an unpublished autobiography. Madison, Wisconsin: Wisconsin Historical Society.

Sosnik, Harry. Interview by Barbara Hogenson for the Columbia University Oral History Research Office, May 1985.

Stein, Jules. Unpublished draft of a memoir, based on interviews with Stein by Murray Schumach.

Wasserman, Lew. Interview by Steven Spielberg, Dec. 12, 2002.

CHAPTER 2: MONOPOLY POWER

Documents

Dalitz, Morris Barney. Documents obtained through Freedom of Information Act requests to the U.S. Department of Justice and the Federal Bureau of Investigation.

Factor, John. Documents obtained through Freedom of Information Act requests to the U.S. Department of Justice and the Federal Bureau of Investigation.

Hearings before a Special Subcommittee of the Committee on Education and Labor, House of Representatives, "Jurisdictional Disputes in the Motion-Picture Industry," 1947–1948.

Hearings before the Select Committee to Investigate Organized Crime in Interstate Commerce, U.S. Senate, 1951. (Kefauver Committee Hearings).

Korshak, Sidney. Documents obtained through Freedom of Information Act requests to the U.S. Department of Justice and the Federal Bureau of Investigation.

MCA, Inc. Documents obtained through a Freedom of Information Act request to the U.S. Department of Justice.

United States of America v. MCA Inc., U.S. District Court for the Southern District of California, Central Division, 1962.

Books

Bilby, Kenneth. *The General: David Sarnoff and the Rise of the Communications Industry.* New York: Harper & Row, 1986.

Dunne, Philip. *Take Two.* New York: Limelight, 1992.

Eisenberg, Dennis, Uri Dan, and Eli Landau. *Meyer Lansky.* New York: Paddington, 1979.

Evans, Robert. *The Kid Stays in the Picture.* New York: Hyperion, 1994.

Friedrich, Otto. *City of Nets: A Portrait of Hollywood in the 1940s.* New York: Harper & Row, 1986.

Lazar, Irving, with Annette Tapert. *Swifty.* New York: Simon & Schuster, 1995.

Moldea, Dan E. *Dark Victory: Ronald Reagan, MCA, and the Mob.* New York: Viking, 1986.

Navasky, Victor S. *Naming Names.* New York: Viking, 1980.

Puttnam, David. *Movies and Money.* New York: Alfred A. Knopf, 1998.

Reagan, Ronald, with Richard G. Hubler. *Where's the Rest of Me?* New York: Karz, 1981.

Rose, Frank. *The Agency.* New York: HarperCollins, 1995.

Smith, Sally Bedell. *In All His Glory.* New York: Simon & Schuster, 1990.

Touhy, Roger, with Ray Brennan. *The Stolen Years.* Cleveland: Pennington, 1959.

Weaver, Pat, with Thomas M. Coffey. *The Best Seat in the House.* New York: Alfred A. Knopf, 1994.

Articles

Champlin, Charles. "All the Way with MCA." *Los Angeles Times,* 1966.

Doherty, James. "Parole Scandal Reveals Capone Gang's Crime Empire." *Chicago Tribune*, May 13, 1948.

Frankel, Stanley, and Holmes Alexander. "Arvey of Illinois." *Collier's,* July 23, 1949.

Gelman, David, and Alfred G. Aronowitz. "MCA: Show Business Empire." *New York Post Daily Magazine,* June 4–10, 1962.

Gould, Jack. "Tempo at the Top: Fast." *New York Times,* Dec. 19, 1965.

Hellman, Geoffrey T. "A House on Gramercy Park." *New Yorker,* Apr. 8, 1950.

Liebling, A. J. "Action in the Desert." *New Yorker,* May 13, 1950.

MacKaye, Milton. "The Big Brawl: Hollywood vs. Television." *Saturday Evening Post,* Jan. 19, Jan. 26, and Feb. 2, 1952.

"More Trouble in Paradise." *Fortune,* Nov. 1946.

"Paramount: Oscar for Profits." *Fortune,* June 1947.

Robb, David. "New Info on Reagan, MCA Waiver Probe." *Variety,* Apr. 18, 1984.

Thompson, Edward. "There's No Show Business Like MCA's Business." *Fortune,* July 1960.

Tosches, Nick. "The Man Who Kept the Secrets." *Vanity Fair,* April 1997.

Trebay, Guy. "Stein's Way." *Vanity Fair,* July 1991.

U.S. News & World Report staff. "Robert Kennedy Speaks His Mind." *U.S. News & World Report,* Jan. 28, 1963.

Velie, Lester. "The Capone Gang Muscles into Big-Time Politics." *Collier's,* Sep. 30, 1950.

Whiteside, Thomas. "The Communicator." *New Yorker*, Oct. 16 and Oct. 23, 1954.

"Wilbur's Dream Joint." *Time,* May 8, 1950.

Miscellaneous

Clare, Ralph. Letter to the editors of *Los Angeles Tidings,* May 9, 1947.

Dunne, Father George H. "Christian Advocacy and Labor Strife in Hollywood." Interviewed by Mitch Tuchman, UCLA Oral History Program, 1981.

Dunne, Father George H. "Hollywood Labor Dispute: A Study in Immorality."

Kennedy, Jacqueline. Notes to Doris and Jules Stein, quoted in Jules Stein's unpublished draft of a memoir.

Migden, Chester. Interview by Terry Sanders. Legacy Documentation Program, Screen Actors Guild Foundation, May 1989.

Schary, Dore. Interview. Popular Arts Project, Series 1, Volume 6, Part 3. Oral History Research Project, Columbia University, November 1958.

Smith, Sandy. Unpublished manuscript.

Sorrell, Herbert Knott. "You Don't Choose Your Friends: The Memoirs of Herbert Knott Sorrell." Interviewed by Elizabeth I. Dixon, UCLA Oral History Program, 1963.

Stein, Jules. Unpublished draft of a memoir, based on interviews with Stein by Murray Schumach.

Warner, Jack. Letter to Lew Wasserman. Jack L. Warner Collection, University of Southern California Cinema-Television Library.

Warner, Jack, and Lew Wasserman and Jules Stein. Exchange of telegrams. Jack L. Warner Collection, University of Southern California Cinema-Television Library.

CHAPTER 3: POLITICAL MIGHT

Documents

Documents obtained through a Freedom of Information Act request to the National Archives, regarding Watergate Special Prosecution Force, Campaign Contributions Task Force Numerical File No. 522, "Movie Industry."

House Judiciary Committee Hearings, Watergate Investigation, and Report on Impeachment.

Nixon, Richard. Address to the Nation on the Situation in Southeast Asia, Apr. 7, 1971.

Nixon Presidential Materials, National Archives. Textual materials (office files, memoranda, letters, documents) and White House tapes.

Testimony to the Senate Select Committee on Presidential Campaign Practices.

United States of America v. Columbia Broadcasting System, Inc. et al., U.S. District Court, Central District of California, 1972.

Weekly Compilation of Presidential Documents. *The President's Remarks at a Reception Given by the President and Mrs. Nixon at Their California Home, "La Casa Pacifica,"* Aug. 27, 1972.

White House Press Conference of Peter Flanigan, Charlton Heston, Jack Valenti, and Taft Schreiber, Apr. 5, 1971.

Books

Ambrose, Stephen E. *Nixon: Ruin and Recovery, 1973–1990.* New York: Simon & Schuster, 1991.

Beschloss, Michael R. *Taking Charge.* New York: Simon & Schuster, 1997.

Brownstein, Ronald. *The Power and the Glitter.* New York: Pantheon, 1990.

Cannon, Lou. *Reagan.* New York: G. P. Putnam's Sons, 1982.

Casey, Al. *Casey's Law.* New York: Arcade, 1997.

Cohen, Edwin S. *A Lawyer's Life.* Arlington, Virginia: Tax Analysts, 1994.

Garment, Leonard. *Crazy Rhythm.* New York: Times Books, 1997.

Haldeman, H. R. *The Haldeman Diaries: Inside the Nixon White House.* New York: G. P. Putnam's Sons, 1994.

Kutler, Stanley I. *Abuse of Power.* New York: Touchstone, 1997.

Lukas, J. Anthony. *Nightmare.* New York: Viking, 1976.

Morris, Edmund. *Dutch.* New York: Random House, 1999.

Rains, Bob. *The Human Side of Hollywood Stars.* Danville, Illinois: Three Lions, 1999.

Reeves, Richard. *President Nixon.* New York: Simon & Schuster, 2001.

Articles

Berges, Marshall. "The City." *Time*, Dec. 18, 1964.

Bruck, Connie. "The Personal Touch." *New Yorker*, Aug. 13, 2001.

Canby, Vincent. "Czar of the Movie Business." *New York Times Magazine*, Apr. 1967.

———."Is Hollywood in Hot Water?" *New York Times*, Nov. 9, 1969.

———."Sure, Hollywood Is Collapsing, but . . ." *New York Times*, May 2, 1971.

Cheshire, Maxine. "Problems of a Presidential Adviser." *Washington Post*, Oct. 15, 1972.

Curtis, Charlotte. "The Jules Stein Party: A 3-Day Extravaganza for 600 Fashionable Guests." *New York Times*, Mar. 30, 1969.

Drinkhall, Jim. "Reagan's Riches." *Wall Street Journal*, Aug. 1, 1980.

Gent, George. "Big TV Networks Amazed by Move." *New York Times*, Apr. 15, 1972.

———."Major TV Networks Face Antitrust Suits Charging Entertainment Monopoly." *New York Times*, Apr. 14, 1972.

Gottlieb, Bob. "How Lew Wasserman Foiled the Wicked Witches and Became the Wiz of MCA." *Los Angeles Magazine*, Jan. 1979.

Gussow, Mel. "Excitement Fills Premiere of 'Dolly.' " *New York Times*, Dec. 18, 1969.

Haber, Joyce. "Model Soiree at Western White House." *Los Angeles Times*, Aug. 29, 1972.

Kael, Pauline. "On the Future of Movies." *New Yorker*, Aug. 5, 1974.

Kohn, Howard, and Lowell Bergman. "Reagan's Millions." *Rolling Stone*, Aug. 26, 1976.

Loehwing, David. "It's the Reel Thing—Motion Picture Producers Are Making a Solid Comeback." *Barron's*, Jan. 24, 1972.

McPhee, John. "New Kind of King." *Time*, Jan. 1, 1965.

Murphy, A. D. "Tax Change Benefits Film Biz." *Variety*, Sep. 10, 1971.

Overend, William. "U.S. Judge Real; The Court of No Nonsense—A Verdict." *Los Angeles Times*, May 27, 1985.

Penn, Stanley. "Movie Producers Complain to Justice Unit on Network, National General Film Plans." *Wall Street Journal*, Oct. 5, 1967.

Pinkerton, W. Stewart, Jr. "Hollywood's Glamour and Prosperity Wane with Movies' Decline." *Wall Street Journal*, June 27, 1969.

Shanahan, Eileen. "Trust-Busters in Prime Time." *New York Times*, Apr. 17, 1972.

Smith, Robert M. "TV Suits Put Off Year and a Half." *New York Times*, Apr. 15, 1972.

Miscellaneous

Finch, Robert H. Letter to the editor of the *Los Angeles Times*, Franklin D. Murphy Papers, Department of Special Collections, Charles E. Young Research Library, University of California, Los Angeles.

Hunter, Ross. Oral history, Ronald L. Davis Oral History Collection on the Performing Arts, DeGolyer Library, Southern Methodist University.

Krim, Arthur. Oral history, interviewed by Michael L. Gillette, Lyndon Baines Johnson Library Oral History Collection, 1981–1983.

LBJ Library: Macy File, White House Central file, White House Social file.

Stein, Jules. Letter to Franklin Murphy, Franklin D. Murphy Papers, Department of Special Collections, Charles E. Young Research Library, University of California, Los Angeles.

Stein, Jules. Unpublished draft of a memoir, based on interviews with Stein by Murray Schumach.

Valenti, Jack. Oral history, interviewed by T. H. Baker and Joe B. Frantz, LBJ Library Oral History Collection, 1969-1972.

Wasserman, Lew. Interview by Steven Spielberg, Dec. 12, 2002.

Wasserman, Lew. Oral history, interviewed by Joe B. Frantz, LBJ Library Oral History Collection, Dec. 21, 1973.

Weisl, Edwin L., Sr. Oral history, interviewed by Joe B. Frantz, LBJ Library Oral History Collection, May 13, 1969.

CHAPTER 4: DOMINION

Documents

General Explanation of the Tax Reform Act of 1976, prepared by the staff of the Joint Committee on Taxation, Dec. 29, 1976.

Legislative material, 122 Congressional Record §13,384, Aug. 4, 1976.

Articles

Anson, Robert Sam. "Hurricane Charlie." *Vanity Fair,* Apr. 2001.

Berges, Marshall. "Lew and Edie Wasserman: The Movie Usher Grew Up to Be Chairman of the Board." *Los Angeles Times,* Dec. 2, 1973.

Gottschalk, Earl C., Jr. "If It's Show Business, Chances Are MCA Inc. Is Deeply Involved in It." *Wall Street Journal,* July 10, 1973.

Hersh, Seymour M., with Jeff Gerth. "Double Life of Sidney Korshak." *New York Times,* June 27–30, 1976.

Maslin, Janet. "Film: Golden Ages; Just Before They Invented the Blockbuster." *New York Times,* May 1, 1994.

Scheer, Robert. "Line Drawn Between Two Worlds." *Los Angeles Times,* Jan. 30, 1978.

Schuyten, Peter J. "How MCA Rediscovered Movieland's Golden Lode." *Fortune,* Nov. 1976.

Steiger, Paul E. "Sidney Korshak: Man Who Makes Things Happen." *Los Angeles Times,* Sep. 15, 1969.

Miscellaneous

Stein, Jules. Letter to the Trustees of the Jules Stein Eye Institute, Franklin D. Murphy Papers, Department of Special Collections, Charles E. Young Research Library, University of California, Los Angeles.

Stein, Jules. Unpublished draft of a memoir, based on interviews with Stein by Murray Schumach.

CHAPTER 5: WASSERMAN & SON

Documents

United States of America v. Columbia Pictures Industries, Inc.; Getty Oil Company; MCA, Inc.; Paramount Pictures Corporation; and Twentieth Century-Fox Film Corporation, U.S. District Court, Southern District of New York, 1980.

Books

Pye, Michael, and Lynda Myles. *The Movie Brats.* New York: Holt, Rinehart & Winston, 1979.

Reischauer, Edwin O. *The Japanese Today: Continuity and Change.* New York: Longitude, 1995.

Articles

Articles in *Mainichi Shimbun* and *Yomiuri Shimbun,* October–December 1990.

Bruck, Connie. "Leap of Faith." *New Yorker*, Sep. 9, 1991.

"Down to the Wire on Fin-Syn." *Broadcasting*, Oct. 24, 1983.

Egan, J. "A Hollywood Thriller: MCA v. the Sharks." *U.S. News & World Report*, Sep. 7, 1987.

Fabrikant, Geraldine. "A Movie Giant's Unfinished Script." *New York Times*, Oct. 20, 1985.

Harris, Kathryn. "MCA Takes the Cautious Road as Competitors Plunge Ahead." *Los Angeles Times*, Nov. 22, 1981.

Kroll, Jack, with David T. Friendly. "The Wizard of Wonderland." *Newsweek*, June 4, 1984.

Lardner, James. "The Betamax Case." *New Yorker*, Apr. 6 and Apr. 13, 1987.

"Networks Nervous over Reagan Briefing from FCC's Fowler." *Broadcasting*, Oct. 10, 1983.

Robb, David. "Evans Paints 'Picture' of Korshak 'the Consigliere.'" *Hollywood Reporter*, Aug. 19–21, 1994.

CHAPTER 6: LOST EMPIRE

Articles

Archerd, Army. "Home Is Close to Edie's heart." *Variety*, July 9, 1996.

Bruck, Connie. "Bronfman's Big Deals." *New Yorker*, May 11, 1998.

Davis, David. "A Well-Nourished Mogul." *Los Angeles Magazine*, Oct. 27, 2002.

Deutsch, Susan. "LEW!" *California Magazine*, Mar. 1985.

Dunne, Dominick. "The Last Emperor." *Vanity Fair*, Apr. 1996.

Farhi, Paul. "The Man Who Remade Hollywood; Lew Wasserman Fades Out Quietly After Changing the Face of Show Biz." *Washington Post*, July 23, 1995.

Rose, Frank. "Twilight of the Last Mogul." *Los Angeles Times*, May 25, 1995.

Miscellaneous

Wasserman, Lew. Oral history, interviewed by Joe B. Frantz, LBJ Library Oral History Collection, Dec. 21, 1973.

Index

Page numbers in *italics* refer to illustrations.

Universal made-for-TV movie deals
and, 206, 207–9, 210, 211, 249,
285, 305, 393, 401
National Cultural Center, *see* John F.
Kennedy Center for the Perform-
ing Arts
National Endowment for the Arts
(NEA), 279, 336
National Lampoon's Animal House,
397
New Jersey Casino Control Commission, 392
New West, 458
New Yorker, xiii, 128
New York Stock Exchange, Stein's seat
on, 10, 35, 153
New York Times, xiv, 8, 168, 188,
193, 201, 207, 209, 250, 252–53,
259, 304, 318–19, 344–45, 373,
388, 417, 418, 468
nightclubs, Outfit and, 18, 22–23,
31–34, 55
Night Gallery, 471
Nightmare (Lukas), 301, 303, 308,
316
Nixon, Pat, 306
Nixon, Richard, xii
fund-raising for, 268, 270, 275, 283,
291–92, 301–3, 306–7, 308–12,
314, 315–19
Haldeman and Ehrlichman fired by,
313
movie industry and, 270–89,
300–301, 302–12, 313–19, 364
and network antitrust suit, 286–88,
303–6, 314
resignation of, 313, 318
and sale of ambassadorships,
316–17
Schreiber and, 268–73, 275, 279,
281, 282–83, 286, 288–89, 290,
291–92, 293–94, 299–300,
301–3, 306–7, 308–14, 319
in White House tapes, 275–76, 313
Nixon: Ruin and Recovery,
1973–1990 (Ambrose), 295
Nizer, Louis, 121, 232, 236, 245, 285,
304–5
Novak, Kim, 56
Nugent, Luci Johnson, 227
Nugent, Pat, 227
Nype, Russell, 116, 117

O'Bannion, Dion, 18, 30
O'Connell, Helen, 378
O'Connor, Ann, 364
Olson, Culbert, 100
Oppenheimer, Gerald, 248, 252
Oppenheimer, Harold, 268
Outfit, 21–22, 25
anarchy and, 26, 30, 45–46
FBI's secret taping of, 195–205
federal indictments of, 25, 58
in Havana, 85, 86, 163–64
kidnapping and, 23, 26, 29–31, 45,
56, 87, 201
in Las Vegas, 139–43, 163, 195,
196–205
LW and, xii, 141, 154, 163, 229,
237, 473, 474, 475
MCA and, 6, 18, 23, 31–34, 37,
40–41, 85–86, 139–43, 163–64,
255–56, 463–64
in movie industry, xii, 29, 56–61,
62–65
nightclubs and, 18, 22–23, 31–34, 55
police, courts, and politicians
bought off by, 18, 19, 21–22, 25,
30
R. Kennedy's war against, 195–205,
217
Sinatra and, 84, 85
Ovitz, Michael, 396, 422–30, 433,
434–39, 442, 444, 449

Pabst Blue Ribbon Casino, 32
Pacino, Al, 298
Paint Your Wagon, 250
Paley, Babe, 126, 163
Paley, William, 124–26, 163, 446
Paley Raids, 124–26
Palmieri, Edmund, 304–5
Paramount Communications, MCA in
merger talks with, 421–22
Paramount Decree (1948), xii, 111–13,
174
Paramount Pictures, 217, 250, 343
CIC and, 345–51
in IA-AMPTP contract negotiation,
385–86, 387
MCA's acquisition of film library of,
173–76, 185, 404, 468
pay TV and, 404–6
principal shareholders in, 46, 82–83,
117

CONNIE BRUCK has been a staff writer at *The New Yorker* since 1989; she frequently writes about business and politics for the magazine. In 1996, her profile of Newt Gingrich, "The Politics of Perception," won the National Magazine Award for reporting. She has won two Front Page Awards from the Newswomen's Club of New York for her 1990 piece "Deal of the Year" and her 1997 piece about Tupac Shakur. She has also won a 1991 Gerald Loeb Award for excellence in business reporting, and a 1991 National Magazine Award for Reporting. Bruck is the author of two books: *Master of the Game,* about Steve Ross and Time Warner, which was published in 1994, and *The Predators' Ball,* published in 1988, about junk bond impresario Michael Milken. She lives in Los Angeles.

ABOUT THE TYPE

This book was set in Sabon, a typeface designed by the well-known German typographer Jan Tschichold (1902–74). Sabon's design is based on the original letter-forms of Claude Garamond and was created specifically to be used for three sources: foundry type for hand composition, Linotype, and Monotype. Tschichold named his typeface for the famous Frankfurt typefounder Jacques Sabon, who died in 1580.